THEOSOPHICAL SIFT

(T. P. S.)

VOL. III.

1890-91.

𝕷𝖔𝖓𝖉𝖔𝖓:

THE THEOSOPHICAL PUBLISHING SOCIETY,

7, DUKE STREET, ADELPHI, W.C.

Path. 132, Nassau Street, New York, U.S.A.

———

1891

Phil 29.7 (3)

CONTENTS.

———:o:———

CAPITAL PUNISHMENT.

BY

FRANZ HARTMANN, M.D.

THE OLD, OLD STORY.

London:

PUBLISHED BY THE T.P.S., 7, DUKE STREET, ADELPHI

1890.

CAPITAL PUNISHMENT.

WHILE a wave of spiritual enlightenment is passing over the world, calling forth various reforms in the political and social relations of humanity, there is one extremely dark spot in the mind of mankind, into which this light does not seem to be able to penetrate, namely, the idea of killing criminals for the purpose of punishing them. This idea is a superstition, arising from an entire ignorance of the true nature of man; a relic of the Dark Ages, a blot on the character of humanity. It was to be expected that in consequence of the rapid spreading of progressive ideas, disseminated by Theosophical literature, this remnant of a barbaric custom would gradually disappear. Instead of that, the Austrian lawmakers have just revised the penal code, retaining capital punishment, and, the faculty of medicine having memorialized the Minister of Justice recommending the cutting off of the heads of criminals in the place of hanging them. In the most progressive country of the world—the United States of America—legal killing by means of electricity is about to be introduced, while in other so-called civilized countries the carelessness of allowing oneself to be caught for committing a crime is punished by hanging, garrotting, shooting, or by the guillotine.

The first question which arises in the consideration of this subject is: "What is the object of killing a criminal?" The second question is, "Is that object attained?" The only imaginable objects in killing a criminal are: 1. To inflict punishment on him for having acted against the law; 2. To render him incapable to do further mischief, and thereby to protect society.

The age in which criminals were tortured has passed away; the authorities are content upon finding a way by which the death penalty can be inflicted with the least possible suffering to the delinquent; and even inflicting mental suffering upon the candidate for death is avoided, because, instead of causing him to get frightened by imagining the horrors of hell, everything is done to make him believe that his sins are forgiven, and that he will be received with open arms in the celestial kingdom. The "punishment" is, therefore, evidently not intended to produce physical or mental suffering, and if the criminal is a man of courage, and does not fear death, there will be no horror of dying, there will be no suffering, and the only possible punishment for him is the loss of his life. Now the medical fraternity inform us that as soon as the heart and the brain of a person are paralysed, there is an end to his consciousness. If this is true, then the criminal, as soon as he is killed, is unconscious of ever having lived; he is unconscious of ever having lost his life, and where, then, is the punishment in causing a man a loss of which he is not aware, and in taking away from him something that he will never miss? It is like taking away from a person something that never belonged to him, and of which he does not even know that it exists.

Seen from this point of view, capital punishment is a total failure, because, besides frightening a timid criminal for a few hours or days before his death, there is no pain inflicted upon him; and even this mental torture, if any, is not inflicted by the law, but merely by the criminal's own imagination, and by his belief regarding the state after death. The capital punishment being, therefore, merely an imaginary punishment, does not fulfil its object as a punishment, and the only remaining question is whether society can protect itself better by killing a criminal than by shutting him up in a prison and seeking to educate him and to improve his character. At a time when no convenient prisons existed, and when the only means of protecting oneself was to kill the aggressor, the killing of criminals may have appeared to be useful and necessary; but at the present state of civilization, where the country abounds with prisons, there is, to say the least, no necessity for killing an offender against the law; nor is there any financial profit arising from killing him, because, besides the cost of the execution, the Government loses his labour.

There is still another reason given by the advocates of capital punishment for its continuation, namely, the " wholesome effect which it will have of frightening other criminally-inclined people into remaining virtuous "; but it is very doubtful whether the defenders of such an argument believe it themselves, or whether they have ever seriously considered it; because it is well known that the law does actually never punish a crime unless the criminal is caught, and, therefore, the punishment is rather for having committed the crime in a bungling manner, which involved discovery, than for committing it; and the only thing which the captured criminal regrets is that he was not cunning enough to avoid being caught, and the only sincere resolve which he forms in his own mind is to be more careful the next time, so as not to be caught again. Moreover, the morality of a people which is based only upon cowardice arising from fear of punishment is worth very little, and the passions, merely restrained and pent up by fear, accumulate and grow in strength. The pent-up passions of a nation restrained by fear resemble a mine loaded with dynamite, waiting for a favourable moment to explode, when the result will be such as has been witnessed during the horrors of the French Revolution.

Thus, seen from a merely external and " materialistic " point of view, capital punishment is useless and unnecessary; but a correct conception of its true nature and consequences can only be formed if we look below the surface appearances and study the true nature of " life " and of the constitution of man.

There is nothing more irrational than the attempts which have been made by our modern " rationalists " of separating science from philosophy. In doing so, science, so-called, condemned itself of being merely a science of external appearances and phenomena, relegating the causes of such external appearances to the region of the " unknowable." It is admitted by all modern and ancient philosophers that a tree is the result of something capable to produce a tree ; i.e., of the action of some invisible principle, or " potentiality," residing in a kernel and capable to develop into a tree ; and likewise that the organism of man is the result of something invisible in connection with a power whose manifestation is called " life " ; but material science, in disregarding and denying the existence of causes which she cannot see with material eyes, makes of every man and of every tree a miracle whose existence cannot be explained. Occult science says that the principle which causes the appearance of a tree, or which manifests itself in the human form as a man, is the real thing of importance which is to be taken into consideration ; and that the external form, be it that of a man or of a tree, is nothing else but an external form whose importance does not transcend the plane whereon it exists. She says that while the form or appearance perishes, the power which caused that form to exist remains, and will be capable, under favourable conditions, to produce another similar form, be it a man or a tree, exhibiting the same qualities as the former. There is only this difference, that while the seed of a tree may be destroyed, the spiritual " seed " which produces the soul of a man cannot be destroyed by capital punishment, but will, under favourable conditions, produce such a man again as sure as the seed of a thistle will produce nothing else but a thistle. All this is taught by the doctrine of Reincarnation, a doctrine with which our scientists ought to make themselves familiar, if they do not prefer to remain in ignorance regarding that which is of supreme importance in studying the nature of man. This doctrine, then, teaches us that, in depriving the spirit of a criminal of his physical body, we do not kill the cause that produced the criminal, and that this cause will in due time produce another criminal of the same kind, if not of a still worse character, as the unjust act of robbing him of his life will have caused a sense and desire of revenge and an embitterment of the spirit. By capital punishment we, therefore, at best, defer the manifestation of an evil cause for some future time, and give to a future generation an evil inheritance, with which we ourselves ought to have contended, and which we ought to have sought to ameliorate. This is, however, not all. It might be said that we do not care about the troubles that will affect future generations, and that it is all we can do to protect and take care of ourselves ; but a deeper investigation in the invisible nature of man will show us that in killing the body of a criminal we do not get rid of the powers that constituted him a criminal, and that these powers, after having been deprived of one instrument for their manifestation, will continue to manifest themselves in other still less convenient ways. To understand this it will be necessary to throw a glance at the constitution of man, as it is taught by those who have the capacity to know it; and for the sake of those who are not familiar with the doctrines of Occultism, we will attempt to outline that constitution in comprehensible terms. According to the doctrines of the sages, Man is a fourfold manifestation of consciousness, or, in other words, a trinity of spirit and body, with the intermediary link called the " soul," the latter being divisible into the purely animal and the divinely human soul. To the former belong the animal emotions and passions, to the latter the higher powers of the mind. We may, therefore, classify these four states of consciousness as four principles, giving them the following familiar names:

1. GOD, the *Atma*, the "divine Self," *i.e.*, the Divinity in man, a universal power, existing in the majority of the criminals, only, so to say, in a dormant or latent state, and not having arrived at a state of self-consciousness in them. This means that the criminal is not a saint, and does not know the god that is hidden in him, and whom to awaken to consciousness is the object of human life, an object frustrated by the execution of the criminal. This principle, whether awakened or not, cannot be executed and killed; it is the real and true Self, and returns to its divine source after the death of the body, as is also taught by the Church, which, at the funeral service, relegates "the body to Earth, and the spirit to God."

2. The MIND. This we understand not to be the thinking faculty of the brain, but that principle which manifests itself as thought and will in the material brain, *i.e.*, that which enables the brain to think by the aid of the physiological processes taking place in the living subject. Even if the head is cut off and the brain with which man used to think is destroyed, the thought-producing principle cannot be killed; but after being deprived of its instrument for manifestation, it enters into its own state of being, which in criminals of the ordinary kind is presumbly that which is called *Devachan*, where it rests in its subjective condition until the time arrives when it will be reincarnated upon the earth, and evolve a new physical body with the same tendencies which it possessed in its former life.

3. The ASTRAL SOUL. It is well known that the physical body or " corpse" of a man is not the man himself, but merely an instrument formed by nature, in and through which the consciousness of man may manifest its mental and physical powers; in other words, man is not himself his own nature, but he has an everchanging organism, in which his (temporary) nature is mani-

festing itself. The same is the case with his astral soul, the seat of his passions and emotions. The astral soul is not the man himself, but merely a principle wherein the good and evil powers existing on the astral plane are manifesting themselves, in the same sense as cold manifests itself in an icicle; to destroy the icicle does not destroy the cold, even if that piece of ice were broken into a thousand pieces; and if the icicle is molten and evaporated, the same cold will be able to cause the vapour to condense and to freeze into ice again. This means to say that in the astral plane of the world there exist certain influences of a good and an evil kind, comparable to miasmas in the physical atmosphere of our planet; and as those miasmas will be attracted to those who are especially susceptible for them, and cause epidemic diseases, likewise these astral influences are attracted to those animal souls in men and women where they find a congenital soil to grow and develop, just as the life principle in a cherry tree attracts from the soil and the atmosphere all that is necessary to build up a cherry tree and nothing else. The animal soul of a hardened criminal is a fruitful soil where evil astral influences are readily attracted to and developed. These evil tendencies are not the man himself; they merely belong to his nature and are acting in and through him. They cannot be killed by killing the body, but if the physical form wherein they are active is destroyed, these powers for evil are liberated and free to be attracted to and to manifest themselves in other human souls where they find points of attraction, in the same sense as the cold liberated by evaporation will cause water with which it comes into contact to freeze and crystallize. If we kill a malefactor, we liberate his own essential ego of the evil influences which had possession of him, and we enable these influences to fasten upon the souls of innocent but sensitive persons, in which they create evil inclinations and thoughts, and which may then repeat the same crime for which the criminal was executed. The world is full of such sensitive and mediumistic persons, and it is a known fact that crimes sometimes become epidemic, and that if a criminal has been executed for some especially atrocious crime, crimes of a similar nature are often heard of soon afterwards. The execution of a criminal in this respect has the same effect as pouring out a stinking fluid upon the public thoroughfare with the good intention of getting rid of the evil odour, and thereby poisoning the whole community by the (psychic) stench that was at first confined to only one place.

4. The PHYSICAL BODY. The " corpse "—the external form with its inherent life principle and " magnetic body," or " perisprit." This is merely an external instrument for the inner man, and incapable *per se* to do anything good or evil, unless made to act by the astral soul or the mind. It is merely an innocent victim of the natural forces acting therein, and to punish it for sins which the inner man committed through its instrumentality is like hanging

a stick with which a murder has been committed, or tearing to pieces the overcoat of a thief.

If the above is taken into due consideration, it will be seen that in executing a criminal nobody is actually punished except those sensitive and innocent people who are deficient of the power of self-control, and who may become infested with the evil influences arising from the liberated animal soul of the criminal, and which may cause them to become criminals themselves. The other persons that are punished by the performance of such an official act are the judge, the jurors, and the executioner, together with those that sanctioned the infliction of " capital punishment," and the degree in which they punish themselves will depend on whether they are thus sinning consciously or unconsciously, and whether or not they are aware of the true nature of capital punishment and its consequences. This is explained by the action of the law of *Karma*, a law which every lawyer and judge ought to know above all, as it is the supreme law for administering justice in the universe. It teaches that the universe is a whole, and that no individual can inflict the slightest injury upon any other individual without experiencing himself the full effect of his acts ; or, as Edwin Arnold expresses it in his " Light of Asia," which, even if it is a poem, nevertheless embodies the most undeniable truths :—

> " By this (law) the slayer's knife did stab himself ;
> The unjust judge hath lost his own defender ;
> The false tongue dooms its lie ; the creeping thief
> And spoiler rob to render.
>
> " Such is the law which moves to righteousness,
> Which none at last can turn aside or stay ;
> The heart of it is love ; the end of it
> Is peace and consummation sweet. Obey ! "

The law of Karma is the law of justice and retribution, by which the harmony in the universe, which has been broken, is restored. It is a law which is administered by nobody—neither by a God nor by a man—and its action is therefore not to be avoided or thwarted, neither by bribes nor by prayers or arguments. It is the Law itself, and administers itself without partiality, its effects being in exact accordance with the causes that produced them. There is, therefore, an adequate punishment for every sin, and there is no necessity that any mortal man should presume to put himself in the place of the law and judge over the destiny of the soul of another human being. All that a man has a right and a duty in regard to criminals is to teach and instruct them, to educate and aid them to get rid of their own evil inclinations ; for it ought to be kept in mind that as long as a man has no perfect self-knowledge, his will cannot be perfectly free. The ignorant man does nothing good or evil himself; he follows the thoughts that lead him. The man who has no mastery over himself is mastered by the influences which are controlling him. It is not our object at present to investigate the various methods which are employed to enforce prison discipline. They may be good or they may be bad; they may or may not be adapted to teach criminals; but surely the killing of a criminal can teach him nothing; it can only arouse in his soul a spirit of fear, embitterment and revenge, because he instinctively knows that no man has a right to rob him of his life.

The law of Karma is the law of impartial justice, which claims an eye for an eye and a tooth for a tooth, and which says that he who kills with the sword shall perish by the sword. Being a universal law, it applies itself alike to a criminal as to a judge on the bench; it is no respecter of persons; it pays no reverence to judicial wigs and gowns, and even Royalty is not exempt from premature deaths produced by the action of the Karma of former lives. He who condemns a fellow-being to death will necessarily suffer for it, either in this or some future life upon the earth. He may condemn a man, having, at the same time, the best of intentions, and he may have his own life cut short while he still has the best intentions.

Some poet asks the question about man in the following words :—

> " Out of Earth's elements, mingled with flame,
> Out of Life's compound of glory and shame,
> Fashioned and shaped by no will of our own,
> Helplessly into life's history thrown,
> Born to conditions we could not foresee,
> Born by a law which compels us to be,
> Born by one law, through all Nature the same,
> What makes us differ and who is to blame ? "

Our answer to this query is that humanity, being a unit, the condition of the whole is responsible for the condition of each single individual, and that unit being made up of individuals, each individual is responsible for the conditions which affect the whole, and the responsibility of either is in exact proportion to its capacity to teach and enlighten the other. Therefore, instead of killing one another, we ought to aid each other in coming to life, for no one can be said to be truly alive as long as he does not know his own divine self, and that true Self embraces and includes the whole of creation, because God is in, and through, and above All.

F. HARTMANN.

THE OLD, OLD STORY.

THERE are few lives into which there has not at one time entered a ray of sunshine, or that have not at some time been illumined by the light of love. There may, indeed, be found barren and loveless lives, but even these may yet discern on the dim horizon of the past the light of one bright star; a morning star, whose orbit no longer coincides with the zodiac of the present. The star of memory or the star of hope can only be quenched by despair. Man lives on hope or on memory; a vision of the future or a shadow of the past continually cheat the soul and hide the everlasting reality from the eternal now.

Memory and hope, as compared with the light of Love, are as will-o'-the-wisps compared with the light of the sun; they delude and lead us astray; but so long as we are unable to bear the light of the sun these alone make human life possible in the darkness and gloom, and endurable in the face of continual disappointment. Love is a mystery which the philosopher strives in vain to explain, and those equally who accept or reject his explanation, who pretend to scorn, or who are enthusiastic followers of the God, are equally deluded and finally equally discouraged. Love is a frenzy, a subtle madness in the blood that brings out the best and the worst that is within its victim.

The theme of the poet and painter, the dream of youth, the solace of prime, and, too often, the disappointment of age, can this also be the theme of the Theosophist? This is, indeed, the theme of themes, as it is the riddle of riddles.

Where love is there can be no disappointment, no old age, no decay, no death. It is love alone that makes us immortal. Here lies the great secret. It is not love that disappoints us. Life disappoints us because it is without love, because we allow love to die in us; yet it is not love that dies, but we who die toward love. When we can no longer excite or experience love we are growing old; the freshness and bloom of spring has been replaced by the sere and yellow leaf.

Love is determined not by what we can get out of life, but by what we can put into it; not by desire, but by sacrifice. Desire is selfish and doomed to disappointment, Love is altruistic and blooms immortal. Disappointed love is the monument we build in pain and tears to our own selfishness. The sighs and groans of unrequited love differ in degree but not in kind from the faintness that accompanies hunger. It is the need of our animal nature for food, of our human nature for sympathy, rather than of our Divine nature to give, to help, and to bless other lives. Love overflows like a full fountain; desire consumes like a fierce fire. He who is no longer the victim of desire, but who is the master of love, can rule the forces of life. There is but one rival of love, and hat is hate. We are equally carried out of ourselves by the one as by the other. Desire is earth-born, the victim of time, the servant of circumstance but both love and hate " enter within the veil" and marshal unseen forces of weal or woe. " The Voice of the Silence " cries: " Kill out desire, kill out all sense of separateness"; but only the shrill voice of hate bids us kill Love, for love is the silent voice, the harbinger of every Golden Precept. The face of the black magician glows with the baneful fires of desire and hate; the face of the white magician beams with the pure light of love. The plume of the one is the red comb of the cock set in the feathers of the raven. The insignia of the other is the white wings of the dove touched with the azure blue of heaven.

For most of us, life is one continual round of disappointments. Disappointed love, disappointed ambition, disappointed greed. In seeking thus to draw all things into ourselves we at last become but Dead Sea apples, emptiness, blackness and despair. With no more, at best, than faint intuitions born of former lives, we allow selfishness to smother these, till the *ennui* and imbecility of age make us relinquish life itself, and then we talk of " some other clime," some fairer land, where love shall bloom immortal!

O! know ye the land where the flowers of Love
   Perpetually bloom near life's river?
O! know ye the heaven where the wings of the dove
   Are shorn of their bright pinions never?

Is the land far away in the mists of the past?
   Is it lost in the dim distant future?
Are all of these visions too fickle to last?
   And is there no rest for earth's creature?

Ah! the land is just here; ye but journey in vain,
   Who hunt through the realms of creation;
Ye are doomed to despair; ye are pilgrims of pain,
   Whate'er be your lot or your station.

The god whom ye seek has oft passed you at morn,
  His garment hath brushed you at even;
At noon in the broad glare of day he is born,
  No Earth can confine him, no heaven.

His feet are unsandaled, his head it is bare,
  And his face is concealed as tho' shrouded.
And ye never will know how exceedingly fair
  Is the god till your soul is unclouded.

Seek him not here or there, for he scorneth approach
  No building of man can contain him;
But when his own temple is void of reproach,
  Thou wilt find that naught else can restrain him.

He will lead from this temple the bride of his soul,
  A true virgin, whose lamp is still burning.
And thou wilt know then no part, and no whole,
  When thy soul has once learned true discerning.

LOVE'S SACRIFICE.

A child-soul sweet as breath of Flowers
Fell softly on this world of ours;
To try its wings, and learn its powers.

A tiger seized it in his claws;
Beast! unrestrained by human laws,
With purring breath and cruel jaws.

O stricken heart! O wounded dove!
O starving soul for breath of love!
Black lowers the Karmic sky above.

O moaning seas of scalding tears!
O hearts awreck by hopes and fears!
Love shall redeem the vanished years.

LOVE'S ALTAR.

Be true to Love, and not to me,
O Soul! adrift on Karmic Sea,
Spinning the threads of Destiny.

O Soul of Flame! O subtle breath!
O Love! more strong than life or death,
No wavering flame thine altar hath.

Feed well the flame through day and night
With oil of love, in garments white,
That wandering souls may see the light.

O Queen of Flame! O white-robed priest
The god ye serve is not the Beast.
Your star shines brightly in the East.

Above love's alter's upper rim,
. Spread wide the wings of Cherubim;
List to the sacred Marriage Hymn.

No sound of lute, no sensuous dance,
No weaving Nautch-girls' am'rous glance
Enters our altar's broad expanse.

No sinuous snake in human form,
No tiger's claw, no power can harm
Where love can light and love can warm.

Warmed by loves altar's steady glow,
Led by love's light through frost and snow.
Come stricken souls who hunger know.

We pile for you love's fuel higher,
We fan the flame by strong desire;
Come nearer, starving soul, come nigher.

The wedding feast, the marriage hymn,
The welcoming wings of Cherubin,
And Soma's cup filled to the brim—

'Tis thus love's ruined altars rise,
With beacon light from Eastern skies,
And Brotherhood the golden prize.

What inexpressible sorrow in the faces of the little loveless children, what hopeless despair in the bended form and wrinkled face of age, drooping toward tho dust and ashes, instead of looking outward toward the light and upward toward the stars. The child faces his old Karma, the battle to be won, the Karma of the aged is at his back, the battle lost if only evil deeds drag him down to earth and the silence of the grave. And all of this for lack of love! Only the middle or mature of age can make either of these conditions possible. These it is who beget the children in a moment of strong desire without love; these are they who, journeying on through disappointment to despair, become the stranded wrecks on the further shore of time, and these are they who talk of love! The lesson is not so hard that it cannot be understood. These are all bewildered souls who have lost their way. There is little hope for the aged. We may minister to them, but

> " The cup of life is drawn
> And nought remains but lees."

Love may, indeed, minister to them, but it cannot be so kindled in them as to chase away the shadows of memory and rekindle the desire of unselfish deeds. It is too late for them to learn self-forgetfulness. " Their sorrows are many, their pleasures are few." A host of infirmities have need of many nurses, and the habits of a life-time cannot be changed in a moment. They are victims of desire, pilgrims of passion, aliens to peace, wanderers from heaven. Let them sleep! " He giveth His beloved rest "; and again, as little children, will they be filled with fresh desire, and seek again the Immortal *Amrita*. Gathering intuitions from vague memories of pain, led gently by Infinite Love, they will at last enter the abodes of peace and hear the " Voice of the Silence."

To the young, to men and women in their prime, and through these to the little children is the message and the opportunity.

Learn, then, the lesson well. Life is barren without love, and love is impossible without self-forgetfulness. Be undeceived, oh, eager Soul! Desire seeks, Love gives; desire leads inevitably to satiety; satiety to disgust; disgust to despair, despair to death, and death to oblivion! So rapid runs the scale from birth to death. Now, listen to the scale from birth to Life. Love seeketh opportunity, opportunity seeketh action, action begetteth zest, zest begets inspiration, and these aspire toward the light of life, the *Amrita* of the gods, and the springs of Immortal Life. These are the two poles of one being, and man is himself the arbiter of his own fate. This is no strained philosophy, no subtle mysticism, but the one law of action, the Perfect Law of Love. Between this and the law of hate are only walking shadows, Maya, delusions all. Here lies the secret of happy homes, of restful lives, of beautiful children, of a redeemed humanity.

That man or woman walks in a bewildering delusion that leads only to sorrow and repentance, who imagines that by scorning the common task, or neglecting the obligation already voluntarily assumed, a higher life can be attained. If one finds himself chained to a beast by a voluntary act, the price of his liberation is to lead the beast up toward humanity, not by brutish goads, or superior scorn, but by the light of love. When every task is accomplished, and every duty done, and discouragement rests upon that soul toiling patiently with heavy burden, lo! the dawn of humanity in the one is the birth of divinity in the other. This is, indeed, the Way and the truth of The Life.

Other religions and all other associations of men drive many beings more or less asunder, build high and hard walls, and beget pride, and cast and creed. The old Wisdom-religion draws men together like the living elements of one body. No true Theosophy ever rent asunder even an unhappy, because an inharmonious, home; but rather it everywhere and at all times commands that harmony be brought out of discord, love out of desire, life out of death. Those who keenly feel discord and find themselves in the midst of it, are there for the sake of opportunity, and if they, too, fall into discord, how shall they proceed to action, and from action to zest, and so on to the fountains of life. Only they who have proved faithful over a few things shall be rulers over many, Shall he who knows no discipline be captain of a company or general of an army?

It is to the young, in whom desire is strong, and love an unknown realm, that the higher life promises most, no matter whether they seek the mystic realm to become lovers of mankind, or seek in quiet ways the common path as builders of happy homes and parents of healthful and happy children, and so help to redeem the world. The field of life lies virgin all before them, and the one bar to happiness, the one bar to love, is *Self*, just as it is also a bar to theosophical progress. In the common lot of man and woman in married life, if each will demand nothing, and give all; if each will forget the desire of self before the good and the happiness of the other, they will find themselves drawing more closely together instead of wider and wider apart. Each will outdo the other in deeds of kindness and words of love. Having thus nourished the sacred flame of love to the mastery of themselves and the putting down of Self, their lives will broaden and their sympathies extend, till their influence embraces other lives, and inspires other homes, thus helping on the reign of Brotherhood. Love may thus illumine every spot and inspire every life. It is thus that Theosophy teaches the law of love and the reign of Universal Brotherhood. It is, indeed, the law of the heart rather than of the head, and yet none so sure to know and to understand as the unselfish. The lower *Manas*, mere intellectuality, anchored to sensation and to desire, is always blind to the higher truths; it grovels and is hemmed in by the narrow bounds of sense and time. Self is the partition wall by which man separates himself on the one hand from human kind, and on the other from his higher self. It is thus that man is at war with himself, as with all below and all above him. It is thus that man suffers and grows old and dies. The law of his life is at war with the conditions of his environment. This is indeed the old, old story. Disappointment follows desire as its shadow, till the shadow becomes the substance, and impotent desire now wasted to a shadow hangs upon the heels of despair, and life itself is vanquished!

What sufferings are endured in this primary school of life! and yet with what willing feet and beating hearts do men and women enter the lists unwilling to save their lives by burying self : longing for love like blind children wailing for the tender mother whom they cannot see ; putting it aside when it is within their very grasp ; seeking it through earth, and hell, and heaven, when they have closed its golden portals within their own souls.

> Open, then, the golden gate !
> And let the god of Love come in ;
> And the old story shall beome the new song.

The Third Volume of the T.P.S. having now commenced, those whose subscriptions are due on the 1st of March are requested to renew as soon as possible, otherwise no further copies can be sent to them.

ALLEN, SCOTT AND CO., Printers, 30, Bouverie Street, London, E.C.

SOME PRACTICAL SUGGESTIONS FOR DAILY LIFE.

SOME HINTS ON THE THEOSOPHICAL TRAINING OF CHILDREN.

London:

PUBLISHED BY THE T.P.S., 7, DUKE STREET, ADELPHI

1890.

PREFACE.

————

THE T. P. S. desires to inform its readers that the quotations of which the following pamphlet is composed were not originally extracted with a view to publication, and may therefore appear somewhat disjointed.

They are now published in the hope that others may take the hint, and make daily books of extracts for themselves, thus preserving a lasting record of the books read, and rendering their reading of practical value. By following this plan, the reader would concentrate in a brief space whatever has appealed to him as being the essence of the book. It would also be a pleasant thing to turn the pages of such a book of reference, and compare his thoughts and sympathies with those of earlier days, noting by what means, and along what lines, he has progressed.

We may also suggest the plan of reading a set of quotations each morning, trying to live up to them during the day, and meditating upon them in leisure moments.

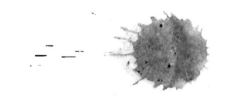

SOME PRACTICAL SUGGESTIONS FOR DAILY LIFE.

SUNDAY.

RISE early, as soon as you are awake, without lying idly in bed, half waking and half dreaming. Then earnestly pray that all mankind may be spiritually regenerated; that those who are struggling on the path of truth may be encouraged by your prayers and work more earnestly and successfully, and that you may be strengthened and not yield to the seductions of the senses. Picture before your mind the form of your Master as engaged in Samahdi. Fix it before you, fill in all the details, think of him with reverence and pray that all mistakes of omission and commission may be forgiven. This will greatly facilitate concentration, purify your heart and do much more. Or reflect upon the defects of your character: *thoroughly realize their evils and the transient pleasures they give you,* and firmly *will* that you should try your best not to yield to them the next time. This self-analysis and bringing yourself before the bar of your own conscience facilitates in a degree hitherto undreamt of your spiritual progress. When you bathe, exercise during the whole time your will, that your moral impurities should be washed away with those of your body. In your relations with *others* observe the following rules. 1. Never do anything which you are not bound to do as your duty; that is, any unnecessary thing. *Before* you do a thing think whether it is your duty to do it. 2. *Never speak an unnecessary word.* Think of the *effects* your words might produce before you give utterance to them. *Never allow yourself to violate your principles by the force of your company.* 3. Never allow any unnecessary or vain thought to occupy your mind. This is easier said than done. You cannot make your mind a blank all at once. So *in the beginning* try to prevent evil or idle thoughts by *occupying your mind with the analysis of your own faults,* or the *contemplation of the perfect ones.* 4. During meals exercise your will, that your food should be properly digested and build for you a body in harmony with your *spiritual* aspirations, and not create evil passion and wicked thoughts. Eat only when you are hungry and drink when you are thirsty, and *never otherwise.* If some particular preparation attracts your palate, do not allow yourself to be seduced into taking it simply to gratify that craving. Remember that the pleasure you derive from it had no existence some seconds before, and that it will cease to exist some seconds afterwards; that it is a transient pleasure, that that which is a pleasure now will turn into pain if you take it in large quantities ; that it gives pleasure only to the tongue ; that if you are put to a great trouble to get that thing, and, if you allow yourself to be seduced by it, you will not be ashamed at anything to get it ; that while there is another object that can give you eternal bliss, this centreing your affections on a transient thing is sheer folly ; that *you* are neither the body nor the sense, and therefore the pleasure and the pains which *these* endure can never affect you really, and so on. Practice the same train of reasoning in the case of every other temptation, and, though you will often fail, yet you will achieve a surer success. *Do not read much.* If you read for ten minutes, reflect for as many hours. Habituate yourself to solitude, and to remain alone with your thoughts. Accustom yourself to the thought that *no one beside yourself can assist you*, and wean away your affections from all things *gradually.* Before you sleep, *pray as you did in the morning. Review the actions of the day*, and see wherein you have failed, and resolve that you will not fail in them to-morrow.*

MONDAY.

The right motive for seeking self-knowledge is that which pertains to *knowledge* and not to *self.* Self-knowledge is worth seeking by virtue of its being knowledge, and not by virtue of its pertaining to self. The main requisite for acquiring self-knowledge is *pure love.*† Seek knowledge for pure love, ‡ and self-knowledge eventually crowns the effort. The fact of a student growing *impatient* is proof positive that he works for *reward*, and not for love, and that in its turn proves that he does not deserve the great victory in store for those who really work for pure love. §

The "God" in us, that is to say the Spirit of Love and Truth, Justice and Wisdom, Goodness and Power, should be our only true and permanent *Love*, our only reliance in everything, our only *Faith*, which, standing firm as a rock, can for ever be trusted ; our only Hope, which will never fail us if all other things perish ; and the only object which we must seek to obtain, *by our Patience, waiting contentedly until our evil Karma has been exhausted* and the divine Redeemer will reveal to us his presence within our soul. The door through which he enters is called *Contentment*; for he who is discontented with himself is discontented with the law that made

---

* Theosophist. August '89, p. 647.   ‡ So as to be able to help mankind.
† Altruism ?   § Theosophist, August, '89, p. 663.

him *such as he is ;* and as God is *himself* the Law, God will not come to those that are discontented with Him. If we admit that we are in the stream of evolution, then *each* circumstance *must* be to us *quite right.* And in our failures to perform set acts should be our greatest helps, for we can in no other way learn that calmness which Krishna insists upon. If all our plans succeeded, then no contrasts would appear to us. Also those plans we make may all be made ignorantly and thus *wrongly,* and kind Nature will not permit us to carry them out. We get no blame for the *plan,* but we may acquire karmic demerit by not accepting the impossibility of achieving. If you are at all cast down, then by just that much are your thoughts lessened in power. *One could be confined in a prison and yet be a worker for the cause.* So I pray you to remove from your mind any distaste for present circumstances. If you can succeed in looking at it all *as just what you in fact desired*† then it will act not only as a strengthener of your thoughts, but will act reflexly on your body and make it stronger.‡

To act and act wisely when the time for action comes, to wait and wait patiently when it is time for repose, put man in accord with the rising and falling tides (of affairs), so that with nature and law at his back, and truth and beneficence as his beacon light, he may accomplish wonders. Ignorance of this law results in periods of unreasoning enthusiasm on the one hand, and depression and even despair on the other. Man thus becomes the victim of the tides, *when he should be their Master.*§

Have patience, Candidate, *as one who fears no failure, courts no success.* ‖

Accumulated energy cannot be annihilated, it must be *transferred to other forms,* or be transformed into other modes of motion ; it cannot remain for ever inactive and yet continue to exist. It is useless to attempt to *resist* a passion which we cannot control. If its accumulating energy is not led into other channels, it will grow until it becomes stronger than will and stronger than reason. *To control it,* you must lead it into another and *higher* channel. Thus a love for something vulgar may be changed by turning it into a love for something high, and *vice may be changed into virtue by changing its aim.* Passion is blind, it goes where it is led to, and reason is a safer guide for it than the instinct. *Stored up* anger (or love) *will* find some object upon which to spend its fury, else it may produce an explosion destructive to its possessor ; *tranquility follows a storm.* The ancients said that *nature suffers no vacuum.* We cannot destroy or annihilate a passion.

---

* T. P. S., No. 8, Vol. 2, Hartmann, p. 9.
† " You " meaning the Higher Self. We *are* as we make ourselves.
‡ Path, August, '89., p. 131.
§ Path, July, '89. p. 107.
‖ Voice of the Silence, p. 31.

If it is *driven away another elemental influence will take its place.* We should therefore not attempt to destroy the low, without putting something in its place; but we should displace the low by the high; vice by virtue, and superstition by knowledge.*

TUESDAY.

LEARN that there is no cure for desire, no cure for the love of reward, no cure for the misery of longing, save in the fixing of the sight and hearing on that which is invisible and soundless.†

A man must believe in his innate power of progress. A man must refuse to be terrified by his greater nature, and must not be drawn back by his lesser or material self.‡

All the past shows us that difficulty is no excuse for dejection, much less for despair, else the world would have been without the many wonders of civilization.§

Strength to step forward is the primary need of him who has chosen his path. Where is this to be found? Looking round it is not hard to see where other men find their strength. Its source is profound conviction.‖

Abstain because it is right to abstain, not that yourself shall be kept clean.¶

The man who wars against himself and wins the battle can do it only when he knows that in that war he is doing the one thing which is worth doing.**

"Resist not evil," that is, do not complain of or feel anger against the inevitable disagreeables of life. *Forget yourself* (in working for others). If men revile, persecute, or wrong one, why resist? In the resistance we create greater evils.††

The immediate work, *whatever it may be,* has the abstract claim of duty, and its relative importance or non-importance is *not to be considered at all.*‡‡ The best remedy for evil is not the suppression, but the *elimination of desire,* and this can best be accomplished by keeping the mind constantly steeped in things divine. The knowledge of the Higher Self is snatched away by engaging the mind in brooding over or

---

* "Magic," p. 126, Hartmann.
† Light on the Path, Karma, p. 35.
‡ Comments, Light on the Path.
§ Gates of Gold, p. 69.
‖ Gates of Gold.
¶ Light on the Path.
** Gates of Gold, p. 118.
†† Path, August, '87, p. 151.
‡‡ Lucifer, Feb., '88 (p. 478).

contemplating with pleasure the objects which correspond to the unruly sense.*

Our own nature is so base, proud, ambitious, and so full of its own appetites, judgments, and opinions, that if temptations restrained it not, it would be undone without remedy; therefore are we tempted to the end that we *may know ourselves and be humble.* Know that the greatest temptation is to be without temptation, wherefore be glad when it assaults thee, and with *resignation,* peace, and constancy, resist it.†

Feel that you have nothing to do *for yourself,* but that certain charges are laid upon you by the Deity, which you must fulfil. Desire God, and *not anything that he can give.*‡ Whatever there is to do, *has* to be done, but not for the sake of enjoying the fruit of action.§ If all one's acts are performed with the full conviction that they are of no value to the actor, but are to be done simply because they *have* to be done—in other words, because it is in our nature to act—then the personality of egotism in us will grow weaker and weaker until it comes to rest, permitting the knowledge revealing the True Self to shine out in all its splendour.§

One must not allow joy or pain to shake one from one's fixed purpose.‖

Until the Master chooses you to come to him *be* with humanity, and unselfishly work for its progress and advancement. This alone can bring true satisfaction.¶

Knowledge increases in proportion to its *use*—that is, the more we teach the more we learn. Therefore, seeker after Truth, with the faith of a little child and the *will* of an Initiate, give of your store to him, who hath not wherewithal to comfort him on his journey.**

A disciple must fully recognize that the very thought of individual rights is only the outcome of the venomous quality of the snake of Self. He must never regard another man as a person who can be criticised or condemned, nor may he raise his voice in self-defence or excuse.††

No man is your enemy, no man is your friend. *All alike are your teachers.*‡‡ One must no longer work for the gain of any *benefit,* temporal or *spiritual,* but to fulfil the law of being which is the righteous will of God.§§

---

* Page 60, Bhagavad Gita. (All quotations are taken from Mohini's translation)

† Molinos, Spiritual Guide. ‡ P. 182, Bhagavad Gita.

§ Introduction, Bhagavad Gita. ‖ Comments. Light on the Path.

¶ Path, December, '86, p. 279. ** Path, Dec. '86., p. 280.

†† Lucifer, p. 382, Jan. '88. ‡‡ Light on the Path. p. 25.

§§ Bhagavad Gita. Introduction.

WEDNESDAY.

Live neither in the present nor the future, but in the *eternal.* The giant weed (of evil) cannot flower then; this blot upon existence is wiped out by the very atmosphere of eternal thought.* Purity of heart is a necessary condition for the attainment of " Knowledge of the Spirit." There are two principal means by which this purification may be attained. First, drive away persistently every *bad thought ;* secondly, preserve an even mind under all conditions, *never be agitated or irritated at anything.* It will be found that these two means of purification are best promoted by *devotion* and *charity.* We must *not* sit idle and make no attempt to advance because we do not feel ourselves pure. *Let everyone aspire,* and let them work in right earnest, but they must work in the right way, and the first step of that way is to purify the heart.†

The mind requires purification whenever anger is felt or a falsehood is told, or the *faults of another needlessly disclosed ;* whenever anything is said or done for the purpose of flattery, or anyone is deceived by the insincerity of a speech or an act. ‡

Those who wish for salvation ought to avoid lust, anger and greed, and cultivate courageous obedience to the Scriptures, study of Spiritual philosophy, and *perseverance* in its practical realization. §

He who is led by selfish considerations cannot enter a heaven where personal considerations do not exist. *He who does not care for Heaven, but is contented where he is, is already in Heaven,* while the discontented will in vain clamour for it. To be without personal desires is to be free and happy, and " Heaven " can mean nothing else but a state in which freedom and happiness exist. The man who performs beneficial acts induced by a hope of reward is not happy unless the reward is obtained, and if his reward is obtained his happiness ends. There can be no permanent rest and happiness as long as there is some work to be done, and not accomplished, and the fulfilment of duties brings its own reward. ‖

He who thinks himself holier than another, he who has any pride in his own exemption from vice or folly, he who believes himself wise, or in any way superior to his fellow-men, is incapable of discipleship. A man must become as a little child before he can enter the Kingdom of Heaven. Virtue and wisdom are sublime things, but if they create pride and a consciousness of separateness from the rest

---

* Light on the Path, Rule 4.   ‡ Bhagavad Gita, p. 235.
† Theosophist, Oct., '88, p. 44.   § Bhagavad Gita, p. 240.
‖ " Magic," intro., p. 34, Hartmann.

of humanity, they are only the snakes of self reappearing in a finer form. The sacrifice or surrender of the *heart* of man *and its emotions* is the first of the rules, it involves "the attaining of an equilibrium which cannot be shaken by personal emotion." Put, without delay, your good intentions into practice, never leaving a single one to remain only an intention. Our only true course is to let the motive for action be in the action itself, never in its reward; not to be incited to action by the hope of the result, nor yet indulge a propensity to inertness.

" Through *faith* the *heart* is purified from passion and folly; from that comes mastery over the *body*, and, *last of all*, subjugation of the senses.†

The characteristics of the illuminated sage are, 1st., he is free from all desires,‡ and *knows* that the true Ego or Supreme Spirit *alone* is bliss, *all else* is pain. 2nd. That he is free from attachment and repulsion towards whatever may befall him, and that he acts without determination. *Lastly* comes the subjugation of the *senses*, which is useless, and frequently injurious as breeding hypocrisy and spiritual pride, without the second, and that again is not of much use without the first.§

" *He who does not practice altruism*, he who is not prepared to share his last morsel‖ with a weaker or poorer than himself, he who neglects to help his brother man, of whatever race, nation, or creed, *wherever and whenever* he meets suffering, and who turns a deaf ear to the cry of human misery; he who hears an innocent person slandered, and does not undertake his defence as he would undertake his own, *is no Theosophist.*

THURSDAY.

No man does right who gives up the unmistakable duties of life, resting on Divine command. He who performs duties, thinking that if they are *not* performed some evil will come to him, or that their performance will remove difficulties from his path, works for result. Duties should simply be done *because commanded by God*, who may at any time command their abandonment. So long as the restlessness of our nature is not reduced to tranquility we must work, consecrating to the Deity all fruit of our action, and attribute to Him *the power to perform works rightly*. The *true* life of man

---

* *I.e.*, knowledge, and this comes by the practice of unselfishness and kindness.

† P. 95., Bhagavad Gita.

‡ This can best be accomplished by keeping the mind constantly steeped in things divine.

§ P. 61, Bhagavad Gita.

This must be taken in its *widest* sense also, *i.e.* spiritual knowledge, etc.

is *rest in identity with the Supreme Spirit.* This life is not brought into existence by any *act* of ours, it is a reality, "the truth," and is *altogether independent of us.* The realization of the non-existence of all that seems opposed to this truth is *a new consciousness* and not an act. Man's liberation is in no way related to his acts. In so far as acts promote the realization of our utter inability to emancipate ourselves from conditioned existence, they are of use; after this stage realized acts become obstacles rather than helps. Those who work in obedience to Divine commands, knowing that the power thus to work is a gift of God, and no part of man's self-conscious nature, attain to freedom from the need of action. Then the pure heart is filled by the truth, and identity with the Deity is perceived. A man must first get rid of the idea that *he himself* really does anything, knowing that all actions take place in the " three natural qualities,"* and *not* in the soul at all. Then he must place all his actions on *devotion.* That is, sacrifice all his actions to the Supreme and not to himself. He must either set *himself* up as the God to whom he sacrifices, or the *other* real God—Krishna, and all his acts and aspirations are done either for himself or for the All. *Here comes in the importance of motive.* For if he performs great deeds of valour, or of benefit to man, or acquires knowledge so as to assist man, and is moved to that merely because he thus thinks *he* will attain salvation, he is only acting for his own benefit, and is therefore sacrificing *to himself.* Therefore he must be devoted inwardly to the All; knowing that *he* is *not* the doer of the actions, but the *mere witness* of them. As he is in a mortal body he is affected by doubts which *will* spring up. When they do arise, it is because he is ignorant about something. He should therefore be able to disperse doubt " by the sword of knowledge." For if he has a ready answer to some doubt he disperses that much. *All doubts come from the lower nature,* and *never* in any case from the higher nature. Therefore as he becomes more and more *devoted* he is able to know more and more clearly the knowledge residing in his Satwa (goodness) part. For it says: " A man who is perfected in *devotion* (or who persists in its cultivation) finds spiritual knowledge spontaneously in himself in progress of time." Also, " A man of doubtful mind enjoys neither this world nor the other (the Deva world), nor final beatitude." The last sentence is to *destroy* the idea that if there is in us this Higher Self it will, even if we are indolent and doubtful, triumph over the necessity for knowledge and lead us to final beatitude in common with the whole stream of mankind.†

---

* Of the *body, i.e.,* Goodness, Badness, and Indifference.

† Path, July '89, p. 109.

True prayer is the contemplation of all sacred things, of their application to ourselves, our daily life and actions, accompanied by the most heartfelt and intense desire to make their influence stronger and our lives better and nobler that some knowledge of them may be vouchsafed to us. All such thoughts must be closely interwoven with a consciousness of the Supreme and Divine Essence from which all things have sprung.*

Spiritual culture is attained through *concentration*. It must be continued daily and *every moment to be of use*. *Meditation* has been defined as " the cessation of active external thought." *Concentration* is the entire life tendency to a given end. For example, a devoted mother is one who consults the interests of her children and *all* branches of their interests in and before all things; not one who sits down to think fixedly about *one* branch of their interests all the day. Thought has a self reproductive power, and when the mind is held steadily to one idea it becomes coloured by it, and as we may say, all the correlates of that thought arise within the mind. Hence the mystic obtains knowledge about any object of which he thinks constantly in fixed contemplation. Here is the rationale of Krishna's words. " Think constantly of me; depend on me alone, and *thou shall surely come to me*." Life is the great teacher: it is the great manifestation of Soul, and Soul manifests the Supreme. Hence all methods are good, and all are but parts of the great aim, which is Devotion. " Devotion is success in actions," says the Bhagavad Gita. The psychic powers, as they come, must also be used, for they reveal laws. But their value must not be exaggerated, nor must their danger be ignored. He who relies on them is like a man who gives way to pride and triumph because he has reached the first wayside station on the peaks he has set out to climb.†

———

FRIDAY.

It is an eternal law that man cannot be redeemed by a power *external to himself*. Had this been possible, an angel might long ago have visited the earth, uttered heavenly truths, and, by manifesting the faculties of a spiritual nature, proved a hundred facts to the consciousness of man of which he is ignorant.‡

Crime is committed *in the Spirit* as truly as in the deeds of the body. He who for *any* cause hates another, who loves revenge, and will not forgive an injury, is full of the spirit of murder, though none may know it.

---

* Path, Aug. '89, p. 159.   † Path, July, '89, p. 111.
‡ Spirit of the New Testament, p. 508.

He who bows before false creeds, and crushes his conscience at the bidding of any institution, blasphemes his own divine soul, and therefore " takes the name of God in vain " though he never utters an oath. He who desires, and is in sympathy with the mere pleasures of sense, either in or out of the married relation, is the *real adulterer*. He who deprives any of his fellows of the light, the good, the help, the assistance he can wisely give them, and lives for the *accumulation of material things*, for his own personal gratification, is the real robber ; and he who steals from his fellows the precious possession of character by slander, and any sort of misrepresentation, is no less a thief, and one of the most guilty kind.*

If men were only honest with themselves and *kindly disposed* towards others, a tremendous change would take place in their estimate of the value of life, and of the things of this life.†

Develop thought. Strive, by concentrating the whole force of your soul, to shut the door of your mind to all stray thoughts, allowing none to enter but those calculated to reveal to you the unreality of sense, life, and the Peace of the Inner World. Ponder day and night over the unreality of all your surroundings and of yourself. The springing up of *evil* thoughts is less injurious than that of idle and indifferent ones. Because as to evil thoughts you are always on your guard, and, having determined to fight and conquer them, this determination helps to develop the will power. Indifferent thoughts, however, serve merely to distract the attention and waste energy. The *first great basic delusion* you have to get over is the identification of yourself with the physical body. Begin to think of this body as nothing better than the house you have to live in for a time, and then you will never yield to its temptations. Try also with consistent attempts to conquer the prominent weaknesses of your nature by developing thought in the direction that will kill each particular passion. After your first efforts you will begin to feel an indescribable vacuum and blankness in your heart ; fear not, but regard this as the soft twilight heralding the rise of the sun of Spiritual bliss. Sadness is not an evil. Complain not ; what seem to be sufferings and obstacles are often in reality the mysterious efforts of nature to help you in your work if you can manage them properly. Look upon *all* circumstances with the gratitude of a pupil.‡ All complaint is a rebellion against the law of progress. That which is to be shunned is *pain not yet come*. The *past cannot* be changed or amended ; that which belongs to the experiences of the *present* cannot and *should* not

---

* Spirit of the New Testament, p. 513.

† Theosophist, July, '89, p. 590.

‡ T.P.S. No. 3, Vol. 2, '89.

be shunned; but alike to be shunned are *disturbing anticipations* or *fears of the future,* and every act or *impulse* that may cause *present or future pain* to ourselves or *others.*[*]

SATURDAY.

There is no more valuable thing possessed by any individual than an *exalted ideal* towards which he continually aspires, and after which he moulds his thoughts and feelings, and forms *as best he may* his life. If he thus strives to *become* rather than to seem, he cannot fail to continually approach nearer his aim. He will not, however, reach this point without a struggle, nor will the real progress that he is conscious of making fill him with conceit of self-righteousness; for if his ideal be high, and his progress towards it real, he will be the rather humiliated than puffed up. The possibilities of further advancement, and the conception of still higher planes of being that open before him, will not dampen his ardour, though they will surely kill his conceit. It is just this conception of the vast possibilities of human life that is needed to kill out *ennui,* and to convert apathy into zest. Life thus becomes worth living for its own sake when its mission becomes plain, and its splendid opportunities are once appreciated. The most direct and certain way of reaching this higher plane is the cultivation of the *principle of altruism,* both in *thought and life.* Narrow indeed is the sweep of vision that is limited to self, and that measures all things by the principle of self-interest, for while the soul is thus self limited it is impossible for it to conceive of any high ideal, or to approach any higher plane of life. The conditions of such advancement lie *within* rather than without, and are fortunately made *independent of circumstances and condition* in life. The opportunity therefore is offered to *everyone* of advancing from height to height of being and of thus working with nature in the accomplishment of the evident purpose of life. [†]

If we believe that the object of life is simply to render our material self satisfied, and to keep it in comfort, and that material comfort confers the highest state of possible happiness, we mistake the ow for the high, and an illusion for the truth. Our material mode of life is a consequence of the material constitution of our bodies. We are "worms of the earth" because we cling with all our aspirations to earth. If we can enter upon a path of evolution, by which we become less material and more ethereal, a very different order of civilization would be established. Things which now appear indispens-

---

[*] Pantanjali Aphorisms 16, book 2, Q. E. Judge.
[†] " Man," J. Buck, p. 106.

able and necessary would cease to be useful; if we could transfer our consciousness with the velocity of the thought from one part of the globe to another, the present mode of communication would be no longer required. The deeper we sink into matter, the more material means for comfort will be needed; the *essential* and powerful god in man is *not material*, and independent f the restrictions laid upon matter. What are the *real* necessities of life? The answer to this question depends entirely on what we imagine to be necessary. Railways, steamers, etc., are now a necessity to us, and yet millions of people have lived long and happily, knowing nothing about them. To one man a dozen palaces may appear to be an indispensable necessity, to another a carriage, another a pipe, and so on. But *all such necessities are only such as man himself has created*. They make the state in which man now is agreeable to him, and *tempt him to remain* in that state, and to desire nothing higher. They may even hinder his development instead of advancing it. Everything material must cease to become a necessity if we would really advance spiritually. It is the *craving* and the *wasting of thought* for the *augmentation* of the pleasures of the lower life which prevent man entering the higher one.*

---

* " Magic "; Hartmann, p. 61.

SOME HINTS ON THE THEOSOPHICAL TRAINING OF CHILDREN.

" Ye open the Eastern windows,
That look towards the sun."

In these two lines a great poet expresses one of his thoughts about children, and the idea is full of suggestion to anyone who has come in contact with the fresh and natural mind of a child, who has watched its intuitive powers, and its simple faith that accepts truth without question,—nay, not only without question, but with clear understanding, as if, indeed, it still retained some glow from those " trailing clouds of glory " which so soon grow dim and " fade into the light of common day." These little ones do, indeed, "open the Eastern windows " for us, letting in sunlight and air on our shadowed and stifled lives ; and by our very love for them they draw us into a higher life, and often do more to educate us than we do to train them.

We see in the natural child the unconsciousness of self that we have lost —the simple regard for things as they are stripped of the world's opinion of them—the frank, outspoken word and revealment of their thought, which puts to shame our use of language to conceal thought, the natural modesty and refinement which is as far as possible removed from our grown-up propriety, which is measured only by what other people say. All these contrasts between ourselves and them bring before us many thoughts.

And two specially prominent questions occur to us : (1) Why do we not make ourselves more child-like ? (2) Why do we not endeavour to keep our children child-like ? If we are earnest Theosophists—that is, if we are earnestly trying to live up to the spiritual truths in our own form of religious belief, which it is one of the great aims of Theosophy to show us—we have already answered the first question by trying to cultivate the teachable mind, the open heart and clear spirit, without which very little growth can go on ; we are trying to make thought and life harmonious, to put aside shams and selfishness, prejudice and pride, and in very truth to " become as little children." And our efforts with ourselves, our struggles in our own growth, bring forcibly home to us the need for looking seriously into the defects in modern methods of educating children. Seeing the hard task of uprooting so much that has become ingrained in our characters, the difficult warfare against habits, mental and bodily, which we have only just begun to try and conquer—seeing all this, we must ask ourselves, Can we not save our children the same long, hard struggle, or, at any rate, mitigate it by equipping them at the outset with proper weapons, and teaching them how to use them ?

Whilst we are striving to become more child-like, we see the children growing rapidly into old men and women, becoming hard and materialistic, almost before they can speak plainly, and losing that lovely freshness and clearness of soul so valuable to the aftergrowth, so necessary to spiritual development.

To acknowledge the evil is the first step, to remedy it, a harder task, but one that as earnest Theosophists we must not shirk. For, as each one of us has to find the truth *within* himself—and only so can it be perceived and known —so it behoves us to help our children to keep the clear mirror of the soul untainted, and free from everything that can distort the Divine images reflected on its surface.

Our first aim should be to promote the harmonious development of all the faculties; to strive after bodily, mental, and spiritual perfection, and to endeavour to make the advance equal in each. If we strain the mind and starve the body, we warp and destroy both. To starve the mind and soul produces equally disastrous results; but perhaps our worst error nowadays is the excessive stimulation of the mind, especially the lower critical faculty, and the almost total disregard and stunting of the imagination.

The senses should be cultivated; indeed, they are not trained sufficiently, but, at the same time, they should not be regarded as the only avenues to knowledge. To train a child to *see*—really to see an object on which its eye rests—not only quickens and sharpens the sense of sight, but gives it a power of creating and holding mind pictures which stand out clear and strong, and also develops higher powers and greater capacity for abstract thought than we can have any idea of until we have tried the experiment upon ourselves; so with all the senses. We do not want our brains burdened with confused masses of facts and images, and half-blurred memories, a kaleidoscopic tangle of colours and forms and ideas coming and going whether we wish it or not. How much more, then, should we try to train the young growing brain of a child, to give it few ideas, and those clear ones—few images, and those distinct—to nourish its mind with a small quantity of easily digested food, instead of pouring a perpetual stream of miscellaneous knowledge into its brain, the very amount alone preventing its being of any use. Pouring in—not drawing out—such is modern education to a very great extent. Together with this cultivation of the senses should the reasoning faculties grow, but kept in subjection as half-developed powers, not dragged into prominence, otherwise conceit and self-confidence shut out further knowledge. In children, and in uneducated people, the intuitive powers are strong; but as the logical faculty develops, the intuition becomes less prominent, and, if resolutely set aside, disregarded, and unused, will wither and lie entirely dormant; and as an unused limb hampers and warps the body, so will this dormant faculty hamper and warp the soul. The logical powers, trained side by side with the intuitional, will produce the highest form of intellect—the intellect that may be more rightly named genius. A natural child is humble and anxious to learn, ready to reverence and respect what is higher and wiser than itself, and this reverence should be fostered and carefully guarded, not by parents and others in auth rity setting themselves up on a pedestal, and all the time allowing the child to see weaknesses and want of dignity that destroy the authority and re pect at once, but by influencing and commanding their obedience and regard by showing them that we are fallible as they are, struggling against temptation and faults, doing wrong and getting punished for it like themselves, but still trying to follow a high ideal, and reverencing all that is wiser than ourselves. If we show them ourselves thus striving, we step down and take them by the hand and draw them upwards with us, instead of tanding on what is to a child an unreachable level of supposed goodness, with the chance of the child losing all faith in that goodness by seeing we are but human after all.

First, then, train the senses in due order and with full knowledge of their limitations, letting the child see that where these stop short, faith begins—that side by side with the visible, tangible world, lies that larger and more real invisible world, to be believed in first, and afterwards to be apprehended and known as the child grows and develops. So we lay a groundwork on which to build *self-knowledge,* and together with this must be built its inseparable companion, *self-control.*

From the very beginning a child should be taught this, and the little efforts at self-command and the conquest of uncontrolled impulses give a child a sense of power, strength and reliance that cannot be given by any outward authority. Let it see that faults and tendencies to wrong-doing are not to be excused on the ground of natural defect or bad example of others, but as so many difficulties to be overcome, so many opportunities for self-conquest, so many lessons set for us to learn, for our final good and well-being. Never let a child say, " I cannot do this." Put in its way only such tasks as are within its power, and see that the required effort is made, or better leave it unattempted. For succcessful effort braces and inspirits the whole being, and gives confidence, whilst nothing so deteriorates the character as half-done work. Unquestioning obedience is another most necessary factor in education. But commands should be few and certain. Wavering indecision in issuing commands is fatal to authority. No child should be irritated with a host of petty orders and rules, but the habit of instant obedience, when once the word of command has gone forth, should be established early. No one can rule till he has learned to obey.

It is difficult in a short space to touch on the wide and important question of punishment, but a few general remarks may be made.

Theosophists should bear in mind the law of Karma, and carry it out in their training.

Punishments should rather be called *consequences*—the inevitable result of a cause. A child should be made to see that certain effects follow certain of its actions as surely as night follows day. And due warning of the effect should be given. If you do such or such an action, this or that penalty will follow! Parents should never punish in anger, never lose temper with a child; but calmly administer the previously threatened payment for breach of law. Children are very quick to perceive, and the *certainty* of the effect is the only deterrent to the act in future.

Punishments depriving children of food or play, or any of the necessaries of life, should be avoided, likewise long tasks that try the brain or nerves; and, of course, all threats of unknown bogies or other methods of working on their fears are as wicked as they are useless.

Too many people punish offences against custom and manners as heavily, if not more so, than moral delinquencies. This gives a child a very false idea of the relative proportion of human and Divine law.

In all our action and attitude towards children, love, and love alone, should be apparent as our motive power. Discipline and teaching alike prompted by our desire for their final welfare. Pain and sorrow, pleasure and happiness, given in the same loving spirit, for the same wise and good end; and the more we realize that our own education goes on in the same way, the more will our children see and understand the use of our discipline.

And here we touch on the root of the whole subject. It is *our* growth, *our* education, that affects them. It is what we think and what we believe that has most effect on them. When we realize, as all students of Occultism must realize, that our unspoken word, our most secret thought, is given out by us unconsciously, and either taints or purifies the subtle atmosphere around us, and takes effect for good or evil on those with whom we come in contact, then, and then only, do we wake up to our terrible responsibilities, and the need for the most searching cleansing of those thoughts, the need for high and lofty ideals, for perpetually dwelling in thought on all that is good and beautiful, that no inward taint of ours may sully their purity, nor infect them with evil. They can in this way imbibe our faith, our deepest religious beliefs, our love of and trust in the Divine, just as they will no less surely catch our want of faith, our doubt and cynical discontent with life.

Let us, then, as children too, members of the one great family, by our striving, our own growth in goodness, our own sense of the unity and harmony of all things, make an atmosphere of sunshine and purity for our children to live in, and from the very beginning of their young lives inculcate those larger lessons of universal Brotherhood which Theosophists are endeavouring to teach, so shall we no less than they open windows towards the East for them and for ourselves.

March, 1890.   FRANCIS ANNESLEY.

PRINTED BY ALLEN, SCOTT AND CO., 30, BOUVERIE STREET, E.C.

A SUMMARY OF

BERTRAM KEIGHTLEY'S LECTURES

IN AMERICA.

———————

AUM.

———————

London :

PUBLISHED BY THE T.P.S., 7, DUKE STREET, ADELPHI.

1890.

A SUMMARY OF BERTRAM KEIGHTLEY'S LECTURES IN AMERICA.

WE are all interested in efforts to spread, as widely as possible, the benefits that result from a knowledge of Theosophy. But when these efforts are attended with such marked success as that which has followed the addresses of Mr. Bertram Keighley in the United States it is felt that a permanent record of the good work done will be welcomed. It will, moreover, answer two purposes. In the first place an epitome of lectures delivered to audiences for the most part ignorant of the scope and objects of Theosophy, will be useful to put into the hands of inquirers; in the second it will permit the expression of heartfelt esteem and sympathy with one who has thrown aside all considerations of personal ease to devote himself untiringly to the interests of humanity.

An attempt will be made to put before the reader a complete statement of the ground covered by Mr. Keightley; and only such additions will be made to the lecturer's words, as reported in the American press, as may serve to link together parts which would otherwise appear disjointed.

The Theosophical Society was founded in 1875, by Colonel Henry S. Olcott, and Madame Blavatsky, a Russian. The first is a soldier of eminence, who has held high places of honour and trust in this country, and the second is a lady of rank and family in her native land. It would seem strange that the organization should have taken the name of Theosophy, when it does not accept any of its dogmas. The explanation is found on consideration of the ancient meaning of the word. It was first used in Alexandria, and its fundamental idea was the union of all religions. As the Society is founded on universal brotherhood, it accepts the idea of the unity of religions, and strives to bring them into harmony. The Society is a protest against the materialism of the day, and the aim of its members is to recall to men the spiritual side of life.

The chief principle of the Society is co-operation, and its mission is to establish in the world a true feeling of that brotherhood which binds all men into one common family. The Society has no creed, tenets, or religion. In non-sectarianism it is absolute, and it requires from its members exactly the same toleration in regard to the opinions of others as each claims for his own. In reference to Theosophy, it is an ancient system of thought, embodying an accurate, scientific, and experimental knowledge of those planes of nature which transcend the observation of the physical senses. It is as old as the human race, and its existence can be traced from the earliest time of which we have any recollection. Madame Blavatsky, by her literary works, has been largely instrumental in putting the system into a form suited to our present mental tendencies. Theosophists do not regard her writing as infallible, but as a text-book and guide, to assist the student in his own researches. The endeavour of Theosophists is to follow the rule laid down by Gautama Buddha: " Do not believe a thing because I say it. Do not believe a thing because the Scriptures teach it. Do not believe a thing because others believe it. But believe it only when you have satisfied your reason in regard to it." Theosophy is not Buddhism, however, any more than it is Mohammedanism or Christianity. It is the essential truth underlying all these, for, in the opinion of Theosophists, religion is merely the science of those planes and states of being which lie beyond the cognisance of our physical senses. Theosophy differs from modern science in that it analyses the universe into three factors instead of two. Materialism regards the universe as built up of matter in motion, and endeavours to trace the origin of intelligence from this matter in motion. But Theosophy recognises three co-existing factors in nature : matter, motion, and mind, or, substance, energy, and intelligence. In its application to human life, Theosophy recognises as its mental doctrine the idea of evolution, though it differs from the Darwinian school in many parts of detail. It teaches the growth and development of the human individual through successive reincarnations or re-embodiments of this spiritual individuality upon this earth. The circumstances and surroundings of each re-incarnation, as well as the inborn faculties, aptitudes and tendencies of the child being the result of his own action in preceding lives upon this earth. As our lives are composed of days and nights, and there are days and nights of the universe of immense duration, and practically infinite to our comprehension, although really only as drops of water in the mighty ocean. The out-breathing of the universe becomes an intelligent power which informs all being and nature. There is no such thing as creation out of nothing. We trace manifestations of ideas, forms, types, species, varieties, and individuals. This process is sometimes referred to as the descent of spirit into matter, for matter is the crystallization of spirit. In stones and rocks, modern science recognises vibrations of atoms, but Theosophy teaches that a consciousness exists in stone or rock which, to our finite minds, is absolutely inconceivable. The material aspect undergoes a change at last, in the return cycle, and ultimately the universal return to the great mother, resting in her bosom till the time comes for the dawn of a new day upon a more perfect scale. The law of harmony, or the law of equilibrium, is the basis of all form of law recognised by science. For what purpose is all this ? The primary fact is a spiritual monad, which is eternal in the past as well as in the future. It has descended into matter under every form of manifestation. In past cycles the spiritual monad has evolved upward through all stages of plants, and animals, up to man himself. It then crystallizes and acquires immortality. This constitutes the individuality of the true inner man, which is *per se* immortal. Individuality is not the same as personality, the latter being only the experience which pertains to a single physical life, as Mr. Smith or Mr. Jones. The goal of man, or selfless immortality, is directly opposed to selfishness, which is death and destruction. Union of the personal self with the divine self forms what Buddhists term Nirvana, or conscious bliss and rest in eternity. The individual is like an actor who plays different parts on successive nights. The actor is always one and the same, but he identifies himself successively with the various parts he performs. To-night he is Hamlet, to-morrow King Lear, next Macbeth, and the following, Mark Antony. So the individuality manifests in one life as Mr. Smith, next as Mr. Jones, and so on in another form until it has simulated every type of experience possible on earth. The monad is sexless and androgynous. On our plane it manifests through male or female, the sexes usually being alternate in successive incarnations; though there are some exceptions to this rule. In regard to a human being, Theosophy sees in him seven modes of manifestation. First, his gross material body, which we perceive through material senses; second, his vitality; third, the ethereal form in which, and through which, his grosser or physical manifestation, is built; fourth, the animal instincts and passions; fifth, the mind or intelligence; sixth, the spiritual soul or the most subtle and the highest form in which matter can exist; seventh and last, that divine ray or animation that traverses life after life, through the other six, and finally constitutes all, the sum of previous incarnations.

Re-incarnation means the re-embodiment of the true ego, or the individuality, and this re-incarnation is brought about under known laws, called Karma. It is obvious to everyone who will pause a moment, that one life, even if it be extended a hundred years, is not adequate to experience all the things necessary to beautify and develop the individuality; besides, re-incarnation gives a clear solution of many mysteries in human nature which cannot be explained by heredity or any other principle. At the present time re-incarnation is the belief of two-thirds of the human race, and in early times it was probably accepted by a still larger proportion. It is a Christian doctrine, as is manifest from the conversation between Jesus and Nicodemus, the instance of the man born blind, and several other passages in the Gospel. It was held by Justin Martyr, Clement of Alexandria, Origen, and, to some extent, by St. Augustine. It is the basis of the doctrine of original sin, and sheds light upon the double nature of man, and the continual contest between flesh and spirit.

In a word, that it alone adequately solves the problem of life. Many people object to the doctrine of re-incarnation on the ground that we do not remember any prior state of existence, but Theosophy teaches that is only due to the fact that the physical brain can be conscious only of what has been registered upon it. The physical brain is a new formation in each life, and is in most people not sufficiently sensitive to register impressions proceeding from the spirituality and individuality within man. But what is called the voice of conscience is, in truth, nothing but the impulse communicated to our physical consciousness by our inner selves. As the human race evolves, the physical mechanism will respond more readily to these impressions, and we shall regain the memory of our past lives. There are men living who, by a special course of life and training, have acquired that faculty, and they state that re-incarnation is a fact. Theosophists maintain that the doctrine of re-incarnation may be reasonably accepted by men, because it affords the best and only satisfactory explanation of the inequalities of birth, and of the innate tendencies with which every child is born, and of many other of the mysterious problems of life. But remember that these are not the doctrines of the Theosophical Society, but the conclusions arrived at by many of its members as the result of investigation and research. Certain experiments prove that consciousness can be preserved at a distance from the physical organism; that the greater part of the eternal universe is transcendental to our physical senses, as demonstrated by dream life and somnambulism. Space cannot be eliminated from human consciousness. It must be omnipotent and infinite; lying at the foundation of all phenomena that we see in nature, under the three aspects of eternal substance or matter, eternal motion or energy, and abstract, absolute consciousness. These are not separate things, but one, everywhere present at every point. The personal self is embraced in a larger whole. The true ego preserves all that is highest and best in numerous incarnations. The theory that the earth moves round the sun is accepted because it best explains all the facts observed. For a similar reason the doctrine of reincarnation should be received. It is a matter of re-collection to some persons, particularly children.

Theosophy teaches that after death the human ego passes into a subjective condition, and there enjoys the complete fruition of all its higher affections, loves, and aspirations. All the animal passions, impulses, and desires are left behind in an intermediate state before the ego passes into the subjective condition in which the ego is wholly absorbed in the bliss of its present experience. It does not realize the fact that it has left the physical world, and is too fully occupied to reflect upon and think about the actual state, which is like that of the man who is absorbed in listening to a strain of beautiful music. His attention is too completely engaged to permit him to be conscious of anything except the music to which he is listening. While he remains in that condition he is oblivious to his actual surroundings, and will even be unaware that someone is speaking to him. But remember the experience of the ego in the subjective world are real to it, and many times more vivid than are any of the experiences of the earth-life, of which we are familiar. Since the ego is in a subjective condition, it cannot meet and recognise departed spirits in the ordinary sense of the meaning of those words; but all those to whom it has been attached, or whom it has loved during earth-life, will be present as really and actually as if they were still living together in actual life. And this, whether those persons are already dead or still living upon the earth. The best analogy to guide one in forming a correct conception of the subjective state of existence may be found in the study of our dream-life. In a vivid dream we are conscious of elaborate scenery and surroundings. We hold long and animated conversations with persons living and dead, or even with strangers, and while we are dreaming, the whole experience is as actual and real to us as our waking life. But, nevertheless, there can be no question that we are ourselves both the creator of the scenery and surroundings of our dreams, and of the personages who figure therein, and we are the inspirers of the thoughts which they express. It is in a manner analogous to this that the ego creates its own objective world, and the personages who play their parts in this subjective life. In this way alone is it possible for the after-death state to be one of perfect bliss. Take, for instance, the case of a husband and wife, when the husband is deeply in love with the wife, but she does not reciprocate that affection. If the husband dies, he certainly cannot be happy without the companionship of the wife he has loved. But should the wife happen to be in love with some other person, she will not want her husband with her. However, when both are dead, the wife will figure as a part of the husband's subjective experience, but the husband will play no part in that of the wife. Supposing a woman has had three or four husbands, and had truly loved each one, they will all play a part in the wife's after-death dream in the same order in which she loved them, and to the extent to which she was attached to them; and similarly, each of the husbands, who had truly loved his wife, will have her as a part of his experience when he passes into the subjective condition. Nature is an absolutely just, yet a kindly mother, to her children, and while she requires at the hand of every man the payment of his just debts to the uttermost farthing, she yet provides for him a long period of blissful rest and refreshment before he is called upon to take up anew the burden of earth-life, and to pay the penalties which he has deserved through his own actions. The larger part of what we term sin and evil proceeds from, and, is confined, to the animal nature and instincts within us, and although these must of necessity produce their appropriate consequences, on the physical plane, in subsequent lives, yet the higher nature of the man is not so deeply stained by them as to render him, as a rule, unfitted for a blissful subjective condition after death. It requires a Satan in human form to deserve a subjective hell. The vast majority of human beings pass into a blissful condition after death, but the intensity of the bliss they experience will depend upon the extent to which the man has developed his spiritual aspirations. Theosophy holds that men are more often sinned against than sinning, and since we suffer personally for deeds done by our egos in past existences, of which we have no recollection, justice requires that the personal consciousness of man should in some way be compensated for the sufferings which his inner self, or spiritual ego, has deserved. Moreover, a large part of our suffering is due to the fact that many of our better and nobler aspirations and longings can find no fulfilment in earth-life, owing to the pressure of circumstances, and it is just these which find their complete fruition in the subjective world.

Theosophy accepts as genuine the phenomena known as spiritualistic, excepting, of course, those cases which are proven to be frauds. But it differs from spiritualism in the explanation it gives of them. Theosophy teaches that the physical phenomena of the *séance* rooms are not produced by the spirits of the departed, with the exception, however, of the occasional intervention of suicides in these productions. With regard to the intelligence manifested in many so-called spirit communications, Theosophy holds that it is derived from the higher consciousness of the medium or one of the sitters present. In reference to the phenomena of materialization, Theosophy says they are produced mainly through the medium's astral body, which oozes out from the left side, and assumes the form of some person whose picture is vividly impressed on the mental sphere of one of the sitters present, or else moulds itself upon the astral corpse, which the ego leaves behind in the subtile world before it passes into the subjective condition. But Theosophy holds that it is possible for the spirit of a living human being to take up the mental vibrations proceeding from an entity in the subjective world, and so to reflect, as it were, the mental conditions and surroundings of that ego; but the ego in question is not conscious of such communication taking place, because in that condition the faculty of self-analysis or self-reflection is dormant. It must be remembered that psychic phenomena existed long before the manifestations in modern times. The Costatics, Swedenborg, Jacob Böhme, and others, gave evidence of abnormal faculties and powers which we term psychic. So, also, Paracelsus, Van Helmont, and the Albigenses, the Pythonesses and Sybils of Greece. The Jews had their schools of the prophets for the training of the faculties. The Egyptian, Persian, and Indian schools had systematic plans of training. What was it that was taught in these mysteries? Every great writer of antiquity has borne witness to the value of the science of nature and man. All the great inventors, teachers, and leaders of men, have taught the same. The Egyptians possessed knowledge of electricity, and probably of steam also. Hypnotism or mesmerism is mentioned in the oldest Vedas and books dating back to the earliest night of time. Pythagoras and Plato spoke of these mysteries in the highest terms. Theosophists maintain that this is the beginning of a more spiritual cycle, and that within the next few years mental evolution will make extraordinarily rapid advancement, supplemented by great scientific discoveries and the demonstration of finer forces in nature. The experiments of the famous Charcot in hypnotism illustrate the scientific awakening to the importance of occult forces. The psychological researches of Ribot and Binet are of equally great importance The comprehensive philosophy more or less expounded by numerous Theosophic publications is a preparatory course for the esoteric teachings given to her pupils by Mme. Blavatsky, and involves the basic laws of reincarnation and Karma. Much of the superficial literature of the day embodies in a crude form theories promulgated by Theosophists, such as refer to manifestation of the magnetic and electrical forces, to the phenomena of clairvoyance, clairaudience, somnambulism and mesmerism. Popular taste craves the exaltation of the senses thus afforded, and feeds its hunger for the marvellous, but isolated students are making unimpassioned and careful expeditions into the psychological realm- collecting the fundamental laws of biology, and preparing text-books for the coming generation.

Possibly not another century will pass before the attributes of ether will be as familiar to man as those of gas, and his intelligent manipulation may develop cognition of new functions and potencies in himself, fulfilling the ancient prophecy that all nature shall be subordinate to man.

There is nothing mystic in the study of Theosophy; it is simply investigation of natural laws and the development of natural powers, latent though they be in every soul, and in the present state of thought, when the minds of men are in a constant ferment, and the development of new and strange powers and faculties is rapidly taking place among us, a scientific study of the knowledge possessed by our forefathers will be of inestimable value to mankind.

The immediate advantage of the pursuit of Theosophy is the impetus it affords humanity toward self-analysis and self-study—a positive knowledge of the present in place of vague beliefs and useless speculations upon future existence—a just estimate of man's relation to society and his duties to himself; for "the study of mankind is man," and although his life is but an infinitesimal fraction of the whole, it shares with it the attribute of endlessness.

And this brings us to the question of religion. Now, the first point which I wish to say to you in regard to religion is that it must be scientific. Our tenets must conform to strict logic and be capable of rational explanation. We must accept nothing on faith, and must not surrender our minds to bigotry or prejudice. In the search of this rational and scientific religion, the leaders of our organization are teaching now a system of Theosophy, not as a dogma, but as a means of assisting the members of the society in arriving at religious conclusions, which they can formulate for themselves into distinct and logical creeds.

The Theosophist's comprehension of diety is pantheistic, but the ultimate fact is one absolute, unknown and unknowable. Deity is a reality, and of it man does not, nor ever can he know. In order to understand him, it is necessary to be his equal, and it is no use to talk of an infinite knower, for if infinite, nothing can exist out of him, nothing is then to be known.

In the West the good done by the society has been chiefly in giving a standing room for those whose intellectual lives are darkened by the materialistic creeds of the day. It has nothing to offer to the selfish mind. Its principles of co-operation are rather for the altruistic than for the egotistic. It furnishes a congenial companionship for all who are struggling toward a newer and truer light. The individual who attempts to stand alone cannot have that support which is found in the presence of companions. In this, as in all things else, union is strength. The Theosophical Society stands in a better position than any other ever founded, to carry on the war for the intellectual freedom of humanity. Many societies for this purpose have been founded from the earliest ages, but hitherto all have failed.

In considering what the society has done towards developing a spirit of brotherly benevolence throughout the world, we must turn first to the East. In no part of the world has there been so much race and theological prejudice as in India. Here the spirit of caste has separated man from man by a chasm which made united effort impossible, and rendered the country helpless in the hands of every conqueror. In this country the society has already wrought great changes. It has, by inculcating the unity of all religions, brought many of these people into concord with one another, and is enabling them to act together and in harmony for the general good of the country and its people. And not the least part of its work has been to break down prejudices in European minds in regard to the races of the East, and familiarize the Eastern and Western races, and thus make their relations more real and close. One thousand years ago the Hindus were split up into small subdivisions, and no co-operation was possible except among small clans. Since the Theosophical Society commenced its work, men of all four castes meet together and co-operate on the platform, in hospitals, dispensaries, schools, etc. The society has brought into co-operation the conquered Hindus and their Mohammedan conquerors; also the Buddhists of Ceylon, who were expelled 800 years ago. Among the Buddhists there have been two churches, as widely separated as Roman Catholics and Protestants. A reconciliation has been brought about between these two churches. In the East men of every creed—Hindus, Parsees, Buddhists, Mohammedans, Chinese and Japanese—all meet together, forgetting their differences, and co-operating in establishing knowledge of the truths of nature.

I may say right here that a part of the good work done by the Theosophists in the East has been to counteract the evils wrought by the missionaries of the established churches of Christianity. These by the example of the missionaries and by the doctrine of vicarious atonement have done much to corrupt the natives. The Christianized people of India have been degraded rather than elevated by a belief which teaches them that they are to be saved not by their own works, but by the atonement of Christ.

In India there are 175 branches of the Theosophical Society, and in Ceylon, also, a great work has been performed, and a new stimulus given to life, which has shown itself chiefly in the advance of womanhood in that island, where there are twenty branches, with an average of fifty members to a branch. The Society is growing rapidly. No proselytizing is done. It is not a matter of conversion; it is a matter of growth and development. When a mind becomes receptive to higher religious truths, it will seek them, and until it does become receptive, there is no use trying to force them into it. During a recent tour of Japan, Colonel Olcott, the president of the Society, lectured before twelve Buddhist sects, and in temples where no American or European ever before set foot. He went by invitation from the Buddhist sects there. They formed a joint committee to receive him and organize his tour. They sent a deputation to escort him from Ceylon. He took with him letters of credence and introduction from the High Priest of Ceylon, head of the Southern Buddhist Church. He was received royally by the Japanese people, spoke three times a day to native audiences numbering several thousands each, was entertained in temples, and when he left was presented with many rare books, pictures, and manuscripts for the library at Adyar, the headquarters of the whole Theosophical Society. We have in the Society Hindus of all castes and sects, Buddhists, Mahommedans, Parsees, besides Christians of the Protestant and Roman Catholic Churches of every sect, creed and denomination. Right here in the United States we have lawyers, physicians, generals, railway men, and men at the head of large commercial enterprises. All these have their individual beliefs, but are active members of the Society. Our rules permit the broadest and most varied individual beliefs, and require only that all shall unite in working for the cause of universal brotherhood, and that each shall exercise the same toleration towards all that he expects to receive for himself. Remember that Theosophy is not the creed or religion of the Theosophical Society, since the Society has, and can have, no creed or religion whatever.

On the other hand, it is not a school of magic, and has nothing to offer to those bent on purely selfish ends. Yet it must not be supposed that we expect the Theosophist to be free from selfishness at the beginning of his membership. There are three stages of his life. We find in the first stage students who have joined through finding in Theosophy a clue to much that is dark in the Western system of metaphysics; students of science who have joined for the sake of light on the genesis of man and the elements, on the relation of the moon to the earth and kindred topics; together with others who have joined through interest in its teachings as to religious symbolism. These find in one another's society sympathetic and elevating influence, yet they gradually become satiated with intellectualism, with words and phrases, and come to think that they are making no headway, and that Theosophy is all empty talk. They are to blame for this satiety. When a man has taken in a certain amount of knowledge he cannot receive more without giving out some of his store. When they come to understand this truth and to act upon it they progress to the second state.

In this state the Theosophist desires to experience a love of the universal brotherhood of mankind, and, therefore, wants to serve his fellows, and to learn how best to do so. To this end it is that he who seeks for broader knowledge. And just as he works for others does he improve spiritually. His sympathies quicken, his grasp of spiritual truth grows firmer, and his consciousness of spiritual joy grows more acute. Then it is that possibilities of usefulness to the human race productive of pure delight, superior to worldly wealth and honours, open more and more clearly to his view. The most of our members are in this state, and for them the dawn of spiritual perfection has come.

The results of the Theosophist's life in this stage are calm self-study, growth of charity, increase of tolerance, and a readiness to take truth wherever found. With the deeper insight into spiritual law comes less resentful feelings as to the trials and sorrows of the world. Hope grows as he comes to see the true path more clearly, and there comes, besides, determination to so prepare conditions as to increase his usefulness to others in the lives that are before him.

Progressing, he passes by self-study into the third state, where the main object of life is not his fame, fortune, family, or the like, but the service of the whole human race, life being dedicated to duty.

In this stage the Theosophist must neglect no duty to his fellows, even to promote his own spiritual welfare. Few have yet attained to this stage, and few of the few—perhaps only one or two—have ever reached true unselfishness, which is the desideratum of Theosophy. But in the recognition of the high ideal, a man places himself against the stream of modern thought in every form,

If he is beaten down, who shall wonder or complain ? The man who breasts the tide is the man who knows how strong the current is. I hope that when the day comes for the record to be written there will be not a few who will desire the epitaph which Mrs. Besant formulated : " We have tried to follow truth."

And to this goal all the teachings of his philosophy lead him, for he is taught " If the 'Secret Path' is unattainable this 'day,' it is within thy reach to-morrow," and the doctrine of Karma serves as the strongest incentive and untiring effort, for this law is simply the law of cause and effect on the moral and spiritual planes of nature, and runs through all lives and connects them, so that absolutely what a man sows that shall he also reap. This is an immutable law, and in connection with re-incarnation explains the apparent injustice and inequalities which prevail in life. The conception of Karma renders a man self-reliant and self-dependent, because it teaches that he is what he has made himself by his own actions in other lives, and that his present acts determine his future. In this you see there is no room for vicarious atonement, or a death-bed escape from the consequence of one's own actions be they good or evil. Absolute justice is the keynote of nature.

The circumstances and environment of each path as well as the innate tendencies, faculties and aptitudes of a new personality are determined by Karma, which teaches man's absolute responsibility for his every action. If this is not a superior precept to the doctrine of vicarious atonement, we have mistaken the truth, for we believe that more good will result to the human race from the eradication of this erroneous conception than can be readily conceived. More harm has been done by causing men to believe that they can escape from the consequences of their own acts by shifting those consequences on to the shoulder of some other being than from any other single source. This idea weakens and demoralizes men, enfeebles their sense of personal responsibility, and holds out delusive hopes of escape from the operations of the laws of nature.

Treating of social problems, Mr. Keightley told how his heart leapt within him when he read " Looking Backward." He felt that the right chord had been struck, the people's ear gained. But could the dream of Edward Bellamy be at once carried out, that process would not of itself radically change human nature, since human nature changed but slowly. Yet, to institute a system of living, whose object lessons taught helpfulness rather than intensified selfishness, would accelerate progress. It would, too, clarify the atmosphere render it more healthful. The passions, emotions, thoughts of man were real forces in nature, producing physical effects. How different the physical atmosphere of a home where the members worked harmoniously together from one where this was not the case !

All human beings are fundamentally one, and it is absolutely impossible for the individual to rise without raising the whole race. The great struggle in which man has been engaged is between the divine and the animal. Theosophy is self-forgetfulness. Self must be subdued and conquered and replaced by universal co-operation.

If anyone, laying aside all prejudice, would inquire into the ancient histories of China and other countries, they would find there had been co-operation; but, unfortunately it had been overthrown by the internal decay of corrupted greed and not from any external cause.

Looking at Christianity, it would be found that at first it was purely unselfish, but, holding companionship with human selfishness, it fell into decay by allowing a number of persons to remain as they were, while becoming nominal members of the church.

Selfishness is self-destructive. It is human, but it is greatly aggravated by our present evil system of competition. Give a man a sound basis to work on, with congenial surroundings, and he will steadily work forward, till ultimately the millennium is reached.

Co-operation may be urged as the solution of the pressing problems of humanity, and you naturally appeal to the selfish element of humanity; that is, under co-operation, how much better off you will be; and that no one will then suffer as they do now. But, after all, you leave untouched the brutal selfishness of humanity. You simply substitute one form of selfishness for another. Theosophy, however, takes up this selfishness and attempts to eliminate it, it holds that men are one; that there is a unity in humanity, and that it is impossible for the individual to leave the mass or advance alone without the whole of humanity advancing. You oppose competition by the spiritual or divine law of co-operation. Theosophy does the same. But Theosophy is more; it is the elimination of selfishness. One of the greatest obstacles to co-operation has been religious differences. There has been no greater impediment since the commencement of the Christian era. Before this period there was no such opposition as there has been since—to go no further back than the Roman Empire, an organization of various tribes in a single State. The gods of other nations were adopted, and the religions of subjected nations were recognised. Strange to say, the change which has come from the Middle Ages is due not to Christianity, but to Judaism, which has rendered Christianity what it is. Dogmatism, which has burdened Christianity since the days of Constantine, has caused wars, persecutions and exclusiveness. It has checked co-operation, and rendered impossible the unification of mankind. It is the systematic growth of individualism as opposed to co-operation. The fundamental idea of salvation is a conception more opposed than any other to solidarity of the race.

Now, latterly, as dogmatic religion has lost its hold on the Western mind, we have witnessed an enormous growth of materalism. There is supposed to be nothing beyond matter known to the physical senses. The ancient conception was that each nation had a right to its own religion. No religion was believed to be superior to any other. All religions were acknowledged to be forms of one and the same truth. Plato and Pythagoras studied nature under Egyptian priests. Appollonius of Tyana was instructed by Brahmins of India. All thoughtful men recognised the idea that the gods were various conceptions of facts in nature.

The moment a man begins to think, he says that all cannot be right. A few minds have grasped the conception that the number of men who have attained salvation along the generally accepted paths was an infinitesimal fraction of mankind. You have only to read the lives of saints of the Roman Catholic and Protestant Churches, and also the lives of Mohammedans, Brahmins, Buddhists, and Chinese to find that every form of religion has had sincere devotees, whose lives have been miracles of devotion.

The spirit of materialism is found opposed to co-operation because its whole tendency is centralization upon self; with no larger or more permanent hope, no future, no punishment, no reward. The tendency is to live for the moment only, increasing the growth of selfishness and individualism. The history of the last fifty years is a demonstration of this statement, although men are often better than their beliefs. Many materialists have been the examples of the purest of Christians. To oppose this growth of selfishness by sound philosophy, the Theosophical Society was founded in New York in 1875. Its fundamental idea is co-operation, the first object being to formulate a nucleus of a universal brotherhood. There is no requirements of its members except that they should exercise the same toleration towards others which they claim for themselves. The essence of the Theosophical Society is intellectual co-operation along certain lines. Our founders chose as a basis the intellectual or spiritual field, rather than the political or social platform. Ideas rule the world. If men think aright, they are sure to reach universal brotherhood sooner than by any other way. Although the churches to-day have given up burning people at the stake, they have not abandoned social ostracism.

We have, however, in America at this age the beginning of a new race. How different this race is from the old is shown by the success achieved by faith cures, metaphysical healers, Spiritualists and others. The success of these things in this country proves that the American has undergone some deep-seated physiological changes rendering his nature susceptible to finer vibrations and more mystical influences than those of the people of Europe. There are a greater number of psychics in America than in Europe. In the Eastern States there are probably ten times as many sensitives as in Europe, and in California twice as many as in the Eastern States. It is not so much the " glorious climate " as the result of the miixng of Spanish, Indian, and other bloods. These are the forerunners of another race, the sixth sub-race of the Aryan stock. By the development of this new race we hope to arrive at a psychic stage which will enable us to make scientific tests of the super-physical world which lies everywhere around us.

Any reform to be permanent must be deeply laid in its basis or it will not stand the test of time. All students of history have noticed that development and progress have been the watchword of mankind. The family is the first step in co-operation ; then the tribe is formed ; then the city is organized by the tribe ; and finally the nation is formed by tribes of the same blood. Next we find the race, and eventually the larger and nobler idea of humanity as a whole.

But ambition and a desire for power is an inherent idea in human nature, and if the struggle for existence is removed, it does not remove selfishness. The only thing which has been removed is that which keeps ambition down, and humanity will have more chance to gratify ambition under a system of co-operation than now.

Human nature only changes slowly, and is influenced above all things by the ideal. If that ideal is simply selfishness, all the animal characteristics of humanity will work out, and your system will fall to pieces.

Mr. Bellamy recently pointed out that Christianity is essentially co-operative, but it made a compromise with selfishness in the early days and fell into decay. It soon became permeated with the worst forms of selfishness.

The study of Theosophy will show men that selfishness is self-destruction, and that the only true way to happiness is through the practice of altruism. This being translated into action from generation to generation will bring about a change in human nature. Then the noble goal of self-renunciation shall be reached and the ambition of man shall be to live among men, for men, with men, and through men, till at last the soul may enter upon other cycles and universes, having fulfilled its lower existence, and having from man become God.

A U M .

AUM is the most sacred and mysterious syllable of the Vedas. It is the first letter of the Sanscrit alphabet, and it is said to be the first sound produced by the breath of a new-born child. The daily prayers of the Brahmins begin and end with this word ; according to the sacred books, it is the word which the gods themselves use when calling on the great Unknown One.

In the Kandogya Upaneshad we find its praises set forth in the following words : " Man, meditate on the word one called *udgita ;* (2) it is the best of all essences — the supreme one — that which holds the place of honour, the eighth."

He is then recommended to meditate on this syllable as representing the two kinds of breath which animates the body. The vital breath and the ordinary breath of the mouth or lungs for this meditation provokes wisdom and the perfect accomplishment of the sacrifice. We read in verse 10 : " It would therefore seem that both he who knows the real meaning of one and he who is ignorant of it perform the same sacrifice. But this is not the case, for knowledge and ignorance are two different things. The sacrifice is more powerful if we make it by the aid of science, faith, and the Upaneshad."

Outwardly, both accomplish the same thing, but he who is wise, having meditated on the hidden meaning of Om, gives to his actions the qualities inherent in Om, which requires this psychic force to be able to manifest itself and become active. When a jeweller and a peasant sell a precious stone, the knowledge of the first must produce a better result than the want of it in the latter.

Sanbaracharya, in his " Sharir Bhashya," treats at length of the syllable Om, and devotes to its consideration a whole chapter of the Vayu Purana. As Vayu means air, it is easy to understand the mental attitude of those who occupy themselves with this Purana. They analyse the sound, an analysis which should discover some interesting relations as existing between the physical and spiritual constitution of man. Sound possesses tone, and tone in nature possesses supreme importance and profound meaning. It is by inarticulate cries that man in his incipient state of early childhood expresses his sentiments, and that animals proclaim their distinctive characters; the voice of a tiger differs from that of a tortoise; the tones of the voices of the animal world differ as much from one another as their natures, and possess meanings which distinguish different objects; the study of the laws which lie hidden under these different sounds cannot be considered puerile if it leads to the distinguishing of fundamental characteristics descriptive of the nature of animal life.

The Padma Purana says : " The word Om is the queen of prayers; it should, therefore, be pronounced at the beginning of all prayers "; and the laws of Manu order that " a Brahmin should always pronounce the syllable Om at the beginning and end of the reading of a lesson in the Vedas. For if Om does not begin it then the meaning will escape him; and if Om does not end it, then nothing will be retained for any length of time."

This is what the celebrated Raja Ramohun Roy says in treating of this subject : " Om, considered as only one letter, and pronounced by one articulation, symbolises the supreme Spirit. One letter (one) is the emblem of the Most High. (Mann ii., 83.) But considered as a three-lettered word, made up of *a u m*, it symbolises the three Vedas, the three states of the nature of man, the three divisions of the universe, the three gods Brahma, Vishnou, and Siva, which are the agents of creation, conservation, and destruction on earth; or, more properly speaking, the three attributes of the Supreme Being personified by these divinities. In this sense it implies that the Universe is under the control of the Supreme Being."

We may picture to ourselves the immensity of universal space as traversed by a simple and homogeneous vibration of sound which acts with an awakening and vivifying energy, and rouses into motion every molecule of ether. This is represented in every language by the vowel *a*, which takes precedence over all the others. This is the word, the verbum, the logos of the Christian's St. John: "In the beginning was the Word, and the Word was with God, and the Word was God." (St. John, chap. i., v. 1.) It is Creation, for without this resonance, without this movement amongst the quiescent molecules, there would have been no visible universe. That is to say, on this sound, or as the Aryans call it, this Nadu Brahma (divine resonance) depends the evolution of the visible from the invisible.

But this sound *a*, as soon as it is produced, becomes transformed into *au*, so that the second sound, *u*, is that which the first produces through the continuation of its own being. The vowel *u*, a compound one itself, represents, therefore, conservation. And the idea of conservation is entirely contained in that of creation, because nothing which had not previously come into existence could be preserved. If these two sounds, combined in one, could be indefinitely prolonged, we should do away with the nature of destruction. But they can only be continued for the duration of one respiration, and whether we press onr lips together, the tongue against the roof of the mouth, or make use of those organs which lie further back, there must always be a closing in at its finish like the sound of the letter *m*, which, with the Aryans, received the signification of a " stoppage "; and with this final letter we have the destruction of the whole word or letter. We can quickly prove experimentally that it is impossible to utter the letter *m* without first opening the mouth and thus emitting the two vowels *au*. Without fear of contradiction, we may assert that every word commences with *au* and ends with *m*. The word tone is derived from the Latin and Greek words signifying sound, and possessing also another signification. In Greek the word *tonos* means the act of spreading or radiating. While in its general character the word tone is used indifferently to characterise high notes, low notes, sharp and flat, or soft and hard ones, in music it shows the quality of the sound produced, and is employed in alluding to the difference of pitch between two instruments. In medicine it is used to denote a physical state, such as that of strength, elasticity, or tension. We can easily reconcile this physical meaning of the word to that divine resonance of which we have spoken, for we can consider tension to apply to the vibration or quantity of vibration which allows the ear to perceive a sound, and if the whole organism were gradually to weaken until it became non-existent, the result obtained would be a dissolution of this collection of molecules.

In painting, tone indicates the general character of a work; and the same may be said of morals and customs. We say " bon ton "; the English use the expression " high-toned sentiments," " a general tone of politeness "; so that we find the meaning of this word applicable to both good and evil, to the supremely great and the infinitely little. The only letter capable of expressing all this is the sound *a*, modified in different ways, as *long*, *short*, or *medium*. Just as the tone of manners, morals, of painting, and of music means their true characteristics, in the same way tones of different animals, including man, express their real character; and all these together, combined in the deep murmur which nature throws up, swells into the Nada Brahma, the divine resonance, that which we call the music of the spheres.

Meditating on the tone, as expressed in the Sanscrit syllable, Om leads us to the knowledge of the secret doctrine. In the human voice we find the seven divisions of the Divine essence for the microcosm, being a copy of the macrocosm; our halting measures contain collectively that of the whole, in the seven notes of the scale. This brings us to the seven colours, and so on, step by step, from stage to stage, until we reach the divine radiation itself, or Aum. For this divine resonance of which we have spoken is not actually the same as Divine light in its perfection. Resonance is but the expression of the complete sound Aum, which continues for, according to what the Hindous term, the duration of a day, and night of Brahma, and which they give as 1,000 ages. It not only acts as the force which excites and animates the molecules of the universe, but also as an incitement to the evolution and dissolution of man, and of the animal and mineral kingdoms and solar systems. In the planetary system, the Aryans represented this force by Mercury, which has always been held to represent the ruler of the intellectual faculties and stimulator of universal life. Some old authors mention that it is pictured in the skies by Mercury and reproduced in humanity in the universal chatter of women.

Wherever the divine resonance has been stopped by death or other changes, Aum has been intoned. These expressions of Aum are simply the innumerable microscopic utterances of the word, which is only completely pronounced and finished, according to mystical and hermetic language, when the great Brahm ceases to breathe, and ends his word with the sound *m*, causing universal dissolution. This universal dissolution is known in Sanscrit and in the secret doctrine by the name of Maha Pralaya, or Grand Dissolution. Having pronounced the sacred syllable, the ancient Rishes of India said, " Nothing either begins or ends; all is change, and that which we call death is trans formation." These words, applied to manifested life, the so-called death of a sensible creature means only the transforming of energy, the changing of manner and place in the manifestation of the Divine Resonance. So that we see that even in these early ages of the history of our race, the doctrine of conservation of energy was known and applied.

The Divine Resonance, or the sound *au*, the universal energy which remains constant in quality during the continuation of each day of Brahma, and which, when the great night falls, is reabsorbed in the All. Appearing and disappearing continually, it transforms itself incessantly, covered at intervals by the veil of matter, which we call its invisible manifestation, and which is never lost, but is always changing one aspect for another.

We may now comprehend both the beauty and the utility shown in the construction of Sanscrit words. Nada Brahma is the divine resonance; if, after having pronounced the word Nada, with the word Brahm, we should naturally conclude that the final *m* symbolised the Pralaya, and this would contradict our hypothesis that the divine resonance is everlasting, for if it stops it is lost. For this reason an *a* is added to the end of the word Brahm in order to indicate that under the title of Brahma the second will continue to exist. But space is wanting in which to examine this question as we should like to. and these few allusions have no other aim than to indicate the real and practical meaning of Aum.

For us, Om is a real and living fact. It represents the continuous *courant* of that silent meditation which man should follow, even while occupying himself with the duties and necessities of life. There is one constant effort common to all finite beings towards a given end, and this we do not even confine to them alone, but include the whole animal kingdom ; for these inferior beings only await their turn to evolve to a superior condition, and unconsciously, perhaps, but none the less effectively, do they assimilate the same nourishmen .

" Having grasped the bow, the mighty weapon, place upon the string the arrow pointed by devotion. Then, drawing it, aim, oh ! my friend, at the mark, directing your thoughts to the Indestructible. Om is the bow, the Ego is the arrow, Brahma is the mark. He who hits shall be free from illusion, and, then, as the arrow becomes one with the might of its energy of projection, it will become one with Brahmam. Learn that he alone is the true Ego and renounce all other words. He is the bridge which leads to immortality. Meditate on the *I am I* as Om. All hail to thee, and mayest thou safely traverse the ocean of shadows."

HADJI-ERINN (M.S.T.)

" Aum "—(Thos. Williams, F.T.S., Translator.)

ALLEN, SCOTT AND CO., Printers, 30, Bouverie Street, London, E.C.

THEOSOPHICAL SYMBOLOGY.

ON DYNASPHERIC FORCE.

London:
PUBLISHED BY THE T.P.S., 7, DUKE STREET, ADELPHI.

—

1890.

THEOSOPHICAL SYMBOLOGY.

SOME HINTS TOWARDS THE INTERPRETATION OF THE SYMBOLISM OF THE SEAL
OF THE SOCIETY.

" A combination and a form, indeed,
    Where every god did seem to set his seal,
    To give the world assurance of a MAN."

As the question is often asked, What is the meaning of the Seal of the
Society, it may not be unprofitable to attempt a rough outline of some of the
infinite interpretations that can be discovered therein. When, however, we
consider that the whole of our philosophical literature is but a small contribu-
tion to the unriddling of this collective enigma of the sphinx of all sciences,
religions and philosophies, it will be seen that no more than the barest outlines
can be sketched in a short paper.

In the first place, we are told that to every symbol, glyph and emblem
there are seven keys, or rather, that the key may be turned seven times, corresponding to all the septenaries in nature and in man.

We might even suppose, by using the law of analogy, that each of the
seven keys might be turned seven times. So that if we were to suggest that
these keys may be named the physiological, astronomical, cosmic, psychic,
intellectual and spiritual, of which divine interpretation is the master-key, we
should still be on our guard lest we may have confounded some of the turnings
with the keys themselves.

If it can be demonstrated that these symbols are the formulæ of the laws,
forces, and powers of nature and man, we shall have established a rational
basis for their use, and shall restore to their ancient dignity these monarchs
who have been dethroned by superstition and cant into the dungeons of an
artistic æstheticism.

In our attempt, let us follow the time-honoured and spiritual method of
proceeding from universals to particulars. Let us take the primitive type of
the serpent with its tail in its mouth. This we find in all symbology to be the
circle, the most mysterious and universal of all symbols. Taking it in its

highest interpretation, it stands for the absolute, or Absoluteness, of which we can predicate nothing. Yet as the mind of man, in order to preserve its reason and growth, continually fights against the paralyzing inanity of a blank negation, it is ever striving to advance the circumference of its knowledge, unconscious that at the same time the circumference of its ignorance is proportionably increasing. Till at last, tired with this endless quest for the external and that which is not, in despair it turns upon itself to know the knower and the subject of that object which it thinks *not self*.

Thus, by analyzing self-reflection, an ultimate is reached—pure thought.

Yet there is one factor which cannot be destroyed. From thought the idea of Space can never be eliminated. Therefore, as in all deductions we start from pure thought, and as that thought is the *Self*, and yet cannot eliminate from itself the idea of Space, Space is taken as the first aspect of the Absolute, as far as *Self* is concerned. Still, as the *Self* is essentially of the nature of the Absolute, it leaves open the path of progress to ITSELF by retaining the idea of that which is neither *space* nor *self*, but Space and Self as a unity. This from the standpoint of *Self*, or pure thought, is ABSTRACT SPACE.

This, then, is the highest interpretation of the circle, whose centre is everywhere and circumference nowhere. And its centre, which is equally itself, is the first potentiality of all that may be evolved in Space and Time, and which may be represented by the symbols which the serpent surrounds in our Seal. Thus, then, the Circle represents the type of abstract Space, and this primordial type is assumed by the serpent which swallows its own tail. The Serpent is not the Circle, but assumes the form of the Circle.

This is, of course, from the highest and most metaphysical standpoint, when the circle is taken to typify the Absolute. Nor must we be misled by the term " space " as meaning anything of a material nature, for we might equally endeavour to explain it by the graphic symbol of the " Great Breath," or Absolute Motion, meaning thereby Absolute Consciousness, in that Consciousness cannot be conceived by us without the idea of change, and change is *motion ;* or, again, we might (to coin a word) call it " Beness," or that which underlies and comprehends both being and non-being.

We must further remember that this Absolute Circle includes every idea of Space and Time, that it is Abstract Space and Time, or Duration. Hence we see that the perfect type of space is a sphere or globe, as it was also the type of perfect man. Thus we have the same figure for the Macrocosm, or Great World or Universe, as for the Microcosm, Little World or Man. The heavenly bodies are spheroidal, as are also their paths, and the perfect, or heavenly Man, is typified by a globe, as Plato has said and the Egyptians have everywhere testified in their hieroglyphics.

Moreover, seeing that the Circle has no end and no beginning, it is a fit symbol of eternity, eternal Time, or Duration, the ever-present type of Time as we know it. Hence, also the circles, or cycles of Time which play so important a part in all ancient systems and in all astronomical calculations, are but manifestations of this one eternal type. Further, the terms " wheels," planetary chains, rings, rounds, etc., are all synthesized by this comprehensive symbol. Truly, as Plato says, the Deity geometrizes.

Again, from a mathematical point of view, zero becomes a number only when preceded by one of the nine figures to manifest its potency. Zero by itself is no number.

To put it mathematically :

$$\text{The Deity} = O.$$

As Oken says, " There is only one essence in all things, the O, the supreme identity, but there is an infinite number of forms. The ideal nought is absolute, or monadic unity, not a singularity, like an individual thing or number 1, but an indivisibility, or absence of number, in which can be discovered neither the 1 nor the 2, neither line nor circle—a pure identity. The mathematical O is the eternal. It is not subjected to any definition of time or space, it is neither finite nor infinite, neither great nor small, neither at rest nor in motion, but it is and is not all these. The eternal is the *nothing* of nature."

Mathematical readers might do well also to reflect on the formula

$$x^0 = 1.$$

Here x may stand for any unity or collection of unities, in fact, for all differentiation. Therefore, all things in their essence are a unity, for the formula is true for *all* values of x.

We will now consider more particularly the meaning of the serpent. In its highest aspect it is the symbol of Wisdom. " Be ye therefore wise as serpents," says one of the Masters. Do we not find thronghont the Greek and Roman classics that the serpent was regarded with the greatest reverence, and frequently guarded within the sacred Adytum of the Sanctuary ? Everywhere the same legends and traditions in Egypt and Chaldea, among the Druids and Norsemen, with the ancient Mexicans and Peruvians. In India the folklore teems with legends of the cobra. These sacred reptiles almost invariably guard *hidden* treasure, for is it not the Initiates who guard the *occult* secrets of nature ?

Throughout the whole of antiquity the Serpent was sacred to the Gods of Wisdom, and we find that Isis has the asp in her head-dress.

What matters though the sacred genii of the Temples and the quiet dwellers in the fanes of Æsculapius appear as hissing vipers in the hands of the Pythoness and Sibyl, or in the locks of Medusa, or of the Eumenides and the frenzied Bacchanals ! They were all typical of one and the same force of Inspiration.

Then, also, the Initiates in all ages were called Serpents or Dragons, of which, indeed, the reason may appear in the sequel.

In the first place, as the serpent is oviparous, it was regarded by the ancients as a symbol of the Divinity which issues from the egg of Space, as, for instance, the Ophio-Christos of the Alexandrine Mystics.

As the *Secret Doctrine* tells us : " The Spirit of God moving on Chaos was symbolized by every nation in the shape of a fiery serpent breathing fire and light upon the primordial waters, until it made it assume the annular shape of a serpent with its tail in its mouth."

Moreover, as the serpent sloughs its skin, it was taken as the type of rejuvenation and immortality. In other words, it symbolized the immortal individuality, or Ego, of man, or the Christ-principle which is the silent Watcher of each of us—our conscience. This it is which is the sun whose ray forms this or that personality, and as the snake sheds its skin, so does the spiritual individuality shed its various personalities in its pilgrimage, or cycle, of reincarnation.

In Indian symbology the serpent is seven-headed, even as the Gnostic Dragon has seven " Vowels " above its crest. These vowels typify the seven planes of Cosmos, the seven principles in man, and all the septenates in nature.

Moreover, in symbolism, the serpent and dragon are interchangeable, so that in the Chinese Theogony we find Kwan-shi-yin, the " Logos," " the Son identical with his Father," called the Dragon of Wisdom.*

In the Greek, the word δράκων (Dracon) means " watcher " or " Seer," thus giving a key to the symbol as applied to the Initiates, or Epoptæ, of the Greater Mysteries.

Still following out the higher meaning of the symbol, we find it typifying the " Fallen Angels "; the Serpent, or Dragons of Wisdom, who fell into generation, or hell; or, in plainer words, our spiritual Egos incarnating into the prison of the body, the marriage of the Heavenly Man with the Virgin of the World or Nature.

It would take too long to enter into the astronomical interpretation of the constellation of the dragon, one out of the seven keys to this protean symbol, with which, indeed, the solar mythologists are so content that they deny all others. Neither can more than a glance be given at the variants of the Serpent symbol as, for instance, the tenth zodiacal sign, which, in India, is represented by Markara, the Crocodile, and in its correspondence with the human principles is the most mysterious of all signs.

The comprehensiveness, again, of the symbol may be seen by the fact that the Milky Way, the Ecliptic, Tropics, and the Cycle of the Great or Sidereal Years were called Serpents by the Astrologers and Adepts.

But as everything has its opposite, so the " Divine Serpent " has its contrary, the Serpent of Evil, even as the Ophites had their Agatho-dæmon, or Good Spirit, and their Kakodæmon, or Evil Spirit. If there is a Universal Medium, or Primor-

---

*See Secret Doctrine, i. 472.

dial Substance which pervades, comprehends, or surrounds all things, and which we may conceive of more correctly by considering it as a Universal Force, then we may look upon this comprehending *something*, as fitly symbolized by a serpent which bites its own tail. As such it is neither good nor evil. But seeing that all things are differentiated, and that the law of their differentiation is septenary, as we shall see in the symbolism of the interlaced triangles, it follows that this one substance can only in its higher essence be considered as pure and good.

This plastic medium, which the Hindus call Akash, impinges upon the earth in its most differentiated form, and is, moreover, stained and discoloured by the evil thought-emanations of the earth's inhabitants. This it is which Occultists call the " Astral Light."

Thus the Norse mythology allegorizes a great truth when it tells us that the Midgard Snake encircles the earth, coiled at the bottom of the seas, for the seas are the planes of this primordial force, or matter, and the Midgard Snake is the Astral Light. This, then, is the lower serpent without man corresponding to the serpent within, and typifying the lower nature of each man, his personality, which has to be slain, even as St. George and St. Michael slew the dragon, Bellerophon the Chimæra, and Œdipus the Sphinx—the dragon of Self must be slain by every Initiate, or son of God. And, indeed, in battling with this serpent of the lower nature, no quarter is asked or given by him who would become a Dragon of Wisdom, and change this corrupt body for an incorruptible. So also those who are developing the psychic senses, if they get ensnared within the coils of the Serpent of the Astral Light, will have no quarter given them, but will either fall willing victims to the subtle draughts of this mayavic nectar, or lose their senses before the awful visions that their own impurity attracts. For the *psyche* is of a truth " earthy, sensual, devilish."

To have true vision, this Guardian of the Threshold must be passed—true vision lies beyond. Thus we can plainly see that of a truth *Demon est Deus inversus*, and thus also why the first Matter of the *Magnum opus* of the Alchemists was to be *pure*, even as their Mercury.

In Egyptian hieroglyphics, the God Nahbkhoon is represented as a snake erect on human legs. The name signifies the " uniter," and denotes this medium which unites the human to the divine monad.*

We see, then, that the serpent typified both the Upper and Lower Lights, and accordingly that it is on the one hand the " healer " and on the other the " destroyer."

To take a very familiar instance, the allegory of the brazen serpent in the Books of Moses shows the existence of that ever great struggle between the Initiates and the orthodox Jewish priesthood, typified by Moses holding up the

---

* See " Secret Doctrine," i. 472.

Serpent in the wilderness, and so saving the people from the bites of the fiery serpents, or Levitical caste, who were tempting Israel to sin ; and with a larger interpretation, it typifies the true teacher, who, by his power, can heal the wretched victims of the fiery serpenst, or the passions of their lower natures. Moreover, the skin of the serpent is covered with scales, which may fitly suggest by their forms the facets of diamonds, and thus typify the various religions, philosophies, and sciences of the world, which are but facets of the one immutable truth. Or, again, they may represent individuals who make up the whole of humanity or the microcosms which compose the macrocosm, each reflecting but so much of the rest, and, therefore, capable of appreciating and reflecting but a portion of the wisdom of the whole.

It is also to be observed that the serpent bites or swallows its own tail, typifying thereby the descent of spirit into matter, and the ascent of matter into spirit, as also the incarnation of the Manasaputras, or mind-born sons of the great intellectual Soul of the Universe, into the Amanasa, or mindless men-animals, the production of nature. For, if "nature, unaided, fails," it must be that Divine Intelligence should aid her in her work. And yet both are from one source, the head and tail of the serpent are both essential parts of the reptile.

Evolution and involution are correlations. The Great Breath is out-breathed and in-breathed ; and its in-breathing makes every point and atom of its out-breathing conscious as each re-enters into itself.

Thus, at this point of balance, is self-consciousness ; and the ancient wisdom which bade its disciples " know thyself," knew that Mind could know Mind and the Knower, Knowing and Known become one in that Trinity, which is essentially a unity. These symbolical serpents are also connected with trees, and interchangeable with them. Thus we have the Tree of Life, or Spirit, in the midst of the Garden of human Principles, and also the Tree of knowledge of Good and Evil, the tree of Matter. For had not the Serpent of Matter tempted the Divine Androgynes Adam and Eve to fall into generation and disobey the law of Sameness, they could never have gained that knowledge of Self-Consciousness which was required by the law of progress. For the descent of spirit into matter is followed by the ascent of matter into spirit, as has been said, even as the pendulum swings back upon its own path to its starting-point. Therefore, following the law of creation, or action, the " Fall " of our progenitors into creation, or generation, was necessary as soon as it had been initiated by their creator. As a varient upon this symbol, there is an old Hermetic glyph in which the circle is formed by two serpents swallowing each other's tails. Everyone will recollect the Caduceus of Hermes, the Psychopompus, or conductor of the Souls of the dead from and to Orcus. This is composed of a rod with a knob at the top, entwined with two serpents, but in the original symbolism it was composed of *three* serpents, the three *Fires*, which are also seven and forty-nine.

In this connection it may be remarked that Kundalini, one of the powers latent in man, is said in the " Voice of the Silence " to be called the " Serpentine, or annular power, on account of its spiral working. . . . . . It is an electric fiery power, the great pristine force, which underlies all organic and inorganic matter."

Therefore, when Thomas Vaughn, in one of his alchemical receipts, says, " Take our two serpents, which are found everywhere on the face of the earth," he may not be quite an ignoramus as the moderns imagine, and, after all, there may be something more in Alchemy than our material scientists are prepared to admit.

We will now leave our circle, and, bearing in mind that the serpent is a dual Symbol in that it shadows forth both Spirit and Matter, will proceed to consider the symbol of the interlaced triangles.

Let us again refer to Oken, and see how he traces the connection between the O and this duality. " (+ ---)," he says, " is nothing else than the definition of O. This duality is the monad itself under another form. In multiplication, it is the form alone which changes. The Eternal becomes the real by a dual division of itself. Once manifested it is either positive or negative. Nought differs from infinite unity only because it is not affirmed.

" + presupposes O ; — presupposes + and O ; but O presupposes neither + nor — . Purely negative quantities are nonentities, for they can only be connected with positive magnitudes. — is the retrogression of + into O."

If + be taken to represent Spirit or the Purush of the Hindu philosophies, then the triangle with its apex pointing upwards will have the same signification. For has it not the shape of a tongue of flame or fire ?

Truly as + it is the everlasting Yea of Teufelsdröch, the positive pole of the Universal Magnet.

In like manner, the triangle with its apex pointing downwards is the — or negative pole of the Universe, Matter, or Prakriti, the Everlasting Nay of the Philosopher of Old Clothes. As, also, the Above is Fire, so the Below is Water ; but this metaphysically. Yet these two triangles are essentially one and as a distinct duality, unthinkable. For there must be a Centre of Indifference, a Synthetical Something, whether we express it by the all-containing circle of the Serpent, or by the central point expanded into the symbolism of the Crux Ansata of ancient Egypt. Thus the Higher is reflected in the Lower, which is essentially itself, and we have a duality of trinities which are essentially a unity, which unity in itself is nothing (O).

This pantacle portrays the generation of all numbers, and is, therefore, the type of the Universe. For example, the point within, or the whole figure, is 1 ; the two triangles are 2 ; each triangle has three sides ; the three sides of one triangle with the other as a unity, or the three sides of each triangle with the centre point common to both produce 4 ; the common property of three sides, and the duality of the triangles yield 5 ; there are 6 points to this hieroglyphic hexagram, which, together with the central one, make 7 ; and if we proceed to place the tail in the Serpent's mouth by adding the extremes we obtain :—

$$1 + 6 = 7. \qquad 2 + 5 = 7. \qquad 3 + 4 = 7.$$

This trinity represents the three lower, or manifested, planes of cosmos, and the synthesizing fourth plane, corresponding with each of which are two human principles, and the seventh, which is universal.

It matters not by what name the pantacle is called, for there are hundreds, and we are not among those who consider that " names " are " things," it is always the symbol of the Macrocosm, or Universe. The interlacing of these triangles forms an interior plane six-sided figure, or hexagon, which is typical of the manifested universe synthesized by the central Symbol of the Microcosm, or Man, seven in all. The sides of this plane figure form the bases of six triangles, of which the apexes touch the Serpent of Wisdom. From one point of view, these are the seven rays of the Logos, or Word, the six and the synthesizing seventh, each a trinity which becomes a septenary, thus typifying the forty-nine Fires. For analogy is the first law of symbolism, and there are ever three unmanifested, or formless planes, and three manifested or of form, and one that is both formless and of form, both subjective and objective, and yet neither one nor the other. These lower planes, or states, again, in their turn, are of a like nature, each relatively being both spiritual and material, spiritual towards the interiors and material towards the exteriors, and of neither nature, yet of both natures, at their laya, or zero points, where one passes into the other.

Moreover, as shown above, we may regard either triangles as a unity in its oneness, or as a trinity with respect to its sides, each unity of Sameness with its trinity of Difference forming a quaternary, or Tetractys, the one towards Spirit being the Supernal, and the one towards Matter being the Infernal.

Seeing also that there are an infinite variety of triangles, of which the equilateral is the only perfect figure, the inequality of the sides will represent the infinite variety of triple qualities, which form each entity.

Therefore, each triangle typifies the three fundamental Gunas, or qualities, of the Hindu philosophies, viz., *Satva, Tamas* and *Rajas,* of which Satva correlates with wisdom, goodness, purity, light, spirituality, and sameness ; Tamas with ignorance, evil, impurity, darkness, materiality, and difference ; and Rajas with foulness, or passionate activity, a transformation of the mysterious Eros and Kama. These are the Preservative, Destructive, and Creative energies in nature, as typified by the *Trimurti,* or Trinity, of the Hindus under the personifications of Vishna, Shira and Brahmâ.

Moreover, the six points of the interlaced triangles are the six directions of Space, North, South, East, and West, the Zenith, and Nadir ; or, before, behind, right, left, up and down, synthesized by the point in the centre, which is no direction, yet potentially all directions. And this universe of three dimensions and seven directions is surrounded by the great circle of Time or Death, the Devourer; for even the great cosmos, endless though it may seem to our finite intelligence, is confined within the bounds of finitude and change, and with the removal of time, will in the Ever-Present resolve itself into its primordial Source, and the circle " Pass not," being broken, will cease " becoming " in the perfection of the great day " Be with us."

Seeing, again, that the lower triangle is a reflection of the upper, this pantacle symbolizes the great Hermetic axiom, " As above, so below." Moreover, the lower triangle is reversed. Thus we have a symbol of a binary in nature, without which manifestation were impossible. Among which opposites we may mention the terms personal and impersonal. The personal is limited and finite, while the impersonal is unlimited and infinite. Therefore, the Occultist refuses to entertain the idea of a personal deity as the expression of the Universal Divine, of which, indeed, he can predicate nothing—not even that, and IT is impersonal. For to predicate anything of the unspeakable and the unthinkable is to depart from its nature and create the uncreated. Yet in this war of terms, that which points towards the progress of thought and frees itself from the shackles of matter and finiteness should have the preference, and the spiritual or impersonal be predicated of one Deity rather than the material or personal. Now everything exists by its opposite, light by darkness, liberty by necessity, good by evil. And if this polarity of the universe were destroyed, *existence* would cease and all would *be*. As Eliphas Lévi says : " If the shield of Satan did not stay the spear of Michael the power of the angel would lose itself in the void, or manifest itself in infinite destruction. If, on the contrary, the foot of Michael did not keep down Satan in his efforts to ascend, Satan would dethrone God, or rather, lose himself in the abysses of the height." Returning to our triangles, if they are gradually pulled apart until their bases coincide, we have the quaternary traversed by a diameter. Remove this diameter, and the subtle being separated from the fixed, we have a facet of the symbol of the philosophers' stone, or the cube.

We will now proceed to give some meaning to the curious symbol which is near the mouth of the serpent. It is called in India the Jaina Cross, the Svastica, and the Chackra, Discus, or Wheel of Krishna, in which sense it overlaps the meanings of the interlaced triangles, which are sometimes called by the same name. In the West it is known as the Gnostic Cross, and is identical with the Wheels of Pythagoras and Ezekiel.

It is also the Miölnir, or Hammer of Thor, in the Scandinavian mythology, the magic weapon forged by the Dwarfs in their war with the Giants. In other words, the Titans, or forces of matter. When the Ases are purified by the fire of Suffering, Miölner will lose its virtue. This " Hammer of Creation," and in another sense of Destruction, is sung by the bards of ancient Aryava ta, in India's great epic, the Mahabharata, Book I., Chapter xv.

" In the midst of this dreadful hurry and confusion of the fight, Nar and Narayan entered the field together, Narayan beholding a celestial bow in the hands of Nar, it reminded him of his Chakkra, the destroyer of the Asuras. The faithful weapon, *ready at the mind's call*, flew down from heaven with direct and refulgent speed, beautiful yet terrible to behold, and being arrived, glowing like the sacrificial flame, and spreading terror around, Narayan, with his right arm formed like the elephantine trunk, hurled forth the ponderous orb, the speedy messenger and glorious ruin of hostile towns, who, raging like the final all-destroying fire, shot bounding with desolating force, killing thousands of the Asuras in his rapid flight, burning and involving like lambent flame, and cutting down all that would approach him. Anon he climbeth the heavens from whence he came."

The turning back of its ends denotes its revolution. It is therefore the symbol of evolution and progress as Krishna says in the *Bhagavad Gita :* " He who in this life does not cause this cycle, thus already revolved, to continue revolving, lives to no purpose a life of sin, indulging his senses."

Round this quaternary are *two* circles, the outer, the infinite, all-comprehending, the inner the circle, &c., the circle of necessity surrounding the quaternary of matter ; between are the three arupa or formless and spiritual planes. From the microcosmic or human standpoint it typifies the " divine pilgrim " upon the wheel of matter, or the Christ crucified on the cross, or the tree of the lower quaternary or personality.

The form of this cross is sometimes found in this shape :—

Here we see the quaternary of matter represented by the simple Svastica and the divine Tetractys, or quaternary, manifested by the four mathematical points. Each material cell, or principle, has a germ of spirituality within it, for in Occultism even a blade of grass has all its seven principles, though some are latent. So long as man is drawn by *tanha*, or his thirst for life, into the meshes of matter, so long will he continue to tread his sorrowful pilgrimage upon the wheel of re-incarnation. To be freed from this necessity the four arms, or spokes, must be drawn within the hub, and the base metals transmuted into gold. Further this symbol denotes the four mystic elements of the ancients—earth, water, air, and fire, surrounded by Ether " the lining " of Akâsa, which we may describe, though in fear of being misunderstood owing to the materialistic bent of modern thought, as cosmic electricity. The four beings who mysteriously preside over these four points of the compass, to use the most material of all descriptions, are mysteriously connected with Karma, of which they are the agents, and, in another sense, are the protectors of mankind. To trace the meanings of the cross, even superficially, would take volumes, and the object of this paper is merely to give a few hints towards the comprehension of a few of the infinite meanings of the hoary symbolism collected into the seal of the Society; it will, therefore, be better to combine the interpretation of the Svastica and the Crux Ansata, the handled cross or Tau, the central symbol. Perhaps, however, it may be said that in relation to the whole, the Svastica should be interpreted as a cosmic, and the Tau as a human symbol. If that be so, we will leave the Macrocosm, and proceed to consider the symbol of the Microcosm, or man.

In the first place we observe that the Tau differs fundamentally from the Svastica in that it has only three arms. The horizontal and vertical lines do not cut each other, but merely meet. When they cut the vertical, or spiritual, is immersed in the horizontal, or material, the fall into matter is accomplished. With the " handle," or superimposed circle, it signifies life or spirit. We find that in ancient Egypt the initiated adept who had successfully passed all his trials was bound upon a cross of this shape, upon which he remained for three days plunged in a deep and sacred trance, during which his higher principles, or spiritual soul, were supposed to hold communion with the gods. For three days the body remained in the crypt of the temple or pyramid, and on the morning of the third day, just as the sun rose, the Tau and its burden was set so as to catch the first rays of the luminary, and the glorified initiate was brought back to earth-life. In this connection, then, the circle of the handle typifies the immortal spiritual Ego which was also symbolized by a winged globe.

But let it not be supposed that these dramas of initiation were peculiar to ancient Egypt. In Antiquity the Mysteries were the most sacred institutions of all nations, and all the knowledge of the ancients was derived therefrom. In their purity, their tradition and apostolic succession contained in an unbroken chain without missing links, until, with the arrival of Kali Yug, they began gradually to lose their purity. The poison of materiality gradually infused itself, and so closed veil after veil of the temple of Isis until mankind began to deny that there ever were such things, and clamoured that the only realities were surfaces, and that these contain no within.

But though, from lack of knowledge, the generality denied these mysteries, yet they remained; for, though the school had ceased for want of fit pupils, the masters had still to watch and wait; they could not leave their self-appointed task until they were relieved by volunteers who would continue to guard the portals of knowledge from the unworthy, and point the way to worthy aspirants. Hence the traditions that a magician could not die until he has passed the " word " to his successor.

Yet this symbolism and these mysteries were in vain if they but pointed to mere external forms and ritual. The spiritual interpretation of them must be for all time, and must point to something ever present. And if the latter is the case, as we believe, we can never over-estimate the wonderful efficacy of these magnificent heirlooms left us by our predecessors.

The true interpretation of a symbol is that which applies " now and within," and we shall find that this Crux Ansata contains a wonderful mystery and a virtue that can raise humanity from the animal to the divine. For the dark crypt in which the crucified one *was* placed, *is* the body. The body was plunged in a death-like trance, and the cross of the passions was still and lifeless, for this was the last trial, and the lower nature was to be for ever subdued by the higher. So too if we can send the three-headed Cerberus of the passionate nature or principles to sleep, we shall be glorified by the awakening of the spiritual senses, and so overthrow the old dragon.

There is another form of this symbol, viz :

♀ or alchemically,

This is also the Ansated Cross, and is a symbol of man, generation and life. The androgyne has separated into male and female, and man has stepped out of the circle of Spirit. It is thus the symbol of septenary man, the 3 and, the 4. It also symbolizes Venus-Lucifer, the morning and evening star. Venus or Lucifer may be looked upon as the *alter ego* of the earth, for their symbols are the same except with this remarkable difference, that they are reversed, and that whereas in the case of the former spirit dominates matter, with the latter it is the material quaternary which crowns it in triumph. There is much food for reflection in this strange fact. How verily art thou fallen from Heaven, Lucifer, Son of the Morning !

If, however, it is remembered that the fallen angels are in reality the incarnating and spiritual souls of men, it will be easy to see that their reflections, our evanescent personalities, are their counterparts reversed in the ocean of matter or Mâya, illusion and ignorance, the permanent above the impermanent below. Therefore, to be at one with our higher natures we must reverse this tendency of our lower natures, and let the circle or triangle of spirit dominate the quaternary of matter. The Ansated Cross, therefore, is the symbol of regenerated man, who, when thus purified, remains in the midst, knowing all things in the universe.

Returning to our symbol as a whole, let us treat it from the exteriors to the interiors, remembering at the same time that in so doing we really proceed from the interior to the exterior of things as manifesting the eternal idea.

First we have the Serpent, which, as a unity, represents the one substance, the Mother-Father, of the stanzas of the Book of Dzyan in the *Secret Doctrine*. This substance is purely metaphysical, and is not matter ; but the one Something which, as has been said, is for us pure thought. Then, as Brahmâ, the supreme being divides himself into two, and in his female half Vach creates Viraj, who, when born, immediately exclaims " I am Brahm," thus producing the illusion of " I am I," as distinguished from the reality " I am," so the one Substance becomes two, or Mother and Father, and immediately results in the Son, or the Universe, symbolized in our seal by the double-circled Svastica, which is further portrayed and expanded by the Seal of Solomon or the interlaced triangles. And as the Serpent bites its own tail, so the Universe enters within itself in man, the central symbol, who is the intelligent and self-conscious centre of the arc of evolution.

It will further be seen that the seal of the Society includes its three objects for as it shows the centre of the universe as man, so it shows that all men are essentially one, thus portraying its first object of establishing a basis of universal brotherhood.

Moreover, in uniting into one symbol the symbolism of all the great world religions, it shows their essential unity, which is the basis of Theosophy, the synthesis of all systems ; thus it fitly typifies the second object, which is the study of comparative religions, sciences, and philosophies.

And, lastly, as the powers of Cosmos, or Nature and Man, or of the Macrocosm and Microcosm, are shown forth especially in the symbology of the Serpent, so our seal declares the third object, which is a study of the undiscovered laws of nature and the powers latent in man.

And if anyone inquire what good is this study of symbolism and this revival of the superstition of the ancients, it may be replied in the words of one of the greatest of the moderns, viz., of Thomas Carlyle, " of kin to the incalculable influences of Concealment, and 'connected with still greater things, is the wondrous agency of symbols. In a Symbol there is a concealment, and yet a revelation ; here, therefore, by Silence and by Speech acting together, comes a double significance. And if both the Speech be itself high, and the Silence fit and noble, how expressive will their union be! Thus in many a painted Device, or simple Seal-emblem, the commonest Truth stands out to us proclaimed with quite new emphasis."

And further on : " Another matter it is, however, when your symbol has intrinsic meaning, and is of itself *fit* that men should unite round it. Let but the God-like manifest itself to sense. Let but Eternity look, more or less visibly, through the time Figure! Then it is fit that men unite there, and worship together before such a symbol ; and so from day to day, and from age to age, superadd to it new divineness."

In speaking of the keys of the mystery-language and of symbolism, the author of the *Secret Doctrine* says :

" The comprehension of the Occult Doctrine is based upon that of the seven sciences, which sciences find their expression in the seven different applications of the secret records. . . . . . Thus we have to deal with modes of thought on seven entirely different planes of Ideality. Every text (and symbol) relates to, and has to be rendered from, one of the following stand-points :—

1. The Realistic plane of thought.
2. The Idealistic.
3. The purely Divine or Spiritual.

The other planes too far descend the average consciousness, especially of the realistic mind, to admit of their being symbolized in terms of ordinary phraseology. There is no purely mythical element in any of the ancient religious texts ; but the mode of thought in which they were originally written has to be found out and closely adhered to during the process of interpretation. For it is either symbolical (archaic mode of thought), emblematical (a later, though very ancient mode of thought), parabolical (allegory), hieroglyphical, or, again, logogrammical—the most difficult method of all ; as every letter, as in the Chinese language, represents a whole word.

Thus we see that, of all writings, symbols are of the most universal application, and how that the ancients, by their symbology, created vehicles for the Infinite, with which, indeed, they were in closer touch than the moderns, who rejoice in the exact verbosity of modern scientific and legal phraseology, whereby we strive to narrow and confine all things. Like, also, as the spiritual science of Alchemy left its gross body to the material science of Chemistry, and Astrology bequeathed its shell to mathematical Astronomy, so has symbology projected its shadow in the science of Geometry and Algebra. If, then, the material expression of these sciences is so potent that it has enslaved the intellectual world of the nineteenth century, what must be the spiritual potentialities within them !

Herodotus is called the Father of History, and his writings are revered by scientific chroniclers as the rise of the sun of intellect over the fields of super-stition, mythology, and allegory. But was the method of the ancients so irrational ?

For them the events of history were but the fleeting and impermanent show-ng forth of great laws of nature ; for them the form was nothing, the spirit that manifested, alone was worth the remembering ; causes were nearer truth than effects. Therefore, they refused to stamp the evil of the past upon the minds of men, for they knew full well that seeing there was more of evil in the world than good, and that the events of history and the hate-bred warfare of the nations was the result of the passionate side of human nature, they refused to perpetuate the progeny of these passions by clothing them in the protecting garments of history.

They refused to perpetuate national hatred by feeding the fire of discord by the fuel of history. For they knew that by the law of the association of ideas the passions of the past would thus inoculate the thought of the present. But mankind required a demonstration of the truth of these laws, of which the majority were gradually losing the knowledge. Thus following the law of ebb and flow, the pendulum has swung into the materiality of realism, and, having now reached the end of its arc, commences to return upon its path with the added knowledge of its experience. It is now being daily demonstrated that results are infinite and that their study requires longer time than the life of the individual allows, therefore it becomes imperatively necessary to reduce this infinity, and confine it within some limit, if we are not to lose ourselves in the void. In plain words, the details of sciences, religions and philosophies have to be classified and synthesized; and a beginning in this direction has been already made in the introduction of the comparative method. Thus the swing of the pendulum begins to return, and at this returning point a moment of pause is given us, where we have the chance of a brief respite from the overpowering rush of collective thought. At such moments we can view the landscape and choose; we can even ascend the shaft of the pendulum, and so, for ourselves, lessen its velocity.

Of this ascent the simplicity of symbolism is a type; for in a symbol may be included the whole science of life, and therefore, the adoption by the Society of a Seal which includes the chief symbols of the past is a potent sign of the tendency of thought to-day. Moreover, it is the gauntlet thrown down to materialistic negation by serving as a practical method for the training of that intuitive faculty which is the bridge between the material and spiritual mind, the path from the Satanic to the Divine.

G. R. S. MEAD, B.A., F.T.S.

ON DYNASPHERIC FORCE.

From LUCIFER, v. 3., No. 13.

RECENT scientific research has proved conclusively that all force is atomic. That electricity consists of files of particles, and that the interstellar spaces contain substance, whether it be called ether, or astral fluid, or by any other name, which is composed of atoms, because it is not possible to dissever force from its transmitting medium. The universe, therefore, and all that it contains, consists of matter in motion, and is animated by a vital principle which we call God. Science has further discovered that these atoms are severally encompassed by an ethereal substance which prevents their touching each other, and to this circum-ambient interatomic element they have given the name of dynasphere— but inasmuch as it has further been found that in these dynaspheres there resides a tremendous potency, it is evident that they also must contain atoms, and that these atoms must in their turn be surrounded by dynaspheres, which again contain atoms, and so on *ad infinitum.* Matter thus becomes infinite and ndestructible, and the force which pervades it, persistent and everlasting.

This dynaspheric force, which is also called etheric, is conditioned as to its nature on the quality of the atoms which form its transmitting media, and which are infinite both in variety and in their combinations and permutations. They may, however, be broadly divided into two categories, the sentient and the non-sentient atoms.

Dynaspheric force, composed of non-sentient atoms, is the force that has been already mechanically applied by Mr. Keely to his motor, and which will probably ere long supersede the agencies now used for locomotives, projectiles and other purposes; when the laws which govern it come to be understood, it will produce materially a great commercial and industrial revolution. There is no hard-and-fast line between the sentient and non-sentient atoms; just as zoophytes are a connecting link between the animal and vegetable creation, so there is a graduated scale of atoms between those which, although animated by the divine life, are not sentient, and those which are as highly developed relatively to them as man is to a cabbage. For the highest class of sentient atoms through which divine force is transmitted are in the perfect human form. They are infinitesimal bi-sexua innocences male and female, two in one. The tradition of fairies is the lingering consciousness, come down from a remote past, of this fact.

Owing to the unhappily debased condition of our planet, this force is not now operant upon it, except to a very limited and imperfect degree—it is struggling, however, to penetrate into the human organism through the channel provided for it, and this channel must, of necessity, partake of the nature of the forces operant within it—in other words, it must be a bi-sexual channel. It was this bi-sexual channel which Christ came to restore by his mission to earth; and thus to inaugurate a process by which man should regain his lost bi-une condition. That process has now partially achieved its consummation in the advent of the complementary half of man whom we call the *sympneuma.* It is only through the sympneuma that the dynaspheric force, consisting of bi-sexual atoms, can be projected into nature. It comes for the healing of the nations, and is all the more necessary now because the conditions of nature have of late years undergone such a change as to render possible the invasion of the human organism by forces similar in character, with this one difference, that the atoms of which they are composed are not bi-sexual. These forces exhibit themselves in the phenomena of hypnotism, thought-reading, telepathy, mesmeric healing, spiritualistic manifestations, and in divers other ways, and depend for their quality on the source of their projection in the invisible and the human medium through whom they are transmitted—where both are bad, the atoms are in the form of infusoria, or predatory animalculæ, who prey upon each other, and work moral and physical malady. Where both are relatively good, they are in the form of separate uni-sexual beings, depending for their quality upon the medium, and partaking of what moral taint his nature may possess. It must be said that the same remark applies to the bi-sexual atoms of the sympneumatic force; but, although imperfect, there is this guarantee for their superior quality, that it is not possible for a human being to enter upon sympneumatic conditions, excepting after a long and arduous discipline and self-sacrifice for his neighbour, and of great sufferings.

The sympneuma visits none who have not been thus prepared, and who do not live exclusively for the service of humanity, to the extinction of private affections, personal ambitions, or worldly considerations of any kind.

A false sympneuma may, however, visit those who are wholly engrossed by self; such are the succubi and incubi—well-known by the Church—and the force acting through them is the most fatal which can operate upon earth.

There are methods, however, not necessary to enter upon here, by which the true can be distinguished from the false with absolute certainty. All human emotion is atomic, and it has never been possible that it should be otherwise. The peculiarity of the atomic force of the present day is, that it has received an immense accession of energy, through changes which have operated in the invisible.

It is these changes which render will-force, and magnetic influence so much more powerful now than they were formerly; and hence it becomes of such tran-scendent importance that persons who find themselves in possesssion of this re-inforced energy, and able to operate upon others hypnotically or for curative purposes, should realise the character of the agency they are dealing with—for it is quite impossible for them to project this will-force, or magnetic influence, into the organism of another, without projecting the atoms with it. Now, these atoms vary in quality from the predatory animalculæ to the human form through an infinite variety of types; none of them pure and good, though some are far purer and better, relatively, than the others—still no magnetiser is so perfect that his magnetism does not convey to his patients the atoms of the vices and defects peculiar to his own nature, of which they may have been comparatively free.

It may thus happen that a magnetiser, while healing the body of a patient, may work irreparable moral injury to his soul, and this while animated with the best intentions, and quite unconsiously to himself. It often happens, moreover, that the progress of the soul can only be achieved by an attenuation of the external structural atoms, thus producing physical disease; to heal a person thus under-going moral treatment, directed from the unseen world, by a sudden and pre-mature exercise of will-force in this one, applied to his surface organism, is to render him a fatal service. Again, it may be that the welfare of a person's soul is dependent upon its removal from the body at a certain juncture; here, again, human interference, by the operation of the human will being free, and yet under specific law, that free operation cannot be arbitrarily hindered in defiance of the law under which it acts.

The reason why material remedies of all kinds may be employed with safety and propriety, is because the curative forces they contain are not composed of sentient atoms, and can be controlled from the unseen in quite a different manner from those which are—which may, to a certain extent, be influenced by them, but cannot be controlled. When a person has reached the point, which may be attained after a long sympneumatic training, and a life passed under the influence of that training, of having no will but that of God operating freely in him, as his own, he may, under a pressure, which he will recognise as a divine impulse, put forth a healing power, but he will have no personal desire connected with it; the healing force will be put through him irrespective of any conscious will he used; the energy he projects will convey bi-sexual atoms, which may prove a seed sown as a preparation for a sympneumatic descent.

At such moments the operator will hold himself exclusively open to Christ, for it cannot be too earnestly insisted upon, that Christ is the one source and channel of sympneumatic life, and the healing which comes through it, when a person's moral condition renders such physical healing desirable.

In the presence of the rapid development which dynaspheric force is acquiring, and of the great interest which it is attracting, especially among good and earnest truth seekers, who are only investigating it with the object of turning it to account for the benefit of humanity, it has seemed to me necessary to make these remarks. I have done so in the hope that they might serve as a warning and an encouragement—as a warning of the dangers that beset the unwary explorers into these little known and almost untrodden regions; and as an encouragement as indicating the immense potentialities now descending upon the world for its succour in the hour of its approaching need.

If I seem to have written with the certainty of conviction, it is with no desire to impose my authority arbitrarily upon my readers, but in all humility to give them the facts as they have been revealed to me, after an arduous struggle and investigation into the methods of operation of these forces, which has lasted nearly twenty-five years.   Laurence Oliphant.

Theosophical Publishing Society, 7, Duke Street, Adelphi, W.C.

VIVISECTION.

CONTENTMENT.

London:

Published by the T.P.S., 7. Duke Street, Adelphi

1890.

[THE T. P. S. has been requested by a member of the Anti-Vivisection Society to insert the following articles in "Theosophical Siftings." The T. P. S. is pleased to be able to afford a wider scope for the untiring efforts of these lovers of the defenceless brute creation. As this subject is also of great interest to many Theosophists, the T. P. S. sincerely hopes that they will give their sympathetic approval.]

VIVISECTION.

The following is an attempt to give a short account of Vivisection in England. It is a sad task, for one unavoidably reverts to former days, when our people, as a nation, shuddered at the whispered rumours of Majendie's atrocities in France, and we, alas! perhaps plumed ourselves upon our superiority to our neighbours. A speech in the House of Commons of Mr. Martin, M.P. for Galway, February 24th, 1825, describing one of Majendie's experiments, too horrible to copy, was received with cries of " Shame!" and manifestations of great disgust. About the same time Dr. John Reid, of Edinburgh and St. Andrews, pursued a similar course of long protracted unmitigated tortures, but mark this, it was done secretly, shyly, conscience did not then speak, but he knew that the best men in Scotland, and also the general public voice, would condemn the practices and shun the perpetrator. How changed is Scotland now; yet still there are in it hearts and voices which protest unceasingly against what is now unblushingly avowed, and, protected by license, done with full impunity.

One cheering thing I must thankfully record,* Dr. Reid's deep heartfelt repentance. The warning came through long-continued agonies in the same tongue-nerves upon which he had specially operated, and this, he owned, was not for expected relief of human sufferings ; the motive always being scientific fame. His full and sorrowful confession must lead us to deep pity and thankfulness for such a change of heart, would that it might prove a salutary warning. The discovery of chloroform, etc., gave rise to illusory hopes, but hear what Dr. George Hoggan says : " I am inclined to look upon anæsthetics as the greatest curse to vivisectible animals. . . . They indeed prove far more efficacious in lulling the public feeling towards the vivisector than pain for the vivisected." Dr. Hoggan also refers to curari, which paralyzes voluntary motion and heightens sensation. We well know this now, we also know how innumerable are the experiments depending on the actual pain caused by them.

---

* Life of Dr. John Reid, by George Wilson, M.D.

Let us turn to the brighter side and the efforts made to resist these atrocities when creeping in to our hospitals and medical schools. In 1870, at the meeting of the British Association at Liverpool, resolutions in the biological section were drawn up minimizing experiments to a great degree.

Of course these well-intended resolutions possessed no legal authority, the sorrowful comment is shown by the 1874-5 Reports of Experiments in our London University College, Guy's Hospital, and Westminster Hospital Medical School, this latter adds, " Gentlemen will themselves perform the experiments so far as opportunities permit."

The disgusting Norwich experiments, conducted by Dr. Magnan, upon two dogs, by the injection of absinthe and alcohol in 1874, and the subsequent trial, aroused the public at last, and the result was the Royal Commission in 1875—1876, where the friends of animals had small chance of an impartial hearing. Its results was the Cruelty to Animals Act of 1876. This, when introduced by Lord Carnarvon into the House of Lords was a far more satisfactory measure than after its changes in the House of Commons, where the Medical Profession proved too strong for Ministers.

The Bill was, and is in itself, stringent, but the exceptional clauses obtained completely cancel each safeguard in succession. The Bill now only serves to mislead the public. Probably no Act for Restriction could have prevented evasions, this one is utterly futile, it has an Inspector, himself a vivisector, who simply receives and transmits the statements of the operating Vivisectors themselves, they of course, report the smallest possible amount of suffering in all their experiments.

Meanwhile the London Anti-Vivisection Society, after much private effort in the same cause, had been inaugurated in June, 1876, on the ground of the entire Prohibition of Vivisection.

This, the earliest London Society, was quickly followed by the International Society for the same object. At that time many humane persons flattered themselves that Government measures, sooner or later, would do all that was needful. Thus the Victoria Street Society " for the Protection of Animals" acted, doing their best for poor animals whilst waiting for amendments which never arrived. This position became at last unbearable, and at a meeting in August, 1878, under the presidency of the late honoured Earl of Shaftesbury, the principle and the resolution of the Total Prohibition of Vivisection was proposed and carried. After a time the International joined the Victoria Society on this firm common ground, common alike to them and to the London Society. All can now work with redoubled zeal in the same noble cause. It is very encouraging likewise to remark that in the United States similar results have followed The friends of Animals began there with efforts to restrict vivisection. They came very soon to the English and Scotch conclusion, viz., that the one only safe reliable standpoint for the protectors of dumb helpless creatures is the Prohibition of Vivisection, for this they continually work they can be content with no less.

I must not trespass on more space, or it would be easy to show the danger of small beginnings, the impossibility of real safeguards, and the moral, as well as physical evils arising from this sinful practice, from which we desire to keep our own nation, and to utter a voice of kindly warning to every land, distant or near.

ELEANOR M. JAMES.

"VIOLATIONISM;" OR, SORCERY IN SCIENCE.

BY

ANNA KINGSFORD, M.D. (Paris).

[In view of the recent attempt of the British Chloroform Commission, under sanction of the Nizam of Hyderabad, to debauch the people of India by introducing among them the practice of painful experimentation upon animals in the alleged interests of physiological research, the following address delivered in London, in 1882, by the late Dr. Anna Kingsford, possesses a peculiar interest.]

Believers in the conclusions of the exponents of physical science, are apt to bring against the students of Spiritual Science, the charge of reviving the old tricks and evil doings of sorcery. Some persons who make this allegation believe that sorcery, whether ancient or modern, never had, nor can have, any other basis, than mere imposture and ignorant credulity; others believe or suspect that it represents a real art of an unlawful and abominable character. I propose to shew that sorcery has indeed been revived in modern times to a considerable extent, but that its revival has taken place, not in the domain of Spiritual Science, but in that of physical science itself.

A further object of my address is to suggest to those who, like myself, hold as a fundamental doctrine of all Spiritual knowledge, the Unity of Substance, and who think it incumbent on them to give the knowledge of that doctrine practical expression in universal sympathy with all forms of sentient being, that it is high time for them to enter the lists actively against the worst manifestation of Materialism and Atheism the world has yet seen, and to declare their recognition of the simple and obvious moral issue of faith in a good God, namely—the duty of Love for all incarnations of the Divine Substance, and horror and reprehension of cruelty as such, whatever plea may be advanced for its practice.

It would be difficult to find stronger evidence of the banefulness of the influence exerted by the materialistic spirit of the day, than that which is furnished by the apathy and uncertainty of the public generally in regard to the practice know as vivisection. To the vitalized minority of persons, the spectacle thus afforded is as amazing as it is deplorable. That any human being, claiming to be civilized, should, through indifference or doubt, hesitate to condemn an organized system of torture, on whatever plea instituted, is in itself sufficiently surprising. But when all the aggravating circumstances are taken into the account—especially the innocence and helplessness of the victims—the prevalent attitude of the public mind becomes explicable only as the result of some moral epidemic.

From the ordinary point of view, the utilitarian and the moral, this question has already been amply discussed, and with these it is not now my purpose to deal. There is a third aspect of it, especially interesting to the student of psychological and occult science, and one which, for want of a more precise definition may be described as the Spiritualistic Persons to whom the chronicles of the modern vivisector's laboratory and the records of ancient and mediæval sorcery are alike familiar, must doubtless have noted the family resemblance between the two, and will need only to be reminded that the practice whose ethics are now so prominently canvassed in medical conclaves, and on popular platforms, represents no new feature in the world's history, but is in every detail a resuscitation of the old and hideous cultus of the Black Art, whose ghost was deemed to be for ever laid.

The science of medicine, placed originally under the direct patronage of the Gods, whether Egyptian, Oriental, Grecian, or Teutonic, and subsequently under that of the Christian Church, was among all nations in the days of faith associated with the priestly office. The relation between soundness of soul and soundness of body was then held to be of the closest, and the health-giving man, the therapeut, was one who cured the body by means of knowledge, Divine alike in its source and in its method. In Egypt, where the order of the Theraputæ seems to have had its origin, healing was from the earliest times connected with religion, and there is good reason to believe that the practice of medicine was the exclusive and regularly exercised profession of the priesthood, the first hospital of which we have any record being within the consecrated precincts of the temple, and the sick being placed under the immediate care of its ministrants.

More than one deity was associated with medical and therapeutic science. According to Diodorus (lib. i.) the Egyptians held themselves indebted for their proficiency in these respects to Isis. Strabo speaks of the methodical treatment of disease in the Temple of Serapis, and Galen makes similar observations with regard to a temple at Memphis, called Hephæstium. As is well known, the name Pæan, the Healer, was one of the most ancient designations of Apollo, in his capacity of Sun-god. This title, and the function it implies, are ascribed to him in the Orphic hymns, in the Odes of Pindar, and in the writings of Hippocrates, Plato, and all the later poets and historians, both Greek and Latin. Ovid attributes to Apollo the declaration:—"Medicine is my invention: throughout the world I am honoured as the Healer, and the power of the herbs is subject to me."

Æsculapius, reputed the son of Apollo, gave his name to medical science ; and his temples, the principal of which were at Titana in Sicily, at Epidaurus in Peloponnesus, and at Pergamus in Asia Minor, were recognised schools of medicine, to whose hierophants belonged the double function of priest and physician. These medical temples were always built in localities noted for healthiness, and usually in the vicinity of mineral springs, that at Epidaurus, the most celebrated of them all, being situated on an eminence near the sea, its site having been determined doubtless rather by the beauty of the scenery and the purity of the air, than by the tradition that Epidaurus was the birthplace of Æsculapius himself.

The course of treatment adopted comprised hydropathy, shampooing, dieting, magnetism, fumigations, gymnastics, and herbal remedies, internally and externally administered, these remedies being in all cases accompanied with prayers, music, and songs called νόμοι. In the hospitals of Pergamus and Epidaurus the use of wine was forbidden, and fasting was frequently enjoined. It was also held indispensable that the professors of so divine an art as that of medicine should be persons of profound piety, and learning, of sound moral and spiritual integrity, and therefore of blameless lives. It was, as Ennemoser observes in his "History of Magic," deemed necessary that the aspirant after medical honours should be "a priest-physician. Through his own health, especially of the soul, he is truly capable, as soon as he himself is pure and learned, to help the sick. But first he must make whole the inner man, the soul, for without inward health no bodily cure can be radical. It is therefore absolutely necessary for a true physician to be a priest."

This was also the idea of the early Hebrew and Christian Churches, whose physicians always belonged to the sacred order. Many of the primitive Christian religion communities were schools of medicine; and the visitation of the sick, not only in the priestly, but in the medical capacity was held to be a special function of the clergy. The custom still survives under a modified form in Catholic countries, where "religious" of both sexes are employed in hospitals as nurses and dressers, the higher duties of the calling having been wrested from them by the laity—often too justly designated the "profane."

Such, universally, was the early character of medical science, and such the position of its professors. "Priest" and "Healer" were religious titles, belonging of right only to initiates in Divinity. For the initiate only could practice the true magic, which originally, was neither more nor less than the science of religion or the Mysteries, that Divine knowledge won by reverent and loving study of Nature, which made the Magian free of her secrets and gave him his distinctive power.

Side by side with this true magic, sanctioned by the Gods, taught by the Church, hallowed by prayer, there grew up, like the poisonous weed in the cornfield, the unholy art of the black magician or sorcerer, whose endeavour was to rival, by the aid of sub-human or "infernal" means, the results obtained legitimate by the adept in white or celestial magic.

And, as on the one hand, in order to attain the grace and power necessary to perform Divine works or "miracles," the true Magian cultivated purity in act and thought, denying the appetites, and abounding in love and prayer; so, on the other hand, in order to achieve success in witchcraft, it was necessary to adopt all the opposite practices. The sorcerer was distinguished by obscene actions, malevolence, and renunciation of all human sentiments and hopes of Heaven. His only virtues—if virtues they can be called—were hardihood and perseverance. No deed was foul enough, no cruelty atrocious enough, to deter him. As the supremacy of the Magian was obtained at the price of self-sacrifice and unwearying love and labour for others, so the sorcerer, reversing the means to suit the opposite end, sacrificed others to himself, and cultivated a spirit of indiscriminate malignity. For the patient and reverent study by means of which the Magian sought to win the secrets of Nature, the sorcerer substituted violence, and endeavoured to wrest from her by force the treasures she gives only to love. In order to attract and bind to his service the powers he invoked, he offered in secluded places living oblations of victims the most innocent he could procure, putting them to deaths of hideous torture in the belief that the results obtained would be favourable to his wishes in proportion to the inhumanity and monstrosity of the means employed. Thus as Ennemoser observes, " the sorcerers inverted nature itself, abused the innocent animal world with horrible ingenuity, and trod every human feeling under foot. Endeavouring by force to obtain benefits from hell, they had recourse to the most terrible of infernal devices. For, where men know not God, or having known, have turned away from Him to wickedness, they are wont to address themselves in worship to the kingdom of hell and to the powers of darkness."

Such, precisely, is the part enacted by the vivisector of to-day. He is, in fact, a practitioner of black magic, the characteristic cultus of which has been described by a well-known writer on occult subjects as that of vicarious death. " To sacrifice others to oneself, to kill others in order to get life,—this was the great principle of sorcery." (Eliphas Lévi.) The witches of Thessaly practised horrible cruelties ; some, like Canidia, of whom Horace speaks, buried infants alive, leaving their heads above ground, so that they died of hunger ; others cut them into pieces and mixed their flesh and blood with the juice of belladonna, black poppies, and herbs, in order to compose ointments deemed to have special properties. The well-known history of Gilles de Laval, Seigneur of Retz and Marshal of Brittany in the fifteenth century, may serve as an illustration of the atrocities perpetrated in secret by professors of sorcery. This man distinguished for the military services he rendered to Charles VII., and occupying an honoured and brilliant position in the society of the day (as also do most of our modern sorcerers), was yet, like the latter, guilty of the most infamous practices conceivable. More than 200 children of tender years died in torture at the hands of the Marshal and his accomplices, who, on the faith of the doctrines of sorcery, believed that the universal agent of life could, by certain processes conducted under approved conditions, be instantaneously fixed and coagulated in the pellicule of healthy blood. This pellicule, immediately after transfusion was collected and subjected to the action of diverse fermentations, and mingled with salt, sulphur, mercury and other elements,* (Eliphas Lévi.)

An almost exact parallel to the modern vivisector in motive, in method, and in character is presented by the portrait thus preserved to us of the mediæval devil-conjurer. In it we recognise the delusion, whose enunciation in medical language is so unhappily familar to us, that by means of vicarious sacrifices, divinations in living bodies, and rites consisting of torture scientifically inflicted and prolonged, the secrets of life and of power over nature are obtainable. But the spiritual malady

---

* These formulæ, prescribed by the ancient science of alchemy, have reference, of course, to truths of which the terms used are symbols only. But the sorcerer, not being an initiate, understood these terms in their ordinary sense, and acted accordingly.

which rages in the soul of the man who can be guilty of the deeds of the vivisector, is in itself sufficient to render him incapable of acquiring the highest and best knowledge. Like the sorcerer, he finds it easier to propagate and multiply disease than to discover the secret of health. Seeking for the germs of life he invents only new methods of death, and pays with his soul the price of these poor gains. Like the sorcerer, he misunderstands alike the terms and the method of knowledge, and voluntarily sacrifices his humanity in order to acquire the eminence of a fiend. But perhaps the most significant of all points of resemblance between the sorcerer and the vivisector, as contrasted with the Magian, is in the distinctive and exclusive solicitude for the mere body manifested by the two former. To secure advantages of a physical and material nature merely, to discover some effectual method of self-preservation in the flesh, to increase its pleasures, to assuage its self-induced diseases, to minister to its sensual comforts, no matter at what cost of vicarious pain and misery to innocent men and animals, these are the objects, *exclusively*, of the mere sorcerer,—of the mere vivisector. His aims are bounded by the earthly and the sensual ; he neither cares nor seeks for any knowledge unconnected with these. But the aspiration of the Magian, the adept in true magic, is entirely towards the region of the Divine. He seeks primarily health for the soul, knowing that health for the body will follow ; therefore he works through and by means of the soul, and his art is truly sympathetic, magnetic, and radical. He holds that the soul is the true person, that her interests are paramount, and that no knowledge of value to man can be bought by the vicarious tears and pain of any creature soever. He remembers above all things, that man is the son of God, and if for a moment the interests of Knowledge and of Love should seem to be at variance, he will say with equal courage and wisdom : " I would rather that I and my beloved should suffer and die in the body, than that to buy relief or life for it our souls should be smitten with disease and death." For the Magian is priest and king as well as physician ; but the sorcerer, whose miserable craft, divorced from religion, deals only with the lower nature, that is, with the powers of darkness, clings with passionate despair to the flesh, and, by the very character of his pursuits, makes himself incapable of real science. For, to be an adept in this, it is indispensable to be pure of heart, clear of conscience, and just in action. It is not enough that the aim be noble, it is necessary that the means should be noble likewise. A Divine intention presupposes a Divine method. As it is forbidden to man to enrich himself by theft, or to free himself by murder, so also is it forbidden him to acquire knowledge by unlawful means,—to fight even the battles of humanity with the weapons of hell. It is impossible to serve humanity by the sacrifice of that which alone constitutes humanity—justice and its eternal principles. Whenever the world has followed the axioms of the vivisector, whenever it has put sword and flame and rack to work in the interests of truth or of progress, it has but reaped a harvest of lies, and started an epidemic of madness and delusion. All the triumphs of civilisation had been gained by civilised methods: it is the Divine law that so it should be, and whoever affirms the contrary is either an imbecile or a hypocrite. The vivisector's plea that he sins in the interests of humanity is, therefore, the product of a mind incapable of reason, or wilfully concealing its true object with a lie. That, in the majority of cases, the latter explanation is the correct one is proved beyond doubt by the nature of the operations performed, and by not a few incautious admissions on the part of some of the school itself. To multiply pamphlets, "observations," and "scientific" discussions; to gain notoriety among followers of the cultus, to be distinguished as the inventor of such a "method" or the chronicler of such a series of experiments, and thereby to earn wealth and position, these constitute the ambitions of the average vivisector. And, if he go beyond these, if some vague hope of a "great discovery" delude and blind his moral nature as it did that of the miserable Seigneur de Retz, we must in such case, relegate him to the category of madmen, who, for the poor gains of the body, are willing to assassinate the soul. Madness such as this was rife in those mediæval times which we are wont to speak of as the "dark ages," and the following examples, selected for the striking resemblance they present to the "scientific" crimes of the nineteenth century, may, with the instances already given, suffice as specimens of the abominations which the delusions of sorcery are able to suggest.

"The Taigheirm was an infernal magical sacrifice of cats, prevalent until the close of the sixteenth century, and of which the origin lies in the remotest times. The rites of the Taigheirm were indispensable to the worship or incantation of the subterranean or diabolic gods. The midnight hour, between Friday and Saturday, was the authentic time for these horrible practices; and the sacrifice was continued four whole days and nights. After the cats had been put into magico-sympathetic (surexcited) condition by a variety of tortures, one of them was put alive upon a spit, and, amid terrific howlings, roasted before a slow fire. The moment that the howls of one agonized creature ceased in death, another was put on the spit—for a minute of interval must not take place if the operators would control hell—and this sacrifice was continued for four entire days and nights. When the Taigheirm was complete, the operators demanded of the demons the reward of their offering, which reward consisted of various things, such as riches, knowledge, fame, the gift of second sight, etc."—*Horst's "Deuteroscopy" and Ennemoser's "History of Magic."**

Let the following extracts from publications circulated among the vivisectors of to-day be compared with the foregoing, and the reader will himself be enabled to judge of the exactness of the parallel between the black art of the past and of the present.

"Dr. Legg's experiments on cats at St. Bartholomew's Hospital included a great variety of tortures. Among others, their stomachs were opened, while the cats were pinned alive on a table, their livers were pricked with needles, the stomachs were then sewn up, and the cats left in that condition until death ensued from prolapse of the bowels; some of the animals surviving the torture as long as twenty-six days."—*St. Bartholomew Hospital Reports.*

"Burns were produced by sponging the chests and bellies of dogs with turpentine five or ten times in quick succession, setting fire to it each time; and scalds, by pouring over the dogs eight ounces of boiling water nine times in quick succession. All the dogs died, either in a few hours, or at the latest, after five days."—*Edinburgh Medical Journal*, 1869.

"Delaroche and Berger baked hundreds of animals to death in ovens, the heat being gradually increased until death ensued. Claude Bernard invented a furnace for roasting or baking animals to death, the details and diagram of which apparatus are given in his 'Lessons on Animal Heat.' Magendie has also shown by numerous experiments that dogs perish at the end of about eighteen minutes in a furnace heated to 120° (centigrade), and at the end of twenty-four minutes in one heated to 90°; or in one at 80° at the end of thirty minutes."—*Beclard's "Treatise on Physiology,"* and *Gavarret's "Animal Heat."*

"Professor Mantegazza has recently investigated the effects of pain on the respiratory organs. The best methods for the production of pain he finds to consist in planting nails, sharp and numerous, through the feet of an animal in such a manner as to render the creature almost motionless, because in every movement it would feel its torment more acutely. To produce still more intense pain, it was found useful to employ injuries followed by inflammation. An ingenious machine,

---

* Among the practices of Japanese sorcerers in the present century, the following is cited in Mr. Pfoundes' book "Fu-so Mimi Bukuro":—"A dog is buried alive, the head only being left above ground, and food is then put almost within its reach, thus exposing it to the cruel fate of Tantalus. When in the greatest agony and near death, its head is chopped off and put in a box."

constructed expressly for the purpose, enabled the professor to grip any part of an animal with pincers with iron teeth, and to crush or tear or lacerate the victim so as to produce pain in every possible way. One little guinea-pig far advanced in pregnancy, endured such frightful tortures that it fell into convulsions, and no observations could be made on it. In a second series of experiments, twenty-eight animals were sacrificed, some of them taken from nursing their young, exposed to torture for an hour or two, then allowed to rest an hour, and then replaced on the machine to be crushed or torn for periods varying from two to six hours. Tables are appended by the Professor in which the cases of 'great pain' are distinguished from those of 'excessive pain' the victims of the last being 'larded with nails in every part of the body.' All these experiments were performed with much patience and delight."—
"*Of the Action of Pain,*" &c., *by Prof. Mantegazza, of Milan,* 1880.

The two following experiments are cited from Baron Erst de Weber's " Torture-chamber of Science," and also from the *Courrier de Lyon,* June 8th, 1880 :—

" The body of a pregnant bitch at the point of delivery was cut open to observe whether in her dying and mutilated condition she would not attempt to caress and lick her little ones."

" The forehead of a dog was pierced in two places with a large gimlet, and a red-hot iron introduced through the wounds. He was then thrown into a river, to observe whether in that state he would be able to swim."

Professor Goltz, of Strasburg, writes :—

" A very lively young dog which had learnt to shake hands with both fore-paws had the left side of the brain extracted through two holes on the 1st December, 1875. This operation caused lameness in the right paw. On being asked for the left paw the dog immediately laid it in my hand. I now demand the right, but the creature only looks at me sorrowfully, for he cannot move it. On my continuing to press for it, the dog crosses the left paw over, and offers it to me on the right side, as if to make amends for not being able to give the right. On the 13th January, 1876, a second portion of the brain was destroyed; on February 15th, a third; and on March 6th, a fourth, this last operation causing death."

M. Brachet writes :—

" I inspired a dog with a great aversion for me, tormenting him and inflicting on him some pain or other as often as I saw him. When this feeling was carried to its height, so that the animal became furious every time he saw and heard me, I put out his eyes. I could then appear before him without his manifesting any aversion; but if I spoke, his barkings and furious movements proved the indignation which animated him. I then destroyed the drums of his ears, and disorganized the internal ear as much as I could. When an intense inflammation had rendered him completely deaf, I filled up his ears with wax. He could now no longer hear or see. This series of operations was afterwards performed on another dog."

The prize for physiology was, by the French Institute, awarded to the perpetrator of the above "experiments."

In "Cyon's Methodik," a "Handbook for Vivisectors," we read the following :—

"The true vivisector should approach a difficult experiment with joyous eagerness and delight. He, who shrinking from the dissection of a living creature, approaches experimentation as a disagreeable necessity may, indeed, repeat various vivisections, but can never become an *artist* in vivisection. The chief delight of the vivisector is that experienced when from an ugly-looking incision, filled with bloody humours and injured tissues, he draws out the delicate nerve-fibre, and by means of irritants revives its apparently extinct sensation."

Have we in this nineteenth century indeed expunged from among us the foul and hideous practice of sorcery, or rather, if comparison be fairly made between the witchcraft of the "dark ages" and the "science" of the present, does it not appear that the latter, alike for number of professors, ingenuity of cruelty, effrontery and folly, bears away the palm ? No need in this "year of grace" to seek in the depths of remote forests, or in the recesses of mountain caves and ruined castles, the midnight haunts of the sorcerer. All day he and his assistants are at their work unmolested in the underground laboratories of all the medical schools throughout the length and breadth of Europe. Underground indeed, they needs must work, for the nature of their labours is such that, were they carried on elsewhere, the peace of the surrounding neighbour-hood would be endangered. For when from time to time a door swings open below the gloomy stone staircase leading down into the darkness, there may be heard a burst of shrieks and moans, such as those which arose from the subterranean vaults of the mediæval sorcerer. There still, as of old, the Wizard is at his work, the votary of "Satan" is pursuing his researches at the price of the torture of the innocent, and of the loss of his own humanity.

But between the positions of sorcery in the past and in the present is one notable and all important difference. In the past it was held a damnable offence to practise the devil's craft; and once proved guilty, the sorcerer, no matter what his worldly rank or public services, could not hope to escape from death by fire. But now the professors of the Black Art hold their Sabbat in public, and their enunciations and the recitals of their hideous "experiments" are reported in the journals of the day. They are decorated by princes, fêted by great ladies, and honoured with the special protection of State legislation. It is held superstition to believe that in former ages wizards were enabled by the practice of secret abominations and cruelties to wrest knowledge from nature, but now the self-same crimes are openly and universally perpetrated, and men everywhere trust their efficacy."

And in the last invention of this horrible cultus of Death and Suffering, the modern sorcerer shews us his " devils casting out devils," and urges us to look to the parasites of contagion—foul germs of disease—as the regenerators of the future. Thus, if the sorcerer be permitted to have his way, the malignant spirits of fever, sickness, and corruption will be let loose and multiplied upon earth, and as in Egypt of old, every living creature, from the cattle in the field to the firstborn son of the king, will be smitten with plague and death. By his evil art he will keep alive from generation to generation the multitudinous broods of foul living, of vice, and uncleanness, none of them be suffered to fail for need of culture, ingrafting them afresh day by day and year by year in the bodies of new victims; paralysing the efforts of the hygienist, and rendering vain the work of the true Magian, the Healer up, and the teacher of pure life.

VIVISECTION IN INDIA.

From REIS AND RAYYET *(Prince & Peasant), Calcutta, Saturday,*
March 15, 1890.

DEAR MR. EDITOR,

Knowing you to be a true friend of dumb animals, and an ardent upholder of the Law of Mercy wherever it is possible for mercy to be exercised, I venture to call your attention to the feeling with which the report of the Hyderabad Chloroform Commission (so-called)—in reality a Commission for Vivisection—has been received in this country.

It is not a noisy feeling, or one that is to any great extent represented in the daily newspaper press; but among the calmest and most resolved friends that India has in the British Islands, (and I am sure the same remark will apply to America, and to several European nations, when once the facts are known), it has a depth and intensity which I do not remember to have been equalled, in any like case, in my experience of public affairs.

The feeling is one of simple horror that India, of whose gentleness and mercifulness many Englishmen have strongly, and often spoken, should have been selected for experiments which it has been publicly asserted would not be permitted in this country, lax as English law is with regard to the system of secret torture which goes under the name of vivisection.

The *Lancet* states that in Hyderabad 490 dogs, horses, monkeys, goats, cats and rabbits had been *used*—(kindly notice the word that I have italicised), and that 600 experiments had been carried out, under the direction of this Commission. The same animals had, in some cases, been used more than once, after an interval, say of three or four days. Every intelligent reader of the words knows what this means.

"In order" (the Report says) "to test the alleged danger from shock during chloroform administration, the Committee performed a very large number of those operations which are reputed to be particularly dangerous in this connection—such as extraction, evulsion (tearing out) of nails—section of muscles of the eye, &c. In many cases the operations were performed after the animals were merely stupefied by chloroform and not fully insensible." The stories of the fiendish cruelties inflicted by vivisection as we know it in England, I shall not attempt in any case to re-narrate, They are too horrible to keep before one, or to dwell upon.

I am quite sure that the Nizam cannot know what, in its naked deformity, vivisection really is, and how it has been depicted and stripped of its pretences, by men of the highest character and culture, both in science and literature, in this country. The vivisectors say that the operations are in many cases painless. They do not say in all cases; and for what they do say their word is not accepted. From all parts of the British Islands have come words as direct as these—" *We do not believe you!* The power, and the exercise of the power, of secret torture are in their very nature brutalising; and neither you nor any other men are to be trusted to draw the line at which you suppose that there is no suffering. No such power as you claim ever was entrusted to any human beings without leading step by step to cruelties far beyond what was at first contemplated, or at least avowed."

We are pointed also to the fact that some eminent men have carried on these operations. I reply that eminent men have condemned these operations; and that for one vivisector who might perhaps be trusted to reduce the suffering to its smallest possible limits, there must, in the nature of things, be scores of vivisectors who do not care in the least what amount of suffering they inflict, or how long their helpless victims suffer.

There are many strong and unanswerable arguments against the practice of vivisection in any hands. I will mention three. Eminent doctors, and scientific men, testify that, in their opinion, Nature does not give up her secrets to the vivisector; that her way to knowledge, for any purposes of mercy to man never can be the way of cruelty and suffering intentionally inflicted on any other living creatures.

Another argument is that in the medical profession, (in many cases distinguished by gentleness and pitifulness, and in which these qualities are so greatly needed and so deeply prized) there is great danger that even the habitual sight of cruelty and torture will harden the heart to the cry of suffering, and turn the mercy into cruelty, the kindness into callousness.

Other points, with undeniable examples from history, to the fact that the love of cruelty grows; and that people who have begun by torturing animals which cannot speak, have generally ended by torturing helpless human beings.

Each of these arguments is, I think, worthy of consideration from its own point of view; and the concluding one is surely of great importance to India, which depends so much on its power to protect itself from every form and kind of cruelty. What may not be the consequences if these practices are allowed? You know that the kidnappers of half a century ago found in eminent doctors customers for dead bodies, Allow vivisection to prevail in India and we may have a new system of Thuggee, sanctioned by the Law and blessed by Science—till the evil thing is found out. This is but one reason among many which will occur to your readers why India in particular should not have vivisection forced upon it on any plea whatever. For the protection of India itself, and especially of its poor people, I plead against this unholy experiment.

But, Sir, these arguments, strong as they may be, do not include the one which I venture to submit to the Nizam, and to you, and to the intelligent men of India, as the strongest and highest argument of all. That we have no warrant, in the faiths of India, any more than in the faith of England, or in any instinct of the human heart, for the claim to inflict torture on any living thing, be the presumed, or asserted, benefit to man what it may. The cowardly plea that the vivisector may, by his researches, learn something useful to mankind has been dealt with by many earnest and gifted speakers and writers; and I am sure it will be met in the same spirit by many of the true men of India, and by none more earnestly than the generous writer who sketched the picture of the " Bengalee *pariah*, my poor Tom."

I can fancy poor Tom under the vivisector's knife, and fastened to a board, every limb bound down so that he could not stir, and his mouth gagged so that he could not cry. Can you, Mr. Editor, fancy this, and then fancy the writer who drew Tom's picture looking on, like a philosopher, callous to suffering? The latter fancy is beyond me. I can fancy that writer flying at the vivisector's throat, and trying conclusions with him, man to man.

I earnestly appeal to the Nizam, on behalf of many English ladies, whose feeling I know that these words all too weakly represent, and of many Englishmen, ardent defenders of India's just rights, that he will reconsider the permission he has given to this Chloroform Commission ; that he will consider the danger of opening the door to vivisection in India ; the value to India, " Prince and Peasant " alike, of the law of mercy, which never before ran so great a risk of being set at nought in your land.

I am, Dear Sir,
Yours truly,

Carmarthenshire.   JAMES ROUTLEDGE.

P.S.—One other thought I might have mentioned. There is, I think, no doubt that many vivisectors push their experiments to the utmost extent that a living being can endure and live, or endure before death, the object being to gauge the limit of endurance. I leave this fact to speak for itself.

J. R.

CONTENTMENT.

From the THEOSOPHIST, *October*, 1889.

WHAT a pleasure it is to meet anyone possessed of this rare and lovely virtue! Such a restful and yet, at the same time, bright and invigorating atmosphere surrounds them, blessing with refreshment and strength all with whom they come in contact.

What is the secret of its attainment and maintenance? Is it only the fruit of natural disposition and temperament? There is, truly, a species of contentment which seems to be the product of the constitution; the mere result of a harmonious compound of mental and physical elements, suitably environed. But this sort of contentment will soon wither in the rude, cold blasts of life. It requires sunshine, fair weather; and under stress of sorrow is very apt to give way utterly, and to leave the sufferer on a level with the born grumbler and hypochondriac. Is it that the person possessing it has no ambition, no desires, no stirrings after an unattained good, and so is content with anything? That is indifference, not contentment. Content implies satisfaction, which again implies fulfilled desire. It is something other and more and greater than these.

What is most commonly understood by it may perhaps be thus defined—"the feeling which arises upon the satisfaction of our ordinary and natural wishes and desires";—such as the attainment of success in our work in the world, the creation of congenial surroundings, the realizing of the love for which we sigh, and the like. Aye? But time after time experiences rudely give the lie to our fond expectation of entering into rest by these means. How seldom to any, and to most how scarcely ever, are these "ordinary" desires even approximately satisfied! And when they are, is contentment the invariable result? Anything but it. The longed-for treasure grasped, we awake to find ourselves unsatisfied still; there is something within us which is restless and still unsatisfied. We imagined that these desires were the strongest we had, that these longings arose from the secret depths of our nature; and we find it is not so. The Inner, Higher Self is truer to its innate divinity than the Common Self believed; it refuses to be—it cannot be—content with such satisfaction. There is a thirst within the soul which the waters of earth may not quench; we rise from the feast, hungry still; the fuller our hands become, the emptier they are. This is not misty theorizing; every-day experience shows us that there are desires in the heart deeper, stronger than the desires of comfort, wealth, knowledge, fame, power, love. And it is felt, vaguely, sadly that the hardest thing remains yet to be done—namely, to discover first what these desires are, and then how they may be satisfied. Till this has been done, contentment is to us a word of eleven letters, and nothing more.

This desire of desires, then, is—what? The yearning of the Divine spark which is the core of the soul, as the soul is the core of the body, which refuses to be ignored or smothered, which ever struggles to return to the Central Fire, whence it emanated that it might by the accumulation of new experiences add to infinity—if so wildly paradoxical a phrase may be permitted.

"Son of Eternity, fettered in time, and an exile, the Spirit
"Tugs at its chains evermore, and struggles like flame ever upwards."

Only when the desire dies away into the fruition of consummation, when "the Dewdrop slips into the Shining Sea," will perfect contentment, the fulness of the "peace that passes understanding," be known. But even here and now foretastes of that crowning bliss may be realized. In proportion as the aspirations of the Spirit are encouraged, in strictly answering proportion will the man come to feel the blessedness which is is birthright.

Yes! Even here and now it is possible for us to attain to a state in which joy shall have lost its power to intoxicate, sorrow its power to prostrate; and this, without becoming insensible to either joy or sorrow. The surface of the sea may be ruffled, but down underneath, deep, calm, utter content will be the habitual state. We can so live that we shall be satisfied without the pleasures of life, if they fall not to our lot; not that we have ossified ourselves, cauterized the heart till all capacity of feeling has gone out of it: but because, possessing the greater, the soul can do without the less. Content, too, mark well, with a bright, cheerful contentment, not with a mere passive calm; the soul so rich in its possessions that it is invigorated with a gladsomeness that gives it strength to endure and bear all things; to delight in all pure joys, to rise above sorrows, and to shed an influence on all around, to bring with it an atmosphere of happiness and peace. This was that of which Paul wrote when he said he had learned, in whatsoever state he was, therewith to be CONTENT.

"LEARNED!" Mark well the word. Not in a day, not in a year, can this lessons of lessons be learned. But at any time, so good is the Soul of Things, the first beginning can be made. Just where and as we are we can open our book and begin the study. To struggle is to rest, to renounce is to enjoy, to aspire is to be content. Why fret our hearts to death over trifles, when by devotion to the One Reality we can attain all in one?   GRACE HAWTHORN.

Theosophical Publishing Society, 7, Duke Street, Adelphi, W.C.

THEOSOPHY AND MODERN
WORLD PROBLEMS.

THE ROSICRUCIANS.

London:
Published by the T.P.S., 7, Duke Street, Adelphi.

1890.

(The T. P. S. desires to state that the writers of signed articles are alone responsible for the views therein expressed.)

THEOSOPHY AND MODERN WORLD PROBLEMS.

IT is more than likely that what I have to say may bring down the wrath of many worthy members of the T.S. It seems so very simple, when one has a fad, and when one has learned to persuade oneself that in one's own fad lies the solution of all that is called wit in the world, to proceed to the further conclusion that the exploiting of that particular fad is the divinely appointed mission of Theosophy, the purpose of its existence at this time and upon this planet. And yet nothing can be more clear than that gigantic schemes for the reconstitution of society and repairing the mistakes committed by the directing forces of the world have nothing whatsoever to do with Theosophy, and of this nature are nearly every one of the prevalent fads to which I have alluded. The panaceas of social and political quacks have attracted so much attention and proved so fascinating to mankind in all ages that we need not wonder when we hear on one side that some form or other of socialism is the acme of Theosophy, being the only real altruism ; whether it be the strange but seductive dream which is embodied in Bellamy's " Looking Backward," or the theories of Henry George, or the modern gospel of salvation by strikes, each prophet exploits his pet nostrum ; or on another platform we hear that the true purpose of Theosophy is the emancipation of women, elsewhere it is the universal adoption of a pure diet and the utter prohibition of killing of animals for food or for sport or for science ; again, it is the absolute abolition of all intoxicating drinks. And so one faddist raves against another, and all claim by the divine light of Theosophy to solve the problems of the world. And the lines of every one of the fads are similar, certain axioms are laid down, predicating exactly the meaning and purpose of the world and the reason for the presence in it at this time of the human life monad. Then follow sundry statements of the present conditions of humanity, whence it is triumphantly proved that the existence of a particular group or section of humanity offends against the basic principles of the present manvantara, which cannot continue its upward evolution so long as that section continues to exist.

Now, were it not that one meets faddists of this type constantly among Theosophists, one would say that the whole principles and conception of Theosophy were opposed to such fads. One would say that the most rudimentary understanding of the law of Karma would negative them altogether ; but seeing how widespread and how apparently fascinating to good Theosophists this faddism is, it is worth while to examine it closely and see what germ of truth, or it may be perversion of truth, underlies it all.

If we consider, for instance, the dream of the Socialist we see how it is founded on a presumed intention of the ruling spirit of the world that all human beings should be born free and equal. The exact meaning of "freedom" in a state of existence whose very necessity it is to be *conditioned* is a subject of considerable dispute, and equality never has been the condition of human beings, their inequality presenting, in fact, a problem utterly insoluble save by theosophic teachings grounded on the law of Karma. Such teachings, however, the Socialist waives aside with a lofty scorn. He says, and he is perfectly right in saying, that the poor have been for centuries growing poorer and the rich growing richer, and that the contrasts have never been so sharp as they arc at present, that all wealth is accumulated into few hands, and those, as a rule, the hands of men who do the very least for the well-being of humanity, financiers, speculators, contractors, and the like, the bulk of whom might be swept off the earth by a sudden cataclysm, and leave it none the poorer. The truth of all this may be readily granted and the outcome of occult learning appears to be that whatever conditions of earth life are most favourable for the development of the life monads, which at any given time are pressing into incarnation, will undoubtedly subsist, and that when those peculiar conditions cease, from any change in the necessities of the monad, to be requisite for its evolution, then these conditions will cease to subsist. Thus some of the races of mankind, when their function as sheaths or vehicles of the incarnating monad is no longer required, utterly cease to exist. Vain is any endeavour of man to alter or to retard by one hour the effect of this law, vain his attempt to save the

Maori or the Redskin from becoming extinct. Meanwhile the woolly-headed African, seemingly at first sight a lower type than either, so far from perishing before the white man, thrives and multiplies alongside of him, as in America to-day. The Theosophist knows that the purpose of the Maori is accomplished ; that of the negro has yet to be completed.

And as with races so it is with classes. In the middle ages there were classes of men in England whose degradation and sufferings would not be believed now. Like the races above mentioned, they have ceased to exist, and, for the same reason, there is now no need for them ; the life monads to whom those peculiar human bodies were necessary no longer press for incarnation. Be it observed no human law has anything to do with this

It would be easy to show from history, if time sufficed, how law after law has been passed for ameliorating the condition of certain classes, or for abolishing certain classes considered to be so degraded as to be a reproach to humanity, and every law has been a dead letter until the proper time arrived, and then in many cases the result simply took place without a single legislative change. To this day there are on the Statute Book unrepealed laws which, if put in force, would make earth a hell for whole classes ; these laws are out of date and dead, and the classes whom they would have oppressed exist no more, for the need of them in the cosmic economy is past. It may be asked, then, whether it is wrong to try and improve the condition of humanity, and the answer is certainly not wrong, but so far as the endeavour implies an attempt to change the conditions under which humanity exists before the human life monads coming into those conditions are changed, it is for the Theoso-phist, who should know better, infinitely foolish, as being a waste of time and power, trying to do that which no human strength or skill can accom-plish before the right time, but which at the right moment will be accomplished in natural evolution without any human effort.

Multitudes of Socialistic schemes have been launched within the last hundred years, but not one has come to anything, "because of the selfish-ness of man," says the Socialist. Precisely !—and until man is less selfish every scheme will similarly fail.

But, it may be said again, the first followers of Christ were Socialists. True again ! for those first followers had attained a height of unselfishness which made it possible in their little community, but they never proclaimed it as a lesson for the whole world in its then condition of self-seeking cruelty and tyranny.

Many years ago a pamphlet was published by a half-crazed philan-thropist, which began by pointing out in graphic language the number of poor creatures in London who suffered torments or actually died from cold, then proceeded with elaborate scientific reasoning to show that under the whole of London, below the stratum of the green sand, lay a vast reservoir of water, and below this again the central fires of the globe burned perpetually; bore deep enough, this was the conclusion of the pamphlet, bring the water and the fire together, and you have a perpetual supply of boiling water sufficient, if carried in pipes around London, to form a vast heating apparatus for the whole metropolis. It would make coal unnecessary and render it impossible that anyone should suffer from cold again.

Of such sort, to the mind of a Theosophist, are the Socialistic schemes.

Are we then to sit unmoved and irresponsive gazing on the misery of the world, and merely saying " Kismet." By no means, for those who seek practical work in the way of benevolence there is plenty to be done. Feed the hungry, cloth the naked, comfort the afflicted, but do not waste time and force in grand schemes to banish hunger and cold and sorrow from this planet. There is one grand scheme, and Theosophy shows us what it is, " bear one another's burdens " ; so will you aid, as fully as the power given to you admits of, to kill selfishness out of the world, and teach others the same sublime lesson, and when this lesson is fully learned the Socialists' dream will come true.

Meantime you want some grander, more exhaustive scheme for bringing the millennium to mankind at once. Examine your motives closely. Is not your real desire that your own name may be linked to some such scheme, that you may have the adulation of the multitude ; is it not, in a word, a miserable personal vanity, an accentuated separateness, that actuates you? A very natural, very human sentiment ; but beware, O human brother ! that you deceive not yourself by calling it love of humanity. Only when all desire of personal glorification or recognition of services is destroyed can the work for humanity be really begun on the lowly and unnoticed lines that are the true spirit of theosophy.

And as it is with Socialism, so is it with all the other fads above mentioned, and many another besides. A truly noble object is the emancipation of women, but not one to be accomplished by legislation or platform speeches. Theosophists should know well the theory of the evolution of sex and all it involves, and why the reincarnating life monad is attracted to a female rather than a male body. Let those who do not know something of this study occult works until some meaning of the problem begins to dawn on them, and they will then see the conditions on which the emancipation of women can become practicable.

When social and political questions are looked at in the clearer and stronger light of Theosophy many proposed reforms will seem very much like going into a gymnasium and removing therefrom all the apparatus for the more difficult exercises.

Not that one should blame reformers, they have their uses; indeed even while we realize their mistakes and know that we cannot follow them, we know that they are indispensable factors of evolution. But Theosophists should not be reformers of such a type as has been indicated ; the clearer light, the higher qualities which enable them to be Theosophists indicate a higher grade of usefulness, for which there is no reward of man's praise, no premium such as the self-seeking separateness of the individual demands, but rather that far higher blessing which is shared by the whole universal brotherhood, and means one more step gained towards the final attainment of Para-nirvana.   J. W. BRODIE-INNES.

THE ROSICRUCIANS.[*]

IT is a remarkable historical fact that the Rosicrucian order sprang into existence, some three centuries ago, like Minerva from the head of Zeus, completely formed and organized without any visible source whence the exoteric world might trace its beginnings. Indeed the members of the order themselves are by no means certain as to its precise origin, and the most far-fetched theories thereupon are to be found in their writings.

All the accounts, however, agree in pointing to an origin outside Europe in Oriental lands, and for this opinion there must have been some historical grounds that have been either lost or completely shrouded beneath the veil of symbolism. On the one hand, it is impossible that a detailed constitution such as that of the Order, together with a system of occult science that embraces every domain of transcendental knowledge, should have been the product of a single man and a single epoch. There must rather have been the co-operation of many men of high spiritual attainments; and thus those hypotheses which attribute the foundation of the Order to a single man such as Studion or Valentine Andrea are untenable, and can only have arisen through the prevailing ignorance about the Order.

It is known that every form of occultism was cultivated among the Egyptian priesthood, that magic, magnetism, astrology, and the secrets of chemistry found their votaries in the temples. Since Moses was said to be learned in all the wisdom of the Egyptians, which wisdom, as we know, included magic, there is no inherent improbability in the kabbalistic tradition according to which Moses, with whom the Rosicrucians claim a certain connection, communicated his knowledge to certain chosen members of his nation. Perhaps we ought to consider the Essenes and the Therapeutæ of the earliest Christian times, as bearers of the Mosaic

* Translated from the " Sphinx," and reprinted from the " Theosophist "

tradition, while the depositaries of the Egyptian temple secrets must be looked for in the Neo-Platonists, especially Jamblichus.

It is certain that from some such elements as these, among Europeans of Greco-Roman culture, there existed in the first centuries of our era a secret society, the principal aim of which was, together with magico-mystical studies, the transmutation of metals or alchemy. Such a society is referred to in the following passage from Thoelden's (Tollii) " *Coelum reseratum chemicum* " : " Our ancestors again united themselves in the time of Valerius Diocletian, in the year 248. This tyrant reigned twenty years, and during his reign many of the good old men were martyred through his cruel rage, which not only learned men but others also were compelled to flee for safety to other lands with their wives and children, etc." Reference is plainly here made to a mystical society, which was in course of time destroyed through hostile circumstances, but afterwards reconstituted.

This view is supported by Professor Kopp in his " History of Chemistry" and " Materials for a History of Chemistry." Kopp accounts in this way for the remarkable fact that, from the fourth to the sixth century, there was quite a flood of alchemical writings in the Greek language containing an amount of practical chemical knowledge, of which the prose writers of the classical age, such as Diodorus Siculus, Pliny, Dioscorides, and others, give no indication that they knew any-thing. This is further confirmed by the fixity of chemical symbolism and the mystical properties attributed to certain chemical substances, so that we are obliged to suppose that these things were more universal and of more ancient origin, because isolated searchers, during the con-fusion of the great migrations, would hardly have been able to find either leisure for such studies or a receptive public to appreciate them. We can therefore only conclude that the long course of experimental research undertaken by a closed body was written down, and thus communicated to the new members, who were admitted from time to time into its ranks.

As we find that the Arabians were the guardians of the sciences, so we find existing among them various secret unions having mystical and alchemical studies as their object. These are referred to in the different accounts of the schools of magic at Toledo, Salamanca, Barce-lona, and other places, the existence of which is confirmed by Bernhard Basinus in his " *De cultibus magicis* " and by Martin Delrio in his " *De disquisionibus magicis*," both these writers being Spaniards living at a time when these schools were still flourishing. It is needless to mention that these schools of magic were not establishments where instruction was given in the art of "raising the devil," but centres of meeting for societies such as have been already described. It is well known that the Arabians were deep students of alchemy, magic, astrology, etc., and in proof that this was so I need only mention the names of Geber, Avicenna, Rhases, and Averrhoes.

As Christendom began to shake off the chains of barbarism in Europe, young men of all nations turned their eager steps to Spain, to sit at the feet of the great masters and learn from them the secret sciences. Such a student was Gerhard of Cremona (about 1130), who first translated Aristotle and Ptolemy into Latin ; also the celebrated doctor of medicine Arnald of Villanova (about 1243), and Petrus of Agano (died 1403), and lastly the celebrated Raymond Lully, who died in 1336, and Pope Sylvester II., a native of Lorraine.

All these men were deeply versed in the secret sciences, whence they were reputed to be magicians. They naturally sought to spread the knowledge they had acquired, and at that epoch this could only be accomplished through the means of secret societies.

Of the existence of such societies we find proofs from the writings of these men. Thus in the " *Theoria* " of Raymond Lully, printed in the " *Theatrum chemicum Argentoratum* " (1613), there is a passage in which mention is made of a society, *Societas physicorum*," and of a " *Rex physicorum*," and in the " Rosary " of Arnald of Villanova, written about 1230 and included in the fourth volume of the " *Theatrum Chemicum*," we find traces of a similar society a century before the days of Lully, as we find mention made of "sons of the Order."

In the same volume (page 1028) we further find a bishop of Treves, Count von Falkenstein, spoken of as " most illustrious and serene prince and father of philosophers" in the fourteenth century. That the above was one of the titles of the higher officers of the Rosicrucian Order is proved by the title of a manuscript in my possession called " *Compendium totius Philosophiæ et Alchemiæ Fraternitatis Rosæ Crucis ex mandato Serenissimi Comitis de Falkenstein, Imperatoris nostri Anno Domini* 1374*.*"

This manuscript contains an exposition of alchemical theories in accordance with the science of the time with a collection of such processes as are of value in practical alchemy. Although it contains no philosophy or theology in the modern sense of the words, this manuscript has still a certain historical value, as in it we find the first use of the title "Imperator" as applied to a member of the Order, and also this is the earliest extant mention of the name " Fraternitas Rosæ Crucis " (Fraternity of the Rosy Cross). It is probable that the old secret brotherhoods of Alchemists and mystics had this name at the time of the appearance of the many " Rosaries " produced by such men as Arnald, Lully, Ortholanus, Roger Bacon, etc., and united the symbol of the rose which represents the secret as well as ineffable bliss, with the cross or symbol of the Christian faith.*

The earliest extant accounts of the Order of Rosicrucians are about contemporaneous with this manuscript, and the actual history of the Order may thus be said to commence from this time. This, however, is not very extensive, as the Order, entirely free from worldly aims or ambition, devoted its whole energy to the elevation of mankind and the search after the secrets of nature. The writer is, however, in a position to furnish some interesting facts connected with the Order, as his great-grandfather was long one of its most zealous members and held the office of Imperator. During the years from 1764 to 1802 he copied out the chief contents of the archives of the Order, and this manuscript library is still in my possession.

About the year 1378, Christian Rosenkreutz, a knight of noble family, newly returned from the East, established a secret society at some place now unknown. Rosenkreutz, who had learned many secrets during his travels in Arabia and Chaldea, was the head of this order, and its object was the study of the higher chemistry or the search for the " Philosophers' Stone."

The society began with four members, their number being afterwards increased to eight. These lived with Rosenkreutz in a building erected by him called *Sancti Spiritus*. Under a pledge of secrecy Rosenkreutz dictated to the other members the secrets he had learnt, and this knowledge was written out in books. Although it may have contained other similar manuscripts of older date, these books formed the nucleus of the library of the Order, and in my collection there are a number of manuscripts, beginning from the year 1400, each inscribed with the date at which it was written and the name of the Imperator by whose orders it was prepared.

The rules of the society founded by Christian Rosenkreutz were as follows : The members were to heal the sick without accepting remuneration for so doing. There was to be no distinct uniform worn by members

---

* Similar proofs, though of a less striking nature, that the Rosicrucians are descended from the above-named societies, may be found in the book of the great Kabbalist Pico de Mirandole " *De Oro*," which went through many editions, and is to be found in all large libraries.

of the brotherhood as such, but each was to dress in accordance with the customs of his country. At a certain day in every year all the brothers were to meet in the building above mentioned, or assign good reasons for their absence. Each was to choose out a worthy person to be his successor in case of death. The letters R. C. were to form their seal and watchword. The brotherhood was to remain a secret one for a period of one hundred years.

Rosenkreutz is said to have died at the age of 106. The other members knew of his death, but they did not know where he was buried, it being a maxim with the first Rosicrucians that their place of burial should be concealed even from the members of the Order. In the same building other masters were chosen as necessity required, and the society continued for about 120 years, never having more than eight members, new ones being admitted only to take the place of those that died, under an oath of silence and fidelity.

After this time a door was discovered in the building (probably somewhere in South Germany), and on its being opened it was found to lead to a burial vault. The door bore the inscription " *Post annos CXX patebo.*" The vault had seven sides and corners, each side being five feet broad and eight feet high. It was lighted by an artificial sun. In the middle, instead of a tomb-stone, there was a round altar, and on it a small plate of brass bearing the inscription, "A. C. R. C. *Hoc Universi Compendium vivus mihi Sepulchrum feci.*" (While alive I made this my sepulchre the compendium of the universe.) Round the edge was " *Jesus mihi omnia.*" In the middle were four figures with the inscription : " *Nequaquam vacuum. Legis Jugum. Libertas Evangelii. Dei gloria Intacta.*"

The vault was divided by the brothers into roof or sky, wall or sides, and earth or pavement. The roof and the pavement were in triangles towards the seven sides, and each side was divided into ten squares, which were to be explained to those newly admitted. Each side had a door to a chest in which different things were kept, especially the secret books of the Order and other writings, which latter also might be seen by the profane. In these chests were found among other things, "mirrors possessing many virtues, little bells, burning lamps, all so arranged that even after many hundred years, when the whole order had been destroyed, it could, by means of the things in this vault, be again restored."

Under the altar, after removing the brass plate, the brothers found the body of Rosenkreutz, undecayed and uninjured. In his hand he held a book written on parchment with golden characters, with the letter T on the cover,* and at the end signed by eight brothers "in two different circles, who had been present at the death and burial of the father of the Rosicrucians."

In the *testament* the society offers its secrets to the whole world; it declares that it belongs to the Christian religion, but to no particular sect; that it honours all government; "that the making of gold is but a small thing to them, and that they have a thousand better objects." The writing ends with the words: "Our building *Sancti Spiritus*, though a hundred thousand men have seen it, shall remain for ever undisturbed, undestroyed, unseen, and well hidden from the godless world."

The manuscripts in my possession are the only record of the doings of the Rosicrucians during the fifteenth century. Among these there is especially a *Clavis Sapientiæ* (key of wisdom) or "a dialogue on wisdom (Alchemy) with a scholar of note." This is dated 1468, and bears the name of the Imperator Johann Carl Friesen; it contains a collection of important alchemical processes of which some few were known, though in an incomplete form, to the celebrated chemist Johann Kunkel von Loewenstern,† who, as is stated in the chapter on Antimony, and Crocus Martis, in his "*Laboratorium chymicum*," made gold from one of them.

At the beginning of the sixteenth century there appeared in Paris a secret society founded by Henry Cornelius Agrippa of Nettesheim in 1507. This society was connected with the Rosicrucians, and the Rosicrucian Irenæus Philalethes, when writing in 1650, expressly calls Agrippa Imperator.

The Rosicrucians were re-organised by Theophrastus Paracelsus. During his long travels in the East he had evidently become acquainted with the Indian secret doctrine, and he drew after him in Europe a large number of disciples among the learned men of the day, and united the Rosicrucian system with the older teachings, though we cannot now easily trace how far this was done.

This "Luther of medicine" is not only called in my manuscripts Imperator, but also *Reorganisator*. Moreover, the title *Monarcha Secretorum*,

---

* Perhaps the original of the manuscript in my possession, entitled "Testamentum Fratrum Rosæ et Auræ Crucis," the above-mentioned dictation of Rosenkreutz, which, next to the Bible, was considered the most precious treasure of the Order.

† Kunkel von Loewenstern was the discoverer of phosphorus. He was alchemist to the Kurfurst Johann George II. of Saxony, to Frederick William and Frederick III. of Brandenburg, as well as Charles XI. of Sweden, who ennobled him on account of his eminent services.

adopted by Paracelsus and used against him as a proof of his insanity, points to the same circumstance.

Paracelsus was inclined to be a free-thinker in ecclesiastical matters, and was more attracted to the teachings of Luther than those of the orthodox church, and from his time we find many protestants in the ranks of the Rosicrucians, such as the doctors of medicine, Adam von Bodenstein, Michael Toxicates, Johann Hufer, Michael Maier, and Conrad Khunrath, who edited editions of the works of Paracelsus, and in a numerous collection of writings worked for the spread of the Rosicrucian doctrines.*

We also find some theologians among the Rosicrucians, such as Johann Arndt, the celebrated author of " The true Christendom," who in 1599 wrote a Rosicrucian book, a copy of which I possess, entitled '' Zweytes Silentium Dei." In this manuscript is taught the preparation of the philosophers' stone without artificial fire, by only using the heat of the sun, concentrated, by means of burning mirrors· Whatever may be thought of the value of their aims in general, it is an interesting scientific fact that the Rosicrucians were acquainted with the use of burning mirrors a century before Tschirnhausen, which mirrors were quite equal in power to the celebrated work of this Saxon philosopher who was a contemporary of Augustus the Strong.

The members of the Order must have been widely distributed in the year 1590, for in that and the following year we find the French alchemist Barnaud travelling about Germany to seek out the Hermetic masters of the Rosy Cross.

In the year 1601 he had a Latin letter printed, addressed to all the Rosicrucians in France, warmly recommending to them King Henry IV. and Maurice of Nassau. From this we must gather that Barnaud had entered into close relations with the Order and may even have been its Imperator, as also that Henry IV. and Maurice of Nassau had evinced no unfriendly disposition towards it. It is remarkable that the Emperor Rudolph II., who was known to be an eager student of magic, alchemy, and astrology, was never a member of the Order, and this is the more remarkable since he had Rosicrucians as his physicians in Gerhard Dorn, Thaddeus von Hayeck, and Michael Maier.

---

* There is a good catalogue of these works in Schmieder's " History of Alchemy," but they have no interest for the modern reader, as the symbology used in the description of persons and things at the beginning of the seventeenth century is now entirely incomprehensible.

In 1604 a certain Simon Studion, born at Urach in Wurtemburg, wrote a mystical work, only extant in manuscript, entitled "*Naometria.*" By this he means a new worship of the inner and outer temple—that is to say, a mystical description of the inner and outer man who is taken as the temple of God. The writer has many mystical things to say about the rose and the cross, and produces a set of allegories and apocalytic calculations that are perfectly unintelligible. Studion was a man who was given to seeing visions, and who was affected with a sort of religious mania. Notwithstanding this, his curious work has been ignorantly supposed to be the foundation of the Rosicrucian system, and he has been looked upon as the founder of the Order.

Similar claims have been made on behalf of the well-known Wurtemburg Doctor Johann Valentine Andrea (1586-1634), a man of high culture and learning, who wrote a "*Fama et Confessio fraternitatis Rosæ Crucis,*" as well as his better known work, the "Chemical Marriage of Christian Rosenkreutz," and also a "General Reformation of the Whole Word."

These works made a great impression, and were immediately translated into other languages—the *Fama* was translated into five different tongues, The utility of these works is about equal to those of Studion mentioned above. In the *Fama* and *Confessio* the history of the knight Rosenkreutz is related with a number of allegorical embellishments. The "Chemical Marriage" is a very abstruse alchemical book in which the universal alchemical process is taught under the figure of a marriage. The setting is, however, so *bizarre*, all direct reference to chemistry being avoided, that no one—that is, no one living at the present day—can make the least sense out of it. In the "General Reformation" he gives a plan of an Utopia on a christian-theosophical basis; but the book is as unsatisfactory as his other works.

The fact that these works were translated into so many languages shows that there must have been a large number of persons who possessed the key to their dark symbolism, so that in spite of their oracular obscurity these books were a source of commercial profit to the publishers. Among those initiated into the mysteries of this hieroglyphical language there may have been a large number of exoteric alchemists, who vainly tortured their brains to arrive at the real meaning of the allegories without being ever able to tame the "red lions." All that we of this age can say is that the key to these mystical writings is now lost.

The works of Andrea were the precursors of a whole literature, in which the Rosicrucian Order was either defended or attacked. To this belong especially the "Five Letters to the Worshipful Brotherhood of the Rosy Cross"

(Lintz, Austria, 1615) and the "Answer to the Enlightened Brotherhood of the Worshipful Order of the R. C." dated 12th January, 1615, in which is projected a reformation of the arts and sciences—especially of the healing art.

One of the chief studies of the Rosicrucians of the second system was that of magico-magnetic healing. The imperial physician Michael Maier, in his book entitled "*Silentium post Clamores*"* has an important passage on this subject: "Nature," he says, "is still half veiled. Many of her manifestations and secret methods of working, especially those of which a knowledge is necessary for the healing art, are still quite hidden. There is especially a lack of experiment and observation, for our senses alone are unable to trace out the inner being and its qualities. Much gratitude is therefore due to the Rosicrucians, those '*Indagatoribus scientiæ naturalis*' for working to supply this much-felt need. Their secrets are no other than those that every one, who is but to some extent acquainted with philosophy, must discover that they enable him by researches into the unknown to complete the known and use it to advantage."

About the year 1620 Michael Maier travelled in England in order to carry on the Rosicrucian propaganda. He was very well received, and made the acquaintance of the celebrated philosopher Robert Fludd (1575-1637). Fludd was a genial man, master of all the science of his time, and having moreover a strong vein of mysticism in his character. Since about the year 1600 he had begun to study the kabbala, magic, astrology and alchemy, as is proved by his "*Historia utriusque cosmi.*"†

In this work he unfolds a complete transcendental system; and it contains facts and theories of the most important nature. Fludd grasped the Rosicrucian scheme with fiery zeal, and was its most ardent defender in England. He wrote a book called "*Summum bonum,*" in which he drew attention to the Rosicrucian Order, and applied the expressions used in alchemy to the mystical cleansing of the soul according to the Christian gospels. This work gave rise to the view that all alchemy had but a symbolical meaning, and that its teachings were to be interpreted in a spiritual sense only, without any reference to the actual transmutation of metals, an error which shows a complete ignorance of the history of alchemy and of chemistry.

Fludd's "*Summum bonum*" aroused the wrath of the well-known Father Mersennus, the "*Athiestorum Princeps*" and the friend of Ramus, Peirescius and Gassendi, and a bitter feud was created between Fludd and Mersennus as well as Gassendi, Theophilus Schweighardt, and others. The perusal of these controversial writings, collected in the large Oppenheim edition (1617-1638),

---

* Frankfort, 1617, pp. 142.   † Oppenheim, 1617, folio.

is now, however, without interest and almost unintelligible. A passage from the " *Clavis philosophiæ Fluddanæ* " (page 50) is, however, of some importance. From this it appears that the prosperity of the Rosicrucian Order in England was but short-lived, and the transition of the Rosicrucians to the freemasons is at the same time hinted at. From this the rise of freemasonry must be placed about the years 1629-1635; though it is not used by Fludd, it does not seem as if the name of freemason was then adopted. The inventor of the name and the date of its first adoption are alike matters of uncertainty.[*]

In the year 1622 there was a Rosicrucian society at the Hague, where it was established in a palace, and its members lived in wealth. The society also had houses in Amsterdam, Nurenberg, Hamburg, Dantzig, Mantua, Venice and Erfurt. As a sign of recognition the brothers wore a black silk cord in the top buttonhole. This sign was received by neophytes after they had promised under oath, as my manuscript says, to be strangled by such a cord rather than break the silence imposed upon them. " Their other sign is that when they go into company they all wear a blue ribbon, to which is attached a golden cross with a rose on it, and this they are given on being received into the society. This they wear round their neck under their coats so that not much of it is visible. The golden cross hangs down on the left side. The third sign is that on the top of the head they have a shaven spot about the size of a louis d'or, as you may see on myself. Hence most of them wear a wig in order not to be recognised; they are, moreover, very devout and live very quietly. The fourth sign is that on all high festivals, very early at sunrise, they leave their residence by that same door (the one facing the sunrise, *i.e.*, the East) and wave a small green flag. When another of them appears at the place where one lives, he goes to this same place and there they enter into conversation in order to recognise one another, for in the beginning they do not trust one another. Thus they have a certain greeting among themselves which is as follows: The stranger says to the man he is visiting, ' *Ave Frater !*' to which the other answers ' *Rosæ et Aureæ* ' ; then the first says ' *Crucis.*' Then both together say ' *Benedictus Deus Dominus noster, qui nobis dedit Signum.*' Then they have a large document to which the Imperator affixes the secret seal."

I am in a position to give an exact description of this seal, since I was for many years in possession of the one formerly belonging to my great grand father, who, as mentioned above, was Imperator of the order. Unfortunately, it was destroyed in the year 1874 by a fire in my parents' house. It was made of brass, and was about the size of a mark (about as large as half a rupee). It

---

[*] Compare Joh. Gottl. Buhle " *Ueber den Ursprung und die vornehmsten Schicksale des Order der Rosenkreutzer und Freimaurer,*" *Gottingen,* 1802, page 252.

consisted of a shield within a circle ; on the shield there was a cross, at the base of which was a conventional rose with five petals. At top, bottom and sides of the shield was the letter C, and these four letters signify: *Crux Christi Corona Christianorum* (The cross of Christ is the Christian's crown).

The Rosicrucians of these times must not be confounded with the Society of the Rose founded at Paris about the year 1660 by an alchemist and apothecary named Jacob Rose. This did not last, and was dissolved in 1674 in consequence of the notorious Brinvilliers case.

A short summary will be interesting of the chief points in the history of the Order during the seventeenth century.

1604. The twelve tracts of Sendivogius on "The Stone of the Sages" were published at Prague. In 1605 a new edition was issued with an edition addressed by the Wurttemberg councillor Konrad Schuler to the German princes.

1607. Benedict Figulus, the Rosicrucian, printed a " Dialogue of Mercury with a philosopher," a work which made a great impression at the time.

1608. The above-named Konrad Schuler published an " Explanation of the writings of Basil Valentine."

1616. According to a catalogue of this year, some Rosicrucian writings were sold at Prague for the sum of 16,000 thalers.

1619. Gutmann's celebrated mystical work, "Revelation of Divine Majesty," was printed at Frankfort.

1641. Two Rosicrucians who had disclosed their wealth, were tortured to death in Bohemia, in order to extract their secrets from them.

1652. The " *Lumen de Lumine* " of Irenæus Philalethes appeared.

In this work the " Universal Process " is taught.

1667. Johannes Lange published the " *Introitus apertus in régium palatium* " by Irenæus Philalethes, at Hamburg.

1673. The same " *Introitus apertus* " was published at Frankfort in the German language. From this time there is a pause of forty years in Rosicrucian activity.

In the year 1714, as a celebration of the centennial jubilee of the work of the Order from the time of the great impetus given it by the publication of the " *Fama Fraternitas* " of Andrea, the Silesian pastor, Sincerus Renatus (Richter) published a work entitled " The true and complete preparation of the Philosopher's Stone of the Brotherhood of the Order of the Golden and Rosy Cross for the benefit of the Sons of the Doctrine."* In this work there is the

* *Breslau : bey Esaia Fellgiebels sel. Witwe und Erben, 1716.*

important information that " some years ago the Masters of the Rosicrucians went to India, and since that time none of them remained in Europe."*

During the next few years, up to about the year 1762, we have no authentic news of the doings of the Rosicrucians. My grandfather merely makes mention in his writings of an " Adept "† under the cipher F. C. R., who lived in Dresden in a sort of honourable imprisonment, under the care of several officers, and in 1748 made some four quintals of gold for the then prince of Saxony, and left some " Tincture of health " of the bulk of a hazel-nut, and vanished from his prison in some mysterious way. An assistant of this Adept, a certain Johann Gottlob Fried, who was afterwards employed at Taucha, near Leipsic, and who was a serving brother of the R. C., informed my great-grandfather of this fact, and told him that from the crucible employed in making the gold he had got about twenty-one thalers worth of metal, and had also some of the tincture. My ancestor says in a note on the margin of a letter, dated 3rd July, 1765, "that he has no longer any doubt as to the reality of our stone, for he had tried the tincture. It proved to be of lead and quick-silver made into a tincture, and it was found to give true results."

My great-grandfather was made acquainted with the Order, and was ad-mitted as one of its members at Amsterdam by a certain Tobias Schulze, the then Imperator. How this happened I am not able to say, but it appears from the manuscripts that he signed as Imperator from the year 1769. At this time the Order again made some stir in the world though why this was the case does not appear. Many who have inquired into the question, as, for instance, Nicholai, account for it on the hypothesis that the Jesuits, after the dissolution of the congregation by Pope Clement XIV. in 1774, had introduced themselves into the Order. But in contradiction to this hypothesis, it appears from my manuscripts that, so far from this being the case, the Rosicrucians took a mystico-Protestant direction in their theological views, basing their teaching on Biblical grounds and sympathizing with the mysticism of Jacob Boehme. The tendency of these last Rosicrucians is a union of the emanation theories of the Kabbala with the doctrines of Christianity and by this means the Rosicrucians set on foot an amalgamation with the Martinists and the Illuminati. Moreover the connection with the Order of such men as Schrepfer, St. Germain and Cagliostro renders it unlikely that the Jesuits had any relations with it.

It appears from the papers of my great-grandfather that the last of the true

---

* See the same work, page 125.

† " Adept," in the alchemical sense, is a man possessed of the secret of the trans-mutation of metals. Cf. the above-mentioned works of Schmieder and Bopp

Rosicrucians passed their lives in contemplative quiet, votaries of a Christian Theosophy. It is plain that the introduction of masonic elements and the tenets of the Illuminati had shaken the old structure of the Order and forced it out of its former grooves, and from a memorandum in my possession it appears that in 1792 it had been decided to release the brothers from their oath and to destroy the library and the archives. When and where this happened I am unable to say.

In 1801 the well-known author of the " Jobsiade," J. J. Kortum, endeavoured to resuscitate the Order by founding a hermetic society. This attempt was, however, entirely fruitless, for the political ferment of the time had driven all ideas of mysticism out of men's minds, and the few surviving, " *Fratres Rosæ et Aureæ Crucis* " were dying out. It is, however, possible that down to the middle of the present century there were still living some genuine Rosicrucians ; but I do not think it probable that there is any collection of the writings of the Order similar to that of my great-grandfather now in existence. Although on account of the strict statutes of the Order it contains but little historical material, it is most rich in information on practical matters, and one is struck with astonishment on reading of the innumerable secret arts with which the Rosicrucians were acquainted.   KARL KISEWETTER.

HAVE ANIMALS SOULS?

REPRINTED FROM THE THEOSOPHIST.

I.

" Continually soaked with blood, the whole earth is but an immense altar upon which *all that lives has to be immolated*—endlessly, incessantly "..........—COMTE JOSEPH DE MAISTRE. (*Soirées* 1. ii. 35).

MANY are the " antiquated religious superstitions " of the East which Western nations often and unwisely deride; but none is so laughed at and practically set at defiance as the great respect of Oriental people for animal life. *Flesh*-eaters cannot sympathize with total abstainers from meat. We Europeans are nations of civilized barbarians with but a few millenniums between ourselves and our cave-dwelling forefathers who sucked the blood and marrow from uncooked bones. Thus, it is only natural that those that hold human life so cheaply in their frequent and often iniquitous wars, should entirely disregard the death-agonies of the brute creation, and daily sacrifice millions of innocent, harmless lives; for we are too epicurean to devour tiger steaks or crocodile cutlets, but must have tender lambs and golden-feathered pheasants. All this is only as it should be in our era of Krupp cannons and scientific vivisectors. Nor is it a matter of great wonder that the hardy European should laugh at the mild Hindu, who shudders at the bare thought of killing a cow, or that he should refuse to sympathize with the Buddhist and Jain, in their respect for the life of every sentient creature—from the elephant to the gnat.

But, if meat-eating has indeed become a vital necessity—" the tyrant's plea ! "—among Western nations; if hosts of victims in every city, borough and village of the civilized world must needs be daily slaughtered in temples dedicated to the deity denounced by St. Paul and worshipped by men " whose God is their belly ;"—if all this and much more cannot be avoided in our " age of Iron," who can urge the same excuse for sport ? Fishing, shooting, and hunting, the most fascinating of all the " amusements " of civilized life—are certainly the most objectionable from the standpoint of occult philosophy, the most sinful in the eyes of the followers of these religious systems which are the direct outcome of the Esoteric Doctrine—Hinduism and Buddhism. Is it altogether without *any* good reason that the adherents of these two religions, now the oldest in the world, regard the animal world—from the huge quadruped down to the infinitesimally small insect—as their " younger brothers," however ludicrous the idea to a European? This question shall receive due consideration further on.

Nevertheless, exaggerated as the notion may seem, it is certain that few of us are able to picture to ourselves without shuddering the scenes which take place early every morning in the innumerable shambles of the so-called civilized world, or even those daily enacted during the " shooting season." The first sunbeam has not yet awakened slumbering nature, when from all points of the compass myriads of hecatombs are being prepared to salute the rising luminary. Never was heathen Moloch gladdened by such a cry of agony from his victims as the pitiful wail that in all Christian countries rings like a long hymn of suffering throughout nature, all day and every day from morning until evening. In ancient Sparta—than those stern citizens none were ever less sensitive to the delicate feelings of the human heart—a boy, when convicted of torturing an animal for amusement, was put to death as one whose nature was so thoroughly villainous that he could not be permitted to live. But in civilized Europe—rapidly progressing in all things save Christian virtues —*might* remains unto this day the synonym of *right*. The entirely useless, cruel practice of shooting for mere sport countless hosts of birds and animals is nowhere carried on with more fervour than in Protestant England, where the merciful teachings of Christ have hardly made human hearts softer than they were in the days of Nimrod, " the mighty hunter before the Lord." Christian ethics are as conveniently turned into paradoxical syllogisms as those of the " heathen." The writer was told one day by a sportsman that since " not a sparrow falls on the ground without the will of the Father," he who kills for sport—say, one hundred sparrows—does thereby one hundred times over—his Father's will!

A wretched lot is that of all poor brute creatures, hardened as it is into implacable fatality by the hand of man. The *rational* soul of the human being seems born to become the murderer of the *irrational* soul of the animal—in the full sense of the word, since the Christian doctrine teaches *that the soul of the animal dies with its body.* Might not the legend of Cain and Abel have had a dual signification? Look at that other disgrace of our cultured age—the scientific slaughter-houses called " vivisection rooms." Enter one of those halls in Paris, and behold Paul Bert, or some other of these men—so justly called " the learned butchers of the Institute "—at his ghastly work. I have but to translate the forcible description of an eye-witness, one who has thoroughly studied the *modus operandi* of those " executioneers," a well-known French author:—

" Vivisection," he says, " is a speciality in which *torture*, scientifically economized by our butcher-academicians, is applied during whole days, weeks, and even months to the fibres and muscles of one and the same victim. It (torture) makes use of every and any kind of weapon, performs its analysis before a pitiless audience, divides the task every morning between ten apprentices at once, of whom one *works* on the eye, another one on the leg, the third on the brain, a fourth on the marrow ; and whose inexperienced hands succeed, nevertheless, towards night, after a hard day's work, in laying bare the whole of the living carcase they had been ordered to *chisel* out, and *that*, in the evening, is carefully stored away in the cellar, in order that early next morning it may be worked upon again if only there is a breath of life and sensibility left in the victim ! We know that the trustees of the Grammont law (*loi*) have tried to rebel against this abomination ; but Paris showed herself more inexorable than London and Glasgow."*

And yet these gentlemen boast of the *grand* object pursued, and of the *grand* secrets discovered by them. " Horror and lies ! "—exclaims the same author. " In the matter of secrets—a few localizations of faculties and cerebral motions excepted—we know but of one secret that belongs to them by rights : it is the secret of torture eternalized, besides which the terrible law of *autophagy* (mutual manducation), the horrors of wars, the merry massacres of sport, and the sufferings of the animal under the butcher's knife—are as nothing ! Glory to our men of science ! They have surpassed every former kind of torture, and remain now and for ever, without any possible contestation, the kings of artificial anguish and despair ! "*

The usual plea for butchering, killing, and even for legally torturing animals—as in vivisection—is a verse or two in the Bible, and its ill-digested meaning, disfigured by the so-called scholasticism represented by Thomas Aquinas. Even De Mirville, that ardent defender of the rights of the Church, calls such texts—" Biblical tolerances, *forced from God* after the deluge, as so many others, and based upon the decadence of our strength." However this may be, such texts are amply contradicted by others in the same Bible. The meat-eater, the sportsman, and even the vivisector—if there are among the last-named those who believe in special creation and the Bible—generally quote for their justification that verse in Genesis, in which God gives *dual* Adam—" dominion over the fish, fowl, cattle, and over every living thing that moveth upon the earth "—(Ch. i., v. 28) ; hence—as the Christian understands it—power of life and death over every animal on the globe. To this the far more philosophical Brahman and Buddhist might answer : " Not so. Evolution starts to mould future humanities within the lowest scales of being. Therefore, by killing an animal, or even an insect, we arrest the progress of an entity

---

* *De la Resurrection et du Miracle.* E. de Mirville.

towards its final goal in nature—MAN ;" and to this the student of occult philosophy may say "Amen," and add that it not only retards the evolution of that entity, but arrests that of the next succeeding human and more perfect race to come.

Which of the opponents is right, which of them the more logical ? The answer depends mainly, of course, on the personal belief of the intermediary chosen to decide the questions. If he believes in special creation—so-called—then in answer to the plain question—" Why should homicide be viewed as a most ghastly sin against God and nature, and the murder of millions of living creatures be regarded as mere sport ? "—he will reply :— " Because man is created in God's own image and looks *upward* to his Creator and to his birthplace—heaven (*os homini sublime dedit*) ; and that the gaze of the animal is fixed *downward* on *its* birth-place—the earth; for God said—' Let the earth bring forth the living creature after his kind, cattle and creeping thing, and beast of the earth after his kind,' " (Genesis I, 24). Again, "because man is endowed with an immortal soul, and the dumb brute has no immortality, not even a short survival after death."

Now to this an unsophisticated reasoner might reply that if the Bible is to be our authority upon this delicate question, there is not the slightest proof in it that man's birth-place is in heaven any more than that of the last of creeping things—quite the contrary ; for we find in Genesis that if God created " man " and blessed " them," (Ch. I. v. 27—28) so he created " great whales " and " blessed them " (21, 22). Moreover, " the Lord God formed man of the dust of the ground " (II.—7) : and " dust " is surely earth pulverized ? Solomon, the king and preacher, is most decidedly an authority and admitted on all hands to have been the wisest of the Biblical sages ; and he gives utterances to a series of truths in Ecclesiastes (Ch. III.) which ought to have settled by this time every dispute upon the subject. " The sons of men...might see that they themselves are beasts " (*v.* 18)..." that which befalleth the sons of men, befalleth the beasts...a man has no pre-eminence above a beast,"—(*v.* 19)..."all go into one place ; all are of the dust and all turn to dust again (*v.* 20)..." *who* knoweth the spirit of man that goeth *upwards*, and the spirit of the beast, that goeth *downward* to the earth ? " (*v.* 21) Indeed, " who knoweth !" At any rate, it is neither science nor " school divine."

Were the object of these lines to preach vegetarianism on the authority of Bible or Veda, it would be a very easy task to do so. For, it it is quite true that God gave *dual* Adam—the " male and female " of Chapter I. of Genesis—who has little to do with our henpecked ancestor of Chapter II.—" dominion over every living thing," yet we nowhere find that the " Lord God " commanded that Adam or the other to devour animal creation or destroy it for sport. Quite the reverse. For pointing to the vegetable kingdom and the "fruit of a tree yielding seed"—God says very plainly: "to you (men) it shall be *for meat.*" (I., 29.)

So keen was the perception of this truth among the early Christians that during the first centuries they never touched meat. In *Octavio* Tertullian writes to Minutius Felix: " We are not permitted either to witness, or even hear narrated (*novere*) a homicide, we Christians, *who refuse to taste dishes in which animal blood may have been mixed.*"

But the writer does not preach vegetarianism, simply defending " animal rights " and attempting to show the fallacy of disregarding such rights on Biblical authority. Moreover, to argue with those who would reason upon the lines of erroneous interpretations would be quite useless. One who rejects the doctrine of revolution will ever find his way paved with difficulties ; hence, he will never admit that it is far more consistent with fact and logic to regard physical man merely as the recognised paragon of animals, and the spiritual Ego that *informs* him as a principle midway between the soul of the animal and the deity. It would be vain to tell him that unless he accepts not only the verses quoted for his justi- fication, but the whole Bible in the light of esoteric philosophy, which reconciles the whole mass of contradictions and *seeming* absurdities in it— he will never obtain the key to the truth ;—for he will not believe it. Yet the whole Bible teems with charity to men and with mercy and love to animals. The original Hebrew text of Chapter XXIV of Leviticus is full of it. Instead of the verses 17 and 18 as translated in the Bible : " And he that killeth a beast shall make it good, beast for beast," in the original it stands : "life for life," or rather "soul for soul," *nephesh tachat nephesh.** And if the rigour of the law did not go to the extent of killing, as in Sparta, a man's " soul " for a beast's " soul "—still, even though he replaced the slaughtered soul by a living one, a heavy additional punishment was inflicted on the culprit.

But this was not all. In Exodus (Ch. XX. 10, and Ch. XXIII. 2 *et seq.* rest on the Sabbath day extended to cattle and every other animal. "The seventh day is the sabbath...... thou shalt not do any work, thou nor thy... cattle ;" and the Sabbath *year*... "the seventh year thou shalt let it (the land) rest and lie still...... that thine ox and thine ass may rest "—which commandment, if it means anything, shows that even the brute creation was not excluded by the ancient Hebrews from a participation in the worship of their deity, and that it was placed upon many occasions on a par with man himself. The whole question rests upon the misconception that " soul," *nephesh*, is entirely distinct from "spirit"—*ruach*. And yet it is clearly stated that " God breathed into the nostrils (of man) *the breath of*

---

* Compare also the difference between the translation of the same verses in the *Vulgate,* and the texts of *Luther* and *De Witte.*

life and man became a living soul," *nephesh*—neither more nor less than an animal, for the soul of an animal is also called *nephesh*. It is by development that the *soul* becomes *spirit*, both being the lower and the higher rungs of one and the same ladder whose basis is the UNIVERSAL SOUL or spirit.

This statement will startle those good men and women who, however much they may love their cats and dogs, are yet too much devoted to the teachings of their respective churches ever to admit such a heresy. "The *irrational* soul of a dog or a frog divine and immortal as our own souls are!" they are sure to exclaim ; but so they are. It is not the humble writer of the present article who says so, but no less an authority for every good Christian than that king of the preachers, St. Paul. Our opponents who so indignantly refuse to listen to the arguments of either modern or esoteric science may perhaps lend a more willing ear to what their own saint and apostle has to say on the matter ; the true interpretation of whose words, moreover, shall be given neither by a theosophist nor an opponent, but by one who was as good and pious a Christian as any—namely, another saint, John Chrysostom—he who explained and commented upon the Pauline Epistles, and who is held in the highest reverence by the divines of both the Roman Catholic and the Protestant churches. Christians have already found that experimental science is not on their side ; they may be still more disagreeably surprised upon finding that no Hindu could plead more earnestly for animal life than did St. Paul in writing to the Romans. Hindus, indeed, claim mercy to the dumb brute only on account of the doctrine of transmigration, and hence of the sameness of the principle or element that animates both man and brute. St. Paul goes further ; he shows the animal *hoping for* and *living in the expectation of the same* "*deliverance from the bonds of corruption*" as any good Christian. The precise expressions of that great apostle and philosopher will be quoted later on in the present Essay, and their true meaning shown.

The fact that so many interpreters—fathers of the Church and scholastics—tried to evade the real meaning of St. Paul is no proof against its inner sense, but rather against the fairness of the theologians, whose inconsistency will be shown in this particular. But some people will support their propositions, however erroneous, to the last. Others, recognising their earlier mistake, will, like Cornelius à Lapide, offer the poor animal *amende honorable*. Speculating upon the part assigned by nature to the brute creation in the great drama of life, he says : " The aim of all creatures is the service of man. Hence, together with him (their master), they are waiting for their renovation"—*cum homine renovationem suam expectant.*[*] " Serving" man surely cannot mean being tortured, killed,

---

[*] *Commen. Apocal.,* ch. v. 137.

uselessly shot, and otherwise misused; while it is almost needless to explain the word "renovation." Christians understand by it the renovation of bodies after the second coming of Christ; and limit it to man, to the exclusion of animals. The students of the Secret Doctrine explain it by the successive renovation and perfection of forms on the scale of objective and subjective being, and in a long series of evolutionary transformations from animal to man, and upward.........

This will, of course, be again rejected by Christians with indignation. We shall be told that it is not thus that the Bible was explained to them, nor can it ever mean that. It is useless to insist upon it. Many and sad in their results were the erroneous interpretations of that which people are pleased to call the "Word of God." The sentence, "Cursed be Canaan; a servant of servants shall he be unto his brethren" (*Gen.* IX. 25), generated centuries of misery and undeserved woe for the wretched slaves—the negroes. It is the clergy of the United States who were their bitterest enemies in the anti-slavery question, which question they opposed *Bible in hand*. Yet slavery is proved to have been the cause of the natural decay of every country; and even proud Rome fell because "the majority in the ancient world were slaves," as Geyer justly remarks. But so terribly imbued at all times were the best, the most intellectual Christians with those many erroneous interpretations of the Bible that even one of their grandest poets, while defending the right of man to freedom, allots no such portion to the poor animal.

> " God gave us only over beast, fish, fowl,
> Dominion absolute ; that right we hold
> By his donation; but man over man
> He made not lord ; such title to himself
> Reserving, human left from human free."

—says Milton.

But, like murder, error " will out," and incongruity must unavoidably occur whenever erroneous conclusions are supported either against or in favour of a prejudged question. The opponents of Eastern *philozoism* thus offer their critics a formidable weapon to upset their ablest arguments by such incongruity between premises and conclusions, facts postulated and deductions made.

It is the purpose of the present Essay to throw a ray of light upon this most serious and interesting subject. Roman Catholic writers in order to support the genuineness of the many miraculous resurrections of animals produced by their saints, have made them the subject of endless debates. The " soul in animals " is, in the opinion of Bossuet, " the most difficult as the most important of all philosophical questions."

Confronted with the doctrine of the Church that animals, though not soulless, have no *permanent* or immortal soul in them, and that the principle which animates them dies with the body, it becomes interesting to learn how the schoolmen and the Church divines reconcile this statement with that other claim that animals may be and have been frequently and miraculously resurrected.

Though but a feeble attempt—one more elaborate would require volumes —the present Essay, by showing the inconsistency of the scholastic and theological interpretations of the Bible, aims at convincing people of the great criminality of taking—especially in sport and vivisection—animal life. Its object, at any rate, is to show that however absurd the notion that either man or brute can be resurrected after the life-principle has fled from the body for ever, such resurrections—if they were true—would not be more impossible in the case of a dumb brute than in that of a man ; for either both are endowed by nature with what is so loosely called by us " soul," or neither the one nor the other is so endowed.

II.

What a chimera is man ! what a confused chaos, what a subject of contradiction ! a professed judge of all things, and yet a feeble worm of the earth ! the great depository and guardian of truth, and yet a mere huddle of uncertainty ! the *glory and the scandal* of the universe !—PASCAL.

WE shall now proceed to see what are the views of the Christian Church as to the nature of the soul in the brute, to examine how she reconciles the discrepancy between the resurrection of a dead animal and the assumption that its soul dies with it, and to notice some miracles in connection with animals. Before the final and decisive blow is dealt to that selfish doctrine, which has become so pregnant with cruel and merciless practices toward the poor animal world, the reader must be made acquainted with the early hesitations of the Fathers of the Patristic age themselves, as to the right interpretation of the words spoken with reference to that question by St. Paul.

It is amusing to note how the Karma of two of the most indefatigable defenders of the Latin Church—Messrs. Des Mousseaux and De Mirville, in whose works the record of the few miracles here noted are found—led both of them to furnish the weapons now used against their own sincere but very erroneous views.*

The great battle of the Future having to be fought out between the " Creationists " or the Christians, as all the believers in a special creation and a personal god, and the Evolutionists or the Hindus, Buddhists, all

---

* It is but justice to acknowledge here that De Mirville is the first to recognise the error of the Church in this particular, and to defend animal life, as far as he dares do so.

the Free-thinkers and last, though not least, most of the men of science, a recapitulation of their respective positions is advisable.

1. The Christian world postulates its right over animal life; (a) on the afore-quoted Biblical texts and the later scholastic interpretations; (b) on the assumed absence of anything like divine or human soul in animals. Man survives death, the brute *does not*.

2. The Eastern Evolutionists, basing their deductions upon their great philosophical systems, maintain it is a sin against nature's work and progress to kill any living being—for reasons given in the preceding pages.

3. The Western Evolutionists, armed with the latest discoveries of science, heed neither Christians nor Heathens. Some scientific men believe in Evolution, others do not. They agree, nevertheless, upon one point: namely, that physical, exact research offers no grounds for the presumption that man is endowed with an immortal, divine soul, any more than his dog.

Thus, while the Asiatic Evolutionists behave toward animals consistently with their scientific and religious views, neither the church nor the materialistic school of science is logical in the practical applications of their respective theories. The former, teaching that every living thing is created singly and specially by God, as any human babe may be, and that it finds itself from birth to death under the watchful care of a wise and kind Providence, allows the inferior creation at the same time only a temporary soul. The latter, regarding both man and animal as the soulless production of some hitherto undiscovered forces in nature, yet practically creates an abyss between the two. A man of science, the most determined materialist, one who proceeds to vivisect a living animal with the utmost coolness, would yet shudder at the thought of laming—not to speak of torturing to death—his fellow-man. Nor does one find among those great materialists who were religiously inclined men any who have shown themselves consistent and logical in defining the true moral status of the animal on this earth and the rights of man over it.

Some instances must now be brought to prove the charges stated. Appealing to serious and cultured minds it must be postulated that the views of the various authorities here cited are not unfamiliar to the reader It will suffice therefore simply to give short epitomes of some of the conclusions they have arrived at—beginning with the Churchmen.

As already stated, the Church *exacts* belief in the miracles performed by her great Saints. Among the various prodigies accomplished we shall choose for the present only those that bear directly on our subject— namely, the miraculous resurrections of dead animals. Now one who credits man with an immortal soul independent of the body it animates can easily believe that by some divine miracle the soul can be recalled and forced back into the tabernacle it deserts apparently for ever. But how can one accept the same possibility in the case of an animal, since his faith teaches him that the animal has no independent soul, since it is annihilated with the body? For over two hundred years, ever since Thomas of Aquinas, the Church has authoritatively taught that the soul of the brute dies with its organism. What then is recalled back into the clay to reanimate it? It is at this juncture that scholasticism steps in, and—taking the difficulty in hand—reconciles the irreconcilable.

It premises by saying that the miracles of the Resurrection of animals are numberless and as well unauthenticated as "the resurrection of our Lord Jesus Christ." * The Bollandists give instances without number. As Father Burigny, a hagiograph of the 17th century, pleasantly remarks concerning the bustards *resuscitated* by St. Remi—"I may be told, no doubt, that I am a *goose* myself to give credence to such "blue bird" tales. I shall answer the joker, in such a case, by saying that, if he disputes this point, then must he also strike out from the life of St. Isidore of Spain the statement that he resuscitated from death his master's horse; from the biography of St. Nicolas of Tolentino—that he brought back to life a partridge, instead of eating it; from that of St. Francis— that he recovered from the blazing coals of an oven, where it was baking, the body of a lamb, which he forthwith resurrected; and that he also made *boiled* fishes, which he resuscitated, *swim in their sauce;* etc., etc. Above all he, the sceptic, will have to charge more than 100,000 eye-witnesses—among whom at least a few ought to be allowed some common sense—with being either liars or dupes."

A far higher authority than Father Burigny, namely, Pope Benedict (Benoit) XIV., corroborates and affirms the above evidence. The names, moreover, as eye-witnesses to the resurrections, of Saint Sylvestrus, Francois de Paule, Severin of Cracow, and a host of others are all mentioned in the Bollandists. "Only he adds"—says Cardinal de Ventura who quotes him—"that, as resurrection, however, to deserve the name requires the *identical* and *numerical* reproduction of the form,† as much as of the material of the dead creature; and as that form (or soul) of the brute is always annihilated with its body according to St. Thomas' doctrine, God, in every such case finds himself obliged to create for the purpose of the miracle a new form for the resurrected animal; from which it follows that the resurrected brute was *not* altogether *identical* with what it had been before its death (*non idem omnino esse.*)" ‡

---

* *De Beatificatione, etc.*, by Pope Benedict XIV.

† In scholastic philosophy, the word "form" applies to the immaterial principle *which informs or animates the body.*

‡ *De Beatificatione, etc.*, I. IV. c, XI., Art. 6,

Now this looks terribly like one of the *mayas* of magic. However, although the difficulty is not absolutely explained, the following is made clear : the principle, that animated the animal during its life, and which is termed soul, being dead or dissipated after the death of the body, another soul—"a kind of an *informal* soul"—as the Pope and the Cardinal tell us—is *created* for the purpose of miracle by God ; a soul, moreover, which is distinct from that of man, which is " an independent, ethereal, and everlasting entity."

Besides the natural objection to such a proceeding being called a " miracle " produced by the saint, for it is simply God behind his back who " creates " for the purpose of his glorification an entirely new soul as well as a new body, the whole of the Thomasian doctrine is open to objection. For, as Descartes very reasonably remarks : " if the soul of the animal is so distinct (in its immateriality) from its body, we believe it hardly possible to avoid recognising it as a spiritual principle, hence—an intelligent one."

The reader need hardly be reminded that Descartes held the living animal as being simply an automaton, a " well wound up clock-work," according to Malebranche. One, therefore, who adopts the Cartesian theory about the animal would do as well to accept at once the views of the modern materialists. For, since that automaton is capable of feelings, such as love, gratitude, &c., and is endowed as undeniably with memory, all such attributes must be as materialism teaches us " properties of matter." But if the animal is an " automaton," why not Man ? Exact science—anatomy, physiology, etc.—finds not the smallest difference between the bodies of the two ; and who knows—justly inquires Solomon whether the spirit of man "goeth upward " any more than that of the beast ? Thus we find metaphysical Descartes as inconsistent as any one.

But what does St. Thomas say to this ? Allowing a soul (*anima*) to the brute, and declaring it *immaterial*, he refuses it at the same time the qualification of *spiritual*. Because, he says : " it would in such case imply *intelligence*, a virtue and a special operation reserved only for the human soul." But as at the fourth Council of Lateran it had been decided that " God had created two distinct substances, the corporeal (*mundanam*) and the spiritual (*spiritualem*), and that something incorporeal must be of necessity spiritual, St. Thomas had to resort to a kind of compromise, which can avoid being called a subterfuge only when performed by a saint. He says : " This soul of the brute is neither spirit nor body ; it is of a middle nature." * This is a very unfortunate statement. For elsewhere, St. Thomas says " that all the souls—even those of plants—have

---

* Quoted by Cardinal de Ventura in his *Philosophie Chrétienne*, Vol. II., p. 386 See also De Miriville, *Résurrections animales.*

the substantial form of their bodies," and if this is true of plants, why not of animals ? It is certainly neither " spirit " nor pure matter, but of that essence which St. Thomas calls " a middle nature." But why, once on the right path, deny it survivance—let alone immortality ? The contradiction is so flagrant that De Mirville in despair exclaims, " Here we are, in the presence of three substances, instead of the two, as decreed by the Lateran Council ! " and proceeds forthwith to contradict, as much as he dares, the " Angelic Doctor."

The great Bossuet in his *Traité de la Connoissance de Dieu et de soi même* analyses and compares the system of Descartes with that of St. Thomas. No one can find fault with him for giving the preference in the matter of logic to Descartes. He finds the Cartesian " invention "—that of the automaton—as " getting better out of the difficulty " than that of St. Thomas, accepted fully by the Catholic Church ; for which Father Ventura feels indignant against Bossuet for accepting such a miserable and puerile error." And, though allowing the animals a soul with all its qualities of affection and sense, true to his master St. Thomas, he too refuses them intelligence and reasoning powers. " Bousset," he says, " is the more to be blamed, since he himself has said : ' I foresee that a great war is being prepared against the Church under the name of Cartesian philosophy.' " He is right there, for out of the " sentient matter " of the brain of the brute animal comes out quite naturally Locke's *thinking matter*, and out of the latter all the materialistic schools of our century. But when he fails it is through supporting St. Thomas's doctrine, which is full of flaws and evident contradictions. For, if the soul of the animal is, as the Roman Church teaches, an informal, immaterial principle, then it becomes evident that, being independent of physical organism, it cannot " die with the animal " any more than in the case of man. If we admit that it subsists and survives, in what respect does it differ from the soul of man ? And that it is eternal—once we admit St. Thomas's authority on any subject—though he contradicts himself elsewhere. " The soul of man is immortal, and the soul of the animal perishes," he says (*Somna*, Vol. V., p. 164) this, after having queried in Vol. II. of the same grand work (p. 256), " are there any beings that re-emerge into nothingness ? " and answered himself:—" No, for in the Ecclesiastes it is said : (iii. 14) Whatsoever GOD doeth, it shall be for ever. With God there is no variableness " (James I., 17). " Therefore," goes on St. Thomas, " neither in the natural order of things, nor by means of miracles, is there any creature that re-emerges into nothingness (is annihilated) ; *there is naught in the creature that is annihilated*, for that which shows with the greatest radiance divine goodness is the perpetual conservation of the creatures."*

* *Somma*—Drioux edition in 8 vols.

This sentence is commented upon and confirmed in the annotation by the Abbé Drioux, his translator, " No," he remarks, " nothing is annihilated ; it is a principle that has become with modern science a kind of axiom."

And, if so, why should there be an exception made to this invariable rule in nature, recognised both by science and theology, only in the case of the soul of the animal ? Even though *it had no intelligence,* an assumption from which every impartial thinker will ever and very strongly demur.

Let us see, however, turning from scholastic philosophy to natural sciences, what are the naturalist's objections to the animal having an intelligent and therefore an independent soul in him.

" Whatever that be, which thinks, which understands, which acts, it is something celestial and divine; and upon that account must necessarily be eternal," wrote Cicero, nearly two millenniums ago. We should understand well Mr. Huxley contradicting the conclusion,—St. Thomas of Aquinas, the " king of the metaphysicians," firmly believed in the miracles of resurrection performed by St. Patrick.*

Really, when such tremendous claims as the said miracles are put orward and enforced by the Church upon the faithful, her theologians should take more care that their highest authorities at least should not contradict themselves, thus showing ignorance upon questions raised nevertheless to a doctrine.

The animal, then, is barred from progress and immortality, because he is an automaton. According to Descartes, he has no intelligence, agreeably to mediæval scholasticism ; nothing bnt instinct, the latter signifying involuntary impulses, as affirmed by the materialists and denied by the Church.

Both Frederic and George Cuvier have discussed amply, however, on the intelligence and the instinct in animals.† Their ideas upon the subject have been collected and edited by Flourens, the learned Secretary

---

* St. Patrick, it is claimed, has Christianized " the most Satanized country of the globe—Ireland, ignorant *in all save magic*"—into the 'Island of Saints,' by resurrecting " sixty men dead years before." *Suscitavit sexaginta mortuos (Lectio* 1. ii. from the *Roman Breviary,* 1520). In the MS. held to be the famous confession of that saint, preserved in the Salisbury Cathedral (*Descript. Hibern.* I. 11, C. 1), St. Patrick writes in an autograph letter : " To me the last of men, and the greatest sinner God has, nevertheless, given, against the magical practices of this barbarous people the gift of miracles, such as had not been given to the greatest of our apostles—since he (God) permitted that among other things (such as the resurrection of animals and creeping things) I should *resuscitate dead bodies reduced to ashes since many years.*" Indeed, before such a prodigy, the resurrection of Lazarus appears a very insignificant incident.

† More recently Dr. Romanes and Dr. Butler have thrown great light upon the subject.

of the Academy of Sciences. This is what Frederic Cuvier, for thirty years the Director of the Zoological Department and the Museum of Natural History at the *Jardine des plantes*, Paris, wrote upon the subject. " Descartes' mistake, or rather the general mistake, lies in that no sufficient distinction was ever made between intelligence and instinct. Buffon himself had fallen into such an omission, and owing to it everything in his Zoological philosophy was contradictory. Recognising in the animal a feeling superior to our own, as well as the consciousness of its actual existence, he denied it at the same time, thought, reflection, and memory, consequently every possibility of having thoughts (Buffon, *Discourse on the Nature of Animals*, VII., p. 57)." But, as he could hardly stop there, he admitted that the brute had a kind of memory, active, extensive, and more faithful than our (human) memory (*Id. Ibid*, p. 77). Then, after having refused it any intelligence, he nevertheless admitted that the animal consulted its masters, interrogated him, and understood perfectly every sign of his will." (*Id. Ibid*, Vol. X., *History of the Dog*, p. 2).

A more magnificent series of contradictory statements could hardly have been expected from a great man of science.

The illustrious Cuvier is right therefore in remarking in his turn, that " this new mechanism of Buffon is still less intelligible than Descartes' automaton."*

As remarked by the critic, a line of demarcation ought to be traced between instinct and intelligence. The construction of bee-hives by the bees, the raising of dams by the beaver in the middle of the naturalist's dry floor as much as in the river, are all the deeds and effects of instinct for ever unmodifiable and changeless, whereas the acts of intelligence are to be found in actions evidently thought out by the animal, where not instinct but reason comes into play, such as its education and training call forth and renders susceptible of perfection and development. Man is endowed with reason, the infant with instinct; and the young animal shows more of both than the child.

Indeed, every one of the disputants knows as well as we do that it is so. If any materialist avoid confessing it, it is through pride. Refusing a soul to both man and beast, he is unwilling to admit that the latter is endowed with intelligence as well as himself, even though in an infinitely lesser degree. In their turn the churchman, the religiously inclined naturalist, the modern metaphysician, shrink from avowing that man and animal are both endowed with soul and facuities, if not equal in development and perfection, at least the same in name and essence. Each of them knows, or ought to know that instinct and intelligence are two faculties completely opposed in their nature, two enemies confronting each

---

* *Biographie Universelle*, Art. by Cuvier on Buffon's Life.

other in constant conflict ; and that, if they will not admit of two souls or principles, they have to recognise, at any rate, the presence of two potencies in the soul, each having a different seat in the brain, the localization of each of which is well known to them, since they can isolate and temporarily destroy them in turn—according to the organ or part of the organs they happen to be torturing during their terrible vivisections. What is it but human pride that prompted Pope to say :—

> " Ask for whose end the heavenly bodies shine ;
> Earth for whose use ? Pride answers, 'Tis for mine.
> For *me* kind nature wakes her genial power,
> Suckles each herb, and spreads out every flower.
>
>   *   *   *   *
>
> For me the mine a thousand treasures brings ;
> For me health gushes from a thousand springs ;
> Seas roll to waft me, suns to light me rise ;
> My footstool earth, my canopy the skies ! "

And it is the same unconscious pride that made Buffon utter his paradoxical remarks with reference to the difference between man and animal. The difference consisted in the " absence of reflection, for the animal," he says, " does not feel that he feels." How does Buffon know ? " It does not think that it thinks," he adds, after having told the audience that the animal remembered, often deliberated, compared and chose !* Who ever pretended that a cow or a dog could be an idealogist ? But the animal may think and know it thinks, the more keenly that it cannot speak, and express its thoughts. How can Buffon or any one else know ? One thing is shown however by the exact observations of naturalists and that is, that the animal is endowed with intelligence ; and once this is settled, we have but to repeat Thomas Aquinas' definition of intelligence—the prerogative of man's immortal soul—to see that the same is due to the animal.

But in justice to *real* Christian philosophy, we are able to show that primitive Christianity has never preached such atrocious doctrines—the true cause of the falling off of so many of the best men as of the highest intellects from the teachings of Christ and His disciples.

III.

" O Philosophy, thou guide of life, and discoverer of virtue ! "—CICERO.

"Philosophy is a modest profession, it is all reality and plain dealing ; I hate solemnity and pretence, with nothing but pride at the bottom."—PLINY.

THE destiny of man—of the most brutal, animal-like, as well as of the most saintly—being immortality, according to theological teaching ; what is the future destiny of the countless hosts of the animal kingdom ? We

Discours sur la nature des Animaux.

are told by various Roman Catholic writers—Cardinal Ventura, Count de Maistre and many others—that "animal soul is *a Force*."

" It is well established that the soul of the animal," says their echo, De Mirville,—" was produced *by the earth*, for this is Biblical. All the living and moving souls (*nephesh* or life-principle) come from the the earth ; but, let me be understood, not solely from the dust, of which their bodies as well as our own were made, but from the power and potency of the earth ; *i.e.*, from its immaterial force, as all forces are . . . those of the *sea*, of the *air*, etc., all of wnich are those *Elementary Principalities* (*principautés élementaires*) of which we have spoken elsewhere."*

What the Marquis de Mirville understands by the term is, that every " Element " in nature is a domain filled and governed by its respective invisible spirits. The Western Kabalists and the Rosicrucians named them Sylphs, Undines, Salamanders, and Gnomes ; christian mystics, like De Mirville, give them Hebrew names and class each among the various kinds of Demons under the sway of Satan—with God's permission, of course.

He too rebels against the decision of St. Thomas, who teaches that the animal soul is destroyed with the body. " It is a force,"—he says—that " we are asked to annihilate, the most *substantial* force on earth, called *animal soul*," which, according to the Reverend Father Ventura, is * " the most respectable soul after that of man."

He had just called it an immaterial force, and now it is named by him " the most substantial thing on earth."†

But what is this force ? George Cuvier and Flourens the academician tell us its secret.

" The form or the force of the bodies," (form means soul in this case, let us remember), the former writes,—" is far more essential to them than matter is, as (without being destroyed in its essence) the latter changes constantly, whereas the form prevails eternally." To this Flourens observes : In everything that has life, the form is more persistent than matter ; for, that which constitutes the BEING of the living body, its identity and sameness, is its form." ‡

" Being," as De Mirville remarks in his turn, " a magisterial principle, a philosophical pledge of our immortality," § it must be inferred that soul —human and animal—is meant under this misleading term. It is rather what we call the ONE LIFE I suspect.

However this may be, philosophy, both profane and religious, corro-

---

* *Esprits*, 2m. mem. Ch. XII. *Cosmolatrie*.
† *Esprits*—p. 158.
‡ *Longevity*, pp. 49 and 52.
§ *Resurrections*, p. 621.

borates this statement that the two "souls" are identical in man and beast. Leibnitz, the philosopher beloved by Bossuet, appeared to credit "Animal Resurrection" to a certain extent. Death being for him "simply the *temporary enveloping of the personality*," he likens it to the preservation of ideas in sleep, or to the butterfly within its caterpillar. "For him," says De Mirville, "resurrection* is a general law in nature, which becomes a grand miracle, when performed by a thaumaturgist, only in virtue of its prematurity, of the surrounding circumstances, and of the mode in which he operates." In this Leibnitz is a true Occultist without suspecting it. The growth and blossoming of a flower or a plant in five minutes instead of several days and weeks, the forced germination and development of plant, animal or man, are facts preserved in the records of the Occultists. They are only seeming miracles; the natural productive forces hurried and a thousand-fold intensified by the induced conditions under occult laws known to the Initiate. The abnormally rapid growth is effected by the forces of nature, whether blind or attached to minor intelligences sub-jected to man's occult power, being brought to bear collectively on the development of the thing to be called forth out of its chaotic elements. But why call one a divine *miracle*, the other a satanic subterfuge or simply a fraudulent performance?

Still as a true philosopher Leibnitz finds himself forced, even in this dangerous question of the resurrection of the dead, to include in it the whole of the animal kingdom in its great synthesis, and to say: "I believe that the souls of the animals are imperishable,...and I find that nothing is better fitted to prove our own immortal nature."†

Supporting Leibnitz, Dean, the Vicar of Middleton, published in 1748 two small volumes upon this subject. To sum up his ideas, he says that "the holy scriptures hint in various passages that the brutes shall live in a future life. This doctrine has been supported by several Fathers of the Church. Reason teaching us that the animals have a soul, teaches us at the same time that they shall exist in a future state. The system of those who believe that God annihilates the soul of the animal is nowhere supported, and has no solid foundation to it," etc., etc. ‡

Many of the men of science of the last century defended Dean's hypothesis, declaring it extremely probable, one of them especially—the learned Protestant theologian Charles Bonnet of Geneva. Now, this theologian was the author of an extremely curious work, called by him *Palingenesia* § or the "New Birth," which takes place, as he seeks to prove,

---

* The occulists call it "transformation" during a series of lives and the final *nirvanic* Resurrection.

† Leibnitz, *Opera Philos.*, etc.

‡ See Vol. XXIX. of the *Bibliothèque des sciences*, 1st Trimester of the year 1768.

§ From two Greek words—to *be born* and *reborn* again.

owing to an invisible germ that exists in everybody, and no more than Leibnitz can he understand that animals should be excluded from a system, which, in their absence, would not be a unity, since system means "a collection of laws."*

"The animals," he writes, "are admirable books, in which the creator gathered the most striking features of his sovereign intelligence. The anatomist has to study them with *respect*, and, if in the least endowed with that delicate and reasoning feeling that characterizes the moral man, he will never imagine, while turning over the pages, that he is handling slates or breaking pebbles. He will never forget that all that lives and feels is entitled to his mercy and pity. Man would run the risk of compromising his ethical feeling were he to become familiarized with the suffering and the blood of animals. This truth is so evident that Governments should never lose sight of it...... as to the hypothesis of automatism I should feel inclined to regard it as a philosophical heresy, very dangerous for society, if it did not so strongly violate good sense and feeling as to become harmless, for it can never be generally adopted.

"As to the destiny of the animal, if my hypothesis be right, Providence holds in reserve for them the greatest compensations in future states†... And for me, their resurrection is the consequence of that soul or form we are necessarily obliged to allow them, for a soul being a simple substance, can *neither be divided, nor decomposed, nor yet annihilated*. One cannot escape such an inference without falling back into Descartes' automatism; and then from animal automatism one would soon and forcibly arrive at that of man."...

Our modern school of biologists has arrived at the theory of "automaton-man," but its disciples may be left to their own devices and conclusions. That with which I am at present concerned, is the final and absolute proof that neither the Bible, nor its most philosophical interpreters—however much they may have lacked a clearer insight into other questions—have *ever denied, on Biblical authority, an immortal soul to any animal,* more than they have found in it conclusive evidence as to the existence of such a soul in man—in the old Testament. One has but to read certain verses in Job and the Ecclesiastes (iii. 17 *et seq.* 22.) to arrive at this conclusion. The truth of the matter is, that the future state of neither of the two is therein referred to by one single word. But if, on the other hand, only negative evidence is found in the Old Testament concerning the immortal soul in animals, in the New it is as plainly asserted as that of man

---

* See Vol. II. *Palingenesis.* Also, De Mirville's *Resurrections.*

† We too believe in "future states" for the animal, from the highest down to the *infusoria*—but in a series of rebirths, each in a higher form, up to man and then beyond—in short, we believe in *evolution* in the fullest sense of the word.

himself, and it is for the benefit of those who deride Hindu *philozoism*, who assert their right to kill animals at their will and pleasure, and deny them an immortal soul, that a final and definite proof is now being given.

St. Paul was mentioned at the end of Part I. as the defender of the immortality of all the brute creation. Fortunately this statement is not one of those that can be pooh-poohed by the Christians as " the blasphemous and heretical interpretations of the holy writ, by a group of atheists and free-thinkers." Would that everyone of the profoundly wise words of the Apostle Paul—an Initiate, whatever else he might have been—was as clearly understood as those passages that relate to the animals. For then, as will be shown, the indestructibility of matter taught by materialistic science ; the law of eternal evolution, so bitterly denied by the Church ; the omnipresence of the ONE LIFE, or the Unity of the ONE ELEMENT, and its presence throughout the whole of nature as preached by esoteric philosophy, and the secret sense of St. Paul's remarks to the *Romans* (viii. 18-23), would be demonstrated beyond doubt or cavil to be obviously one and the same thing. Indeed, what else can that great historical personage, so evidently imbued with neo-Platonic Alexandrian philosophy, mean by the following, which I transcribe with comments in the light of occultism, to give a clearer comprehension of my meaning ?

The Apostle premises by saying (Roman viii. 16, 17) that " The spirit *itself* " (*Paramatma*) "beareth witness with our spirit " (*atman*) " that we are the children of God," and " *if* children, then heirs "—heirs, of course, to the eternity and indestructibility of the eternal or divine essence in us. Then he tells us that :—

" The sufferings of the present time are not worthy to be compared *with the glory that shall be revealed*." (v. 18.)

The " glory," we maintain, is no " New Jerusalem," the symbolical representation of the future in St. John's kabalistical Revelations—but the *Devachanic* periods and the series of births in the succeeding races when, after every new incarnation we shall find ourselves higher and more perfect, physically as well as spiritually ; and when finally we shall all become truly the " sons " and " children of God " at the " last Resurrection "—whether people call it Christian, Nirvanic or Parabrahmic ; as all these are one and the same. For truly—

" The earnest expectation of the creature waiteth for the manifestation of the sons of God." (v. 19.)

By creature, animal is here meant, as will be shown further on upon the authority of St. John Chrysostom. But who are the " sons of God," for the manifestation of whom the whole creation longs ? Are they the " sons of God " with whom " Satan came also " (See Job) or the " seven angels " of Revelations ? Have they reference

to Christians only or to the "sons of God" all over the world?*
Such "manifestation" is promised at the end of every *Manvantara*† or
world-period by the scriptures of every great Religion, and save in the
Esoteric interpretation of all these, in none so clearly as in the *Vedas*. For
there it is said that at the end of each *Manvantara* comes the *pralaya*, or the
destruction of the world—only one of which is known to, and expected by,
the Christians—when there will be left the *Sishtas*, or remnants, seven
Rishis and one warrior, and all the seeds, for the next human "tide-wave
of the following Round."‡ But the main question with which we are concerned is not at present, whether the Christian or the Hindu theory is the
more correct ; but to show that the Brahmins—in teaching that the seeds
of all the creatures are left over, out of the total periodical and temporary
destruction of all visible things, together with the " sons of God " or the
Rishis, who shall manifest themselves to future humanity—say neither
more nor less than what St. Paul himself preaches. Both include all
animal life in the hope of a new birth and renovation in a more perfect
state when every creature that now "waiteth" shall rejoice in the "manifestation of the sons of God." Because, as St. Paul explains :—

" The creature *itself* (*ipsa*) *also shall be delivered* from the bondage of
corruption," which is to say that the seed or the indestructible animal
soul, which does not reach Devachan while in its elementary or animal
state, will get into a higher form and go on, together with man, progressing
into still higher states and forms, to end, animal as well as man, "in the
glorious liberty of the children of God" (v. 21).

" And this "glorious liberty " can be reached only through the evolution or the Karmic progress of all creatures. The dumb brute having

---

* See Isis, Vol. I.

† What was really meant by the "sons of God " in antiquity is now demonstrated
fully in the SECRET DOCTRINE in its Part I (on the Archaic Period).

‡ This is the orthodox Hindu as much as the esoteric version. In his Bangalore
Picture " What is Hindu Religion ? "—Dewan Bahadoor Raghunath Rao, of Madras,
says : " At the end of each Manvantara, annihilation of the world takes place ; but one
warrior, seven Rishis, and the seeds are saved from destruction. To them God (or
Brahm) communicates the Statute law or the Vedas..as soon as a Manvantara commences these laws are promulgated..and become binding..to the end of that *Manvantara*.
These eight persons are called *Sishtas*, or remnants, because they alone remain after the
destruction of all the others. Their acts and precepts are, therefore, known as *Sishtacar*.
They are also designated ' *Sadachar* ' because such acts and precepts are only what always
existed."

This is the orthodox version. The secret one speaks of seven Initiates having attained
Dhyanchohanship toward the end of the seventh Race on this earth, who are left on earth
during its "obscuration " with the seed of every mineral, plant, and animal that had not
time to evolute into man for the next Round or world-period. See *Esoteric Buddhism*, by
A. P. Sinnett, *Fifth* Edition, *Annotations*, pp. 146, 147.

evoluted from the half sentient plant, is itself transformed by degrees into man, spirit, God—*et seq. and ad infinitum !* For says St. Paul—

"*We* know (" we," the *Initiates*) that the whole creation, (*omnis creatura* or *creature*, in the Vulgate) groaneth and travaileth (in child-birth) in pain until now." * (v. 22).

This is plainly saying that man and animal are on a par on earth, as to suffering, in their evolutionary efforts toward the goal and in accordance with Karmic law. By "until now," is meant up to the fifth race. To make it still plainer, the great Christian Initiate explains by saying :—·

" Not only they (the animals) but ourselves also, which have the first-fruits of the Spirit, we groan within ourselves, waiting for the adoption, to wit, the redemption of our body " (v. 23.) Yes, it is we, men, who have the " first-fruits of the Spirit," or the direct Parabrahmic light, our Atma or seventh principle, owing to the perfection of our fifth principle (Manas), which is far less developed in the animal. As a compensation, however, their Karma is far less heavy than ours. But that is no reason why they too should not reach one day that perfection that gives the fully evoluted man the Dhyanchohanic form.

Nothing could be clearer—even to a profane, non-initiated critic — than those words of the great Apostle, whether we interpret them by the light of esoteric philosophy, or that of mediæval scholasticism. The hope of redemption, or, of the survival of the spiritual entity, delivered " from the bondage of corruption," or the series of temporary material forms, is for *all living* creatures, not for man alone.

But the " paragon" of animals, proverbially unfair even to his fellow-beings, could not be expected to give easy consent to sharing his expectations with his cattle and domestic poultry. The famous Bible commentator, Cornelius a Lapide, was the first to point out and charge his predecessors with the conscious and deliberate intention of doing all they could to avoid the application of the word *creatura* to the inferior creatures of this world. We learn from him that St. Gregory of Nazianzus, Origen, and St. Cyril (the one, most likely, who refused to see a human creature in Hypatia, and dealt with her as though she were a wild animal) insisted that the word *creatura*, in the verses above quoted, was applied by the Apostle simply to the angels! But, as remarks Cornelius, who appeals to St. Thomas for corroboration, " this opinion is too distorted and violent (*distorta et violenta*); it is, moreover, invalidated by the fact that the angels, as such, are already delivered from the bonds of corruption." Nor is St. Augustine's suggestion any happier; for he offers the strange hypothesis that the " creatures" spoken of by St. Paul were " the infidels and the heretics" of all the ages! Cornelius contra-

---

* ..*ingemiscit et parturit usque adhuc* in the original Latin translation.

dicts the venerable father as coolly as he opposed his earlier brother-saints. " For," says he, " in the text quoted the *creatures* spoken of by the Apostle are evidently creatures distinct from men—*not only they, but ourselves also ;* and, then, that which is meant is not deliverance from sin, but from *death to come*."* But even the brave Cornelius finally gets scared by the general opposition, and decides that under the term *creatures* St. Paul may have meant—as St. Ambrosius, St. Hilarious (Hilaire), and others insisted— *elements (! !)—i.e.,* the sun, the moon, the stars, the earth, etc., etc.

Unfortunately for the holy speculators and scholastics, and very fortunately for the animals—if these are ever to profit by polemics—they are over-ruled by a still greater authority than themselves. It is St. John Chrysostomus, already mentioned, whom the Roman Catholic Church, on the testimony given by Bishop Proclus, at one time his secretary, holds in the highest veneration. In fact St. John Chrysostom, was, if such a profane (in our days) term can be applied to a saint, the " medium " of the Apostle to the Gentiles. In the matter of his Commentary on St. Paul's Epistles, St. John is held as directly inspired by that Apostle himself, in other words as having written his comments at St. Paul's dictation. This is what we read in those comments on the 3rd Chapter of the Epistle to the Romans.

" We must always groan about the delay made for our emigration (death); for if, as saith the Apostle, the creature deprived of reason (*mente*, not *anima*, " Soul ")—and speech (*nam si hæc creatura mente et verbo carens*) groans and expects, the more the shame that we ourselves should fail to do so."†

Unfortunately we do, and fail most ingloriously in this desire for " emigration " to countries unknown. Were people to study the scriptures of all nations and interpret their meaning by the light of esoteric philosophy, no one would fail to become, if not anxious to die, at least indifferent to death. We should then make profitable use of the time we pass on this earth by quietly preparing in each birth for the next by accumulating good Karma. But man is a sophist by nature. And, even after reading this opinion of St. John Chrysostom—one that settles the question of the immortal soul in animals for ever, or ought to do so at any rate, in the mind of every Christian—we fear the poor dumb brutes may not benefit much by the lesson, after all. Indeed, the subtle casuist, condemned out of his own mouth, might tell us that, whatever the nature of the soul in the animal, he is still doing it a favour, and himself a meritorious action, by killing the poor brute, as thus he puts an end to its " groans about the delay made for its emigration" into eternal glory.

---

* *Cornelius*, edit. Pelagaud, 1, IX., p. 114.
† *Homélie XIV. sur l'Epitre aux Romains.*

The writer is not simple enough to imagine that a whole British Museum filled with works against meat diet would have the effect of stopping civilized nations from having slaughter-houses, or of making them renounce their beefsteak and Christmas goose. But if these humble lines could make a few readers realize the real value of St. Paul's noble words, and thereby seriously turn their thoughts to all the horrors of vivisection, then the writer would be content. For, verily, when the world feels convinced--and it cannot avoid coming one day to such a conviction— that animals are creatures as eternal as we ourselves, vivisection and other permanent tortures, daily inflicted on the poor brutes, will, after calling orth an outburst of maledictions and threats from society generally, force all Governments to put an end to those barbarous and shameful practices.

H. P. Blavatsky.

THE ASTRAL LIGHT.

THE Astral Light, as the source of all world phenomena, is a theme of no little importance to the student of occultism.

The root of the word "Astral' is to be found in the Assyrian *Istar*, signifying star, and was applied to this element by the Kabalists and later mystics, because they considered the heavenly bodies as the concrete crystallizations of the Astral Light. Some Theosophic writers have confounded the nature of this element with that of Akasâ, while in fact the latter comprehends infinitely more both in quality and quantity. Literally the Sanscrit term Akasâ means the sky, but occultly the *impalpable* Ether or the Soul within the Ether. Our most logical authority, The Secret Doctrine, defines it as the "immortal spirit," the progenitor of Cosmic life and "universal intelligence whose *characteristic property* is Buddhi." Akasâ is the sphere of the pure undifferentiated *Monad*, the essence of wisdom, while the Astral Light at its opposite pole is the abstract atom of matter, the plane of generation, and the great womb out of which issues all planetary life. Ether, which is the highest vibration of the Astral Light, is but as a vehicle for Akasâ, a gross body in comparison.

The functions of the Astral Light are as manifold as the expressed universe. Its nature is dual—the highest Ether forming its positive, and the concrete, or differentiated elements, its negative pole. Its cause reaches back to the root of all causes, and its effects involve all our physical and psychical experiences. We deal with its familiar phenomena in every breath and every motion, while the rare and abnormal phases are as strictly subject to its laws. It is not substantially identical with any one of the material elements of Cosmic matter, but is one degree superior to *Prâkriti* (Nature as apprehended by the senses), and it impenetrates and vitalizes each atom. It is itself the one underlying element in which all other known elements have their source and supply. In its physical aspects it includes the Ether of modern scientists, but in the metaphysical sense they scarcely touch its borderland. For while it is the reservoir of Heat, Light, Magnetism, and Electricity—the field of all degrees of vibration—it is also the sphere of all intellectual life, and the ruling agent in the alchemical process which frees the celebral atom and converts it into thought. Its vibratory rate determines individual mental tendencies, and also establishes our intimate relations in body with the stars. Paracelsus maintains that, " as fire passes through an iron stove, so do the stars pass through man with all their properties, and go into him as the rain into the earth, which gives fruit out of that same rain." While the modern spectroscope reveals the identity in substance of infinitesimal man, and the greatest luminiferous body that glides in vast revolutions through space, no instrument has, as yet, been discovered so sensitive as to register the subtile and evanescent fluid which, by its uniform nature, makes astronomical research and thought-transference possible. Keely's Motor has, however, already foreshadowed such a discovery.

The Astral Light is the great record-book upon whose pages every thought and act of differentiated consciousness is engraven, there to be read by the individual who has learnt the secret of exalting his vibrations until they become synchronous with the waves of this finer element. The definition of Memory which has ever been the enigma of science, a function with an inapprehensible cause, is relegated to the domain of the occultist, who may briefly define it as the correlative vibration of the cerebral centre with the Astral Light. Within this correlation reside all the possibilities of consciousness from the horizon of Maya (illusion) to the zenith of pure Ether or transcendental life. Madame Blavatsky sweepingly states : " The psychic forces, the 'ideomotor' and 'electro-biological powers,' 'latent thought' and even 'unconscious cerebration' theories can be condensed into two words, the Kabalistic 'Astral Light.'" Quesne treated of it as a universally diffused fluid permeating all things, and differing in action only according to the mobility of the organism by which it is confined.

The differentiated *will to live* accompanying each primary monad is the sculptor of the astral images which constitute individual experience. An intense power of concentration makes these images subjective, in which case they are realities only to the operator, but under still more acute and intelligent development, these images may assume a concrete objective form with power of duration proportioned to the original impulse or determined purpose of the projector. " Determined will," says a fire-philosopher, " is a beginning of all magical operations," and the great magician, Abbe Constant, states : " To acquire magical power, two things are necessary: to disengage the will from all servitude and to exercise it in control." He alone can become a master whose physical and psychical organization is attuned to the Astral Key-note—whose self-consciousness has out-grown the limits of personal slavery, and whose will is so cultivated as to act without fear and without desire—intelligent, determined, self-possessed and confident. While the majority of mankind is occupied in mere negative registration of sense-impressions the occultist classifies these, and admits only those most useful to his purpose. Colonel Olcott refers to the manipulation of the Astral Light in his statement, that "the efficacy of all words used as charms and spells lies in what the Aryans call the *vach*, a certain latent power resident in Akasâ. Physically we may describe it as the power to set up certain measured vibrations, not in the grosser atmospheric particles whose undulations beget light, sound, heat and electricity, but in the latent spiritual principle or force—about the nature of which modern science knows almost nothing." As an illustration of this we have the word *Aum*, which, as all students know, has an equilibriating effect which resists the inroad of passion.

The symbol used to express the astral realm by the mystics of all ages is the serpent, or the "fiery dragon." It is stated that long before our globe or even our universe became egg-shaped, "a long trail of Cosmic dust (or fire mist) moved and writhed like a serpent in space." This was the beginning of our Eternity, exoterically expressed by a serpent with its tail in its mouth, or in the act of incubating the *Mundane Egg* with its fiery breath. The Chaldean Oracles refer to the Astral Light as "winding in form," which qualification refers to the vibratory motion that characterizes it. The intense rate of its pulsation may be faintly realized in the rapidity with which successive images are recorded in the dreaming or hypnotized state. An illustration is recounted of a student who was making scientific experiments in this psychological field with a friend. While a drop of water was descending down upon his forehead, he closed his eyes and dreamed that he started out from a harbour upon the wide main, soon passing several beautiful islands full of villages, cities, verdant fields and mountains. The sun was beaming generously, but little by little the sky grew darker and heavier, and drifts of black clouds swept upon the scene. A great gale arose. Consternation and horror pervaded the crew. The waves began to rise higher and higher, until finally the heavens and the sea were blended into one dense chaos.

The crisis was at hand. The dreamer suddenly felt as though the whole sea had burst asunder and drawn him in—he awoke just as the drop of water touched his skin, fallen from the hand of his friend and held but a few inches above his head. He had registered the full episode of dramatic changes during the instant in which the sensor nerve flashed its irritation to the brain. Far more remarkable than this are illustrations on record which cover an extent of years and are recorded in an instant of time, experimentally proven to be less than the period required for transmitting a nervous current. The wondrous rapidity with which feeling and think-ing may be condensed has also been frequently analyzed in the experience of persons nearly drowned, and as Helmholtz has demonstrated that the period in which a nerve-current may be conducted is a *definite* one, we have no alternative but to assume that a far subtler element or vehicle is employed in registering psychic experiences. By the astral current throughout the ayras, around the nerve-centres and nerve-tubes, mind contracts mind, thoughts are flashed in upon us and emotions conveyed. It radiates from the individual man as an impalpable but intelligent aura—the medium of his psychic and intuitional life, by means of which he evinces sympathy and understanding ; while in its higher aspect it is the sensitive plane that records Cosmic ideation, and conveys impressions of truth and of universal law to the human mind.

Experiment with trained sensitives has proven that when an intel-lectual concept is formed, the astral aura photographs it instantaneously, while, when an emotion is evinced, the aura changes in intensity of colour, and, on volition becoming manifest, there is a positive increase of vibration. We, therefore, carry with us all we have ever thought and felt—and *self* is the ever-refining essence of this thought and feeling. From this point of view responsibility assumes enormous proportions, and we perceive why the great Teachers of the world have ever agreed that Man is his own heaven and his own hell.

The great mesmerizer, Du Potet, declares that the faculty of directing this fluid is inherent in certain organizations, that it passes through all bodies, and that everything can be used as a conductor—"*no chemical or physical forces are able to destroy it.*" Treating thus with the merest initial of this latent power, who can say where its further unfoldment will lead the collective consciousness of Humanity ?

In the present age, our science informs us, we perceive in the main only the lowest vibrations and inferior qualities of the Astral Light, because we are in the lower arc of our present cycle, and the energy of the life-wave is at its ebb. Mme. Blavatsky says of Plato's method of expression that he " divides the intellectual progress of the universe during every cycle into fertile and barren periods. . . . When those circulations, which Eliphas Levi calls 'currents of the Astral Light' in the universal Ether, . . take place in harmony with the divine spirit, our earth and everything pertaining to it enjoys a fertile period. The occult powers of plants, animals, and minerals magically sympathize with its superior natures, and the divine soul of man is in perfect intelligence with these inferior ones.

But during the barren periods the latter lose all their magic sympathy, and the spiritual sight of the majority of mankind is so blinded as to lose every notion of the superior power of its own divine spirit. We are in a barren period." Ignoring our latent inherent forces, we drift in negative submission to the lower laws of Nature, suffer deprivation, want of thought, emotion, and volition, while the precious fluid, in mute anticipation, haunts our dreamless sleep, and awaits the dawning of a higher Consciousness. Louise A. Off.

ERRATA.

T.P.S., Vol. III., No. 6, page 3, line 4, for " Wit " read " Evil.'

THE

MASTERS OF WISDOM.

By E. ADAMS, F.T.S.

London:
Published by the T.P.S., 7, Duke Street, Adelphi.
—
1890.

THE MASTERS OF WISDOM.

MAN hath no fate except past deeds,
No hell but what he makes, no Heaven too high
For those to reach whose passions sleep subdued.

AN attempt will be made in this essay to remove from the minds of
air and unprejudiced inquirers into the truths of Theosophy some at
least of the misconceptions and false ideas that now generally cluster
around the names of its Great Teachers in the thoughts of the public.
This task once accomplished to the best of our ability, we have no further
concern with it, the results, whether great or small, will be in the hands
of Karma.

On the sufficiency or otherwise of the evidence we are about to
offer in favour of the existence of the Mahatmas, readers must themselves pronounce, and all our efforts will be directed to setting it forth
in such order, that a fair decision may be reached; we can do no more.
The great Occult Brotherhood, the custodians of the Sacred Wisdom of
the ages, first came publicly into notice this century through the establishment of the Theosophical Society in 1875, and through whom their
philosophy has been given to the world. As soon as their agents
announced the present existence of a body of men living in the East,
possessing certain remarkable attributes which we hope to describe in the
course of this essay, and endowed with great wisdom, the statement was
received with derision and general incredulity, and, except on the part
of a few individuals, no desire was manifested to inquire into the truth
of the matter at all. Considering the nature of the subject and the
character of the age, this conduct was not surprising if we look
below the surface. To bigoted sectarians the idea of the existence
of such beings seemed too absurd to think about, much less discuss,
because, as we shall presently see, the views of sectarian Christianity
and materialistic science as to the meaning of Life and
man's future destiny are vastly different from those of Occult
Philosophy, and that it is only by a proper comprehension
of the latter that accurate and clear views, from an abstrac
standpoint, respecting the Mahatmas (Great Souls) can be attained.

Protestant Theology, as everyone knows, awards all individuals, at death, according to their deserts of faith, elevation to a higher or fall to a lower spiritual condition for ever; a sudden unreasonable leap from finite to infinite life. Roman Catholicism, although approaching closer to Occultism in its doctrines respecting human post-mortem states, yet affords, on the whole, no room in its conceptions for such persons as the "Adepts," especially as they are outside the orthodox pale. The scientists of the evolutionary philosophical school are in no better plight than theologians, so far as viewing the matter impartially at the outset is concerned. For their conceptions of human evolution are confined to the physical, mental, and moral progress of successive generations of mankind, whilst individuals are ruthlessly sacrificed in its attainment. This imperfect and mutilated view of human destiny is presented through lack of knowledge of the law of Karma and Re-Incarnation, and an ignoring of the spiritual element in man. In contrast to the foregoing, Occult Philosophy teaches that each individual Ego passes through great cycles of experiences, obtained through incarnation in some hundreds of personalities, serving as masks for it, and gathering, as it evolves upward in its spiral course, fresh knowledge, powers, and attributes. At the head of this great chain of differentiated human progress stand the "Adepts," the flower of humanity; each the outcome of a mighty struggle "against himself, against all the evils and opposing wills, against all the elements, against all the previous causes whose effects he has destroyed by labours of which those of Hercules are only a pale symbol." Such are the great Masters of Wisdom, the Leaders of the world. The reason therefore of the general disinclination to believe in the existence of the Mahatmas, no matter how good the evidence, lies in the prevailing character of present Religious and Scientific thought; its great difference on this matter, from the teachings of Theosophy, leading to inability to understand the real and proper place of the Adept's nature. As a minor cause, also, the recognition of the existence of such beings as the Arhats necessarily involves the displacement of many popular religious and scientific authorities now looked up to as almost infallible, a mental change for many hard to undergo. Having glanced at the abstract view of the matter, we may now come to the evidence and proofs by which everything must ultimately be judged, apart from all prepossessions either for or against.

THE ADEPTS IN HISTORY.

There are several clues by which the presence and influence of the Adepts and their disciples can be traced in History. The mysteries, for instance, now so much misunderstood, and little known, of all ancient races, were invariably presided over by Initiates, and formed the medium through which pupils were instructed in Occult Wisdom, and such teachings given out to the masses, as their development and circumstances would safely permit. We know that the doctrine of Re-Incarnation was secretly taught by the Adepts in all ages, and appeared masked in exoteric form, as the Transmigration of Souls. The Arhats have from the earliest times called themselves Serpents or Dragons. Thus a Commentary on the Book of Dzyan speaks of the " Serpents of Wisdom whose holes are now under the triangular stones, *i.e.*, the Pyramids. Why is this ? " In every ancient language the word *dragon* signified what it now does in Chinese (*lang*), *i.e.*, " the being who excels in intelligence," and in Greek " he who sees and watches."* The earth in the Aytareya-Brahmana is called the " Queen of the Serpents," referring to the fact that the fire-mist as a long trail of cosmic matter animated by spirit or force once moved writhing.like a serpent in space, before becoming egg-shape. The ancient Adept Hermes regarded the serpent as the most spirit-like of all reptiles. The serpent biting his tail was the symbol of Wisdom and immortality in the Mysteries.

According to the Archaic records, the lost continent of Atlantis was inhabited by two distinct classes of " Adepts," those of the Right and those of the Left hand : White and Black Hierophants. We are told of the Adept astronomers Narada and Asuramâya who lived at Romakapura in Atlantis, also of those White Adepts who instructed the early Aryan race after the destruction of this continent ; the high table lands of Thibet have been inhabited for ages past by the " Arhats." Thibet, called Si-dzang by the Chinese, is mentioned in the oldest books preserved in the province of Fo-kien (the headquarters of the aborigines of China) as the great seat of occult learning in the archaic ages. According to these records it was inhabited by the Teachers of Light, the Sons of Wisdom. The Emperor Yu the Great (2207 B.C.), a pious mystic, is credited with having obtained his Occult Wisdom from Thibet. Chinese literature from Las-tze down to Hiouen-Thsang is filled with allusions and references to Scham-Bhala, the Happy Land, and the wisdom of the Himalayan Adepts. The " Catena of Buddhist Scriptures from the Chinese " mentions the " Great Teachers of the Snowy Mountains, the school of the Haimavatas," and a rule relating to " the great professors of the higher order who live in mountain depths remote from men." A Japanese Cyclopædia in the book of Fo-kone-ky places a Brotherhood of Adepts on the plateau of Pamir, between the highest peaks of the Himalayan ranges. According to tradition the

* Secret Doctrine. Vol. II., p. 210.

Vedas came from the Mansarawara Lake in Thibet, and the Brahmans from the north, the latter claiming descent from the great ancient Rishis (sages). The eminent writers, Strabo, Lucan, Plutarch, Cicero, and Pliny, refer to the Adepts, whom they called Indian Gymnosophists. These great Initiates led a secluded life according to Ammianus Marcellinus, and proofs of their great learning are preserved in numerous volumes in Hindu libraries to this day. Indian literature teems with references to the Rishis and Mahatmas; these terms are interchangeable. The Magi of Persia, who derived their name from the Sanscrit *Mahaji* (the great or wise), have left some deep marks in history. They were not Persians or Chaldeans, and, in the opinion of Orientalists, came to Persia from the *East*. Their schools were divided into esoteric and exoteric sections; the former were devoted to the teachings of practical occultism. There were three classes of Magi, Herbeds (disciples), Mobeds* (masters), Destur Mobeds (complete masters). Initiation consisted of awful and mysterious ceremonies, preceded by a long purification of the candidate. Darius Hystaspes, the monarch who reformed and purified the Persian mysteries, and who was an Adept himself, is said by ancient historians to have been taught by Brahmans. The Akkadian Adepts, who taught Occultism to the Babylonians, came from Upper India according to the archaic records. It should be remembered that at that time Aryan India did not extend southwards beyond the Punjaub. There is no doubt that the Jews acquired all their esoteric knowledge from the Egyptians and Chaldeans. According to Maimonides, the great Jewish theologian, Chaldean Magi were always employed by the Adepts in performing their occult phenomena. Manetho says that Moses was a hierophant of Hieropolis, and a priest of the sun-god Osiris, and that his name was Osarsiph. Jethro the priest, his guru (spiritual guide), gives him Zipporah,† the esoteric wisdom. (Siprah means the shining or resplendent, from Sapar to shine.)‡ Justin Martyr, giving as his authority Trogus Compeius, shows that Joseph learnt magic from the Egyptian Adepts.

The Tanaim were the first Initiates amongst the Jews, and the Books of Ezekiel, Daniel, Enoch and the Revelation of St. John are purely Occult works. The famous Hillel§ was an Initiate. Gibbon demonstrates that the Pharisees believed in the doctrine of the Transmigration of Souls; this shows the Occult influences at work among the Jews.

---

* Sippara, in Chaldea, was the City of the " Sun."
† From Meh-ab, meaning great and noble.
‡ Moses, being an ascetic, could not be married.
§ This Adept had a regular school for teaching Occultism, so had Samuel and Elisha at Ramah and Jericho.

The Sohar teaches practical occultism, through secret signs on the margin. Let us now consider the " Adepts " of Egypt.

According to Herodotus, Orpheus, an " Adept," brought the ancient mysteries from India. Philostratus makes the Brahmin Tarchus say that the Egyptians were originally an Indian race compelled to emigrate from the mother-land for sacrilege and regicide. Diogenes Laertius traces Theosophy to an epoch antedating the Ptolemies, and founded by a Hierophant, Cot Amun (name being Coptic meaning priest consecrated to Amun, god of Wisdom). In both India and Egypt there was a sacred succession of hierophants. " In Egypt each was a Piromis, the son of a Piromis. As in India, at Sringiri " each hierophant is a Sankarâcharya, the son of a Sankarâcharya*." The Egyptian Adepts taught that the soul was re-incarnated after an interval of 3,000 years. The Essenes and healing Therapeutes were followers of the ancient theurgic Mysteries. The Essenes furnished a refuge for the hierophants of Egypt, when the latter from fear of a profanation of the sacred mysteries came amongst them. The Essenes had their greater and minor mysteries at least two centuries before our era. "They rejected pleasures, despised riches, loved one another, and deemed the conquest of the passions to be virtuous," says Dunlap. Over five centuries before the Christian Era, the great Greek Pythagoras journeyed to Upper India for the purpose of studying under the " Wise Brotherhood." On returning, he taught at Croton a system of philosophy identical with that expounded by the " Adepts " to-day. We know the Greeks obtained the Eleusinian Mysteries from Egypt. " All these things," said Zonaras, "came to us from Chaldea to Egypt, and from thence were derived to the Greeks." The great Grecian sages are found constantly travelling to Egypt for instruction, including Plato the great Initiate, whose philosophy contains so many of the ideas of the Eastern sages. We will now cross the Atlantic Ocean in search of traces of the " Serpents of Wisdom." In the Popol-vuh, the sacred book of the Gautemalians, there is sufficient evidence to prove the close relationship of the religious customs of the ancient Mexican, Peruvian, and Egyptian nations. The ancient hieratic alphabets of the Maya and Egyptian languages are nearly identical. In de Bourbourg's work, Votan, the Mexican hero, says that he is the son of a " Serpent," and had visited a serpent's catacomb, like those of Egypt. We find that the Mexicans had their magicians from a remote period. The Popol-vuh mentions a race of men who knew all things at once, and whose sight was unlimited. In the Scandinavian Edda we find the great Earth Serpent Midgard, with its tail in its mouth. The archaic

---

* Lucifer, September, 1889. Art Traces of Ancient India in Egypt.

records teach that Odin was one of the "Sons of Wisdom." The Norse cosmogony is the same as the Indian. Who were the Druids? The Secret Doctrine says: "Like the Hindus, the Greeks, and Romans (we speak of the Initiates), the Chaldees, and the Egyptians, the Druids believed in the doctrine of a succession of worlds and transformations of the face of the earth, and in a seven-fold night and day. Wherever the Serpent with the Egg is found, there this tenet was surely present. Their *Dracontia* are a proof of it." * Pliny calls them the Magi of the Gauls and Britons. " I am a Serpent, I am a Druid," they exclaimed. The Egyptian Karnac is twin-brother to the Carnac of Bretagné, the latter meaning the serpent's mount. We will now turn again to the East.

Near the commencement of the Christian Era, we find Apollonius of Tyana travelling to the abode of the Sages of Upper India. It is related that he found a community of Adepts, wanting nothing, and possessing everything, and wielding marvellous powers. Justin Martyr is a witness to the occult powers of Apollonius, acquired by him as a pupil of the Adepts. "The Christian Gnostics sprang into existence towards the beginning of the second century, and just at the time when the Essenes most mysteriously faded away, which indicated that they were the identical Essenes." † The Secret Doctrine states that the various Gnostic sects were founded by Initiates. They believed in metempsychosis, and the sacred serpent appears on many Gnostic gems. The strong Buddhistic element in their teachings has been noticed by many scholars. As the terms nazar and nazaret meant Adept in ancient writings, the connection between the Initiates and the sect called Nazarenes is apparent. In fact, the secret doctrines of the Magi, of the pre-vedic Buddhists, of the hierophants of the Egyptian Hermes, and of the Adepts of every age and nationality, including the Chaldean Kabalists, and the Jewish Nazars were identical from the beginning.‡ Every nation had two languages; that of the masses and that of the Initiates, which was secret and universal. About the 3rd century of this era, Ammonius Saccas founded the school of the Neo-Platonists, or Eclectic Theosophists. " They united the mystic theosophy of old Egypt with the refined philosophy of the Greeks ; nearer to the ancient mysteries of Thebes and Memphis than they had been for centuries ; versed in the science of soothsaying and divination, as in the art of the Therapeutists; friendly with the acutest men of the Jewish nation, who were deeply imbued with the Zoroastrian ideas, the Neo-Platonists tended to amalgamate the old

* Secret Doctrine. Vol. II., p. 756.
† Isis Unveiled. Vol. II., p. 324.
‡ Isis Unveiled. Vol. II., p. 142.

wisdom of the Oriental Kabala with the more refined conceptions of the Occidental Theosophists." The spiritual illumination of the Neo-Platonists, the ecstatic trance of mystics, the Samadhi of Hindoos are identical in nature. After the downfall of the principal mysteries, which began in Plato's time, the Eastern esoteric societies instituted a kind of international universal Freemasonry amongst their esoteric societies. Finally, through the fanatical persecutions of the Emperor Justinian, the last remnant of the Neo-Platonists fled to the East, comprising the seven wise men, Hermias, Priscianus, Diogenes, Eulalius, Damaskius, Simplicius, and Isidorus. Henceforth the archaic wisdom was represented in Europe by a few secret societies and persons, the great Initiates had all departed for remote places of the Earth. The secrecy preserved by these small lodges, and by the great chief lodge, has always been proportionate to the activity of religious persecutions. From the descendants of the Magi, the Sufis, the mystics amongst the Mahometans derived their knowledge of astrology, medicine, and of esoteric doctrines. In 1118 the order of the Temple was founded, nominally for the protection of pilgrims, but really for the restoration of the primitive mysteries. The red cross on the white mantle, the vestment of the order, pointing to the four quarters of the compass, was the emblem of the universe, a well-known sign to the initiated. In the 16th century we find the famous physician and alchemist, Paracelsus, travelling to the *East*, and instructed in various occult sciences by an Oriental Adept. An examination of his writings and teachings shows their similarity to the philosophical system now given out by the Masters of Wisdom. The 17th century shows the presence of the mysterious Rosicrucians, over whom many modern scholars have spent much time and labour in vain. Why this secrecy ? Because, to be known as a kabalist in that age was to court death from furious religious bigots. We may here quote Swedenborg. " Search for the Lost Word amongst the Hierophants of Tartary and Thibet," said he. According to proofs existing to-day in the archives of St. Petersburg, more than one Russian mystic, at the beginning of this century, travelled in search of knowledge to the esoteric schools in Central Asia ; returning, years later, with a rich store. In this age, " Travellers have met Adepts on the shores of the sacred Ganges, brushed against them in the silent ruins of Thebes, and in the mysterious deserted chambers of Luxor. Within the halls upon whose blue and golden vaults the weird signs attract attention, but whose secret meaning is never penetrated by the idle gazers, they have been seen but seldom recognised. They have been encountered again on the arid and desolate plains of Great Sahara, as in the caves of Elephanta. They may be found everywhere, but make themselves known only to those who have devoted their lives to unselfish study and are not likely to turn back.* The travelling Adepts who from time to time visited Paris during this century were termed by the unsuspecting natives, Boyards, Indian Nabobs, Hungarian Margraves, and *nobles étrangers*. At the present time a mysterious sect, called the Druzes of Mount Lebanon, exists in the East, presided over by initiated wise men called Okhals.† This body is descended from the ancient esoteric societies of the East, and although their mystic doctrines are carefully concealed from outsiders, yet it is known that they closely resemble those of the ancient Gnostics.‡ In the East, now, there are many esoteric societies, sects within sects, all possessing more or less occult knowledge, in addition to the Grand Lodge of Thibet ; thus the archaic mysteries have been continued in the East to our day. It should be remembered, however, as stated in Esoteric Buddhism, that Thibet was not always the great centre of Adept habitation that it is now, although always *a* centre. In the 14th century the great Thibetan Adept reformer, Tsong-ka-pa, introduced a new code of rules for the occult schools, and the Mahatmas began to gravitate towards this region from various parts of the earth. For far more widely was occult knowledge found to be spread than was consistent with the safety of mankind. We have been compelled for want of space to leave the work of the great Indian Adepts unnoticed, even that of the " Great Master," Buddha, who taught " Nirvana and the Law." At the present time in Japan and Siam there are two orders of priests, of which one is public and deals with the people, the existence of the other is known but to a few natives, never to foreigners. The latter are Initiates. Before coming to the evidence of modern eye-witnesses to the existence of the Mahatmas, it will be well to call attention to some special points brought out in the course of our historical survey. We have seen that the ancient mysteries gradually declined, degenerated, and expired in all Western countries, as foretold by the great Adept, Hermes :—" Alas, my son, a day will come when the sacred hieroglyphics will become but idols. *The world will mistake the emblems of science for gods*, and accuse Grand Egypt of having worshipped monsters. But those who will calumniate us thus will themselves worship Death instead of Life, folly in place of wisdom ; fill their temples with dead men's bones as relics, and waste their youth in solitude and tears. Their virgins will be widows (nuns) before being wives, and consume themselves in grief ; because men will have despised and profaned the sacred mysteries of Isis."§ What was the

* Isis Unveiled. Vol. I., p. 17.
† From the Arabic akl, intelligence or wisdom.
‡ See Letter from Initiate, Isis Unveiled. Vol. II., p. 313.
§ Hermes' Tresmegistus xxvii.

cause of this decadence of the ancient schools of the Sacred Science? The following extract from the "Ceylon Gem" may help to explain the matter: "In Ceylon the Adepts counted over thousands in the reign of Dutugamunu. They have gradually ceased to exist, as the keys of those mysteries are lost by the degeneracy of the Buddhist monks of subsequent times, who sought more after worldly renown and glory than the higher spiritual developments." "Men have become wild and wretched by the awful lusts of the flesh, and have consequently lost the secrets of the Law. But those immortal and divine gems of truth were not destined to disappear altogether from the habitation of man, as it was decreed by the departing Arhats to be safely and sacredly kept by the Adepts of the trans-Hymalayan depths until man's condition be adapted to receive it. That time is now drawing nigh; and the custodians of the secret doctrine have thought it fit to send missionaries among mankind to divulge it to them." Throughout our historical survey we succeeded in tracing the connection, direct or indirect, of every ancient school of Occultism, with the great Tibetan Lodge, existing now as then, thus making the existence of the Initiates of to-day quite comprehensible. It is now necessary to review the testimony of modern eye-witnesses respecting the existence of the Mahatmas. From the mass of evidence available in this matter, we can only provide space for a few accounts. In "Five Years of Theosophy," a Hindoo gentleman, Damodar K. Mavalankar, relates the several occasions on which he has seen various Adepts both physically and in astral form. There is also an account, written by himself, of the perilous journey through Sikkhim undertaken by S. Ramaswamier, an Indian official, for the purpose of seeing the Mahatmas, which was successful. We have also the evidence given by Sundook, a pedlar of Thibet, who, on being questioned by several gentlemen, said that there were men living in the mountains beyound Tchigatze and near the city of Lhassa, possessing extraordinary powers distinct from and far higher than the regular lamas of the country. These men, he said, produce many and very wonderful phenomena, and some of their Chelas (pupils) cure the sick by giving them to eat the rice which they crush out of the paddy with their hands, etc. In the presence of a number of respectable witnesses a young Bengali, Brahmachari, gave the following account. On the 15th of the Bengali month of Asar in 1882, he met some Tibetans, called the Koothoompas, and their guru (Teacher), in a field near Taklakhar, a place about a day's journey from the Lake of Manasarawara. The "Master" and most of his pupils wore sleeveless coats over under-garments of red. The complexion of the "Master" was very fair, and his hair, which was not parted, but combed back, streamed down his shoulders. The Master saluted him, and asked him where he was coming from. .On finding that he had not had anything to eat, the guru commanded that he should be given some ground grain and tea. As the Brahmachari could not get any fire to cook food with, the Master asked for and kindled some fuel by simply blowing upon it. The Brahma-chari also said that he had often witnessed the same phenomenon produced by another " Master," at Gauri, a place about a day's journey from the cave of Tarchin, on the northern side of Mount Kailas. The keeper of a flock, who was suffering from rheumatic fever, came to the guru, who gave him a few grains of rice, crushed out of paddy which the Master had in his hand, and the sick man was cured then and there.

The undersigned severally certify that, in each other's presence, they recently saw at the headquarters of the Theosophical Society a brother of the First Section. The circumstances were of a nature to exclude all idea of trickery or collusion, and were as follows. We were sitting together in the moonlight about nine o'clock, upon the balcony which projects from the front of the bungalow. Mr. Scott was sitting facing the house, so as to look through the intervening verandah and the library, and into the room at the further side. This latter apartment was brilliantly lighted. The library was in partial darkness, thus rendering objects in the further room more distinct. Mr. Scott suddenly saw the figure of a man step into the space opposite the door of the library; he was clad in the white dress of a Rajput, and wore a white turban. Mr. Scott at once recognised him from his resemblance to a portrait in Colonel Olcott's possession. Our attention was then drawn to him, and we all saw him most distinctly. He walked towards a table, and, afterwards turning his face towards us, walked back out of our sight. We hurried forward to get a closer view, but when we reached the room he was gone. We cannot say by what means he departed, but that he did not pass out by the door which leads into the compound we can positively affirm; for that door was full in our view, and he did not go out by it. At the side of the room towards which he walked there was no exit, the only door, and the two windows in that direction, having been boarded and closed up. Upon the table at the spot where he had been standing lay a letter addressed to one of our number. The handwriting was identical with that of sundry notes and letters previously received from him in divers ways—such as dropping down from the ceiling, etc. The signature was the same as that of the other letters received, and as that upon the portrait above described. Ross Scott, B.C.S., Minnie J. B. Scott, H. S. Olcott, H. P. Blavatsky, M. Moorad, Ali Beg, D. K. Mavalankar, B. S. G. Mullapoorkar. We now come to the remarkable experience of Mr. Eglinton on board the s.s. *Vega*, the vessel being a long distance from land, which is worthy of notice on account of this gentleman being a thorough disbeliever in the existence of the Adepts before this incident. He relates that one of the Mahatmas suddenly appeared in his cabin, and after some conversation disappeared, taking with him a letter which Mr. E. had written. The letter was as follows :—

"s.s. *Vega*, Friday, 24th March, 1882.

"MY DEAR MRS. GORDON,—At last your hour of triumph has come. After the many battles we have had at the breakfast-table regarding K. H.'s existence, my stubborn scepticism as to the wonderful powers possessed by the 'Brothers,' I have been forced to a *complete belief* in their being living distinct persons, and just in proportion to my scepticism will be my *firm, unalterable* opinion respecting them. K. H. *appeared* to me in person, and what he told me dumbfounded me."

The above letter was received the *same day*, according to the following statement by Mrs. Gordon :—"At nine o'clock on Friday, 24th, Col. Olcott, Col. Gordon, and myself, sat in the room which had been occupied by Mr. Eglinton. We had a good light, and sat with our chairs placed to form a triangle. In a few minutes Col. Olcott saw outside the open window, the two 'Brothers,' whose names are best known to us, and told us so. He saw one of them point his hand towards the air over my head, and I felt something at the same moment fall straight down from above on to my shoulder, and saw it fall at my feet in the direction *towards* the two gentlemen. Col. Olcott and Col. Gordon both saw and heard the letter fall. Col. Olcott had turned his head from the window for a moment, to see what the Brother was pointing at, and so noticed the letter falling from a point about two feet from the ceiling. When he looked again the two 'Brothers' had vanished. There is no verandah outside, and the window is several feet from the ground." In a back number of the *New York World* there is a long account of a reporter's experiences in Forty-seventh Street. The eight or ten persons present saw an "Adept" pass by the window and return. The room was on the second story of the house, and there was no balcony to walk on. The President of the Theosophical Society has publicly declared that he knows fifteen of the Adepts personally. To finish this testimony we may add the following letter :—"Madras, August 7, 1889. Dear sir,—In reply to your inquiries I may say that I certify on my word as a *Sanyassi* that I have twice visited Thibet since the year 1879; that I have personally become acquainted with several Mahatmas, among whom were the two known to the outside world as Mahatma 'M.,' Mahatma 'K.H.'; that I spent some time in their company; that they told me that they and other Mahatmas were interested in the work of the Theosophical Society; that Mahatma 'M.' told me he had been the (occult) guardian of Madame

Blavatsky from her infancy. (Signed) SRIMAN SWAMY, Hon. Sec. Cow Memorial Fund of Allahabad." A lady relates that she saw on one occasion, at a meeting in Paris, one of the Adepts standing for a short time behind the chair of one of the party. It will be noted in an examination of the foregoing accounts that witnesses have seen the Mahatmas under very different conditions, viz., both in physical and astral forms. Their absolute identity, however, in all cases is proved by the immediate recognition by the eye-witnesses of the exact likeness between these forms and the portraits of Adepts in possession of the Theosophical Society. Mention of the ability of the Arhats to transport themselves long distances in astral form brings us to the vexed question of the existence of occult powers, or practical magic. Such, however, is the character of this age, the materialistic education and tendencies of Western minds, that it is difficult to obtain an impartial hearing on this subject. Nevertheless we must try, and commence by showing that occidental science is not in possession of a single *fact* that enables it to deny the possibility of the existence of Practical Occultism. What, for instance, does Physical Science know of Matter and Force? Professor Huxley says, " It is in strictness true that we *know nothing* about the composition of any body, whatever, as it is." Another authority remarks, " What do we know of the atom *apart from its force?*" Does not Professor Agassiz say, " Outside of mathematics the word impossible should never be pronounced?" The Atomic Theory, the very base of gross materialism, has received its death-blow at the hands of Mr. Herbert Spencer. Such confessions of ignorance on the part of eminent scientific authorities, of Nature in its lowest aspect open the door to the possibility of the existence of Practical Magic or Wisdom, understanding the latter to mean, dealing with natural forces of superior power. That such forces exist is the belief of many eminent scientific authorities, of various nationalities, such as the Baron von Reichenbach, Professor Gregory of Edinburgh, Professor Hare of the United States, Thury, Flammarion, Zollner, Butlerof, Aksakoff, Crookes, and A. R. Wallace. And it should be remembered that the opinions of these authorities are founded on many and careful experiments, extending over a long period of time. No doubt to persons unacquainted with the principles of practical Occultism the power of an Adept to transport himself in astral form to remote places, whilst his physical body remains behind, appears a miraculous one, and thorough-going Materialists naturally ridicule the idea. But as the latter on their own confession know nothing of the phenomenon of human consciousness, how it arises, and what it is in itself, suspense of judgment would be more creditable in the matter, especially considering the excellent evidence in existence proving its truth.

No Occultist has ever credited the Adepts with miraculous powers. They have been certainly said to be practical magicians, but never miracle-workers. Miracles are an impossibility. The exercise, however, of rare powers due to a knowledge of occult natural laws is quite another thing. As Professor A. Wilder observes, " The very capacity to imagine the possibility of thaumaturgical powers is itself evidence that they exist. The critic as well as the sceptic is generally inferior to the person or subject that he is reviewing, and therefore is hardly a competent witness. *If there are* counterfeits, somewhere there must have been a genuine original. Let us see, then, what are the principles of this Occult Science.

(1.) There is no miracle. Everything that happens is the result of law—eternal, immutable, ever active.

(2.) Nature is triune; there is visible objective nature; and invisible, in-dwelling, energizing nature, the exact model of the other, and its vital principle; and above these two, *spirit*, source of all forces, alone eternal and indestructible.

(3.) Man also is triune; he is composed of body, soul, and spirit.

(4.) Magic, as a science, is the knowledge of these principles and of the way by which the omniscience and omnipotence of the spirit and its control over nature's forces may be acquired by the individual while still in the body. Magic, as an art, is the application of this knowledge to practice.

(5.) Arcane knowledge misapplied is sorcery; beneficently used, true magic, or wisdom.

(6.) Mediumship is the opposite of adeptship; the medium is the passive instrument of foreign influences, the adept actively controls himself and all inferior potencies.

(7.) All things that ever were, that are, or that will be, having their record upon the astral light, or tablet of the unseen universe, the initiated Adept, by using the vision of his own spirit, can know all that has been known or can be known.

(8.) Races of men differ in spiritual gifts as in other qualities; among some peoples seership naturally prevails, among others mediumship. Some are addicted to Sorcery, and transmit its secret rules of practice from generation to generation, with a range of psychical phenomena, more or less wide, as the result.

(9.) The corner-stone of magic is an intimate practical knowledge of magnetism and electricity, their qualities, correlations, and potencies. There are occult properties in many other minerals equally strange with that in the loadstone, which all practitioners of magic *must* know, and of which ordinary science is wholly ignorant; plants have like mystical properties in a most wonderful degree, and the secrets of the herbs of enchantments are only lost to European science. Magic is spiritual wisdom; Nature the material ally, pupil, and servant of the magician.*

Occult Philosophy asserts that magical powers are not the exclusive property of a few persons and unattainable by the great majority, but are, on the contrary, the natural gifts which the human race will attain as a whole in the course of its future development. The Adepts are men of advanced capabilities, having attained their high position by merit only, and passed by immense efforts unscathed through the fierce fires of experience on this plane during many successive lives.

From the point of view now reached by some of the foremost scientists of the age, the dividing space betwixt ordinary and Occult science is not extensive, taking into consideration the lower powers of the latter, and the proficiency of the worldly men of science in ancient Atlantis† may be soon approached again by our own. At the present time no scientific authority‡ worth naming would deny that natural forces, finer for instance than electricity, may be discovered any day, and, if so, we see how naturally the ordinary and occult sciences join hands. More than one chemist is hunting after the universal substance, believed by many to be that into which all metals can be resolved, along the lines pursued by the ancient Alchemists; nor are these cases by themselves. If time and space permitted, a volume could be filled with reliable accounts of the magical achievements of Ancient Indian, Egyptian, Jewish, and Grecian Adepts and Initiates; of these we have only space for a few. We must here note, however, that the entire history of magical phenomena, from the dawn of history until now, shows their essential oneness throughout, whether they are those ascribed to the Rishis of old India, or of the Egyptian magicians of the time of Pharaoh, or the feats of Simon Magus, Apollonius of Tyana, and Christ§ down to the exploits of the Initiates of to-day. In the 13th century we find some testimony as to the magical powers of the Adepts, coming to Europe from Kublai-Khan, ruler of Tartary. He said, " You see the idolaters (sic) can do anything they please, insomuch that when I sit at table, the cups from the middle of the hall come to me full of wine or other liquor, without being touched by anybody, and I drink from them. They control storms, causing them to pass in whatever direction they please, and do many other marvels; whilst, as you know, their idols speak, and give them predictions on whatever

---

* " Isis Unveiled." Vol. II., p. 590.

† We refer here to those of the strictest school of Materialism who deny even now the reality of all Occult phenomena (p. 75).

‡ Esoteric Buddhism.

§ In Talmudic literature Christ is accused of performing his miracles, not as a Jewish prophet, but as an Initiate of the heathen temples.

subjects they choose."* The magical phenomena of the present day now deserves some attention. Take the feats of the so-called Hindoo jugglers, although as these, be it remembered, are performed for selfish motives (money, etc.), it is the practice of black magic, and note how they transcend all the performances of conjurors. Are not such exploits as the following magical ? (1) To transform a rupee, firmly clasped in the hand of a sceptic, into a living cobra, the bite of which would prove fatal, as an examination of its fangs would show. (2) To cause a seed chosen at random by the spectators and planted in the first semblance of a flower-pot, furnished by the same sceptics, to grow, mature, and bear fruit in less than a quarter of an hour. (3) To stretch himself on three swords stuck perpendicularly in the ground, sharp points upward, and after a short interval the swords removed, and the juggler lies suspended in the air on nothing, a yard from the ground. Such occurrences are not rare in the East, and have been witnessed by hundreds of persons whose veracity is above suspicion. Sir J. Fayrer† admits that the Indian serpent charmers can handle harmlessly cobras with fangs intact, although he is evidently at a loss to account for it. The scholar and traveller, Jacolliot, remarks, " Let it suffice to say that in regard to magnetism and spiritism, Europe has yet to stammer over the first letters of the alphabet, and that the Brahmins have reached, in these two departments of learning, results in the way of pheno-mena that are truly stupefying." The Eastern Occultists gave him this explanation, " You have studied physical nature, and you have obtained through its laws marvellous results—steam, electricity, etc.; for 20,000 years or more we have studied the intellectual forces, we have discovered their laws, and we obtain, by making them act alone or in concert with matter, phenomena still more astonishing than your own." To this day certain Persian sects, the Yakuts of Eastern Siberia, and the Yezidis of Asiatic Turkey, practise Sorcery with horrible and disgusting rites, as Lady Hester Stanhope found out to her cost. Truly the East appears to be the home of magic.

In the West, notably in America, the rise and progress of the Occult phenomena known as Spiritualism has caused a fierce battle, which still continues to rage between the believers and non-believers. On the one hand, some millions of supporters of the phenomena, which they know really occurs ; on the other a great mass of sceptics, very few of whom have investigated, or take the trouble to inquire closely into the matter. It is not here necessary to discuss the attitude of Theosophy

---

* Book of Ser Marco Polo. Vol. II., p. 340

† *Nineteenth Century*, December, 1889.

towards so-called Spiritualism, that is well known; we merely wish to call attention to these magical occurrences, as these bear on our subject. We can certainly find, however, in Mesmerism, now called hypnotism, a justification for the views on magic held by Occultists; it is here, on this point, that opponents and deniers of Practical Occultism must incur complete defeat. For who, in his senses, knowing anything of this subject, will now deny its reality? And what is Mesmerism but the ancient art of enchantment so long derided by sceptics, but which they must now admit without reservation? The victory is therefore won. Practical Magic is. This long digression on the Occult Arts has been necessitated through their intimate connection with the Adepts; no proper view, in fact, of them and their mission could be taken, until the gross misconceptions generally prevailing about Magic had been swept away, and its real character defined. This has now been done. Inquirers into the truths of Theosophy naturally ask many questions, and seek for information respecting the nature and character of its Great Teachers. We shall, therefore, endeavour to deal now with these matters, and solve the various problems arising in connection therewith to the best of our ability.

It has been shown that the high mountain plateau of Thibet, 12,000 to 15,000ft. above the sea level, has been inhabited by the Adepts for an immense period of time. The question is often asked, Why do the Masters of Wisdom live in such a barbarous country remote from civilization? Those who put this query have much yet to learn respecting both the nature of the Mahatmas and their teachings. In the first place, those who call Thibet a barbarous country do not know whether it is or not, as foreigners are excluded. Into that part of Thibet where the Adepts reside not even a native can penetrate. The Masters of Wisdom, on their part, do not think very highly of Western civilization, with its reeking slums, jails and workhouses, and whole nationalities armed to the teeth for mutual destruction. These concomitants of advanced Western progress are certainly lacking in the land of the Sages. "Remember the difference we make between material and spiritual civilizations," says a "Master" in Esoteric Buddhism. The reason why the Mahatmas live in remote mountain regions is easily stated. In such high places the atmosphere is naturally the purest and most refined on the earth's surface, and therefore suitable to the cultivation and development of psychic powers. The powerful magnetism engendered and thrown off by ordinary humanity, especially when crowded together in cities, is extremely trying to the sensitive natures of the Adepts. "What to our physical senses are the odours that hang about sewers and slaughter-houses, that and worse to their spiritual senses are the aura that hang about us." It has been objected that if the Arhats are thus compelled to live remote from ordinary humanity, that they can do nothing by direct means for its elevation. This is an error. The Adepts all work for the progress of the human race, on the spiritual and mental planes, subject to Karmic Law. That they can do this is easily recognised, when we reflect that time and space exist not in the same form on these higher planes of being as they do on the physical ; as the " Key to Theosophy " remarks, the difference between mind and mind can be only one of *state*, not of time or place. It is easy, however, to exaggerate the powers and influence of the Adepts on humanity at large. Hear what one says on this matter : " We are not omnipotent, nay, we are as nothing before the mighty tide of cosmic powers. We can do things to you inexplicable, miraculous, but they are but as the moving of a single mote floating in a wandering sunbeam. Our lives are spent in endeavouring to benefit mankind, but it is only to a limited extent that we can influence the tide of human affairs. As well might one weak human arm seek to stay the rushing waters of the mighty Ganges in flood as we feeble band of Adepts to stem the resistless stream of cosmic impulses. All we can do is, by some groin here, some few hurdles there, somewhat to alter the set of the current, and so avert, here and there, catastrophes that we see impending ; or, again, by tiny canals, here and there, to lead off minute portions of the stream to fertilize tracts that, but for our efforts, would have remained deserts. You have asked how it is that, if this be so, the world knows nothing of us and our deeds ? Like Nature, in harmony with whose laws and inherent attributes all our operations are carried on, we work in silence and in secret. Like Nature, unthanked and unknown, our work must ever be. All earthly rewards for our work—name, fame, 'the applause of wondering senates '— are to us, like the rest of this world's toys, mere illusions, powerless even to *please* those who have once looked behind them into the eternal truths above which they float; for, as your great apostle, himself an initiate, grandly said, ' The things that are seen are transitory, but the things that are unseen are eternal.' And well for us that it is so, since our records afford too many instances of men, well on the upward path we tread, who, their feet caught in these very snares, have fallen irrevocably as regards this life."* We have stated the difference between the narrow and imperfect views held now by the foremost school of Physical Science, and the wide and comprehensive conceptions of Occult philosophy, on the subject of Human Evolution. But even a fair survey of the former will lead to a recognition of the perfectly natural position occupied by the Mahatmas in a world of progress. We see, for instance,

---

* Letter from an Adept.

that the advance of Mankind is accompanied by an immense differentiation among its units. Great indeed is the moral and intellectual gap separating the highest and lowest members of even one race from each other. Assuming, then, as consistent evolutionists are bound to do, that human progress is limitless on this plane, and that the powers and capabilities of ordinary men in the distant future will far exceed those possessed at present, with what show of reason can the possibility of the present existence in the East or elsewhere of highly-advanced men such as the Adepts are be denied ? The long chain of human progress is in this case lengthened at the top, that is all. We readily grant, however, that profound Western conceit often attempts the task. If space permitted it would be easy also to show, from every point of view, excluding that of gross materialism, that the Mahatmas occupy a definite and clear place in Nature, forming a necessary link between ordinary humanity and the intelligences of higher planes of existence, without whom the continuity of the great system of Universal Evolution would not be preserved.

From time to time it has been asked by inquirers why the Adepts do not give us more of their wisdom. Since the publication of the " Secret Doctrine " this question has lost much of its point. But, apart from this, certain formidable difficulties stand in the way of their teaching, especially Western people, what they know. Firstly, the great difficulty everyone encounters who is ignorant of Sanscrit and the metaphysical refinements of Occult Philosophy, in grasping its real meaning ; secondly, the great danger of giving to present selfish mankind the secrets of occult forces, which, if abused, would wreck society. Nor have the Adepts any desire to aid the human race on the path of material progress, which it is now so much inclined to follow ; on the contrary, they desire to assist in the spiritual evolution of Mankind alone. The following statement from them may throw further light on the matter. "There is very little chance of their opinions being accepted by the general public under present circumstances, unless they are supported by such evidence as is within the reach of the outside world. As it is not always possible to procure such evidence, there is very little use in publishing the information which is in their possession until the public are willing to recognise and admit the antiquity and trustworthiness of their traditions, the extent of their powers, and the vastness of their knowledge. In the absence of such proof as is above indicated, there is every likelihood of their opinions being rejected as absurd and untenable ; their motives will no doubt be questioned, and some people may be tempted to deny even the fact of their existence. It is often asked by Hindus as well as by Englishmen why these Adepts are so very unwilling to publish some portion at least of the information they possess regarding the truths of physical science. But, in doing so, they do not seem to perceive the difference between the method by which they obtain their knowledge and the process of modern scientific investigation, by which the facts of nature are ascertained and its laws are discovered. Unless an Adept can prove his conclusions by the same kind of reasoning as is adopted by the modern scientist, they remain undemonstrated to the outside world. It is, of course, impossible for him to develop in a considerable number of human beings such faculties as would enable them to perceive their truth ; and it is not always practicable to establish them by the ordinary scientific method, unless all the facts and laws on which his demonstration is to be based have already been ascertained by modern science. No Adept can be expected to anticipate the discoverie of the next four or five centuries and prove some grand scientific truth to the entire satisfaction of the educated public after having discovered every fact and law in nature required for the said purpose by such process of reasoning as would be accepted by them."* " The Adept has no favour to ask at the hands of conjectural science, nor does he exact from any member of the society blind faith, it being his cardinal maxim that faith should only follow inquiry. The Adept is more than content to remain silent, keeping what he may know to himself, unless worthy seekers wish to share it. He has done so for ages, and can do so for a little longer. Thus he leaves his audience to first verify his statements in every case by the brilliant though rather wavering light of modern science, after which his facts may be either accepted or rejected, at the option of the willing student. In short, the Adept has to remain utterly unconcerned with and unmoved by the issue. He imparts that which it is lawful for him to give out, and deals but with *facts*."† We stated just now one cause for the isolation of the Mahatmas, but it has been asked : Why do they not appear at intervals, and thus confute all disbelievers in their existence ? This query has been well answered in the Key to Theosophy : " The world is neither ready to recognise them, nor to profit by their teaching. Of what use would Professor Clerk Maxwell have been to instruct a class of little boys in their multiplication table ? " Again, " an important reason is the inevitable uselessness of any attempts on their part to deal directly with people not spiritually purified. Though one went to them from the dead they would not believe. If an Adept were to visit an ordinary man a dozen times, would he believe ? If the Adept came in the flesh he would think him an impostor ; if he came in his astral form, and the man's eyes were opened so as to see him, he would persuade himself it was a trick of his own fancy, or of someone

---

* " Five Years of Theosophy," p. 298.
† " Five Years of Theosophy," p. 345.

else's devising. No, the mass of mankind, even the mass of the more highly educated Theosophists, who have in no way purified their spiritual natures, possess that spiritual sense or insight which alone renders *conviction* possible, still only in a potential or dormant state."*

" A moment's reflection will show that they could not come boldly out face to face with the ignorant and superstitious masses of mankind. Did they do so, preach their doctrines and exhibit their powers, then you will admit that, *especially* in this country (India), nine-tenths of the population would protest as the Adepts might—treat these as gods, worship them, and add another, and most rampant one, to the gross superstitions that already cover the fair fields of human souls with a deadly jungle. Of all things they seek to avoid creating any delusions of this kind."†

It is widely supposed by the Western public that the whole body of Adepts is composed of individuals of the same nationality. This is a mistake. In the early part of this century, for instance, an Englishman obtained high rank in the Occult Brotherhood. All ages, all creeds, have produced men with extraordinary powers, through their Divine Selves being partly released from material bonds.

Since the suppression of the archaic mysteries, the Mahatmas make, at stated periods, active efforts on the physical plane to aid the upward progress of mankind through appointed agents. These epochs occur now in the last quarter of each century, and in accordance with the cyclic laws, governing, according to Occult Philosophy, human progress, the " Masters of Wisdom " act. For, as Mr. Judge observes, "during any one cycle the rate or quality of progress appertaining to a different cycle is not possible,"‡ and the Mahatmas are the servants of Karma, and always work in harmony with Nature. Bearing these facts in mind, many incidents in the history of Occultism which appear otherwise inexplicable can be cleared up.

Objection is often raised by critics against the idea that such exalted and wise Beings as the Mahatmas are connected with the Theosophical Society, on the ground that the actions of its Leaders do not seem to be guided by the highest wisdom, at all times, in the conduct of its affairs. This argument shows a misapprehension of the case altogether. No Occultist has ever said that the Mahatmas guide the Society or its Leaders. They watch over and protect it, that is all, foiling every effort made to destroy it, throwing back on the originators every evil influence directed against it. For they look to the future, to the period that must soon come, when the now flowing tide will ebb, and their efforts cease until 1975

---

* " Hints on Esoteric Theosophy," p. 40.

† " Hints on Esoteric Theosophy," p. 35.

‡ Epitome of Theosophical Teaching.

is sounded from the watch towers of time and a new mystic era commences again.

One more link in the chain of evidence proving the existence of the "Masters of Wisdom." Whence comes this stupendous system of Cosmic Evolution, dwarfing all others; as a great critic and sceptic says of the Secret Doctrine: "What Mahatma from his lofty eyrie dictated these volumes of archaic lore, of multitudinous erudition, of Nirvanic teteology, redolent with mammoth strength?"

We predict that, despite the present attitude of bigoted and prejudiced minds, and that of sundry self-appointed leaders of the unthinking multitude, before the next century passes the pre-eminence of the Old Wisdom Religion will be recognised, and the Sages of the Snowy Himavat receive their due from the truth-seekers of every clime.

It is obvious, the Adepts being but mortal men, that the gaps in their ranks caused by death must be filled up from some other source. This supply comes through the promotion of their pupils, of whom there are several classes. Naturally there are many inquirers who wish to know how those willing to qualify can enter the small old path trod by the sages, and finally attain the exalted plane on which the Masters sit. "The Adept becomes, he is not made," says Eliphas Levi. Hard the task, long the way, steep the ascent to that high eminence. True, the beacon light shines from above, but know, O aspirant, that it is from a monster-haunted shore. "The way to it is enveloped with the black cloud of the soul's despair." "No one knows, until he really tries it, how awful a task it is to subdue *all* his evil passions and animal instincts, and develop his higher nature," says One who is on the Path. Great indeed is the conqueror of Self. Many are called, but few are chosen; so must it always be.

But little more now remains to be said. The great sceptic Voltaire says: "A Testimony is sufficient when it rests on—(1) A great number of very sensible witnesses who agree in having seen *well*. (2) Who are sane, bodily and mentally. (3) Who are impartial and disinterested. (4) Who unanimously agree. (5) Who solemnly certify to the fact." Tried by this canon, the evidence we have been able to bring forward, culled from many sources, is enough and more than enough to prove our case. We are content. We have wished that this important task had fallen to abler hands than ours. It has, however, come to us; we have accepted it, remembering Krishna's words—

> This is better, that one do
> His own task as he may, even though he fail.
> To die performing duty is no ill,
> But who seeks other roads shall wander still.

From their mountain home the Masters of Wisdom watch the tides of human affairs ebb and flow. Mighty races come and depart. They view Mankind ardently pursuing the bubbles of the hour, oblivious of the future; mistaking transient illusions, the froth thrown up from the seething sea of life, for realities. Thus will it be until the life cycle of the Aryans must close. When that dread hour, appointed by Great Karma, arrives, and the waves of ocean again roll over the site of our boasting civilization, chanting a solemn dirge for the dead past, then the accounts of the Fifth Root Race will have been balanced by Eternal Justice.

E. ADAMS, F.T.S.

THE TRACT MAILING SCHEME.

THE distribution of Theosophical leaflets by post and hand has been steadily progressing during the past month. Our plan has been to take certain societies and professional men in the first instance, and I am putting a notice in " Light," and in a magazine, to the effect that all applying to me will receive leaflets post free.

Our funds are too precarious to enable us to follow the lead of our American brothers in their wide distribution, but we must hope that those interested will send to my address a few shilling or even halfpenny stamps to help on the movement. It must advance the cause of Theosophy and raise it in the eyes of the public, for the leaflets show the practical side of it, and how its teachings are applied to the necessities of our daily moral life. Such crude ideas are now abroad in connection with the subject that the more people we can reach with even so small a part of our literature as that contained in the leaflets, the more will a reasonable view of our philosophy gain ground. Therefore, any friends who will send us help will be doing the cause a real benefit, and we may be sure some of our seed will fall on good soil.

ALICE GORDON.

7, Nevern Road, Earl's Court.

INAUGURATION

OF THE

EUROPEAN HEADQUARTERS.

THE

STANDPOINTS of THEOSOPHY.

A FEW TRUTHS ABOUT THEOSOPHY.

London :

Published by the T.P.S., 7, Duke Street, Adelphi.

1890.

ON THE SCIENTIFIC IMPORTANCE OF DREAM.

It is extremely interesting, at the present stage of thought, to trace the influence of what we may call "the occult wave" upon the minds of our scientists, and to see how many of them are reluctantly forced to come to conclusions that twenty years ago they would have repudiated with scorn, and how many of them go through long and severe processes of argument and experiment to convince themselves of what to us appear self-evident truths. In several quarters, just at present, the subject of the multiple nature of man has been taken up, and the main object of Baron du Prel's *Philosophy of Mysticism* is to prove that there is a Higher Consciousness in man, and that that Higher Consciousness is identical with Spirit, one and universal. As he approaches his subject from a purely scientific standpoint, and as his book is a long and elaborate one, I have endeavoured to sum up, as briefly as possible, the main points of his argument as based upon the phenomena of our dream-life.

The problem of the work, as Baron du Prel states it in his preface, is the question whether our Ego is wholly embraced in self-consciousness, and his position is, that analysis of the dream-life leads to a negative answer; it shows that self-consciousness falls short of its object, that the Ego exceeds the self-consciousness.

The circuit of the knowledge and self-knowledge possible to an organized being is determined by the number of its senses, and by the strength of the stimuli on which its senses re-act; that is, by what is called the psycho-physical threshold of sensibility, or the boundary-line between the conscious and the unconscious. As life rises into higher forms, so does that threshold rise; that is, the higher a race stands in the scale of being, the wider its limits of knowledge. But this mobility of the threshold in the race must also exist in the individual. This is susceptible of proof from the analysis of our dream-life, but is more strikingly apparent in somnambulism. The displacement of the threshold of sensibility is thus common to the biological process, and to somnambulism, and we may therefore infer from somnambulism not only the mode of existence of our higher consciousness, but also the possibility of a future and more highly developed form of life, where these extraordinary faculties will be normal and usual, instead of exceptional.

It is the rule that only when the activity of the senses is suppressed can the inner working of our higher Ego be perceived, as the stars are first visible with the going down of the sun. This is why the study of the sleep state is so important, particularly in that deepest phase which we call somnambulism. As soon as it is shown that our sleep-life possesses positive characteristics peculiar to itself, it will become the duty of philosophy to make as thorough a study of this third of our existence as it has of our waking life.

The endeavour of the human intellect is to explain the significance of the world and of ourselves, and we find that the moral progress of humanity is thoroughly dependent on the evolutionary capacity of science. The first condition of intellectual progress is that we should realize that true progress is always in the depth, and not in extension on the same level. As Bacon said: " No perfect discovery can be made upon a flat or a level ; neither is it possible to discover the more remote and deeper parts of any science if you stand but upon the level of the same science and ascend not to a higher science."

It was formerly believed, for instance, that the world lay outside of us, and through our senses produced an image of itself upon our brain, and truth was to be captured by study of the object. But when Kant exposed the fallacy of this assumption, and urged the prior examination of the subject and its cognitions, research was begun upon another and a higher plane of investigation.

From the stand-point of every animal organism we can divide external nature into two parts, the lower the grade the more unequal the division, the one including that part of nature with which the said organism is related through its senses, the other that which remains outside this limit, and is therefore transcendental to the organism in question. As development goes on, the boundary of consciousness continually rises. But as there are parts of nature which remain invisible to us, being out of relation to our sense of sight—like the microscopic world, for instance—so there are parts of nature not existing for us, owing to entire absence of relation to our organism.

Science has now herself acknowledged that when she shall have explained the world we see, it is only a represented world that will have been explained, a secondary phenomenon, a mere product of our sense and understanding. Not only are there more things than senses, but things are other than they seem. We are not truly cognizant of *things*, but only of the modes in which our senses re-act upon them. Whence it follows that differently constituted beings must have different worlds.

We may, therefore, conclude that consciousness does not exhaust its object, the world. The second great problem to be explained is man. As the world is the object of consciousness, so is the Ego the object of self-consciousness. Self-consciousness may be as inadequate to the Ego as consciousness to the world; or the Ego may as much exceed self-consciousness as the world exceeds consciousness. This is not only logically thinkable, but has also in its favour analogy, and the doctrine of evolution. If the existence of a transcendental world follow from the theory of knowledge accepted in this age, the theory of self-knowledge belonging to the next age should bring with it the recognition of a transcendental Ego. The question of the soul, which has been stationary for centuries, would be advanced to a wholly new stage if it could be shown that self-consciousness only partially comprehends its object. There are not only boundaries of knowledge which are historically surmountable, but also limitations of consciousness and knowing which are only biologically surmountable.

We stand in the presence of an inexorable alternative: either there is a progress for the future, in which case we must always and à priori grant the existence of facts which contradict our theories, or there are no such facts; and then we must also deny future progress to which, at the highest, only a labour on the level could be ascribed. Owing to the capacity for development, we must expect to be perpetually confronted with fresh problems, for which solution must be sought on deeper lines.

The fact that much that was forgotten emerges again from the unconscious in dreams, proves that in dreaming there is activity in those folds of the brain which in waking are either functionless or whose functions do not result in consciousness. If the deepening of sleep implies the cessation of function in the whole cerebral nerve-system, and yet the inner waking continues and is even exalted, we are forced to suppose, as consciousness presupposes nerves, that in deep sleep the organ of dream is that nerve-system of ganglia, with the solar plexus for centre, which is still so little understood by our physiology.* Physiology cannot demonstrate that the dream organ is incapable of significant dreaming. It has long proved that consciousness is not co-extensive with the material senses; that there is more relation between us and nature than we can be conscious of; tones we cannot hear, colours we cannot see, etc. Sleep can only suspend the *sensuous* relation to nature, but not that which is unconsciously present in waking existence; therefore it may set us free

* Here is certainly an unwarranted jump at a conclusion.

to arrive at the wider consciousness in our inner awakening. Are there, then, forces of Nature of which we become aware in sleep that have escaped the consciousness of sense? We must reply in the affirmative. Wienholt found that healthy sleeping children were disturbed by passes made with an iron key (or other metal object) at a distance of half an inch from the face, or merely approached to the ear. Sleep, therefore, is accompanied by a perception at a distance, and announces the presence of substances which do not excite feeling in the waking man.*

The dreams of deep sleep are lost to recollection, but should be the most significant since the displacement of the threshold of sensibility progresses with the deepening of sleep. Remembering dreams can usually contain only insignificant phantasms, as they are those which immediately follow the falling asleep, or immediately precede the wakening, and are thus connected with the slightest displacement of the threshold. As the failure of memory in the case of deep dream can only be ascribed to the want of a common organ with the waking consciousness, the survival of memory between the light dream and waking must result from at least partial community of organ. The withdrawal of the bridge of memory proves physiologically the change of organ and *vice versâ*.

The dreams of light sleep are remembered because the organ is partly the same as in waking consciousness, and are senseless, because of this mixed activity of the two organs. The dream-organ can only exhibit its unmixed activity in deep sleep. It is in somnambulism that the deep sleep exhibits itself in connection with ideas, and in sleep-walking in acts founded on ideas. It needs only to be proved that sleep, somnambulism, and sleep-walking are intimately related conditions, to dispel the last objection against the possibility of orderly and significant dreams.

In our waking state, a constant, even if slight and unconscious, effort of the will is necessary to keep our attention fixed on the point that immediately concerns us, and this strain is productive of fatigue. But a dream, though ever so long, does not tire, no aim being kept in view, and the inner consciousness being merely passive. Associations, memories, external stimuli, internal agitations of the brain, or of the nutritive processes, are all disturbers of the dream of light sleep, and, therefore, its confusion is very explicable, and the difficulty of retaining incoherent fragments, even in waking, shows how hardly these unconnected bits of dream can be recoverable by memory.

But as the bridge of memory fails between deep sleep (when the dream-organ is undisturbed) and waking, the existence of significant and orderly dreaming can only be proved when the dreamer translates his

---

* Another case where *is* should be *may be*.

dream into acts, as in sleep-walking, or accompanies it with words, as in the somnambulic state, or when, contrary to the rule, it is recollected.

Somnambulism, which splits the consciousness into two persons—the " I " of daily life, and the " I " which emerges only in the somnambulic condition—thus shows us not only that deep sleep is not dreamless, but that our daily consciousness does not exhaust its object.

Schopenhauer says that in dream, somnambulism, and related conditions, we obtain the objectively represented institution by a different organ than in waking, and he speaks, therefore, of a special dream-organ. The teachings of both Fechner and Reichenbach also favour the view that in sleep an organ is active which in waking is either functionless, or whose functions remain below the threshold of sensibility. But even if every impression of consciousness could only be connected with the brain, it must yet be conceded that in deep sleep there must be other avenues of perception leading to the brain than in waking. But if we consider the fact of absence of memory on waking from deep sleep, that fact suggests an actual transposition of the stage of consciousness, and thus an interchange of functions between the brain and the ganglionic system.

If we have two consciousnesses, rising and sinking like the weights in a scale, then from the definition of both can we first attain to the definition of man.

If self-consciousness does not exhaust its object, then corresponding to the transcendental world must be a transcendental Ego, and our sense of personality, by which we know ourselves as mere willing beings, does not coincide with our whole Ego.

Should man be a double being in the sense indicated, with an earthly personality represented by a smaller circle included in the larger circle of the transcendental Ego, the boundary between them being the line between the conscious and the unconscious, these two positions of his being must be related to each other as the scales of a balance, or as the stars, which optically appear only when the sun disappears. And as the emergence of the transcendental Ego can only take place when the empirical Ego is in abeyance, which is the case in sleep, and as sleep forms one-third of our existence, it is evident that the dream-world affords most chance of proving a metaphysical individuality. (The weighty and primary fact is *that we dream;* the content of dream being of secondary consideration.)

Even the empirical Ego must encounter influences from the transcendental world, inasmuch as the two Egos are indeed identical, but for the empirical consciousness such influences are below the threshold of sensibility, and, though we have evidences of its capacity of evolution, it is still only in germ, and even in trance, ecstasy, and similar conditions, it may not be susceptible of a development which would correspond to a biological process of millions of years. This consideration alone should suffice to restrain us from an over-estimation of dreams. And dream-images of true transcendental content can be only symbolical, as they must necessarily clothe themselves in the form of our everyday consciousness.

Still more distinctly than by the alternation of waking and dream is the duplication of our nature revealed by that remarkable class of dreams wherein we are given information by other persons on subjects of which we are ignorant—an example that clearly shows the psychological possibility of the identity of the subject with the contemporaneous difference of persons.

If philosophy, starting from the empirical facts of dream, shall be able to establish the doctrine of the soul, then, and only then, will it be time for it to attack the further question, whether that which is proved in dream in relation to the Microcosm, repeats itself in a larger sphere in relation to the Macrocosm. The question then will be whether there is an all-embracing World-Subject dramatically sundering itself in millions of suns and milliards of beings in space and time, for it is a logical consequence of the dramatic division in dream that the science of the future, far from giving up the conception of soul, much more probably will find itself necessitated to set up, besides the physical aspect and the soul, Spirit as a third element, or a self-consciousness comprehending both body and soul.

In connection with these leading ideas in Du Prel's philosophy of dreams, it will be found interesting to make a brief analysis of an article contributed by him to " Le Lotus " for December, 1888, upon " The Intuition of Time ; or, the Cerebral Clock "; *i.e.*, the faculty of self-waking at a given hour.

In this article, Dr. du Prel undertakes to prove that this faculty, which is common to so many persons, is another proof of the existence of that transcendental Ego that manifests itself in the phenomena of dreams and somnambulism. His argument may be summed up as follows :—

1. The cause of self-waking must be internal, not external ; *something*, but not *some one*.

2. It depends upon three conditions : (a) Consciousness that the time for sleep has passed. (b) Capability of measuring the passing of time. (c) Capability of putting an end to that physiological condition of the brain of which sleep is the result, and introducing into the cerebral consciousness a transcendental idea, that is, an idea outside the limits of our ordinary consciousness.

Only a conscious, willing being can be capable of uniting these conditions. The normal will and consciousness are absent during sleep, therefore they cannot be the cause. If they were, we should need no clocks when awake. (This is another of Dr. du Prel's unwarranted assumptions, because many persons have the faculty of telling the time accurately in their waking hours, and *not*, as Dr. du Prel asserts, by a guess at the amount of time elapsed since some fixed period, but as intuitively as in sleep.) To resume:

1. The cause then must be part of our being, but not in the physiological sense.

2. It is not part of our conscious personality, yet it must be conscious, and especially of time.

3. It is part of our will, but not of our conscious will.

It is then self-conscious, but for us unconscious; it resides in our *being*, and not in our person.

These contradictions can only be reconciled by the assertion that the cause is found in the transcendental subject (or higher consciousness), to which all mystic phenomena must revert.

Like all transcendental faculties, the intuition of time is most exact in somnambulism, where the conscience and will are less active than in the waking state, which proves it to be a problem of the higher consciousness. It must be a continuous condition, for we cannot conceive the sudden and causeless perception of the right moment of waking. To prove this is difficult, because it must be done on the narrow frontier between sleeping and waking; the ordinary consciousness must be able to take cognisance of the *question*; the higher consciousness must be still clear enough to give the correct *answer*. (Dr. du Prel gives two instances of persons who could answer correctly in their sleep when questioned as to the hour.)

It must be proved also that this knowledge of time is not based on clairvoyance—which is only a modified vision (?), the intuitive knowledge of time being a purely internal phenomenon. This has been proved over and over again by many experiments with somnambulists and hypnotized persons, who invariably act upon a knowledge of the true time, and not that of the clocks around them, often purposely altered, as a further test. Furthermore, an order given to a hypnotised person is executed at any given hour after that person has passed out of the hypnotic state, or, as Dr. du Prel puts it : the posthypnotic order is executed by means of the cerebral clock, or the transcendental perception of time. Dr. Beauris, of Nancy (author of *Le Somnambulesine provoqué*) says that such phenomena are among the best known, the most credible, and the most easily produced of the phenomena of hypnotism. He says that this perception of time *" acts like an alarm-clock, which goes off only at the moment for which it is set."*

These facts evidently imply an unconscious faculty of measuring time far more precise than that of the ordinary condition. It is also a well-known fact that somnambulistic patients have not only the intuition of time as to the limitation of their sleep (whether voluntary or induced), but also as to the length of their nervous crises, and the frequency of their recurrence.

This shows that the organic modifications of our bodies, as well as certain maladies, such as intermittent fevers, for instance, must be subject to certain determinate laws of time, and that the transcendental subject (or Higher Self), to which we must attribute the faculty of measuring time, must be conscious of these laws also; in other words, it must be identical with our organizing principle, unless we establish a special principle for the organic activity, and thus transgress that scientific law that forbids the unnecessary multiplication of explanatory causes. The "organizing principle" is explained by Dr. du Prel (in Vol. II. of his *Philosophy of Mysticism*, p. 156) to be the life-principle lying behind all organic nature—"it is transcendental nature, and as in somnambulism it exhibits the faculty of critical self-inspection and cure, it must also be the organizing principle in us, thus a willing, not less than a cognitive being. In a word, the life-principle in us is the transcendental subject.

Our organism has its rhythmic movements, such as respiration and pulsation. It possesses the faculty of measuring time for its periodic func-tions,* such as hunger and thirst; and it oscillates between sleeping and waking, and is thus united to terrestrial life. On the other hand we could not distinguish between one sound and another, or one colour and another, without the unconscious faculty of estimating the difference in the number of their vibratory waves, which would seem to prove, says Dr. du Prel, the identity of the organizing with the sensational principle. The rhythmic movements of the body are insufficient of themselves to solve the problem of the intuition of time; we need besides a special consciousness, which measures them, counts them, and remains unrecognised below the threshold of sensibility; which appertains, that is, to the Higher Self, for the con-tent of our unconsciousness is comprised in our transcendental conscious-ness. Unconsciousness is such only in relation to our sense-consciousness, as is proved by most of the psychic faculties, and especially by this intui-tion of time.

We can see by the evidence of somnambulists, although they do not express their thought directly, but clothe it in the language of sensa-tion, that their indications of time come from the transcendental region to take form in that of cerebral representations, but that they do not originate in the latter. Prof. Wolfart (*Eclaircissements sur le Mesmérisme*) having questioned his somnambulists as to their intuition of time, found

* Is not this an inversion of the right order? Do not hunger and thirst measure time for the organism?

that some reported that they saw before them a brilliant dial upon which they read the hour, some heard a voice, or saw a human form that spoke to them, while others had a perception of the time which they were unable to explain.

We recognise in the reports of these patients of Dr. Wolfart, that ordinary dramatization of internal sensations which makes up a large part of our dream-life. We all know how in our dreams we sometimes seem to be quite other people than our waking selves, and how we more often still, invest the men and women of our dreams with either original and special characteristics, which make them new people to us, or with the bodily and mental characteristics belonging to them in real life; that is, the *dramatis personæ* of our dreams are either entirely creations of our own brains, or characteristic presentments of people we really know. This Dr. du Prel calls "the dramatic separation of the Me in dreams," and maintains that the threshold of sensibility is the plane where this sundering of the Ego occurs, and that which leaves the state of unconsciousness is taken objectively, and ascribed to a foreign source or a foreign speaker. And as we find the explanations of Dr. Wolfart's somnambulists as to their knowledge of time taking this dramatic form, it follows that with them also the sentiment of time must emerge from the unconscious, that is to say, the transcendental consciousness.

That the rhythmic movements of the organism, such as the respiration, are insufficient to explain the problem of the intuition of time is very certain, because the relation between the internal and external rhythm is wanting, as well as the perception of such relation. The ancient Hindus busied themselves with this problem in very remote ages, and they endeavoured to explain the intuition of time by the identification of the transcendental consciousness, or Higher Self, with the Divine, a solution that Dr. du Prel thinks overshoots the mark as far as physiological explanation (*minus* the relation between the internal and external rhythm) falls short of it. He cites a curious passage quoted by Windischmann in his *Philosophie in Fortgang der Weltgeschichte*, III., 1332 : " According to the Hindu conception, the sleeper (*supta*) recognises himself in sleep (*svap*); that is, he becomes conscious of his Higher Self. In the body of the sleeper the five *pranas* are kindled and awakened. To the most secret *prana*, which manifests itself principally by the breath, correspond in the external world, ether (*akasa*) and the luminous sun. *Atma* is the essence, the real being in the sun as in the vital breath ; he who becomes conscious of his *atma* finds therein an internal perception of time by which he can measure the time marked by the external sun. In ordinary consciousness the motion of the sun and that of the internal *prana* are separate. Both accomplish their course, the sun once in twenty-four hours, and the *prana*

21,600 times. As the sun is the *Atma* of the world, and the *prana* is the *Atma* of the body, the first enlightens the world, the second enlightens the body, and the two make up one, which is not realized by those who regard only appearances; they only know that 21,600 revolutions of *prana*, or respirations, are produced during one revolution of the sun, and may be counted thereby; but they who are masters of knowledge, who have complete control over their senses, and can explore their inner nature by their purified *manas*, these unite themselves by *Yoga* with *Atma* (the real being of the sun and the vital breath), and by the movements of their *prana* know the movements of the sun; respiration gives them the knowledge of the solar movement." To this the Editor of *Le Lotus* adds, that the "respiration" spoken of here has little to do with the bodily function so-called: the fact being that there are two systems of *Yoga* practised by the Hindus, the *Hatha Yoga*, or the material, dealing with the functions of the body, and the *Raja Yoga*, or spiritual, dealing with the functions of the soul.

In ordinary language, and setting aside the technical phrases in the Hindu theory quoted, the idea seems to be that "the Masters of Knowledge," they who have purified their whole being, physical, intellectual, and spiritual, can so unite themselves with the Divine Spirit that they partake of its omniscience. This is the "pantheistic explanation" of which Dr. du Prel disapproves, but between which and his own theory of a "transcendental consciousness" persisting during sleep there seems to be very little distinction. He identifies this transcendental consciousness with the Higher Self, which the Hindu philosophers identify with the Divine element in man.

However this may be, this intuitive perception of time during sleep seems to afford a conclusive proof of the truth of the Hindu definition of sleep as a phase of consciousness. In deep sleep the senses and the intellectual faculties are alike dormant, but that *something* of the individual consciousness persists seems to be proved by this power of self-waking, which certainly implies a continuous perception of the lapse of time, and a certain control over the physiological condition of the brain—that is, a certain amount of both will and consciousness. The senses and the intellectual faculties disposed of, there remains only the spiritual element to be accounted for, and as spirit must be identical, whatever and wherever its manifestations may be, is it too much to say that when the soul, by the baptism of its deep sleep, is freed from its earthly impurities, it is enabled to enter into communion with the Divine? This was evidently the idea of the Psalmist in that long-mistranslated passage—" He giveth to His beloved *in* their sleep.*

"The true Self of man (the *homo noumenon*)," says Kant, "is dormant

---

* Or, " while they sleep." And see Job iv., 13.

in dreams, and, therefore, the sense of morality is absent"; for in this state the intellectual faculties hover about the very threshold of consciousness, and are even affected in some degree by sense-impressions, while the spiritual element, the conscience, or Divine voice within, is absent. We can commit any crime in our dreams, or see it committed by others, without the slightest sense of wrong.

Dr. Carpenter, in his *Mental Physiology*, admits that though there is a complete suspension of sensorial consciousness during profound sleep, yet we have no right to affirm with certainty that consciousness is ever entirely suspended even during the profoundest sleep. He also considers that the experiments of Dr. Ferrier on the functions of different parts of the brain conclusively prove the doctrine of unconscious cerebration by showing that important cerebral modifications, of which only the results make themselves known, may take place below the threshold of consciousness (or, as he phrases it, " outside the sphere of consciousness "), and this he asserts to be only the physiological expression of the theory of Sir William Hamilton, Leibnitz, and others, that "the mind may undergo modifications, sometimes of very considerable importance, without being itself conscious of the process, until its *results* present themselves to the consciousness in the new ideas, or new combinations of ideas, which the process has evolved."

This is illustrated by the experience of Dr. Wolfart's somnambulists whose intuition of time emerged from the unconscious plane (or, as Dr. du Prel would say, the transcendental consciousness), to impress itself upon their perceptions either as a sight, or sound, or simply an intellectual conviction.

Whatever deductions we may make from it, spiritualistic or otherwise, this cerebral clock, or intuition of time, is a curious and interesting phenomenon, and one deserving of more study than it has yet received, at least by Western scientists.

KATHARINE HILLARD.

WHY ONE SHOULD JOIN THE THEOSOPHICAL SOCIETY.

THE Theosophical Society is the proper place for many different types of men and women, and for people in varied stages of growth and development.

First. Its broad and non-sectarian basis should attract to it all those who take an intellectual interest in its second or third objects : the study of ancient philosophies, religions, and sciences, and the development and investigations of the psychic powers and faculties latent in many.

Many students of modern western philosophy join its ranks because they find there others who can assist them and throw light upon their difficulties from the standpoint of Oriental philosophy. Students of modern physical science, too, will find in the T. S. those who can co-operate with them, and give them suggestion and sympathy in their investigations. This is especially the case as regards such subjects as Anthropology and Cosmogony, upon which many students of Oriental science belonging to the Society would have numerous ideas to share with their fellow-members.

But among those specially interested in intellectual pursuits, the Society appeals most nearly, perhaps, to such as are oppressed by the intellectual difficulty of the crushing problems of human life, its origin and destiny, the riddles of heredity and the dark mysteries of psychology.

Many members of the Society have given much time to the study of Religions, religious symbolism and dogma, as phases and expressions of the human mind, so that all those interested in such pursuits will find in the T. S. help, stores of information, and many a guiding clue to these labyrinthine mazes. And the same thing applies to those intellectually interested in the study of the abnormal manifestations which occur through the human organism, and in such subjects as Hypnotism, Mesmerism, Clairvoyance, etc., etc.

But the intellect, and the intellectual faculties, by no means embrace the entire human being, and they are far from being the most vitally important of his attributes, great as their importance undoubtedly is; and the Theosophical Society is even more the appropriate place for all those men and women who have the cause of suffering Humanity at heart, than for the purely intellectual student. To lead men on to think for themselves, to assist them to cultivate and develop their nobler and broader aspirations, to aid them in forming a vaster and deeper conception of human life, its laws and its purpose—to do this is true philanthropic work, far more real, more lasting, more important in its results, than to fill their stomachs, to clothe their bodies, or even to minister to their diseases. It is only in the ideas and conceptions as to man and nature which the Society has done so much to popularize, that the poor, the suffering, and the wretched can find a remedy for the sense of bitter wrong, injustice, and cruelty which gnaws so keenly at many a heart.

To assist in this labour of love is a task in which should share all whose hearts beat in responsive sympathy to the mental agony of others. All those of large heart, all the more developed and more compassionate souls of our race should hasten to join in the service of our common humanity, should lay aside all religious and sectarian prejudice, and seek in the ranks of the Theosophical Society the co-operation, assistance, and support which it freely offers to all sincere and ardent lovers of their fellowmen. All such, all who seek as the true goal of effort, to benefit and help others, all who can rise to the broad and lofty ideal of humanity itself as the object of their devotion, can find no truer home, no stronger support, nor more earnest fellow-workers than the Theosophical Society and its devoted members.

The Society has no dogmas, no tenets, no religion; it aims at teaching men the power of co-operation, and demonstrating the value of perfect toleration and mutual aid in the search after truth. Through its many branches, scattered all over the world, it brings together, and focuses at a common centre, the labours and investigations of many minds, and places within reach of the student the labours of others engaged in the same research. Thus it puts into the hands of western students the key to the real comprehension of the religious, philosophical, and scientific knowledge of our Aryan ancestors, while it also opens up the way to a broader and more philosophical comprehension of our own forms of faith in all these directions. No one joining its ranks is called upon to subscribe to any beliefs or doctrines, nor abandon his own, whatever they may be. Theosophy is not the creed of the T.S.; it is only a system of thought studied ardently by many of its members, because they find there that satisfaction for those deeper cravings and longings of their hearts which they have failed to find elsewhere.

It is a commonplace to say that union is strength, yet few

people realize the importance of this truth in the intellectual and aspirational worlds of life. How many a true and noble thought, how many a lofty, unselfish aspiration, how many a longing after a larger and more comprehensive grasp of life have perished, stillborn, for want of the timely sympathy and encouragement of others sharing in like feelings! In moments of weariness and despondency, when the weight of sorrow or suffering forces upon our attention the dark mystery of human life, we feel the need of a friendly hand amid the gloom. In our hours of keen perception, of clear insight, when our hearts are uplifted with the glow of some new thought, some fuller apprehension of the laws which guide our lives, we need kindred minds into which we can pour out our new-found treasures. Such help, such opportunities it is the aim of the T.S. to furnish to all who desire them.

Many minds in our day feel instinctively the desire for some solid foundation on which to rest the aspirations of their hearts in what may be called a religious direction. But they have sought in vain for any firm ground on which to build. To such the T.S. offers opportunities of study and of obtaining what they seek such as no other organization can show. It is true that every man must find his own footing in this search for truth; but much, very much, can be done by mutual assistance, and many errors and mistakes avoided by the free discussion and comparison of views and experiences which the Society exists to promote.

But there are many persons fully in sympathy with the basic ideas of the Theosophical movement, many even who hold such fundamental conceptions of Theosophy as Karma and Reincarnation, who yet do not join the ranks of the Society. Such people are making a very grave mistake, whether their abstention is due to the fact that they do not accept or sympathize with all the teachings of Theosophy, or to a fear of being hampered and limited in their growth or action through belonging to any organization, or again, to the belief that they can get all they need from Theosophical publications and would gain no good by joining the Society. To begin with, no one who joins the Society is expected or asked to believe in or accept anything, except the ideal of Universal Brotherhood. Secondly, no one need fear that he will be hampered or hindered in his growth or action through belonging to the Society, for the whole tendency and spirit of the organization is to encourage and provide for the very largest possible measure of individual freedom of thought and action. Thirdly, those who remain outside the Society under the impression that they can get all they need from books, and have nothing to gain by joining an organization, will sooner or later find out their mistake. For, not only do the magnetic, the mental, and the spiritual currents bind all earnest members of the organization together, so that each is upheld and aided in his progress by the strength of all, not only do the interchange of thought and the mental contact between the members greatly benefit each, but the time is rapidly approaching when the great current of spiritual life and light now sweeping through the world will cease to flow, and those who trusted to themselves alone will find that, not being integral parts of a living whole, their inner life will rapidly die out under these unfavourable conditions.

But these reasons appeal only to selfishness. There is a nobler, a truer, a grander motive which should make all those join the society, who sympathize with the ideal of Universal Brotherhood, or who hold any of the basic conceptions of Theosophy. This is the love of truth and the desire to help others. Nowhere can such a field be found for the action of these two motives as in the Society. No other organization can appeal with half the force to all who love truth for her own sake, to all who long to aid their fellow-men, who desire to uplift the masses of the ignorant and the miserable, who realize that life has a grander, a nobler purpose than eating, drinking, begetting children, and the gratification of selfish desires and ambitions—from all such no organization can claim allegiance with a better right than the Theosophical Society, whose motto is: "There is no Religion higher than Truth," whose foundation stone is the Universal Brotherhood of mankind, and whose maxim for daily life is Altruism.

B. K.

THE TARO.

THERE are three ways of placing the Taro Cards, which may be considered the Body, Soul, and Spirit of the Taro.

The first manner relates to the lower plane, and has reference to questions concerning every-day life, domestic matters, illness and simple queries, etc. For this placing the four Aces and their relative cards are only to be used.

The second manner has relation to Science, Philosophy, Religion, etc. For this, the Aces, with their cards, and the twenty-two keys are to be employed.

For the third manner of placing the Taro, the twenty-two keys only are to be used with the four aces. The cards are to be left out entirely. This mode is to be used when the knowledge sought for is assignable to the Divine Wisdom, and the revelation and unfolding of the inner light, the sacred knowledge of the Occult.

To place the cards in position, the Aces are to be separated from the pack and shuffled by themselves, and are placed face downwards in the centre of the twelve positions, in the order A B C D; the other cards are then to be placed as they arise in the positions numbered consecutively 1 to 12. In all cases faces downwards.

The four aces in the centre form always the Astral key of the knowledge sought for, and each card of the Astral key is allied to the trine of cards which cover the places having the same colour.

The colours were given to show the meaning of the twelve places, and this meaning is intensified or weakened, elevated or lowered, according to the kind of knowledge desired.

The twelve places or thrones are divided into four trines; each of the places of the trine bears harmonious relationship to the other.

The meaning of the portions of the Aces which form the Astral key is as follows: A, coloured red, is the throne of Motion, Action, Will, the proper throne for the Ace of Diamonds. This part of the Key gives action to the Red Trines numbered 1, 6, 11, and will powerfully affect it, if Diamonds fall on the place A.

The red trine is the trine of life.

No. 1 is Present Existence, Action, Being, the Present State or Time.

No. 6 is Life in the Deity, the Source, the Creator.

No. 11 is Life in Posterity, Children, the After-course.

The second Trine is coloured Yellow, and means power, influence, might, and to it belongs that part of the Astral Key which bears the same colour, marked B. The Ace of Clubs is the most powerful occupier of this Throne. No. 2 of this Trine is the place of power, attached to Honour and Majesty.

No. 7. The power given by surroundings, connections, associations, intellect.

No. 12. The power and influence given by Worth or material qualifications.

The third Trine is coloured Green, and has the Ace of Cups as the bountiful and true occupier of its Key—O. This is the trine of love, and the relative positions are numbered 3, 8, 9.

No. 3 is the place of Love, felicity, agreement, delight.

No. 8 is Love in service, reception, bounty.

No. 9 is the place of Favour, Help, Succour.

The fourth place of the Astral Key is marked D, and this with its relative trine signifies afflictions, oppositions, persecutions, punishment, according to the knowledge desired. It has for its significator the Ace of Swords. Should this Ace fall on this throne of the Key in a question of affliction or opposition, and Swords also on the Violet Trine, it would be very adverse.

The first place of this Trine is No. 4, which is the throne of Evil, Sin, the Pit, the casting down of the Mighty Retribution.

No. 5 is the place of Malice, Hatred, Injury, Treachery.

No. 10. The place of Intellectual Death, Idiocy, Mourning.

The common or ordinary meaning of the Aces is: Diamonds=Life, Clubs=Power, Cups=Love, Swords=Affliction.

The meaning of their relative cards is according to their values, and the place and strength of the place where they may fall.

Diamonds—Signify and give Life, Satisfaction, Ability, accomplishments, etc.

Clubs—Power, force, might, the Creative Will.

Cups—Love, beauty, pleasure, enjoyment, favour.

Swords—Affliction, illness, trial, testing, sifting and death.

When the cards have been placed on their thrones, faces downwards, that card of the Astral Key which will most particularly relate to the question, is first to be turned up, and the mind allowed to dwell on the bearings of this first page of revelation. The trine of cards that belongs to this key is then to be shown, and the strength and meaning of the cards is to be read, with the meaning of the place or throne.

The key next in importance with its trine is then to be dealt with and so on with the rest.

Three different packs of cards should be employed, one kept particularly for the Divine Wisdom. This pack, when not used, should be placed away in a small cedar-wood box, wrapped in a linen cloth, and no hand but that of the student to be allowed to touch this pack.

REINCARNATION.

I want to make reasonable the basic hypothesis of Theosophy that men as we now see them are individuals coming out of an immeasurable past, and destined for an immeasurable future; and that just as a school-boy is tied to one class at his school till he knows all that that class can teach, rising therein from the lowest to the highest places, so man lives again and again on this particular planet till he has acquired all that is of value in these conditions of existence.

Suppose a man were placed for the first time in a great forest of oaks. Side by side with gnarled and knotted veterans, impressive in size and suggestive of antiquity, there would be the infantine saplings of yesterday, there would be more developed, but still youthful trunks; in fine, there would be at once before his eye oaks of every degree in magnitude and age. Gazing upon these, would he not be an idiot if he did not guest that at some time in the far past those veterans had been as are now the smaller trees; that as years went by they had grown up through every grade of size now at once exemplified before his eye? He sees the greater, the less, the least; he infers that the greater have once been as are now the lesser and the least.

The parallel is exact. There exist at the same moment men of the noblest scope of intellect and the purest morality, and alongside of these are idiots, criminals, men of the meanest mind and without any morality at all. And midway between the extremes are all the possible gradest Shall we not infer, as with the oaks, that the men largest in intellect and morals were once as the men smallest, and that they grew up through all the stages we now see? If you urge that they have effected all this in one life, in the first place we deny it. Our Herbert Spencers and Father Damien's were not idiot-criminals to start with. And secondly, if it were so, it would remain true that they have developed fastest. How did they acquire the principle of rapid development not shown in idiots and criminals, unless we assume that by the age, say of 21, they have grown up into that fulness of power they had acquired when they left their last life, and can now go on and improve upon that? So the problem remains.

Let us therefore represent a man's intellect and morality, his total size of character at 21, by the figure 100. By the age of 71, he will have expanded into 105. His brother's total character at 21 might perhaps be represented by 90, and he at the age of 71 has only evolved into 93. On the other hand, his sister started life at no less a figure than 120, and at her death was 130. Here then we have three people starting at different levels, and making three different rates of progress. Does it not seem that in some past life our man, who this time started at 100, started *then* as does his brother *now* at 90, progressing perhaps to 93, and that in some future life, starting as does his sister *now* at 120, he may, like her, *then* reach 130? If we do not make this hypothesis, how shall we account for his starting life at 100, and not like the criminal-idiot at 5, 10, or nothing? It is no answer to the difficulty to suggest that the differences between men are due to differences in their heredity, parentage, and environment. Members of the same family have the same heredity, parentage, and environment, yet they may differ in every respect. Even twins, conceived and born in the same hour, are as likely as not to develop radical differences of mind and morals as time goes on. So the qualities of men are due neither to their parents, their ancestry, nor education, nor surroundings, since those who correspond in all those particulars may yet differ. Of this difference the theory of reincarnation affords the only fair explanation, as well as of other innumerable difficulties, otherwise inexplicable. In bar to its acceptance stands one apparent difficulty, and one only. Far from being really a difficulty, however, it is a key-stone of the theory. I refer to the fact that we do not ordinarily remember our past lives. But is the fact of our having forgotten them a proof that we did not live them? Then, also, is the fact that we do not remember our birth a proof that we were not born, and the fact that we remember nothing of our first two years a proof that we did not then exist? If the fact that we are now thirty years old is proof that we were once two years old, then the fact that our present moral and intellectual development may be represented by 100 is proof that it might once have been represented by 50, and we know that in this life we never stood so low as that. There is a story of a certain pike, kept in a large glass tank in the grounds of its owner. Now this fish used to spend the whole of his time in carefully swimming around his tank. On a certain day the owner inserted a glass plate into the tank, so as to shut off half of it from the pike's perambulations. Not seeing the glass, and continuing to circulate, he knocked his nose against it, and this occurred every time he swam round, day and night, for nineteen years. At the end of that time he learned that at a certain point in his journey, pain occurred if he persisted in his circle, so he made it smaller and thus avoided the plate. The owner now removed it, but during the rest of his life of many years he was never known to cross the line where it had been. It is reasonable to suppose that in time he forgot there had been a plate there, forgot the pain he used to have, forgot that he *must not* cross a certain point, and simply *did not* cross it, had no inclination to cross it. He had forgotten the *fact* of the plate, but had learnt and remembered a *lesson* founded on that fact. The first time an infant sees a flame he naturally puts his fingers into it, and gets them burnt. This occurs many times, and at last he learns that flame burns. When he is a man the lesson remains with him that flame burns, but he has forgotten every one of those individual baby finger-burnings that taught the lesson. The lesson remains, but the facts have departed. He might argue that because he could not remember those burnings, they had never occurred ; that his knowledge of the properties of flame had been inherited, or grown up out of his environment, and so on. The illustration is suggestive of the possibility that though the facts of past lives have been forgotten, the lessons, the deductions from those facts, are not forgotten, but are the capital, the 100, with which we start this life. Grant, for a moment, that we have lived many past lives. If we could remember the innumerable details in all those, we should be so lost in a vast and shoreless ocean of memories, as to have neither time nor inclination for present action and thought. But the deductions and lessons from them are few, and have become inherent parts of our characters. But it is not necessary to assume that because they have slipped out of the field of our *present* consciousness, they are past recall. There are on record many statements from those who have been nearly drowned and resuscitated. From these it appears that at the moment of, or just before, death, the whole field of memory is lighted up, and apparently every single fact of every day of the now closing life stands out clearly into consciousness. It may well be that this occurs at the last instant of every life, and that the departing soul reviews its whole career, and assimilates as a lesson the deductions from the panoramic facts of life, which, having served their purposes, are flung into the limbo of empty shells.

But our shop-fronts do not exhibit all the contents of the shop. The mind with which we earn our bread, and laugh, and make love, and think and study with, is not our last possibility, not our eternal mind, not the mind that preserves the record of the many lives we live. Over our heads rests the great globe of the real mind, dipping down a little only of itself into the consciousness of daily life, and the " I " with which we act in daily life is only a little of that great and all-remembering self. Hypnotism, that would-be modern science, will light up for us many of the problems of mental life, and to it for a moment we will now appeal. In the Salpetrière Hospital in Paris, Dr. Charcot, the most important living authority on diseases of the nervous system, with a band of scarcely less eminent physicians, is prosecuting the study of Hypnotism, and the light it throws on disease. The result of their researches is published in a volume of the International Scientific Series by Drs. Binet and Feré. It is there shown by very many carefully conducted experiments that Hypnotism produces a total change of nervous relations. These are of so bewildering a nature, so complex, that without the solution offered by Theosophy they are utterly baffling. So far, nothing has been said concerning the view of Theosophy as to the real constitution of man. Materialists deal with him as a unit; many Christians as a duad, body and soul; St. Paul speaks of him as body, soul, and spirit; Theosophy splits him yet further into seven principles or aspects, or six sheaths and a nucleus, each of the seven having different functions, and being in various relationships in different men. In this division lies the real explanation of Hypnotism, of re-incarnation and the lost memory of former lives. Let us divide a man's mind, his consciousness, into two; representing the total by a great globe over his head, touching his head and dipping into it. Let us suppose that the purpose of repeated lives is that the whole of that conscious sphere of thought shall in successive parts or segments dip into his successive life-brains, and learn somewhat of the world thus each time. At the end of each lifetime the segment that has been steeped into the physical brain, endowing it with

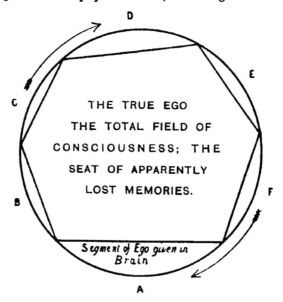

A, B, C, etc., are successional segments of the total field of consciousness, dipping into, and conferring temporary consciousness upon, the brain of each life. The total memories of these lives are thrown into the common

field for devāchanic assimilation. The segments differ in size according to the amount of himself a man can draw into his brain consciousness, and learning thus the facts of each life, on being liberated from that life, pours its knowledge into the common stock in the middle. When the time comes for the man to be born again, the sphere revolves a little, and dips a new clean segment into the new brain of an infant, which then becomes conscious. But that new segment B knows nothing of the doings of the old segment A, though the total mind does. This total mind is, however, not in the brain, but only a little of it. When we say "I," we mean only a small segment of the true or total "I," that segment that is in this temporary brain, and which, therefore, knows nothing of former lives, though the true divine "I" does know and remember. That space of time which lapses between leaving one life and beginning the next is spent in, as it were, entering into the ledger of the eternal or total mind the day-book items of the evanescent segmentary and partial mind of the past life, in drawing from that life any lessons that may be of use for the next. The lesser mind has entered into the inheritance of the vast stores of the greater. Now, Hypnotism does something like this. It partially rees the lesser mind or Ego from the limitations of brain by paralyzing the brain. Therefore, to the extent that Hypnotism is real and deep is the memory expanded. A servant-girl, under the care of Braid, the Manchester surgeon, and a re-discoverer of Hypnotism, while hypnotized, recited long passages of Hebrew, of which, in her waking state, she did not know one word, because many years before she had lived with a Hebrew scholar as his servant. A patient of Charcot's recognised at once, when hypnotized, and correctly named, a physician whom she had not seen since she was two years old, and then only for a short time, during which she was under his care. There is, of course, not now time for the narration of anything like a series of cases, but only for one or two as types. Dr. Richie's great work and the volume already mentioned will give data of any desired fulness, showing that the grasp of real memory upon even the smallest fact is never relaxed. For the memory of waking life is only an infinitesimal fraction of the memory of our entire Ego. Can we get any idea of what the Soul, the Ego, the globe overhead is doing while we are eating, and thinking, and making love in our daily ordinary mind? Let us advance the hypothesis that while we, knowing two facts, laboriously reason to the third, it knows all three at once ; that while we, barely remembering the facts of last year, totally forget our infancy, it knows all the facts of our preceding lives ; that therefore its judgment, if we could only get it, would, from the range of its knowledge, be of infinitely greater value than our own.

Suppose we look at our consciousness during a whole day, and see what elements we can find in it. Lowest of all are the animal emotions, hunger, desire to get money, the impulse to fall in love, sleepiness, etc. ; next above these comes thinking proper, reasoning, deductions of a third fact from two others. Without any other conscious elements than these two sets, we should simply spend life in reasoning as to the best way to gratify our own wishes, to obtain any pleasure and avoid all pain. But on a higher level than either of these two comes an impulse to do duty at any cost, regardless of pleasure or pain, and in the face often of the protests of the reasoning faculty. Assuming brain to be the organ of reason, this call to the performance of duty evidently does not come from brain, but from outside or above it. The hypothesis suggests itself that this call to duty comes from that upper self or globe. Possessing the sum of experiences of all former lives, it judges of our best course in life quite independently of the short-sighted wishes of its limited segment, and what we call obedience to duty is obedience to the course it suggests as in the long run the best for our real evolution. Duty, then, is an impulse whose reason we cannot know. So it remains to prove that outside of ourselves there is an actor, a thinker, a memory, not known to us in our ordinary consciousness, yet a part of ourselves, and occasionally forcing its thoughts upon us and compelling us to act apparently without reason. It cannot be proved, but in a study of Hypnotism we can find strong reason for thinking that this is so. I have to quote two more experiments from the Salpetrière record. A patient being hypnotized was made to promise that in a given number of days, I think as many as 140 after waking, and at a certain hour, she would come in, take up a knife on the table, and stab a doctor in the room. She awoke and departed as usual without memory of the promise. But nevertheless at the appointed time she appeared, entered the room, took up a wooden paper knife and tried to stab the doctor present. Asked to explain her conduct, she stated that she wanted to see how he would look, or gave some other trifling reason, but note that during all that time there must have been in activity *that* in her which had promised an activity not in her consciousness, but of which she was the tool, and which at the appointed time compelled of her the fulfilment of its promise. To explain to herself her own conduct, her brain-mind is obliged to go to work and invent a reason, not the true one. In the next experiment, during the sleep, words were traced on the patient's arm with the blunt end of a probe, and the order issued or promise extracted that on the following day, at four o'clock, blood would issue along the lines of the tracing. At the time named, minute bleeding took place in the prescribed manner, and the words stood dotted out in points of blood. In this case, the power called into activity within the patient, yet not within the field of his waking consciousness, exceeded any that he could in his normal state have used, since no man can control his bloodflow, yet it nevertheless acted punctually and exactly. So Hypnotism will prove that the consciousness of the waking man does not show him anything like the range of his memory or of his powers, and inasmuch as Hypnotism proves that both are existent in hitherto undreamed-of perfection, may we not venture to suggest that some other process so far not known to us might bring into consciousness the immeasurable ranges of past lives, and place in our hands powers like those assigned to saints and seers of the past ? This is the hypothesis of Theosophy. That there exists in man a real and eternal centre, Ego, or Soul, not omniscient, but still learning, not omnipotent, but still acquiring new powers, and that for these purposes it continuously dips into, or mixes itself with matter ; in other words, incarnates or lives. It is the actor who, in successive dramas, or lives, plays successive parts, becoming thereby a better actor, and earning time after time the right to greater parts. We in our ordinary selves are the parts it plays, and mistake the few yards of stage for a real world, and the stage furniture properties and scenery for real and desirable things. These are not in themselves of value, but only as training for the actor. We have, therefore, to recognise that we are not the person of the drama, but the actor who plays it. Suppose the actor while playing his part fell into the delusion that the part was the reality, lived in his dramatic and stagey personality, and could not be waked out of it. He would have lost the lesson in acting that the part could give, he would be fit for no other, and, lapsing into an asylum, he would cease to exist *as an actor*. The strictly materialist hypothesis is that consciousness, and the sensation of " I-ness " is a bundle or succession of impressions coming in from the world without ; not that consciousness or the man, the Ego, *receives* those impressions, but that it *consists* of them ; that the mind *is* a succession of changes without anything changed. Mivart presents us with a humorous analogy. Suppose that we could only conceive of a man as sitting down or standing up. The materialist, being asked what is a man, defines him as a succession of sittings down and standings up? We hold that the materialist has got only part of the matter. The real reincarnating soul projects a little of itself into the bodily brain that it may thus receive impressions from the outer world. Our everyday thinking, then, is a succession of changes or impressions which we call mind, or ourselves. Part of those impressions come from external objects through the senses, part from the body (the bodily desires and sensations), and a part, very few (the impulses to unselfishness and duty), from the true Soul above.

But this Soul is the thing impressed, and the substance whose impressed changes constitute mind. The theory then is this : the parents of a child produce its physical body only, after the pattern of either one or of a combination in different proportions of the two. The body thus produced becomes animated by an Ego or Soul, whose tendencies in its past life-time were such as entitled it to that particular body and environment. The consciousness of the being thus compounded being due to the union of its brain-cells with a portion or segment of the complete Soul is on a lower plane, less in quantity and darker in quality than the pure light of the Soul, since this Soul can only function through the crude and inert brain matter. Hence the brain, though sufficiently animated by the soul to think and know the outer qualities of nature, is unable to know of the past lives of that Soul, and were the facts of those past lives to be photographed into its cells, they would have no room to register the facts of the present life, and we should fool away life in dreams of the past. Hence this brain does not remember the past brain since it does not register its facts. Inaccurately calling the brain the man, we say the *man* does not remember his past life. Let us therefore keep strictly in mind that the man of one life is only an aspect, a segment of the complete man. Suppose we call the man of the past life A, the man of this life B, and the total man or Soul of which they are parts AB. Then, though it seems unjust that B should suffer for the sins of another man A, whom he never knew, and therefore does not remember, yet there is no real injustice, for the aim of nature is not exactly to educate, by suffering, A or B, but AB. The real actor, the individuality, grows and learns by the efforts and pains of its temporary fragments, its personalities, of which our present lives are one. Take the case of a man who in his last lifetime habitually over-ate and over-drank. The child-body into which a man is reborn is that which is in correspondence with the tendencies of his past life. The man in question, the glutton and drunkard, will therefore be attracted towards and animate that infant which has inherited from its parents a diseased liver or weak digestion. With these drawbacks it therefore goes crippled through life, with the habit of melancholy, the clouded brain, that they produce, fails in business, and ends perhaps with suicide. He thinks himself hardly used, but he is the natural outcome of the former man. The real self behind both, the producer of both, which in the first lifetime did so little to elevate its offspring, was so drawn to material enjoyment, is in the next life condemned to an inadequate and heavy vehicle. Hard, perhaps, for that conscious vehicle, but a vitally just and important lesson for the Soul. A man in his boyhood may be an infamous glutton, grow out of it as he gets older, and by old age have forgotten all about it, but his forgetting will not prevent his dyspepsia, the hard penalty of forgotten foolishness. So even in one lifetime we may get punished for forgotten deeds, and do not then think it unjust. Why should it be more unjust because the life in which the deeds were committed is forgotten? And there are few who would grumble at the injustice of being *rewarded* for good deeds in lives past. A brain well-used will be followed by a better one; a brain totally unused or blotted out by drink will be followed by that of an idiot. This is the law that Theosophists call Karma, and in it is the explanation of the diversities and qualities, the abilities and imbecilities of men. We are our own creators, we spend our lives moulding and chiselling a statue, and in our next lives we are that statue, though it has forgotten its creator. Schopenhauer spoke only Theosophy when he said that the World was the product of Will and Idea, The Idea, arising in the eternal Mind, is willing to express itself in matter, is copied or clothed in matter. As a man lives he is unconsciously fashioning a statue. With every act in life he is chipping it into form. If his aims are high, and his efforts great, the statue will gradually become noble in aspect. If he have no aim, but follow the sensual suggestions of his body, his statue grows to be the picture and the work of his sensuality. It is the product of his acts, and as these are prompted by shifting ideas, it comes to represent the total idea or sum of ideas of his life. It is his idea of himself, he dies, and his brain, laden with the facts of life, perishes, but the statue remains. That statue, when he is reborn, he animates with his consciousness; he is his own statue. It has not the facts of his past life, it knows not the acts, but it is their essence, it is a compound of all the ideas and impulses that inspired them. So a man is the creator of his future self, and the continuation of his past. It is in a sense an error to say we do not remember our past lives, for only the facts are forgotten. A man has forgotten the efforts through which he learnt to walk, the falls and aches and bruises, but he has remembered the one important thing—the art of walking. So life is a process of learning, and its pains the cast-aside husk that holds the kernel of knowledge. Every individual of humanity is moving up through his succession of lives towards the perfect final state, moulded thereto by the law of justice called Karma. Into the sources of that law we cannot look as yet; we can only note its tendencies and results. It is strange that the idea of a fixed sum of life on earth has not occurred to many more than the few who have speculated upon it. It has been reckoned axiomatic that the world-population has always steadily increased. But the waste places of the earth are continually displaying the ruins of vast and populous civilisations whose voices have not even reached the beginnings of recorded history; in our own day races are dying down, and the tide that here is flowing is there upon its ebb. If it be objected that the future of the sun will not allow of time for such an evolution of humanity as Theosophy postulates, let it be remembered that science knows no more about the sun than about anything else. It knows neither the reason nor the amount of its heat. Pouillet gives its temperature as 1,461°; Waterston as 9,000,000°. As to the reason, there are as many theories as theorisers. Mr. S. Laing calls them all in question, and Comte regarded it as a for ever insoluble problem. Laing asks, "What is the material universe composed of? Ether, Matter, Energy." "Ether is a sort of mathematical substance which we are compelled to assume in order to account for some phenomena." As to Matter, Huxley says, "We know nothing about the composition of any body whatever as it is." As to Energy, he says, "It is an empty shadow of my imagination." It might almost be said that no scientific statement can ever have any truth. Mr. Edward Carpenter thus analyses two of them. We are told that the path of the moon is an ellipse. But owing to perturbations supposed due to the sun, it is a certain ellipse only for an instant, the next it is a portion of another ellipse. The path is, therefore, an irregular curve somewhat resembling an ellipse. But while the moon is going round the earth, the earth itself is moving round the sun, in consequence of which the path of the moon does not at all resemble an ellipse. The sun itself is in motion round the fixed stars, and they also are moving. So we have not the faintest idea what is the path of the moon. "It is true that if we ignore the perturbations produced by the sun, the planets and other bodies ignore the motion of the earth, the flight of the solar system through space, and the movement of any centre, round which that may be speeding, we may then say that the moon moves in an ellipse. But this has nothing to do with the facts." He then takes Boyle's law of the compressibility of gases. This is the law that under a constant temperature the volume of gas is inversely as to its pressure. How does it work? Firstly, it is not accurate as to some gases, as hydrogen and carbonic acid Then all gases deviate from it when near their liquifying point, so it was concluded that it was true only for perfect gases. This involves the assumption that at a certain distance from their liquefying point gases reach at last a fixed and stable condition. Since then it is discovered that there is an ultra-gaseous state of matter, and that the change in the condition of matter from the solid to the ultra-gaseous states is perfectly continuous. Boyle's law, therefore, applies only at one point in this long ascending scale, one metaphysical point, and at all other points it is incorrect. "Therefore all we can say is that out of the innumerable different states that gases are capable of, we could theoretically find one state that would obey Boyle's law, and that if we could preserve a gas in that state (which we can't) Boyle's law really *would* be true. In other words the law is metaphysical, and has no real existence. This is the method of science. It begins by seizing some salient point, and forms a 'law' round that, neglecting apparently unimportant details. But these details are certain in time to arise and overpower the law thus formed. If you agree to take no account of gases that are approaching liquidity even in a remote degree, and if you agree to take no account of those that are approaching the ultra-gaseous state even in a remote degree, and if you choose your point between these two states with exact regard to the requirements of your problem, and if further you agree not to carry your experiments to great extremes of pressure or the reverse, you may thus by accepting limitation after limitation be able to say you have arrived at Boyle's law. But to represent that this 'law' in any way corresponds with a fact in nature is of course impossible. It is limitation which alone enables the intellect to grasp the situation."

Imagine a man with a scientific turn of mind passing through a long series of reincarnations. In his first lifetime he studies the science of the day, measures, weighs, finds out what he thinks are laws. At last he dies in the fulness of honours. After his death, in the course of years, all the face of science changes and a new set of laws reigns. Being born again, without memory of his former life, he studies and explores with the same innocent energy as before, quite unaware that every line he reads contradicts what in his last life he thought was true, and burnt the Theosophists of that day for denying. Again he dies, is reborn, repeats the same farce, always thinking that this is finality, and so on up to now. Now he is Huxley, but the Huxley of 1,000 years hence will speak with charitable pity of the Huxley of to-day, just as the Huxley of to-day smiles at the theories of Lucretius. Last night he dreamt and while dreaming took his dreams for truth, and even built up some science out of the foolish phantasms of his dreams, forgetting while dreaming that the night before he had also dreamt, and argued, and theorised upon the different, but equally foolish phantasms of *that* dream. But the waking Huxley remembers both dreams and knows them both for foolishness. Our successive lives are successive dreams. While dreaming we do not remember the former dreams, but the waking self knows them all. Theosophists hold that there exist men who have awaked, who have unified knowledge from the chaos of their dreams, who show us the way they have come and the philosophy apprehended by their waking minds. The segment of our souls that is steeped in brain sleeps, and to wake is to live up in the light of the whole Soul. Science is occupied in measuring and weighing the husk of nature, the changes in matter, ether, and energy, whereof it says nature consists. Theosophy holds that behind these lies conscious mind. We know that every thought in our own minds, every change in our consciousness, is attended by the development of heat, and according to science by changes in the atomic relationships in the physical brain molecules, and by the production of magnetic and electric effects. Why shall we not say that the reverse is true ; that wherever in nature there occurs a magnetic or electric change, a molecular re-arrangement or a development of heat, there is behind these a change in the conscious mind of nature? The evolutionary purpose of nature has gathered the primordial nebular matter into the coherency of minerals ; the same law working in the molecules of primordial protoplasm has forced them to develop the complexity of animal life and consciousness ; the same law in the centre of animal consciousness has compelled it to assume the complexity of human mind and consciousness. In the centre of mind is still working that eternal law of which mind is the outcome, which is the producer of mind and therefore above and behind mind, and in which mind lay inherent from the beginning as a seed. To find that fountain of force bubbling up in the centre of consciousness is according to Theosophy the end of reincarnations to which the law known to Theosophists as Karma tends. Science, then, has left mind out of nature, is speaking only of matter, ether, and energy, and has, therefore, to say that in themselves it knows nothing of these, for in themselves they are mind. It will not weigh much with Western minds of to-day that the doctrine of reincarnation is the creed of a majority of mankind now and in the past, nor of all Platinists and Neo-Platonists, from Plato to Emerson, nor of Origen, and other of the early church fathers. It has been, even in the West, advocated by Lessing, Hegel, Boehme, Swedenborg, Giordano Bruno, Leibnitz, Henry More, Schopenhauer, Sir Thomas Brown, Southey, and many others. Henry More says : " I produced the golden key of pre-existence only at a dead lift, when no other method could satisfy me touching the ways of God, that by this hypothesis I might keep my heart from sinking." Modern reincarnationists need not quake for the company they keep. Even Hume, the sceptic, argues the doctrine to be reasonable. " Reasoning from the common course of nature, what is incorruptible must also be ungenerable. The soul, therefore, if immortal, existed before our birth. The metempsychosis is, therefore, the only system of this kind that philosophy can hearken to."

In one sentence we therefore say that reincarnation is the one possible explanation of the moral and intellectual inequalities of men ; that by its aid only can justice be at the root of evolution, or evolution itself be possible for men ; and that in it only lies folded the history of the past of humanity and the promise of the future.

Some use has been made of " The Secret Doctrine," and much more of E. D. Walker's work on " Reincarnation."

THE TAROT CARDS.

It does not require anyone to be deeply read in the profundities of the Zohar to be aware how each several letter of the Holy Tetragrammaton was thought by the Cabbalistic writers to have a mystical significance.

Thus the initial letter of the ineffable NAME, the Yod, was by them regarded as the active principle of the self-creative power, the male; the Hé, the second letter, the passive, or the female; the third letter, the Vau, the mystic union of the first and second principles; and the fourth letter, the second Hé, again repeated, the transition, the ever-recurring continuity of יהוה.

Further, the Cabbalists thought by extending the letters of the NAME on the four arms of an equally membered cross, or on the circumference of a circle, to compare the eternal nature of Jehovah to a wheel or circle ever revolving; and by this symbol the perpetual renewal of His undivided unity, by the mystical action of each of the component principles of His nature flowing in everlasting rotation.

From this idea of a revolving wheel or circle, the Rota of the Mediæval Mystics was probably taken.

Rota is the anagram of Taro, Tora (Thora, in Hebrew, "The Law.")

The well-known magic square

```
Sator
Arepo
Tenet
Opera
Rotas
```

obviously has reference to this word.

There is a symbol of great antiquity, the cross enclosed in a circle, which may perhaps have a similar meaning to that the letters of the Tetragrammaton have when extended on a cross or circle; but the symbol has been in existence long before the time of the Mediæval Mystics, or, indeed, before the Cabbala had been written.

If some of the passages in the Zohar are closely followed and taken in a more literal sense than was perhaps intended by the writers, it will not be difficult to conceive how easily Phallic symbols came to be substituted, for the mystical meanings the Cabbalists connected with the letters of the Tetragrammaton.

It is not pleasant to introduce the Phallic element in reference to the NAME, but it is necessary to do so to understand the meaning of the symbols on the Tarot Cards.

In short, then, the Yod becomes the Phallus ; the Hé the Cteis ; and Vau, a figure similar to the Indian Lingam Yoni, &c.

The wandering tribes known by the various names of Gypsies, Bohemians, Zingari, have for many centuries been in possession of playing cards bearing very singular symbols.

Instead of having the Clubs, Hearts, Spades, and Diamonds of modern playing cards, these cards have in their place, as they are termed by French authors, the Tarot, the Baton, Coupe, Epée, and Denier. (This last represents, or is the name of, an ancient coin or circle.)

The Baton is also described as a staff, club, or budding rod.

The Coupe . . . .

The Epée is generally represented as a sword piercing a crown.

And the Denier, as a disc with a lotus or lily flower in the centre, a centre or a ring.

These cards have been used by the Bohemian gypsies for centuries for fortune telling, and are called Tarot Cards.

A game is still played with ordinary modern cards in Bohemia called Taroc.

It can hardly be a matter of accident that the symbols or hieroglyphics on these Taro cards should so closely resemble, as will be seen, the mystical Phallic ideas which the writers of the Zohar dared to connect with the letters of that NAME which they considered it to be blasphemous to utter.

Take, firstly, the Cabbalistic idea of the extended NAME.

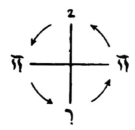

Secondly, the idea of the mystics, who substituted the letters of Taro or Rota for the Hebrew letters.

Thirdly, substitute for these the Phallic idea derived from the Cabbala.

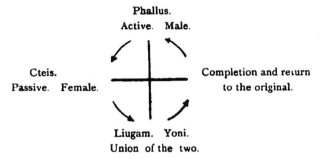

And fourthly, in place of these, substitute the symbols of the Taro.

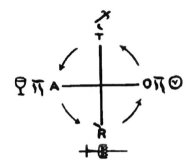

It is almost unnecessary to explain that the Baton, Club, Sceptre = the Phallus.   Coupe, Cup = the Cteis.

Sword piercing the Crown = Lingam.   Yoni Circle = Return of the Divine Nature to itself again in eternal repetition.

The Circle, or Disc, may also represent the double of the Cup; by one Cup being inverted on the other, Generator became Creator.

In modern English cards one of these has perhaps been preserved in the name of Club, and another in that of the Spade.

The double triangle also which forms the Diamond is a well-known sign which, according to mystical authorities, in some degree corresponds to the Circle.

The Heart does not, however, either in form or name, bear any resemblance to the Coupe or Cup of the Tarot.

So far as regards the Cabbalistic origin of these curious signs, an origin which the Count de Gebelin and the more recent French mystics, including the author who writes under the name of Eliphas Levi, have attempted to prove. But have they had their origin from this source ? It seems more probable that these Tarot hieroglyphics had their origin far to the eastward of the land of the Cabbalists or of the authors of the Zohar.   And it is a remarkable thing that, if their origin is from India, they should so closely coincide with the Symbolism, which might be given to the notions of the authors of the Zohar, on the mystical meaning of the letters of the Tetragrammaton. That they are of Indian origin seems more than probable, for does not the Hindù double sexed God and Goddess Arddha-Nari (Isis, Nature) bear in his or her four hands symbols identically the same as those on the Tarot Cards?

The Sceptre or Bâton, the Sword, the Cup, and the Circle or Ring.

The order is not the same, but thus:

Sceptre.	Sword.
Cup.	Ring.

This is no doubt a curious fact, and it goes far also to show that India was the original country of the Gipsy Tribes.

The French writers gave much more importance to these Tarot Symbols than they deserve, and every sensible person will protest against such a profanation of Holy Names, by using authropomorphic emblems such as these.

But the Symbols themselves are curious, and show the similarity of Phallic notions among peoples so far removed from each other by both distance and culture as the Hindûs and the writers of the Zohar.

Every being is at ease when its powers move regularly and without interruption. Now, a rational being is in this prosperous condition when its judgment is gained by nothing but truth and evidence, when its designs are all meant for the advantage of society, when its desires and aversions are confined to objects within its power, when it rests satisfied with the distributions of the universal nature of which it is a part, just as much as a leaf belongs to the nature of the tree that bears it. Only with this difference, that a leaf is part of a nature without sense or reason, and liable to be checked in its operations, whereas is a limb as it were of an intelligent, righteous, and irresistible being, that is all wisdom, and assigns matter and form, time, force, and fortune, to everything in one measure and proportion. And this you will easily perceive if you do not compare one thing with another in every detail, but compare the whole of one thing with the whole of another.

MEDITATIONS—*Marcus Aurelius.*

THEOSOPHY AND DOGMA.

(Reprinted from LUCIFER, *June,* 1889.)

THEOSOPHY has many aspects, and derives its inspiration not from one source only, not from one teacher merely, or from one set of sacred writings, but from all.

This is a fact which it appears most difficult to impress upon the world at large, and upon the opponents of Theosophy in particular. Men are so accustomed to regulate their opinions by some particular creed or dogma, which they suppose to rest upon some *authority* beyond which there is no appeal, that they cannot grasp the wider aspect of human duty and human destiny which Theosophy presents.

If we examine any of those exclusive and contradictory religious systems on which, in some form or another, men blindly rely, we find at once a broad distinction drawn between believers and unbelievers, between those who are within and those who are without the favour of God, betweeen the lost and the saved. But Theosophy knows no such distinctions as these, neither any difference of race, colour or creed.

The spiritual sun shines alike on the good and on the evil, and the water of life descends both on the just and on the unjust. It rests with each individual to make the proper use of those spiritual forces which are ever emanating from the divine source of our being.

We must do this first by faith, and secondly by knowledge. If we have no faith in the divine spark that burns within us, we shall make no efforts to let that spark illumine and guide our life; and on the other hand, if we have faith without knowledge, we shall still be groping in the dark, and will surely mistake the false light of some earth-born system of religion, for the divine light that burns only in the innermost sanctuary of our own hearts.

We must use the spiritual forces in nature in the same way that we make use of physical forces. If a man does not work in harmony with the laws of nature, he will find opposition instead of help; if he sow not in accordance with nature's law, he will reap naught but disappointment and pain. We need faith in the first place, faith in the unity and continuity of natural laws, and faith in our own divine nature, but no amount of faith will enable us to produce the desired result if we do not add to faith knowledge. Theosophy carries this principle right up to the highest spiritual plane, and does not recognise at any point the intervention of an arbitrary personal will, which can make a man other than that which he himself chooses. All are subject to the law of Karma, but Karma is that which each individual makes for himself; it is the law of cause and effect in relation to his own free will.

The will of man is as free as the will of God, and becomes, indeed, that will itself when the man has realised his divine nature, and by crucifying his lower principles has effected the at-one-ment.

It is the most common misconception, then, and the hardest to eradicate, that Theosophy consists in a belief in certain doctrines; that it is in fact nothing more or less than a religious creed.

What then we shall be asked are those doctrines which Theosophists everywhere profess to hold, and which they appear most anxious to teach the world? What is Esoteric Buddhism and the Secret Doctrine, or Reincarnation and Karma, if not a body of doctrines which are intended to supplant other religious creeds and dogmas?

The answer to this is, that these doctrines are the embodiment of certain broad generalisations concerning the history and evolution of humanity; that they are the key which enables us to harmonise certain facts which would otherwise appear isolated and antagonistic. They are in no way analogous to the dogmas and creeds of the religious sects, but answer more nearly to such generalisations of science as the laws of gravity or the conservation of energy. It is not claimed for them that they are necessary articles of belief, neither that they are in their present form accurately and literally true. They are stepping-stones to a higher knowledge of the divine element in human nature, and of the laws physical, psychical, and spiritual by which we are conditioned. If we ask a scientific man what gravity or energy are, he cannot tell us, but no one will deny that the laws which have been formulated respecting their action of manifestation have been most powerful aids in scientific investigations. Now, it is precisely thus with the doctrines of Theosophy. Once these doctrines are understood they give a man an immensely wider view of humanity, and raise him above those narrow and limited conceptions of God and his dealings with individuals, of which so many contradictory assertions are made by various religions, and the innumerable sects into which they are split up.

What practical relation then has Theosophy to our every-day life? We reply that practical Theosophy is identical with practical religion.

It comes from the heart and not from the head. It is the spontaneous love for one's fellow-creatures, which, taking possession of a man, leads to noble acts of self-sacrifice; to right action done simply because it is right, and without any reference to the merit of the act, or any thought of recognition or reward.

Theosophy aims at nothing short of perfection of character; but character as expressed in outward acts is the result of an inward condition. The root of action lies deep down in the inner consciousness. It is the man's thoughts, desires, and innermost convictions which give rise to action. Act does not produce character, is not even a true indication of it, for a right action may be done from a wrong motive. Act is the result of character.

Right action must be based upon right thought, right motive, and right knowledge, and it is just here that the study of the doctrines of Theosophy is of such value to those who are seeking for firm ground to stand upon amid all the conflicting dogmas and controversies of the age, for it provides a basis which is independent of any religious system, and yet includes them all in their inner or esoteric meaning. There is not much difficulty in distinguishing between a right and a wrong action *per se*, but there is a great difference between the man who is merely moral through habit or temperament, and one who is actively beneficent because of the love for humanity which animates him. Moreover, there will be a great difference in the actions of a man who believes in the doctrine of original sin and the atonement, and one who believes in reincarnation and Karma.

Theosophy, therefore, as a system, seeks to influence men by giving them a right basis of thought. It seeks to counteract on the one hand, the materialistic and atheistic teachings of modern science, and on the other hand, the narrow, exclusive, and demoralising teachings of dogmatic and formal religion.

But Theosophy as a system is something even more than this. Theosophy does not seek merely to destroy superstition, but it seeks to build up a new edifice constructed of those very materials which have been so perverted in their uses by centuries of priestcraft and ecclesiasticism. Theosophy is based upon a deeper wisdom, a more interior meaning of those sacred books of all nations, which form the foundation of so many religious systems.

Each one must verify the doctrines of Theosophy for himself, and in doing so will probably find new light and fresh inspiration in those particular records which he has been accustomed to regard as the basis of his faith; and he will also be able to recognise the same meaning in the sacred books of other faiths, which hitherto he may have been accustomed to regard as " heathen," and as being contradictory and opposed to his own.

Theosophy, then, has two main aspects, the theoretical and the practical. These two must harmonise: practice must be based upon theory, and if the theory has been rightly understood, the practice can hardly fail to be in accord with it. Theosophy offers a motive and a moral stimulus free from fear, superstition, or lip worship, but full of divine love. It is practice that makes a Theosophist, and not profession. The Theosophical Society as a body and an organisation seeks to teach the theory, while each individual member must practise so much of the theory as he has been able to assimilate, in his every-day life, in his relations with his fellow-men, and in his inmost thoughts and desires.

Standing free from fear or superstition, let each one make obeisance only to the dim star that burns within. " Steadily, as you watch and worship, its light will grow stronger. Then you may know you have found the beginning of the way. And when you have found the end its light will suddenly become the infinite light."

WILLIAM KINGSLAND,

President of the " Blavatsky Lodge, T. S."

The Press Department of the British Section, Theosophical Society, is not as well served by the Fellows as it should be. Every Theosophist who sees, in any paper, any reference to matters Theosophical, is requested to immediately send a "marked" copy of the paper to MRS. CLEATHER, 19, *Gayton Road, Harrow-on-the-Hill. Each Fellow is asked to regard this as a personal duty, to be rigidly discharged.*

The article on the "Tarot" in T.P.S., v. 3, No. 10, was inserted by the printers in error, after proofs were passed and too late for correction.

CREMATION

CONSIDERED FROM THE POINT OF VIEW OF THE RELIGIONS OF THE EAST.

AN ADDRESS

delivered March 1st, 1890, in the hall of the " Scientific Club " at Vienna, on the occasion of the yearly assembly of the Society of the Friends of Cremation, "The Flame," by FRANZ HARTMANN, M.D.

LADIES AND GENTLEMEN,—

In thanking you most heartily for the opportunity offered me of addressing you on the religious views which form the basis of cremation in India, I must beg of you to permit me to preface the same by a few personal remarks. It happens that the subjects on which I purpose addressing you must appear to most of you quite new and strange, because they refer to facts on which very little light has been thrown as yet in Europe. They refer to mysteries of religions which the Buddhists and Brahmins do not very willingly surrender to publicity, and which, also, are somewhat difficult to understand by the uninitiated. Nevertheless, I shall endeavour to elucidate my subject as clearly as is possible in a short address. I would further beg of you not to think that I intend propagating a new religion. I merely give the results of my own observation, and each one is at liberty to think what he likes about it. There may be possibly some among you who think that the religious views of the Hindus are based only on superstition. Others, again, may have come to the conclusion that these views are founded on the deeper penetration of Indian methods into the secrets of Nature. I do not undertake to give any judgment in this matter. I leave to every one perfect freedom to believe what he thinks right.

The foundations on which the religions of the East are based are still very little known to our Orientalists and philologists. These investigators are, as a rule, occupied with researches into the origin of certain words, or with historical events and other extraneous matters, but certainly not with inquiries respecting Eternal Truth, which is only approachable by spiritual perception. One may have spent one's whole life in India without becoming acquainted with its religious mysteries, just as one may be for long years a diligent church-goer without acquiring a knowledge of the true nature of Christianity. And I also should not have been able to tell you anything about these things had I not joined an association which includes many Brahmins, Buddhists, and others, who enabled me to become better acquainted with the nature of these religions, not only on the surface, but also with the truth which forms their basis.

With regard to Cremation, I must confess that I have hitherto felt an interest in it only so far as its sanitary aspect must attract the attention of a medical man. It is as much a matter of indifference to me whether my body is to be burned or buried after death as what will happen to my cast-off coat. I have also never considered whether *I* ought to be burned or buried, and if any such expression were used it would be incorrect and a wrong mode of speaking, because that which is the real man can neither be burned or buried. That which is interred is only the earthly body, and *one ought not to identify oneself with that even in idea.* Our children who still feel and think naturally, whose nature is not yet spoiled by sophistry, speak more correctly. They say, *e.g.,* " Mamma, Charles is hungry," or " Papa, Mary wants to go to sleep," instead of " I am hungry," etc. In doing so they are right, because the true " I " of man, which (alas!) but few of us know, is not hungry, nor does he want to go to sleep, but he is rather a god raised high above everything that is perishable or transitory. The sages of the East use the same mode of speaking as our children. They say, *e.g.,* " My nature wants this or that ; my body feels ; my mind thinks," etc. The mysterious " I " always remains hidden in the background.

If we investigate more precisely what man really is, we shall find he is made up of many " I's," *i.e.,* of many forms of consciousness, which are continually changing, and that he is always that " I," *i.e.,* that form of consciousness with which he at the time identifies himself. We shall return later on to these different " I's " or forms of consciousness, which, to speak with Goethe, make up " that little world which thinks itself the whole," when we consider the real constitution of man, according to the Indian doctrine ; we shall then find that that " I " of man which is perishable by fire, may stand even after death in a certain connection with that " I " which is imperishable.

To speak first of my own experience, I must say that, although I have never paid much attention to modes of interment, I have, while on my travels, had frequent opportunities of observing them. For instance, nearly thirty years ago I went as ship's doctor to America, lived in different parts of the United States and Mexico ; then travelled through California, Japan, China, and India, and witnessed in these countries, as well as in Ceylon, on many occasions, the ceremony of burying the dead. As well as I remember, one of the first bodies cremated in America was that of the Baron de Palm, which Colonel Olcott had publicly burned, after keeping it concealed for a whole year in his cellar in a barrel of chloride of lime. It is noticeable that in America, although a free country, and not subject to guardianship by Government, reforms are not easily inaugurated. There is there, the same as here, a public opinion which is led by men of letters, clergymen and others, and, as elsewhere, the ground must first be prepared before a new seed or a new idea can take root and be developed. There, as here, a strong opposition was raised. Part of the clergy maintained that cremation was not permissible, as it prevented the resurrection of the body at the last judgment ; others again, more enlightened Theologians, contradicted this by explaining that this resurrection must take place in a living body, not in a decayed one, and that what is meant by this is the spiritual interpenetration of the whole living body by the soul, illumined by the Divine Light. To this must be added that in America there is no State Church protected by the Government, but instead there are about 360 sects, who all differ in opinion and are in mutual conflict. The Church was therefore unable to support its prohibition by force.

The lawyers and doctors maintained, as they do here, that in cases of death by poison, Cremation would render subsequent inquiry impossible as proof of a possible crime. On the other hand, it was well said it were better that once in a way a death by poison should remain unproved than that hundreds of thousands of human beings should lose their lives by an atmosphere made deadly by corpses, or by drinking water poisoned by graves. It could be as readily objected that the body of a man who had died at sea should not be entrusted to the waves, but that it should remain and infect the whole ship, in order that hereafter the possibility should not be interfered with of proving that the patient died in accordance with natural causes.

This view found its support in the fact that the poisoning of towns by churchyards in America was a not infrequent occurrence. It often happens, on account of the quick growth of American towns, a cemetery which has been laid out at some distance, within a few years comes to be situated in the central part of the town. So, for example, in New Orleans, in Louisiana, there are several large cemeteries in the centre of the town. As water is found there within two feet of the surface, the bodies are not interred there, but entombed above the surface, where they poison the atmosphere instead of the water. We see by this that we should purchase, by the prohibition of Cremation, a very small advantage at the price of a very great disadvantage. But that the poisoning of the air and of drinking-water by the interment of the dead is no picture of the imagination, we find amply proved in the East.

When you come to Madras or any other town in India where there are many Mahommedans, who, as is well known, bury their dead, you find that such a town consists, so to speak, of houses and cemeteries. Here a house, there graves; then again a few houses, then more graves, just because the graves of Mahommedans are always dug in the nearest possible vicinity to the houses. Scattered between them are wells; and you can easily believe that the water from these is of such a non-vegetarian character that it is impossible to drink it unless filtered through charcoal. But the poor have no filters, so there are outbreaks of cholera and other diseases, which then spread over Europe.

I had the honour of becoming acquainted, in the course of a journey from Ceylon to Madras, with Dr. Koch, who discovered that cholera is caused by a bacillus. If the same pains had been taken to *discover and prevent the general causes* which *permit* the bacillus to *originate, it would perhaps have been less useful to science, but far more useful to humanity.*

Cremation is universal with the Hindus, and in every town are to be found special places for that purpose. As one meets here in our streets hearses, so one meets there carriers, who are bearing on a litter the dead body unveiled to the cremation place. On arriving there it is laid on a pyre, melted butter (ghee) poured over it, and then burned amid certain ceremonials. Amongst the rich the pyre consists of sandal and other aromatic woods, the ceremonial is magnificent, and the whole proceeding is very costly. Amongst the poor little trouble is taken, and such a Cremation costs only about two rupees. In Burmah each body is placed separately in an old flour barrel, covered with straw and such like material, and is then burned.

In addition to these various modes of disposing of the dead, I will describe that of the Parsees. These allow the body to be taken by birds or dogs. When you go to Bombay you must not neglect to visit the "Towers of Silence." These are the cemeteries of the Parsees. A great tower-like building is provided with a roof which slopes inwards towards the centre of the tower, where there is a deep pit. The bodies are laid upon the roof, and immediately a swarm of carrion vultures, which are constantly on the watch for the arrival of a corpse, swoop down upon it, and devour it within a very few minutes. The well-picked bones then roll down the roof and fall into this deep pit. The idea which underlies this mode of interment is that our Mother—the element earth—should be sacred to us, and that we should not desecrate her with anything that is dead. Besides this, by this mode of interment the component particles which form the human body are quickly incorporated in other living organisms.

Besides Cremation, there obtained in India not long ago the rite of suttee, *i.e.*, the burning of the living widows together with the corpse of the husband, a custom which has now ceased by the intervention of the English. The religious idea which was the foundation of this burning of widows originated in the fact that it is said in the Indian Sacred Scriptures, if husband and wife are united in fire, one hundred thousand years in Swarga (a state of the highest bliss) shall be the result. This sentence in the Vedas was taken quite literally, and produced as its effect this burning of widows. But in reality it has quite a different and much deeper meaning, namely, if we understand "husband" as the male principle, the *thought*, and "wife" as the female principle, the *will*, there is produced by the union of both in the fire of love, that *spiritual perception* the natural effect of which is a state of high and enduring bliss. It is this that is meant by the Indian Sacred Scriptures, which, like our Bible, speak in allegories. This secret interpretation was unknown to the ordinary priests as well as to the laymen, who were incapable of such high comprehension.

As with us a merely dead letter and superficial interpretation of certain biblical passages led to the Inquisition and the burning of witches, so also in India a false interpretation of the Vedas led to various abuses. Amongst these the best known is perhaps the formerly universal evil custom of Jaggernath, namely, on certain days a colossal car, with monstrous wheels, was drawn through the streets by elephants. The populace crowded round to see a supposed dwarf (Jaggernath) contained in the car. During this many were crowded under the wheels and lost their lives, through which they were supposed to acquire eternal bliss. Then, at last, it became the custom that the most believing ones threw themselves under the wheels, and, like so many Christian saints, sought voluntarily the martyr's death. That which lies at the foundation of this religious aberration is as follows:—By the car of Jaggernath is to be understood the human constitution, in the innermost depths of which the Divine Spirit dwells in secret. Whoever recognises this Divine Spirit in himself thereby acquires the Divine Self-consciousness and Conscious Immortality. For this purpose of course it is useless to allow himself to be crushed by an elephant car, just as a Christian martyr does not become either more intelligent or more reasonable for being flayed alive.

It would be easy for me to cite other and varied instances of this kind to show what an amount of evil a false interpretation of Sacred Scriptures can produce. Here in Europe it is customary for us to laugh at this kind of thing, and yet we need not go far to find similar instances.

Also with us the Bible is interpreted superficially, and falsely expounded by both learned and laity, and the true meaning is not grasped. Nowadays there are probably only a few who believe that Adam and Eve in Paradise stole ordinary apples, such as are to be bought here in the fruit market.

It is assumed that this allegory represents how primeval man, who was a high and divine being, plucked the fruit from the tree of the knowledge of good and evil by beginning to think and will for himself, and thereby losing his purely spiritual perception. It was strongly objected to me by learned Brahmins that there are still many more passages in the Bible which are wrongly read by us. For example it says, " Whosoever would follow me must leave father and mother and all things." Now the Brahmins say that this means that we must leave our own prejudices and opinions, which in a certain sense are our own spiritual parents, and also all sinful inclinations, if we would arrive at the knowledge of Eternal Truth. Nevertheless there have been cases where persons have run away from their earthly parents to enter a cloister, and expected that God would reward them for it.

It says, for example, that a camel can sooner pass through the eye of a needle than a rich man enter into heaven. The Brahmins say that that means that he who is rich in opinions and illusions of his own, to which his heart clings, cannot reach that state of contentment and blessedness which is the result of the true knowledge of God in his own heart. But there have been persons (though they have become rarer now in consequence of widespread disbelief) who read the passage superficially, and who gave their possessions to the Church without reflecting that if this superficial reading were the correct one, the *rich* Church would be the very last that could enter into heaven.

A case is known to me in which a man in Illinois attempted to imitate the example of Abraham's readiness to sacrifice his son, because he believed that God also in this case would intervene at the last moment. Had this man first consulted the Brahmins, they would have told him that by Abraham must be understood the universal man, and by Isaac, the self-will, and that when Abraham is prepared to resign his own will completely to the will of God, then God still permitted him to retain his own will, which by this sacrifice had become of a divine nature. But the man referred to above took the passage literally, and as no Divine Being appeared to stop his hand, he actually did slay his son, for which he soon found himself, not in prison, but in a lunatic asylum.

We will not pursue these comparisons any farther. But I would still like to mention that the burning alive of widows was not carried out by force as frequently believed, and that the widow was not cast into the fire against her will. They submitted voluntarily to be burned, and even now, although it has been abrogated, many wives still become victims to suicide at the death of their husbands, not from grief, but from religious conviction. To this should be added that a widow is exposed to the contempt of the rabble, because Hindus and Buddhists are all adherents to the doctrines of Re-incarnation and Karma. In other words, they believe that the personality of man is only a transitory phenomenon, and that sooner or later after death the spiritual force which dwells within him will again call into being another personality (*i.e.*, will re-incarnate), the life of which will have a certain connection with the previous personality. They believe, further, that everything is subject to the Karmic law of Divine Justice, so that when the first personality has led a vicious life, the second personality, possessing a spiritual individuality identical with the first, has to suffer for it. The doctrine of Re-incarnation or Re-embodiment of the spirit in human bodies, and the doctrine of Karma or Divine Justice, of the truth of which about 400 millions of dwellers on this earth are convinced, are too elevated to be fully represented in a short address. To speak briefly, they are based on the idea that the *character* of a thing is the essential, and the *form* in which it presents itself to us is only an appearance.

It is this distinguishing of the true essence from its outward appearance which differentiates the scientific and religious systems of the sages of the East from those of the West. According to certain views of the West, man is a developed ape. According to the views of the Indian sages, which also coincide with those of the philosophers of past ages and with the teachings of the Christian mystics, man is a god, who is united during his earthly life, through his own carnal tendencies, to an animal (his animal nature). The God who dwells within him endows man with wisdom. The animal endows him with force. After death *the god effects his own release from the man* by departing from the animal body. As man carries within him this divine consciousness, it is his task to battle with his animal inclinations, and to raise himself above them, by the help of the divine principle, a task which the animal cannot achieve, and which therefore is not demanded of it.

When I speak of the "religions of the East," I mean by that the broad foundations on which all those religions rest, although there may be in different systems various deviations. We are not concerned with investigating how far the separate religious sects of the East differ from one another. When we know the basis which is common to them all, we have, as it were, a bird's-eye view of the whole, and we shall then perceive that Christianity also rests on the same foundation, because there exists only one sole universal and Eternal Truth, and whatever is true in any religion has its root in this.

The word "Religion" is derived from "religere," and represents the perception of the relation borne by man to his spiritual origin; in other words, religion is the knowledge of the true nature of man and his position in the universe. To study this kind of religion it is necessary to free ourselves from all customary conceptions of that which is called "matter" and to conceive the whole world as merely a mode of manipulation, comparable to a picture that is produced on a wall by a magic lantern, and which disappears again as soon as the light in the lantern is extinguished. We can look upon the world if we choose, with Schopenhauer, who has grasped the Indian doctrine, as a product of will and representation, or, better still, with Jacob Boehme, as the emanation of the Divine Universal Will, the effect of which is Representation. We can also express this in other words, as when we say, *Brahm* (God) *is All* in All. As the pictures of a magic lantern exist by means of its light, so do the material things of which this world of appearances consists originate from the Divine force which dwells within them.

Man also is included in these forms of appearance. According to the Indian doctrine the visible body of man is but a very small part of the real being of man, which is invisible to the outer senses, and may be compared to a nebula in the heavens, which extends over millions of miles, but of which only the innermost shining spot is clearly discernible.

In accordance with these views the world is a universal consciousness, that expresses itself in the most diverse ways in minerals, plants, animals, men, gods, and other beings, and which produces forms corresponding to the character of these beings. Man also is such a form of consciousness. In his thoughts and feelings a continual change of forms of consciousness takes place, a constant swaying to and fro between the higher and the lower. At one time the expanse of his emotional nature is agitated by passions, which again is succeeded by a period of rest. These forms of consciousness produce the various "I's" of man, of which I spoke at the commencement. For man is that which he feels and thinks, and with his feelings and thoughts changes also his form of consciousness, his outward "I." One can, therefore, become also, without re-incarnation, "quite a different person." Only the true, the divine "I," of which most men know nothing, is immortal and eternal.

Hindus and Buddhists, and also the Christian Mystics, divide these forms of consciousness which constitute man into different groups, which I will here refer to cursorily, because, as you will see, Cremation stands in a certain relation to them. I regret that, as my time is limited, I can only convey to you the general fundamental laws of these divisions.

The highest form of consciousness is the Divine *Atma*, or that which we know as God or Christ in man, a form of consciousness which only those possess in whom the divine life has ɔeen awakened—those, in other words, who are *true* Christians, even though they adhere in their outward opinions to the Hindus, Jewish, Mahommedan, or other system, or to no system at all.

You will all easily conceive that the Divine Spirit or *Atma* cannot reveal itself in its perfection in an animal soul. The higher spiritual perception in which the divine in man (Jesus in man) reveals itself is called by the Buddhists "*Buddhi*." It is also taught in Christian doctrine, that no one can go to the Father except through the Son; this means (the Hindus maintain) that man must first have come to divine consciousness (to Christ) before he can conceive the Deity in his true grandeur.

Opposed to this spiritual soul of man is an animal consciousness, or "*Kama-rupa*" (the form produced by the desire for earthly existence), in which the passions and sensual inclinations reside, and which every man feels within himself, although the dissecting knife has not as yet demonstrated this scientifically.

Between "*Atma-Buddhi*" and "*Kama-rupa*" comes the proper human consciousness called by the Buddhists "*Manas*." It is that called "Mind" in English, and in German (incorrectly) the human soul. This is the seat of true human thought and will, and of the intellectual faculties which are contained in it, like the seed grain in a field. It is the "Manas," but not the Divine Spirit, which is constantly influenced by the higher and lower, and in reference to which Goethe says in Faust:—

> " Du bist dir nur des einen Triebs bewusst ;
> O lerne nie den andern (den niedern) kennen.
> Zivei Seden wohnen, ach ! in meiner Brust,
> Die eine will sich von der andern trennen ;
> Die eine hält in derber Liebeslust
> Sich an die Welt, mit klammernden Organen,
> Die and're hebt gewaltsam sich vom Dust
> Zu den Gefilden hoher Ahnen."

The lowest form of consciousness is the animal body. As, according to Hindu doctrine, everything in the world is the expression of the Universal Will, and as a particular consciousness resides in every kind of will, so the body of man can also be nothing else than a certain form of consciousness; but that it has a consciousness of its own, and differing from that of Manas, is shown by the reflex movements, *e.g.*, in epilepsy, where the mind loses its control over the muscles. This body of man, which is the outward expression of the inner man and the object of our anthropology, is the only part of the grand constitution of Man that is accessible to exact scientific investigation, for as exact (*i.e.*, outward) science can only make use of outward means, so it can also only occupy itself with outward things, perceptible by the senses. For a deeper knowledge, an awakening of the inner spiritual senses would be required, *i.e.*, a higher spiritual development.

It is this exterior animal body which is burnt, during Cremation, after it has lost by death its consciousness and sensation, and which should be destroyed as soon as possible, so that it should not be a cause of danger to the living through chemical decomposition.

But between the physical body, which is the seat of the principle of life, and the intellectual principle of man (the Manas), there is another thing, viz., "The astral body," described by Theophrastus Paracelsus, Cornelius Agrippa, and many other mystics, and which is called by the Hindus "Linga Sarira." This astral is a very peculiar thing, and has very extraordinary qualities. It is the exact counterpart of the exterior body, and its consciousness can reveal itself independently of that of the outward body. It is known to some of us as the "Double," and it is the mysterious cause, as yet unexplained by science, of innumerable visions of ghosts and mystical experiences. In a healthy man this astral body is closely and inseparably united to the exterior body. During many forms of illness and other abnormal states its connection with the outward body may, however, become loosened, and such persons then believe that they see their own spirit, or become mediums, so called. It is not at all rare that during severe illness a patient complains that besides him there is another person in the bed, but who really is also himself. To speak briefly, a dividing of consciousness takes place here, which reveals itself as two forms.

It would take us long before we could conclude, if we wished to more particularly enumerate all the qualities which are ascribed to these astral bodies by the Hindus. It will suffice to say for the purpose we have in view to-day that this body, viewed from an outer standpoint, is a semi-material thing which is intimately connected with the exterior body, and which also does not separate from it after death, so long as a trace of the latter still remains.

The Hindu teaches this when the man dies, *i.e.*, when Atma-Buddhi-Manas departs from the body, he leaves behind two corpses, viz., the quite dead physical body, and the astral body, which can be, according to circumstances, quite unconscious, semi-conscious, or even fully self-conscious.

The astral body has namely, like all the other principles which form the constitution of man, its own form of consciousness, which develops during life, according to circumstances, in one direction or another.

In a man, *e.g.*, who, during life, strives only for the noble, the elevated and the spiritual, the consciousness of the astral body (which comprises the merely animal and non-intelligent principle) will only be slight. On the contrary, in another, who yields himself up wholly to the passions, hate, etc., this consciousness of the astral body, which, so to speak, becomes concentrated in him, can persist for a very long time, even when the body is already decomposing. Such a man becomes after death (so say the Indian sages) a " Bhut," *i.e.* a devil, or ghost. He has then no reason by which he can exercise self-control (as this belongs to the higher principles, which have already departed from him), he acts according to his impulse and his nature. It is not my intention to dilate on many marvellous tales of vampires, etc., which are laid to the charge of these God-forsaken Astral men; I will only remark that the most terrible thing a Hindu can represent to himself is, to become after death a *" Bhut."* One can, if one likes, explain away all these things as superstition. But I have known persons who were "clairvoyant," and who maintained that they saw in cemeteries floating forms of corpses buried there, and that this sight was so loathsome that, if everyone had the gift of the inner sight, Cremation would soon become universal, as cemeteries would not be endured any longer.

To liberate this astral body from the corpse and to lead it to its dissolution into the elements of which it is composed, is one of the aims of the Hindus in Cremation.

I have chanced to look to-day into Goethe's " Faust," and the following lines bearing on the above met my eye :—

> " Man kann auf gar nichts mehr vertrauln ;
> Sonst mit tem letzten Athemzage fuhr sie aug
> Tich passt ihr auf, und wie die schnellste Maus,
> Schraps hielt ich sie in festverschlossnen Klauen.
> Nun zaudert sie und will den düstern Oet,
> Des schlechten Leichnams ekles Haus nicht lassen ;
> Die Elemente, die sie hassen,
> Die Reiben sie am Ende schmählich fort."

It is just this that Cremation accomplishes ; that which decomposition only slowly brings about, fire, as the most powerful of all elements, achieves very quickly.

Evidently the "soul" of which Mephistopheles speaks refers to the astral body and to the animal element, " Nephesch," united to it, because the divine in man, " Ruach," cannot be carried off by the devil ; only that which is evil becomes the prey of the evil principles. But that the astral body is something material, but nevertheless pervades the whole physical body, is nothing particularly remarkable, because we are well aware that, *e.g.*, silver is also something very material, but nevertheless pervades, when it is dissolved in union with nitric acid in water, the whole material liquid likewise. And as, by the addition of a little table salt, the silver again separates and becomes visible as chloride of silver, so also a separation or manifestation of the astral body can take place, under various abnormal conditions, in the constitution of man.

The greatest of all German philosophers, Jacob Boehme, from whose writings most of our later philosophers have taken their ideas, compares the astral life to fire—the soul is flame, the spirit is light. Wood is a visible body. Now when light has disappeared with the flame, the wood or the charcoal can still glow for a time, and likewise the fire of passion or desire can, when the spiritual soul has fled, still maintain for a moderate time the lower forms of will in a sort of phantom life.

In conclusion I beg to observe that, according to Hindu doctrine, death is but a change of form. That which is of a divine nature, *i.e.*, immortal, separates from the impure and mortal, and each part continues its own development. That the whole man is not immortal is shown by the simple view of a corpse. But if man has something immortal in him, and if there is something divine in man, then, as God is immortal, the divine in man must also be immortal. But if man is not aware of this divine in him, his immortality will be of as little use to him as it would be to anyone to possess a million of money without having any knowledge of the fact. But whoever finds the divine in himself finds also with it his own immortality, and knows it, and does not require further proof that he is really immortal. Proofs are only necessary for that which one does not perceive. That which is perceived needs no other proof than it is known.

We are assembled here in the Hall of the " Scientific Club," and above me is inscribed " Knowledge is Power." This is perfectly true. Real knowledge gives power outwardly and inwardly. But all is not real knowledge that one is accustomed to regard as such. Much that nowadays is looked upon as science is composed of opinions, which in future will give place to other opinions, as they in their turn took the place of old opinions that were previously looked upon as science. All that we have arrived at by merely logical conclusion, but have not discerned by our own actual perception, I would denote as simply *negative* knowledge, without on that account denying it a certain value. When I say, *e.g.*, three times three are nine, and therefore six times six are equal to thirty-six, I mean by that, that according to the reason given, and the rules of arithmetic, six times six can be nothing else than thirty-six. But that does not by any means say that I know what thirty-six really is, for to know this, I should have first to know what the number *one* is in its real nature. But when I put the question thus, reason comes to a standstill, and can get no farther. It is a question that can only be answered by the inner feeling or intuition.

To learn to know this *One*, *i.e.*, God, is the highest science and art. When we have learnt to know the number *one* in us, then we can also follow up easily all numbers which develop from it. In this perception of the one consists the perception of God in man, *i.e.*, *the self-consciousness of the truth in us.*

The purpose of life is to attain to this self-consciousness of truth ; from death we expect no other gain than liberation from false appearance. Cremation is the most elevated visible sign and symbol of this emancipation ; for as the useless dead body is consumed by fire, and thereby returns again to its mother Nature, so also does the selfishness of man perish in the fire of Divine love, and in the flame of true knowledge the Divine Spirit returns to its primeval origin, the Source of Light.

(Extract from the " Phœnix," of Darmstadt-Frankfort, April, 1890.*)*

SOME BIOGRAPHICAL DATA OF DR. HARTMANN.

A MYSTIC OF THE PRESENT TIME.

I believe I shall engage the interest of the adherents to our purpose if I introduce to them one who has achieved great things in fields of thought, standing in certain relation to our own aim. We shall have an opportunity later on to refer more particularly to these relations. Here we would merely mention that he has at his disposal an amazingly rich fund of material, comprising observations and research in directions which are still, in part, *terra incognita* to us, and which I will endeavour later on to render accessible to a wider circle.

Franz Hartmann, son of Dr. Carl Hartmann, medical officer of the Governmental district of Kempten, in Bavaria, born at the close of the '30's, studied medicine and pharmacy at Munich, at which University he was also named *Doctor medicinæ* and *magister pharmaciæ*.

Thirty years ago he proceeded as a young doctor to France, and went to Havre to see the sea. In the harbour of this town lay at the time a ship just ready to sail for New York, the owner of which was seeking for a doctor for the voyage. Coming accidentally across Dr. Hartmann, he proposed to him to join the ship. Dr. Hartmann agreed to do so, and a few hours later he was on the high seas. On arriving at New York, he was so favourably impressed with American life that he decided to seek his future on that continent.

An inborn love of wandering and of a life of adventure, the interest of becoming acquainted with new countries and conditions of life led him to the Northern and Southern States of North America, to Texas, Mexico, etc., occupying the position of doctor, chemist, or author, according to circumstances. On a journey to New Orleans he was attacked by robbers and lost his fairly considerable savings, reaching that town penniless, and deprived of even decent clothing. Here he had to commence again from the beginning, and was thankful to find a place as medical attendant in an apothecary's shop. But he soon raised himself from this, as New Orleans offered a rich field for his professional activity. In this town he also made the acquaintance of a young lady of good family, whom he married. After a happy married life of only a year and a half he became a widower, and once more the love of wandering awoke within him. Hartmann went to the Rocky Mountains of Colorado, where he lived for many years an active life as a doctor, mining proprietor, and author. In the '70's he removed to San Francisco. There a call reached him from India, where he was already known by his writings on mystical philosophy. He first visited Japan and China, and afterwards reached India for a prolonged stay. In Madras he joined the Theosophical Society, of which he became General Secretary. In this position he had the opportunity of becoming acquainted with countries and people such as seldom falls to the lot of a European, and to penetrate by means of his intimate intercourse with the Guardians of the Ancient Indian Wisdom— learned Buddhists and Brahmins—into the mysteries and unfathomable depths of a culture covering many thousands of years and the cradle of our own.

After 25 years in distant foreign countries, he returned in 1885 to Europe, accompanying Madame Blavatsky, who had already achieved a high reputation by her philosophical works published in the French language. At present Dr. Hartmann resides in Vienna. Devoted to his studies and literary activity, he has for years relinquished his professional work. His domain is that which, at the present time, is only attractive to a very small circle of the "enlightened," viz., the interesting field of mystical and Theosophical Philosophy. Hartmann writes only in the English language, of which he is a master in a way that causes him to be ranked with the leading authors of England and America. His most important works are a *Monograph on Theophrastus Paracelsus von Hohenheim;* some larger works based on the researches of many years on *The Order of the Rosicrucians;* also a *Monograph on the Mystic Jacob Bochme,* and within the last few years, *New Investigations regarding the origin of the New Testament.*

EMIL HIRSCH.

Vienna, March, 1890.

THE POWER TO HEAL.

(REPRINTED FROM THE " THEOSOPHIST," APRIL, 1883.)

It is a striking commentary upon the imperfection of our modern system of medicine that an almost unanimous scepticism prevails among physicians as to the power of healing the sick by mesmeric methods.

By most the thing is declared impossible, and those who maintain its reality are set down as little better than charlatans.

The majority are not satisfied with this exhibition of petty spite ; they do their best to intimidate and ostracize the more candid minority. And they find more than willing allies in the theologians who stand for their especial prerogatives ; and, while claiming to heal by Divine commission, denounce all lay mesmeric healers as either humbugs or sorcerers. It is saddening to read in the literature of mesmerism so many plaintive protests against the prejudiced injustice of the medical profession towards such able scientists as Gregory, Ashburner, Elliottson, and Von Reichenbach. One cannot restrain one's indignation to see how an instinct of narrow selfishness carries professional men beyond all bounds, and warps the moral sense. The case of Newton, the American healer, whose mesmeric cures are recorded by the thousand, and embrace examples of the most desperate ailments instantaneously relieved, is striking. This man has healed in public halls in many American cities as well as in London, not scores, but hundreds of sick people by the simple laying on of hands. His power was so great that he could, by a word and a gesture, dispel the pains of everybody in the audience who stood up when he called upon those who were suffering from any pain to do so. Seventeen years ago he publicly stated that he had up to that time cured one hundred and fifty thousand sick persons. What his present total is—for he is still curing—we cannot say, but it must be larger than the aggregate of all the instantaneous cures effected by all the " Holy Wells " and shrines and professed healers within our historical period. A book* by Mr. A. E.

---

* "The Modern Bethesda"; or, "The Gift of Healing Restored." Edited by A. E. Newton. (New York ; Newton Publishing Company.)

Newton, a respectable gentleman of Massachusetts, which appeared in the year 1879, contains the record of some thousands of cases which yielded to Dr. Newton's tremendous psychopathic power. From a public address of the latter (see pp. 113-4) we learn that " in healing there must be faith on one side or the other. A healer should be a person of great faith, great energy, sympathetic and kind; a man who is true to himself; a muscular man, with a fixed, positive, and determined will. One possessing a good share of these qualities will be successful." The discourse finished, he gave a practical illustration of his healing power. Said he: " Now I ask any in the room that are in pain to rise—only those who are in acute pain." About twenty rose, and the Doctor threw his arms forcibly forward and said, " Now your pain is gone." He then requested " those whose pains were cured to sit down," and they all sat down. His power has been sometimes so superabundant that he had only to touch a paralytic, a club-foot patient, a deaf or blind person, to cure them on the spot, and there he has touched and healed 2,000 in one day. The Curé d'Ars, a good French priest, who died in 1859, healed like Newton for thirty years; during which period he had been visited by 20,000 patients, of all ranks, and from every country in Europe. Dr. Ennemozer, in his most interesting " History of Magic," tells about Gassner, a Romish priest of the latter half of the 18th century, who cured his thousands by the following artifices. " He wore a scarlet cloak and on his neck a silver chain. He usually had in his room a window on his left hand and a crucifix on his right. With his face towards the patient, he touched the ailing part * * * * calling on the name of Jesus * * * * Everyone that desired to be healed *must believe* * * * covered the affected part with his hand, and rubbed therewith vigorously both head and neck." In our days the Roman Catholics have revived the business of miraculous cures on a grand scale; at Lourdes, France, is their holy well, where hundreds of cripples have deposited their sticks and crutches as tokens of their cures; the same thing is going on at the parish church at Knock, Ireland, and last year there were symptoms that the same trump-card was to be played by the fish-collecting priests of Colombo, Ceylon. In fact, the Church of Rome has always claimed a monopoly and made the simple psycopathic law to play into their hands as testimony in support of their theocratic infallibility.

That useful compiler of valuable psychic facts, the Chevalier G. Les Mousseaux, scrapes on this papal violoncello with great zeal. With him all mesmeric healings are effected by the devil. " When the magnetic agent operates upon the evils of the body, experience proves as an infallible truth, that it does not heal them without causing acute pains, or without risk to life, which it often destroys! Its cures are exasperatingly brief; perfect ones are the exception; the evil that it expels from one organ is often replaced in another organ by an evil still more desperate, and the sicknesses it dissipates are liable to cruel relapses." * His several volumes contain hundreds of reports of cases in which the devil has shown his Satanic power by healing the sick and doing all sorts of wonders. And that we may have the most unanswerable proof that the mesmeric fluid has manifested itself similarly in all ages, he collects from the writings of the ancients, the testimonies which they have left on record. Nothing could be more sarcastic than his arraignment of the Academies of Science and the medical profession for their stupid incredulity as to the occurrence of these marvels. Verily this is an author to be studied by the intelligent psychologist, however much he may be disposed to laugh at his Catholic bias and his blind resort to the theory of a non-existent devil to explain away the beneficent power to heal disease which so many philanthropic men in all epochs have exercised. It is not in the least true either that mesmeric cures are impermanent or that one disease disappears only to be replaced by a worse one. If the operator be healthy and virtuous, and knows his science well, his patients will be effectually restored to health in every instance where his or her own constitution is favourably disposed to receive the mesmeric aura. And this leads us to remark that Dr. Newton has not sufficiently explained the curative action of faith nor its relation to the mesmerizer's healing power. The familiar analogy of the law of electric and magnetic conduction makes all plain. If a metallic body charged with + Electricity be brought into contact with a body negatively electrified, the + fluid is discharged from the first into the second body. The phenomenon of thunder and lightning is an example in point. When two bodies similarly electrified meet, they mutually repel each other. Apply this to the human system. A person in health is charged with positive vitality—prana, Od, Aura, electro-magnetism, or whatever else you prefer to call it; one in ill-health is negatively charged; the positive vitality, or health element, may be discharged by an effort of the healer's will into the receptive nervous system of the patient; they touch each other, the fluid passes, equilibrium is restored in the sick man's system, the *miracle* of healing is wrought, and the lame walk, the blind see, deaf hear, dumb speak, and humours of long standing vanish in a moment.

Now, if besides health, power of will, knowledge of science, and benevolent compassion on the healer's part, there be also faith, passivity, *and the requisite attractive polarity* on that of the patient, the effect is the more

---

* "La Magie au XIXme. Siecle," p. 327. (Paris: 1864, Henri Plon.)

rapid and amazing. Or, if faith be lacking and still there be the necessary polaric receptivity, the cure is still possible. And again, if there be in the patient alone a faith supreme and unshakable in the power of a healer, of a holy relic, of the touch of a shrine, of the waters ot a well, of a pilgrimage to a certain place and a bath in some sacred river, of any given ceremonies or repetition of charms or an amulet worn about the neck—in either of these or many more agencies that might be named, then the patient will cure himself by the sole power of his predisposed faith.*
And this rallying power of Nature's forces goes in the medical books under the name of *Vis Medicatrix Naturæ*—the Healing Power of Nature. It is of supreme importance that the one who attempts to heal diseases should have an absolute and implicit faith—(a) in his science; (b) in himself. To project from himself the healing aura he must concentrate all his thought for the moment upon his patient, and

---

* That excellent journal, the *Times of Ceylon*, in its number for February 7th, prints the following facts, which illustrate the recuperative power of the imagination: " I have recently read an account of what is termed ' a faith cure,' which took place with the famous Sir Humphrey Davy when quite a young man. Davy was about to operate on a paralytic patient with oxygen gas, but before beginning the inhalation Davy placed a thermometer under the patient's tongue to record his temperature. The man was much impressed with this, and declared, with much enthusiasm, that he was already much relieved. Seeing the extraordinary influence of the man's imagination, Davy did nothing more than gravely place the thermometer under his tongue from day to day, and in a short time he reported him cured. I can relate a perfect faith cure of a desperate case of dysentery in one of our planting districts, by a medical practitioner well known at the time, Dr. Baylis, who practised on his own account in the Kallibokke Valley and Knuckles district. He had just returned from a visit to India, having left his assistant in charge and on his return was much distressed to learn that a favourite patient of his, the wife of an estate manager, was desperately ill with dysentery, and not expected to live more than a day or two, being almost *in extremis*. She had been gradually sinking under the debilitating effects of the terrible disease, and there was nothing more to be done, as the doctor found the treatment to have been all that he could have adopted.

"Wishing to see the patient before her death, he at once went to the estate, and on seeing him she expressed great pleasure, saying, in faint tones, she knew she should recover now that he had come to attend her, as she had such complete confidence in him. At her request he remained in the house, but no change in her medicine was made. Strange to say, she at once began to recover, and at the end of a week was able to walk with him in the garden.

" Such was the result with the patient. On the mind of the doctor the cure had the effect of causing him to lose all confidence in the efficacy of medicine. He abandoned allopathy as a delusion, took to homœopathy as the only true practice, and necessarily lost many of his patients, and eventually left the country and settled in California as a farmer, where he was drowned a few years ago. The late Dr. Baylis was a marvellously gifted man in many respects, but, like many other clever men, very impulsive. He was inclined to be a believer in Buddhism, and actually named one of his children Buddha."

will with iron determination that the disease shall depart, and a healthy, nervous circulation be re-established in the sufferer's system. It matters nothing what may be his religious belief, nor whether he invoke the name of Jesus, Rama, Mahommed, or Buddha ; he *must believe in his own power and science,* and the invocation of the name of the founder of his particular sect only helps to give him the confidence requisite to insure success. Last year, in Ceylon, Colonel Olcott healed more than fifty paralytics, in each case using the name of Lord Buddha. But if he had not the knowledge he has of mesmeric science, and full confidence in his psychic powers. and the revered Guru, whose pupil he is, he might have vainly spoken his simple religious formula to his patients. He was treating Buddhists, and therefore the invocation of Sakya Muni's name was in their cases as necessary as was the use of the name of Jesus to Pére Gassner and the other many healers of the Romish Church who have cured the sick from time to time. And a further reason for his using it was that the cunning Jesuits of Colombo were preparing to convince the simple-minded Singhalese that their new spring near Kelanie had been endowed with exceptionally miraculous healing powers by the Virgin Mary.

Those who may, after reading our remarks, feel a call to heal the sick should bear in mind the fact that all the curative magnetism that is forced by their will into the bodies of their patients, *comes out of their own systems.* What they have, they can give ; no more. And as the maintenance of one's own health is a prime duty, they should never attempt healing unless they have a surplus of vitality to spare, over and above what may be needed to carry themselves through their round of duties, and keep their systems well up to tone. Otherwise they would soon break down and become themselves invalids. Only the other day, a benevolent healer of London died from his imprudent waste of his vital forces. For the same reason, healing should not be attempted to any extent after one has passed middle life ; the constitution has not then the same recuperative capacity as in youth. As the old man cannot compete with the fresh youth in athletic contests, so he can no more hope to rival him in healing the sick ; to attempt it is sheer folly ; to ask it of him simple ignorance and selfishness. We make these reflections because requests have been made from many quarters that Col. Olcott would visit them and publicly heal the sick as he did in Ceylon. To say nothing of the fact that he is now a man of past fifty years of age, and burdened with a weight of official duty that would break down any person, not sustained like him by exceptional influences, we need only reflect that the suffering sick throughout India are numbered by the tens of thousands, and that for him to be himself known as healer would be to insure his being mobbed and almost torn to pieces in every city. If, in a small place like Galle, our head-quarter building was thronged by two and three hundred patients a day, the road was crowded with carts, litters, and hobbling cripples, and the President was often unable to find time to get even a cup of tea before five p.m., what would it be in our Indian cities, those hives of population, where every street would pour out its quota of invalids ? If, like Newton, he had practised healing all his life, and he could cure by a touch, the case would be different. As it is, all he can do is that which he has been doing, viz., to teach eligible members of the Theosophical Society the secrets of mesmeric psychopathy, on the simple condition that it shall never be used as a means of pecuniary gain, or to gratify any sinister motive.

The T.P.S., having received a donation to the Library and Propagation Fund, will be glad to send Leaflets for distribution to those who can distribute them.

NATIONAL KARMA.

By K. E. MILLS.

ATLANTIS.

(Reprinted from " LUCIFER.")

London;
THEOSOPHICAL PUBLISHING SOCIETY
7, DUKE STREET, ADELPHI, W.C.

The T.P.S. do not ho'd themselves responsible for any opinions expressed in signed articles.

NATIONAL KARMA.

The paper of Professor J. R. Buchanan, M.D., in the *Arena* for August, entitled " The Coming Cataclysm of America and Europe," is of profound interest to Theosophists. The Professor maintains, and to quote from the summary of his article given in the September number of the *Review of Reviews*, " that periodicity is a law of nature, and that we are now approaching our revolutionary period. From 1910 to 1916 America will be devasted by a frightful war—a labour and capital war and black and white war—in which the Church will be shattered and the marriage relation approximated to freedom. . . . The Atlantic coast of the United States will be devastated by a great tidal wave. . . . The greatest horror will culminate at New York and Jersey City. . . . In the midst of all these terrors of war and flood there will occur a geological convulsion, before which all the earthquakes of the past will seem the merest trifles. After six years the war and horror will culminate, after terrible loss of human life and immense destruction of great cities, in the nationalization of everything on Edward Bellamy's principles. Europe, too, has its great calamity. . . . The beginning of the tragedy will approach with the beginning of the century; and the war will develop in about fifteen years. Two years of sanguinary revolution will be her volcanic outburst from the pent-up fires that are smouldering now in human bosoms." And so continues this prophet of woe; and a watcher says, " So be it." To those of us who belong to the Theosophical Society there is hope and salvation for the sin-ridden world, even when we feel that we must walk through the fiery waves of suffering ere we can hope to be purified and consecrated to our glorious task of helping to push the good ship Progress through the surf of the sea of human misery as we aid at the launch of the twentieth century.

Purified through suffering we must be, for *we are not strong enough.*

Honestly, and without self-delusion, let us look at the situation—we English Fellows of the Theosophical Society. We have been called to enter upon a new life. To us has been whispered a secret from the book of destiny. The solidarity of humanity has become an acknowledged fact. The pain of one is the pain of all. The degradation of the meanest tarnishes the lustre of the highest. Upon us, as the banded army of progress, rests the duty of storming the fortress of avarice; of laying low the castle of indolence ; of cutting a pathway and building a bridge that wealth, refinement and knowledge may pass unscathed from the rich to the poor ; that the dignity of toil, the discipline of sacrifice, the beauty of willing service may send its quickening force from the poor to the rich.

Fifteen years of stormy strife have passed over our Society, and, at least, some of our comrades have been enrolled in the army of battle.

While gratefully acknowledging the victories of the past, let us examine the camping-ground of the present.

This is what we see: Vast undulatory plains, and, beyond, great cities, both rich with the wealth of the nation. Those who study these things have stated that, reckoned in pounds, one billion two hundred and fifty million is the total sum of these riches.

Great is the power of wealth—great for destruction and blessing—and those who have sworn to make war to the death on the hydra-headed tyrants of sloth and selfishness, find in this produce of nature, and the labour of man, a subtle foe that paralyses their limbs and sends up its intoxicating fumes to their brains and bewilders their senses. For a curious thing has happened on this field of battle, which, more than all else, shall test the strength and the skill of the army of progress.

Prompt and sleepless to guard their own interest, the dwellers of cities have crept like a thief in the night and laid the stong hand of power on the stores of the nation. And, alarmed at the exit, the burghers run after and snatch what they can for their wives and children.

So at the dawn of the day of battle this meets the eye of the soldiers.

Less than a third of the people have seized and hold nearly two-thirds of the produce. Now here is the problem.

Twenty-five million persons of the poorest and weakest of brain, heart, and soul have got to be taught, clothed, and fed with the pitiful portion that is left from the spoils of the spoiler. Four hundred and fifty million left over to rear and make strong for the struggle for life ; twenty-five million of people. Less, to count heads, than thirty-five pounds a year, and supply all the wants of each adult creature. The problem is perplexing. Not the less so that out from the walls of the wealth-bounded city the " have-alls " keep throwing, when the fancy may strike them, or the wails of the hungry break the calm of their slumbers, gifts, alms, and donations, subscriptions and sermons, all of which are gulped down with a curse for thanksgiving.

But the worst of the trouble is this : we who are banded together to fight against cruelty and wrong are smeared with the mud of that city of wealth and corruption. Most have been reared on the spoil of the spoiler· In our brains are the fumes of the incense our parents have lighted to make thick the air that surrounds us, and keep out the sight of the close-lying sorrow. Our hearts have been seared by the sight of want and distress at our doors. Our ears have been deafened by the cry of our sisters cast out and trodden to death because they were poor and polluted.

We know that poverty, anxiety, and that which springs from these conditions makes the average length of life of the artisan classes little more than half that of their professional brothers. We know that from fifty to fifty-five per cent. of the infants of the working classes *die* before they reach five years old. How should it be otherwise when their mothers are at work, weaving and washing, making all bright and clean, for their rich sisters, who only lose eighteen per cent., or less than one in five, instead of one in two of their dear children? And yet these working-men and women have hearts as sore, as they hear the dull sod fall upon the tiny coffin as would be those of their wealthy employers. We know that the Mansion House Relief Committee Report four years ago told us there would be from seven and eight thousand men apply daily, and *apply in vain*, at the docks of London for labour, for the splendid remuneration of fourpence an hour. We know the smiling, gracefully-clad ladies will ask in all seriousness, "Do you think the working-men do *right* to strike?" Would that politeness permitted the counter question, "Do you think, madam, your white skirt is right to wear while children are *dying* for the want of a portion—only a small portion—of that labour you so thoughtlessly absorb?

Would they see, do we ourselves see, *and act as if we saw*, that at Bethnal Green the infantile death-rate is twice that of Belgravia?

Well, we say, we must be clean, even if all through the summer months the washerwoman toils for sixteen hours a day, and no one asks what becomes of her baby, and if that is clean. We cannot do without house and pretty furniture. We have come to regard these things as a sign of moral worth—as a passport of respectability. Like Carlyle's witness, we must "keep a gig." Have we not been taught from our youth up that the race is to the swift, the battle to the strong? Is not success in the struggle for existence proof positive that we who survive are the "fittest," notwithstanding "when we regard the general tone of feeling of our age, whether as expressed in its literature, in its social intercourse, or even more, perhaps, in its amusements, do we not find ourselves in the presence of a society from which real gladness has well-nigh died out, in which hope is almost extinct?" In spite of our material successes—our victory in the "struggle"—we are human. The sorrows of the crushed and wounded weigh upon our spirits. In our pleasant homes we cannot shut out the thought that "in London there are 60,000 families who live in single rooms, and 30,000 who have no regular homes at all."

In the security of a well-ordered city we are haunted by the re-membrance that 73,000 criminals are yearly arrested, that statistics show that " in 1887 the actual prison population was 14,966, and the total number of persons imprisoned was 163,048. The metropolitan prisons contain about 21 per cent. of the whole prison population."

We may try to console ourselves with the thought that these criminals are more comfortably housed and fed in prison than they would be out of prison; but we fail to convince ourselves that existing prison regulations, splendid as they may be for the physical man, are educational establishments well fitted to prepare the delinquents to create good Karma for the "morrow," when, their term of punishment expired, they shall start afresh on the treadmill of free life outside the prison walls.

As we gather round the social board, and feel a glow of hospitable pride as we glance down the long table, bright with silver and glass, and lovely with flowers, the thought will invade us that we are the leaders of the masses, that our pleasures are also their pleasures. Our feasts are made elegant to the eye; but they appeal to the lower nature of man, and from them, too often, baseness and cruelty result. The softly-lighted banqueting-halls, gay with fruits and flowers, and well-dressed guests, find their counterpart in 180,000 public-houses flashing their garish splendours about the highways and by-ways of "merry England"; and the dark nights find in London alone over 20,000 of these death-traps set to stupefy our people.

As we sip our wine, and join in the flow of happy converse, can we forget that here, in the capital of our boasted civilization, " about 30,000 persons are yearly arrested for drunkenness; of these 15,600 are women?" Fair and bright may look to the glance of the passing stranger the placid interiors of our far-famed English homes, but let us study the reports of the bankruptcy courts; let us read the report of the Registrar-General, no later back than 1889, and we shall see that " in London one person in every five will die in the workhouse, hospital, or lunatic asylum," and from equally reliable resources we can learn that in the third week of December, 1886, no less than 103,968 paupers were relieved, without including vagrants and criminals.

But what, it may be asked, has all this disagreeable fact, which good breeding should teach us to keep out of sight, to do with the army of progress? What have Theosophists to do with these social troubles?

Does not the doctrine of Karma prove beyond dispute that this suffering *must be?* that the sufferers have earned their suffering? that all things are arranged, in this best of all possible worlds, with rigid justice? Are we not told that the "Brotherhood" is to be a fraternity of mind and spirit, not of necessity a Brotherhood of property, where those that have shall share with those that have not ?

Fellow soldiers, comrades in the fight, let us not deceive ourselves! Let us not hug the selfish thought to our hearts. What do our Teachers say ? " Let not the fierce sun dry one tear of pain before thyself hast wiped it from the sufferer's eye. But let each burning human tear drop on thy heart and there remain, nor ever brush it off, until the pain that caused it is removed."

The human tear-drops *have* reached society's heart, and the low sigh of wailing anguish is rushing on the wind. Those who call themselves Socialists may not be right in their attempted remedies for the sin-sick world. We Theosophists do not think they are, but they voice the misery of those who have, and know not how to give wisely to those who have not.

The 25,000,000 persons whose share of the national wealth is less than £35 per head for each adult may be reaping that which they have sown. But we have heard something about national Karma, and we cannot help asking ourselves whether we, the absorbers of the surplus, may not be making each for himself a future of want, and, perhaps, of degradation.

Not only the disciplinary effect of poverty and the perpetual struggle for bread on the toilers has to be considered, but the educational effect of a life of ease and luxury in the midst of want has to be thought of.

Let it be granted that we have the right to all refinements, all the aid in the upward progress which wealth can give us, and the question remains, for each one to answer for himself, whether we are using this wealth, which we may look upon as a condition in mental and moral advancement, in the best manner possible when we absorb it in personal and social luxury. And here it may be well to state that the word luxury is used to denote all expenditure of the common fund of national wealth beyond what is needed for the maintenance of body and mind in the highest state of efficiency, as an instrument for the Higher Ego. We cannot spend our force in two ways at once. Either we must give up all hope of bringing light into Earth's dark places, or we must give up our present habits of labour absorption.

For Theosophists at least, there are questions of Karma to reckon with. There is the Karma now being worked out by the down-trodden masses, worked out in such conditions that it can scarcely fail to renew the crop of evil and generate fresh causes of future suffering. The money that is absorbed in personal luxury would at least do something towards placing some of the children, some of the young men and maidens, in surroundings that would be favourable to the growth of the best, instead of the worst, that is in them. There is the Karma that the rich are generating. Here we face the question. We *know* the state of the country. We *know* that if we expend our forces in nursing and cultivating our already abnormal desires for comfort, for luxury, for the pleasures of the senses, of beauty and sweetness—innocent and good as these may be when not founded, as with us, on hideous sights and sounds, pushed back into the darkness of the alleys, but haunts us still—we know that we are making ourselves bankrupt for the *work that serves*. Not only are we enervated, and so have little power to help, but our reserves are exhausted, and we have no longer the means at our disposal. We have swallowed our cake and then, like children, we lament that we have no bread to feed the hungry. We all think to draw a line somewhere, and balance our personal expenditure with our personal income, so that we have a good margin left over for charity. But in the unconscious competition in which most of us are engaged, the margin is too apt to be encroached upon. A successful speculation, a splendid professional reputation, a good stroke of business, results in a bigger house, in removal to a more fashionable neighbourhood, increased personal expenditure. The coveted picture is bought, or the long-delayed tour is taken ; indulgences before sternly repressed are permitted, with the consoling thought, "we can afford it." But can we? That is the question. True, we may have *money* enough. But have we *character* enough ? Have we built up in the past such a reservoir of virtue that we can afford to miss this golden opportunity of doing loving deeds? Are we so cased in the panoply of mercy that we need not fear that one arrow from the bow of worldly-mindedness can penetrate our armour ? Are we, in truth, quite sure that we have attained the hill top, and are content to be as nothing in the eyes of man ? If we have not reached this goal, we who profess to see in Theosophy the guide of life, we who desire, however feebly, to walk along the path, we, at least, cannot afford it.

And another aspect of the question presents itself to him who is desirous to act "to-day"; to him who sees in the misery of great cities the working of Karma, and who knows that the actions of the present generation are building up a future of happiness or woe for "to-morrow."

Experience of our own weakness, and the object-lesson in constant progress, which is given by our fellow-men, teach that there is practically no limit to our power of labour absorption. The love of luxury grows by what it feeds upon. As he who has set himself to scale the heights of being knows, after ages of struggle and conquest, that he is but at the foot of the mountain, and that before him long vistas still stretch, through which he must toil, so he who is sunk in the pleasures of material existence cannot see the end of the descent into Avernus. Each sense starts up with new and ever [new demands, till eye and ear, taste, smell, and feeling become as so many urging demons tempting man to his destruction.

Now, we are willing to absorb about two lives apiece, that we may " have things decent " around us. It may be, with our love of flowers, our delight in soft draperies, shining silver, glittering crystal, that we could find it in our hardened hearts to absorb any number of lives that our money could buy, and think it no sin. But this shows us the need to place a limit on our desires.

There is no danger like the danger of *drifting*. Modern luxury, self-indulgence, and the sweating-dens, which are their outcome, have been brought about by *drifting*.

Not one woman in a hundred—men may be different—knows, or, at any rate, *realizes* that in her pretty drawing-room, her dainty dinners, her elegant dresses, she is absorbing *lives*. Yet it would be well that our board schools and high schools taught the outlines of political economy, with illustrations taken from life. It would be well that men and women should know that their " being decent " means the neglected babes of the East-end toiler being dead.

Now, what limit shall we put upon our desires ? It is a question of moment for Theosophists. In this incarnation but few of us will gain " the faculty to slay the lunar form at will." But we may attain to some knowledge of self. We may learn a little bit of the lesson of giving up *self* to non-self. We may let our soul lend its ear to every cry of pain like as the lotus bares its heart to drink the morning sun." The first letters of the sweet lesson of Renunciation all may begin to learn.

And it is time to begin. We may confuse ourselves with formulas of " Destiny " and " Karma," and leave the duty that looks afar off undone, till the duty at our doors is forgotten. As a straw shows the way the wind is blowing, so a small thing, relatively, shows that with us Theosophists there must be something wrong—something that needs the personal attention of each one of us.

Charity, it is said, begins at home, but Theosophists do not much care for charity of the money-giving order. But then they care for Justice ; and a person whose expenditure is so regulated that it ignores the claims of justice, stands much in need of a warning to curtail his expenditure.

Have we, who have considered ourselves strong enough to come forward and claim to be enrolled in the band of pioneers to a higher and better life—have we so freed ourselves from the trammels of life as to be able to do our duty bravely and faithfully to our comrades in the fight ? Or do we seek to do battle with the shackles of self-love around us, sitting in easy chairs, and dreaming of the millennium ?   Let facts speak. In the September number of *Lucifer*, Mrs. Besant, as treasurer of the Headquarters Building Fund, has this statement to make : " The burden of the undertaking " (of the establishment of headquarters of the Theosophical Society) " falls very unequally upon those who share its advantages, the members of the staff residing at headquarters who have all given up comfortable private homes and the freedom of individual dwellings, and some of whom have given up in exchange for mere board and lodging appointments at which they earned their living, are those on whom also the chief cost of establishing the new headquarters falls.   It will be seen below (in the statement of account appended to the above in *Lucifer*) that more than half the monetary contributions came from them. In addition to this, the members have each furnished his or her room, and among them have almost entirely furnished the two common rooms—the drawing-room and general work-room. . . . The heavy expenditure has been on building the new rooms required for the work of the Society, altering the interior of the house to accommodate the very large " family " of workers, relaying the drain-pipes, and building necessary sanitary accommodation ; . . . but the Society, whose work makes it necessary that these rooms should be provided and the three secretaries maintained, ought not to allow the main cost of this provision of maintenance to fall on five or six persons, who give their time and work, as well as all else they have, to the Society."

How is it that when a week of self-denial of poor Salvation lads and lasses can bring in £20,000 to the Salvationists' headquarters, a miserable £136 3s. is all that after fifteen years of Theosophic teaching the European Theosophists of the General Society have to offer for their Headquarters Fund?

There can be but one explanation.   More has not been given because " self-denial " is an unknown quantity.   Self-indulgent habits in personal expenditure bring empty pockets.   When the demand comes for some felt want there is no reserve in hand to draw upon.   And justice suffers. For it is not just that some half-a-dozen self-devoted people should have to bear the burden entailed by the work of a society the advantages of which all fellow Theosophists share.   But this small illustration of a gigantic evil is useful to draw our attention to the common national habit of labour-absorption, and to point its inevitable result.

The labourers of the T.S., like the labourers of the nation, have not only to do all the work, but also to furnish the " abstinence " which is the basic foundation of that capital upon which the absorbers subsist. If this state of things is to continue, self-respect, justice, and common honesty will become traditions of the past.

Surely it was with prescience of coming events that the founder of the T.S. wrote in the " Key to Theosophy " these words : " No Theosophist has the right to this name unless he is thoroughly imbued with the correctness of Carlyle's truism, ' The end of man is *action*, and not *thought*, {though it were the noblest,' and unless he sets and models his daily life upon this truth. The profession of a truth is not yet the enactment of it ; and the more beautiful and grand it sounds, the more loudly virtue and duty is talked about instead of being acted upon, the more forcibly it will always remind one of the Dead Sea fruit. *Cant* is the most loathsome of all vices, and *cant* is the most prominent feature of the greatest Protestant country of this century—England."

Well, it certainly looks like it. There are many indications that a general feeling is growing up that common justice would do more for the wretched toilers who " drag the coach " than all the *charity* that is poured out like water.

But what society wants is a recognised limit to legitimate personal expenditure in view of children dying of neglect and millions of beings in the centres of civilization creating individual and national Karma in gin-palaces and places too evil to be mentioned. To those really in earnest in their desire to lessen the misery around them, this limit might be suggested : To take as little as possible from the common stock of the nation's produce, and to give to that stock as much.

Here is a limit at once clear and simple.

It saves vain questioning as to the legitimacy of this or that indulgence ; it reaches the understanding of the meanest intelligence ; it regulates the expenses of the richest as of the poorest. Can any given product of labour be dispensed with without loss to man as a labouring, loving instrument of the silent God ? If the answer is " Yes," then dispense with it.

We may have thought the saying of the Great Initiate, who desired the rich man to sell all that he had and give to the poor, if he would become a disciple, a very hard saying, but it was a simple enunciation of a great truth. The yoke of the follower of the Master is easy, the burden light, but only when the "eye is single." You cannot take your luggage with you into battle. *That* is the burden we bind upon our backs, a burden too heavy to be borne. We Theosophists, with a few bright exceptions, who, with rare insight, have stripped themselves free of useless trappings, think to serve " God and Mammon " ; we will draw to ourselves all the bright glory of Ancient Wisdom ; we will listen to the voice of our Higher-Self, and the divine spark within us shall receive attention. But why should we make ourselves peculiar ? Why give up habits to which we are accustomed ? Why not do as others do ? We are not miracle workers that we can change the conditions of existence and reverse the experience of mankind. " Ye *cannot* serve God and Mammon."

We are standing on the eve of a social revolution, if history is to be relied upon for precedent. The cycle of 600 years has run out, and the signs of social ferment, which accompany these upheavals, are upon us. Let us see what is the lesson of the past, and judge what we must look for in the near future. In 1222, as we know, Genghi Khan personified brute force, swept like a living scourge over the Eastern Continent, changing the face of things from the land we now call Turkey to far Cathay. Six hundred years earlier occurred the Hegira. Move backwards again 600 years, and the Star of Bethlehem arises. Yet, again, look back for a like period, and the Light of Asia, Lord Buddha, throws athwart the gloom his bright and gentle rays. Since then we have travelled slowly into darkness, deep and ever deeper. Now, we look forward to the Revolution that shall herald in the dawn, and having touched the depths of materialism, we prepare for the upward curve that shall bring us to the light of Spirituality. But, if the first lifting of the clouds of night has awakened us, if the very fact of our having turned for guidance to wisdom of the past, which, like its source, is the same yesterday, to-day, and for ever, proves us heralds of the coming day, is it fitting that the rising sun finds us smothered in the down of pillows, stretching our limbs in the soft wantonness of scarcely broken slumber ?

> " Rise ! for the day is passing,
>   And you lie dreaming on ;
> The others have buckled their armour
>   And forth to the fight are gone !
> A place in the ranks awaits you ;
>   Each man has some part to play ;
> The Past and the Future are nothing—
>   In the face of the stern to-day ! "

We are too much inclined to think when we are called upon to take our share of the rough labour of life that the " evolution of society," " division of labour," or some other meaningless formula, muttered with more or less blind faith in its efficacy, will act like a charm and relieve us of our duty. We are inclined to look upon the advise to take as little and give as much to the world's store as the exaggerations of enthusiasm. But it is not so ; for by so doing—for love's sweet sake—we call the hidden force of nature to our aid.

The burdens nature puts upon us she helps us to carry. Those we put upon our own shoulders she lets us faint under, that at last, learning wisdom in the school of experience, we may throw them down.

When we read in " What to Do " that in Russia the harvest cannot be gathered in for want of hands, while men and women are devising amusements to work off their superfluous vitality, we think that things are in a totally different condition here, and that Count Tolstoi's advice to people to leave their recreation and recruit themselves with honest work is inappropriate. But, in truth, things are not so different as they seem. Here the labourers want leaders as well as in Russia. Leaders in labour and leaders in the social amenities which should follow labour in all classes. The poor as well as the rich meet the softening influences of art, of gentle intercourse, of beauty, of sight and sound, the stimulant of music and poetry, to make their lives noble, and enable them to reach the full stature of their manhood. The rich need the discipline of labour, real *productive* toil, not the sham business of unoccupied leisure, which fills up the time of our moneyed classes. It is very good of our public men to come forward and lecture the masses upon the dignity of labour. But something more is wanted. They must show that they honour the calling of the manual labourer by bringing up their children as artisans and labourers if needs be; otherwise they waste their breath. As the rich are, so will those beneath them strive to become. "Already we hear," says the *Pall Mall Budget*, of September 11th, writing on Dr. Rhode's lecture at Leeds, " of harvesting delayed for want of labour. The better class labourers have gone into the towns or the colonies; and we know of villages where old men and boys have the bulk of the field work to do." And it must be so, for the lives of the agricultural labourers, in existing conditions, are little better than the lives of the brutes they tend. We have opened schools, and given the poor a glimpse of a higher state of being, and they leave the soil to rush to towns, let the charmer charm never so wisely from the agreeable altitude of the local platform. How pleasant it is to pass our time in the open air in the warm days of autumn! how lovely are the hop-gardens with their fragrant burdens drooping from the slender poles! Could we not fancy that growing boys and girls might gather hops and health and all the genial influences of Nature once a year, when they crowd from our cities for the summer outing of the poor, without the curse of greed laying its heavy hand upon them, so that the sweet air of heaven becomes laden with a curse, even as the dense atmosphere of slums from which they have fled? But look at this picture given by that trustworthy paper, the *Inquirer*, and noticed in the *Daily News* of September 15th, 1890 :—

"Hop-growers are now compelled by law to provide [hop-pickers] shelter; but in some instances, we are assured, the only protection afforded is some old army tents, through which the merciless rain penetrates when the strong night wind has not blown them away. Many of the hoppers, according to this authority, are received in wooden huts like rows of pig-sties, in which light enters only by the open door or an aperture in the roof that admits wind and rain. In these whole families herd, and male and female assume the indecent habits of brutes. Many of the most wretched concentrate at Maidstone, and the Local Board there philanthropically fastened a strip of thin calico round the verandah of a storehouse which stands in the cattle market ; but during a rough night the calico gets torn to shreds, and sometimes as many as six hundred badly-clad, half-starved people are exposed to the fitful fury of the storm. A year or two ago one poor emaciated woman dragged herself thus far and died during the night. The doctor, at the inquest, said that death was caused by starvation and neglect, and her life might probably have been saved had medical assistance been procured." Now, the death of one poor woman, or of a hundred, does not matter. The load of life must be gladly laid down when carried along in such conditions. What is of consequence is that towns which would pour out money like water for bunting and folly, were some great personage to spend an hour in their neighbourhood, to open a hospital, bridge, or museum, should allow such an object-lesson to be given in its market-place to the rising generation; an object-lesson in callous indifference to human suffering, human misery, and carelessly induced human degradation.

Let the poor suffer in silence, by all means, if such is their Karma, but let not the rich be permitted to absorb their bodies and souls in such fashion as shall generate a fresh crop of evil without protest. It may not be the duty of Theosophists at the present stage of the Society's growth to concern themselves much with physical philanthropy, and it is not for the *bodies* of the toilers I am pleading ; but I want to point out the mental effects which cannot fail to be induced by the possession and *absorption* of wealth amidst the grinding poverty around us.

" Kill out all sense of ' separateness ' ! " Feel that each shivering creature crouching in that cattle market, screened from the gaze of the passing stranger by a thin, wind-torn piece of calico, is indeed a sister, doing battle with the lower nature, striving as best she can to learn the lesson of this earth life that she may the quicker enter into her heritage of God-given womanhood, and ask if her claim on humanity is fully met, if her credit-note is duly honoured, when to her is assigned the open " verandah of a storehouse which stands in the cattle market " for lodging.

Let us not forget in our joyous recognition of the treasures offered to the intellect in the teachings of the wisdom-religion that if through the Hall of Wisdom we would reach the Vale of Bliss, we must close fast our senses against the great dire heresy of separateness that weans us from the rest. Glorious and beautiful are the truths we have to make known, as Theosophists, to a waiting world, but these truths can only be shown with the full splendour of the Light of Love upon them, when by *action* we prove ourselves ready to give what " *is due* to humanity to our fellow-men . . . and especially that which we owe to all those who are poorer and more helpless than we ourselves"; till we show in our lives that we realize that " this is a debt which, if left unpaid during life, leaves us spiritually insolvent and moral bankrupts in our next incarnation."

KATE E. MILLS, F.T.S.

[Reprinted from *Lucifer*, August, 1888.]

ATLANTIS.
FROM THE TIMÆUS AND CRITIAS OF PLATO.

AFTER establishing his famous code of laws, Solon,[*] the renowned Athenian legislator, left his native country for ten years. At Saïs, in the Nile delta, he was honourably received by the priests of Neïth,[†] for both Athens and Saïs were under the protection of the same goddess. In conversing with the learned guardians of the temple on the antiquities of their respective countries, he discovered that there were records in the sacred edifice of events which had happened nine thousand years previously, and in which the inhabitants of his own country had played a conspicuous part. Solon had spoken of the deluge of Deucalion and Pyrrha, giving the orthodox Greek chronology of the time ; on which an aged priest exclaimed: " O Solon, Solon, you Greeks are always children, and aged Greek there is none!" And then he proceeded to explain to the astonished Athenian the astronomical meaning of the myth of Phaëthon, and how that there are successive cataclysms of fire and water, destroying whole nations, and that a noble race had once inhabited the land of Attica, whose deeds and institutions were said to have been the most excellent of all, and how they conquered the inhabitants of the Atlantean island, and both themselves and their enemies were destroyed by terrible earthquakes and deluges. On his return to Athens, Solon composed an epic poem embodying the information he had gleaned from the Saïtic records, but political troubles prevented the entire accomplishment of his undertaking. Now Dropides, his fellow kinsman, was his most intimate friend and fully acquainted with the whole story ; this Dropides was father of Critias the elder, who had many times delighted his young grandson, the Critias of the dialogue and afterwards the most notorious of the thirty tyrants, with a recital of these wonderful chronicles.

Among the many glorious deeds of the noble autochthones of Attica, was their victory over a mighty hostile power from the Atlantic Ocean,

* Circiter 638—558 B.C. † Athena.

which had pushed its conquests over all Europe and Asia. Facing the Pillars of Hercules * was an island larger than Africa and Asia † put together. Besides this main island, there were many other smaller ones, so that it was easy to cross from one to another as far as the *further continent.* ‡ And this continent was indeed a continent, and the sea, the real sea, in comparison to which " The Sea " § of the Greeks was but a bay with a narrow mouth.

In the Atlantic island a powerful confederation of kings was formed, who subdued the island itself and many of the smaller islands and also parts of the further continent. They also reduced Africa within the Straits as far as Egypt, and Europe as far as Tyrrhenia.‖ Further aggression, however, was stopped by the heroic action of the then inhabitants of Attica, who, taking the lead of the oppressed states, finally secured liberty to all who dwelt within the Pillars of Hercules. Subsequently both races were destroyed by mighty cataclysms, which brought destruction in a single day and night, the natural features of the Attic land were entirely changed, and the Atlantic island sank bodily beneath the waves.

Such is the general sketch of this terrible episode in ancient history, given by Critias in the Timæus, and so interested were his audience, that they requested some fuller account of these famous and highly civilized nations of antiquity. To his Grecian hearers the primæval policy and history of their own race was naturally the greater interest. As, however, the Atlantean conflict were the climax of the narrative, Critias proceeds to give an account of their history and institutions. And thus he begins with their mythical traditions :—

In the centre of the Atlantic island was a fair and beautiful plain. In the centre of this plain and fifty stades ¶ from its confines, was a low range of hills. There dwelt an earth-born couple,** Evenor and Leucippe, who had an only daughter, Clito ; after the death of her parents, the god Poseidon, to whom the island had been assigned, became enamoured of the maiden. To make his love a safe dwelling-place, he surrounded the hills with alternate belts or zones of land and water, two of land and three of sea, each in its entire circumference equally distant from the centre· He also caused a hot and cold spring to flow in the centre island and made

* The Straits of Gibraltar.

† As known to the Greeks ; that is to say, the northern coasts of Africa as far as Egypt and Asia Minor.

‡ America. § The Mediterranean.

‖ The Etruscan states in early times extended their sway over the greater part of Italy and furnished Rome with her polity and religious institutions.

¶ Nearly six miles.

** The names were originally Egyptian, but Solon, having studied the science of the power of names, translated them into his own tongue.

every kind of food to grow abundantly. Ten male children were born to the god in five twin-births. When they had grown to manhood, he divided the island into ten parts, giving one to each. And to the first-born of the eldest pair he gave his mother's dwelling and allotment, for it was the largest and best, and made him king [over his brethren and the others governors of land, giving them dominion over many people and great territories. And the eldest he named Atlas, and from him the whole island and sea were called Atlantic. So they and their descendants dwelt for many generations, holding extensive sway over the sea of islands, and extending their power as far as Egypt and Tyrrhenia. By far the most renowned, however, was the race of Atlas, the kings ever handing down the succession to their eldest sons, and being possessed of such wealth as no dynasty ever yet obtained or will easily procure hereafter. Now this wealth was both drawn from foreign tributary countries and from Atlantis itself, which was very rich in minerals, especially its mines of orichalcum, now a mere name, but then the most precious of all metals save gold. The country also was exceedingly rich in timber and pasturage. Moreover, there were vast numbers of elephants. Spices, gums and odorous plants of every description, flowers, fruit trees and vegetables of all kinds and many other luxurious products, this wonderful island, owing to its magnificent climate, brought forth, sacred, beautiful, wonderful and infinite in number. Nor were the inhabitants content with the natural advantages of their glorious island, but displayed a marvellous industry and skill in engineering and the constructive arts. For in the centre island they built a Royal palace, each succeeding king trying to surpass his predecessor in adorning and adding to the building, so that it struck all beholders with the greatest admiration. Now the formation of the zones or belts round the ancient abode of the god was very regular, the circumference of each zone being equally distant from the common centre; and the outermost zones of sea and of land were each three stades * broad, and the next pair of two stades each, the succeeding zone of sea being of one stade, while the central seat itself had a diameter of five shades. And they bridged † over the water zones, making a way from and to the palace, and dug a great canal ‡ from the sea to the uttermost zone of water, wide enough to admit the largest vessels.

They also made water-ways through the zones of land, wide enough for a trireme § to pass, and roofed them over, for the height of the land zones above the water was considerable. Moreover, they enclosed the island, zones, and bridges, with stone walls, placing towers and gates at the

---

* A stade is about 606 feet.

† The width of the bridges was a plethrum, about 101 feet.

‡ Three stades broad, a plethrum wide, and fifty stades long, some six miles.

§ A ship with three banks of oars.

bridges. The stone they quarried from the face of the centre island and from both faces of the land zones, at the same time fashioning a line of docks on each bank of the water zones, leaving a natural roof of rock.

The stone was of three colours, white, black, and red, so that many of the buildings presented a gay appearance. The whole circuit of the wall of the outer zone was covered with brass, which they used like plaster, of the inner zone with tin, and of the acropolis itself with orichalcum, which was of a glittering appearance. The palace within the acropolis was constructed as follows: In the centre was the sacred shrine of Poseidon and Clito, surrounded by a golden enclosure. Hard by stood the great temple of Poseidon * of a different style of architecture to the Greek. The exterior was covered with silver, except the pediments and pinnacles, which were lined with gold. Within, the roof was a magnificent mosaic of gold, ivory, and orichalcum, and all the walls, pillars, and pavements were covered with orichalcum. The most remarkable object of the interior was a gigantic statue of the god, equal in height to the building, mounted on a chariot drawn by six winged horses, and round the car were a hundred Nereïds riding on dolphins; there were also many other statues and numerous votive offerings of the citizens. Round the exterior were placed golden statues of the princes and princesses of the Royal blood, and statues erected by the kings and also by private individuals both of the city and of subject states. There was also an altar of proportionate magnificence. And they had baths for summer and winter, supplied by the hot and cold springs, there being baths for the Royal Family, for men, for women, for horses and other animals. By a system of aqueducts, the water of the springs was carried to the two land zones and utilized for the irrigation of plantations and beautiful gardens. In these zones were many temples of other gods, gardens and gymnasia both for men and horses. Indeed, in the larger belt was a splendid race-course, extending throughout its entire length, a stade broad, and lined on either side with barracks for the household troops. Those, however, of them who were conspicuous for their loyalty, were lodged in the smaller zone, and the most faithful of all in the citadel itself. Moreover, the docks were filled with shipping and naval stores of every description. At fifty stades from the outer water belt or harbour in every direction, another wall was built, enclosing the whole city and meeting the great canal at the sea entrance. The space between this wall and the first water belt was thickly built over and inhabited by a dense population; and the canal and largest harbour were crowded with merchant shipping from all parts, and the din and tumult of their commerce continued all day long and the night through. Such is a general sketch of their wonderful city. Now, as regards the rest of the country; it was very mountainous, with exceedingly pre-

---

* It was a stade long, three plethra broad, and of a proportionate height.

cipitous coasts, and the plain surrounding the city was itself surrounded by mountain chains, broken only at the sea entrance. And the plain was smooth and level, and of an oblong shape, lying north and south, three thousand stades in one direction and two thousand in the other. And the mountains were said to be the grandest in the world for their number, size and beauty; they were inhabited, moreover, by many prosperous and wealthy villages, for there was an abundance of rivers and lakes, meadows and pasturage for all kinds of cattle and quantities of timber. They surrounded the plain by an enormous canal or dike, the size of which is almost incredible for a work of human undertaking.* By it the water from the mountains was conducted round the plain and flowed out to sea near the entrance of the great canal. Moreover, parallel dikes † were cut from the upper bounding canal to that on the sea-side, one hundred stades distant from each other, and these were again joined by transverse water-ways. They also employed the canals for irrigation, and so raised two crops in the year. And the plain was divided into sixty thousand wards or sections, each supplying a certain contingent of men to the army and navy; and the army consisted of war-chariots and a kind of light car, holding two warriors, one of whom dismounted and fought, and the other drove, men-at-arms, archers, slingers, stone-shooters, javelin-men, and light-armed troops. ‡ Such was the military system of the city. And the other nine cities of the confederation had slightly different systems, which it would be tedious to narrate.

Now, as regards the polity of the Atlanteans, the kings exercised an autocracy over the people; but in their dealings with each other and for the common welfare, they followed the traditional law of their divine progenitor, which was also inscribed on a column of orichalcum by the first kings, and the column placed in the temple of the deity. Thither they assembled every alternate fifth and sixth year to decide any disputes that might have arisen between them. And these are the ceremonies they performed before proceeding to their decision. There were sacred bulls grazing in the precincts of the temple. And the ten kings, after first praying to the deity, armed only with staves and nooses, proceeded to capture one of the herd, and sacrificed him on the column over the inscription.

There was also an oath written on the column, invoking dire curses on those of them who infringed the statutes of their divine parent. And filling the sacrificial chalice, § they cast in a clot of blood for each, and

---

* One hundred and one feet deep, 606 feet broad, and upwards of 1,250 miles in length.
† One hundred and one feet broad.
‡ Their standing army consisted of upwards of a million men; their navy of 240,000 and 1,200 ships.　　　　§ Crater or mixing bowl.

purifying the column, they burnt the rest with fire. Then, with golden cups they dipped from the chalice and poured a libation on the fire of sacrifice; and swearing to do justice according to the laws on the column, and neither to rule nor suffer the rule of any of their number, contrary to these ancestral laws, after invoking the prescribed curses both on themselves and their descendants, if untrue to their solemn pledge, they drank and deposited the cups in the temple. Then, having eaten the sacrificial meal and busied themselves with the other necessary offices, when evening grew on, clad in most beautiful dark blue robes, they sat in darkness on the ground round the now cold embers of the sacrificial fire; and through the night they judged and were judged, but when morning came, they inscribed their decisions on a golden tablet and deposited it, with their robes, in the temple as a memorial. And the chief of these enactments were that the kings should never wage war one against the other, but should ever give mutual aid should any of the cities try to destroy the Royal race; and the chief power was assigned to the Atlantic race; nor could any king put to death a kinsman, without first getting a majority of votes from his Royal colleagues. For many generations, then, so long as the nature of their divine ancestry was strong within them, they remained obedient to these laws and well affected to their divine kinship. For they possessed true and altogether lofty ideas, and exercised mildness and practical wisdom, both in the ordinary vicissitudes of life and in their mutual relations; and looking above everything except virtue, they considered things present of small importance and contentedly bore their weight of riches as a burden; nor were they intoxicated with luxury, but clearly perceived that wealth and possessions are increased by mutual friendship and the practice of true virtue, whereas, by a too anxious pursuit of riches, both possessions themselves are corrupted and friendship likewise perishes therewith. And so it was that they reached the great prosperity that we have described.

But when their mortal natures began to dominate the divine within them, through their inability to bear present events, to those who can truly perceive, they began to display unbecoming conduct and to degenerate, destroying the fairest of their most valuable possessions. To those, however, who cannot perceive that true mode of life which leads to real happiness, they appeared most glorious and happy, though actually full of aggrandizement and unjust power. Zeus, however, the god of gods, who rules according to Law, and can perceive such things, wishing to recall a once honourable race to the practice of virtue, assembled all the gods and said :

*   *   *   *   *   *

E. E. O.

[Here, unfortunately, the text of the dialogue ceases abruptly.]

THE MAYAS.

A LECTURE

DELIVERED AT THE

BLAVATSKY LODGE, THEOSOPHICAL SOCIETY,

BY

MADAME A. D. Le PLONGEON.

INDIVIDUALITY AND PERSONALITY.

London;

THEOSOPHICAL PUBLISHING SOCIETY,

7, DUKE STREET, ADELPHI, W.C.

—

1890.

THE MAYAS.

THIS occasion is especially gratifying to us, for besides the pleasure and honour of addressing you, we have the happy certainty of speaking to those who are accustomed to looking beneath the surface of things, to those who rejoice in acquiring knowledge, and who will easily grasp the many facts that we must crowd into this hour's reading. This evening we cannot have the satisfaction of illustrating our subject and thus making clearer our remarks, but if future occasions offer, we have several hundreds of lantern slides ready.

You are aware that Mexico, Central America, and parts of South America are rich in antiquities, the field is indeed so vast, and so neglected, comparatively speaking, that an army of workers is needed there. One of the most interesting spots is certainly that peninsula which the Spanish invaders named Yucatan—now one of the Mexican States, in olden times the seat of a great empire—whose territory seems to have extended N.W. as far as the Isthmus of Tehuantepec, and S.E. as far as the Isthmus of Darien. It is a most interesting fact that the sculptors, in making statues of their monarchs, gave them a posture, as far as the human body could be made to assume it, resembling the contour of that territory, as may be seen by comparing a map with the statue portrayed in Dr. Plongeon's book, " Sacred Mysteries."

We are frequently asked *why* we made up our minds to study the ruins of Yucatan. Well, it was, in fact, a continuation of archæological studies begun by the Doctor as early as 1862, in Peru. There he had reached certain conclusions, and it was in search of further corroboration that he went to Central America, after having also made a close study of old Spanish MSS. in the British Museum.

Arrived in Yucatan, we found there was an immense amount of work to be done, the greater part of it in dangerous places. A few words will make this clear. History tells us that of all the Americans, none so determinedly resisted the Spaniards as those of Yucatan, the Mayas, whose ancestors seemed to have been the most civilized of old American nations. Even at the time of the conquest the natives were far more refined than the Spaniard, who only succeeded in reducing them to slavery after twenty-five years of heroic resistance to cavalry, coat of mail, and fire-arms. Nor would the Mayas then have succumbed, had not the Spaniards found allies in tribes living on the northern coast of the peninsula, and also in a powerful party of Nahualts, at that time likewise in the country.

There is no history more heroic and tragic than that of the Maya people during the last thousand years. After having conquered by force, the Spaniard treated the unhappy people with shameful cruelty and tyranny.

In 1847 the latest great uprisal of natives occurred. After a long and fearful struggle a few thousand freed themselves completely from the white man's control, and built their stronghold in the south-west part of the Peninsula. Not only do they still maintain their liberty, but they are a terror to the white man, and those Indians yet in their service. Their war-cry is " Death to the white monkey!" They have destroyed cities, towns, and villages, driving those under Mexican authority to the northern and most arid part of the land. Unfortunately, many of the ancient ruins are on the territory of these hostile Indians, though the danger is becoming less every year; not only owing to railroads being built, but because the Indians are now carrying on a less active war, and are also decreasing in numbers. They are the miserable vestige of a once noble race! The ruins that we first visited were, at that time, very much exposed. We had to sleep dressed as by day, only removing our boots, and our rifles had to be always close at hand. I need hardly tell you that in those forests I adopted a more convenient apparel than skirts, and I must confess that when obliged to resume these I felt much hampered. It would be a waste of precious time to now talk of our dangers and hardships, illness, hunger, etc., but a few words must be said about our work. We were truly amazed at the perfection of sculptures found in the old city of Chichin Itza, or " City of the Sages," and we heartily wished that it were in our power, not only to save from further decay, but to rebuild the edifices crumbling before us. That being out of the question, what was the next best thing? Surely to obtain what would enable us to make a *facsimile* of their measurements, photographs, moulds. For that we toiled. Our Indian labourers could not understand why we wanted to measure pyramids and terraces, stairs, doorways, and walls; and they could not be trusted to hold the end of the measuring tape exactly where we desired, so we two had to do all that work alone, and some of the terraces were hundreds of feet long, cumbered by felled trees and stones of all shapes, beneath which venomous vipers lurked, while the tropical heat made us dizzy, and tiny wood ticks worked their way into our skin. Taking photographs was not much easier; though well versed in that art, we made about ten plates for every perfect one obtained. True, we wanted them *very* perfect. Many of the sculptures had to be photographed from the top of a ladder supported only by sticks on the edge of a very steep and broken up terrace or pyramid. The longest task was probably the mould-making, because we would not content ourselves with mere squeezes. The result of our work is all that could be wished. We can now build in any part of the world a Maya palace or temple which might be converted into a museum of American antiquities. This is what we should like to see realized . . . We could even place within the walls, besides beautiful sculptures, a few fresco paintings, *facsimiles*, which we were happy enough to rescue from oblivion. Of these there are two tableaux varying in length from one to four feet, the figures being from six to nine inches high. This collection is the only specimen of ancient American paintings. They portray certain events in the history of a family that reigned there many centuries ago. But while at work we were haunted by one desire. On many exterior walls there were sculptured inscriptions. While these remained complete enigmas, we were very much in the condition of persons looking at pictures in the a book, but unable to read the text. Great mystery! Could we not penetrate it ? If we could begin, others might come after to finish. First, in what language were the inscriptions ? We knew that the Maya people were, and are, excessively conservative, to such an extent that this, and their hatred of the Spaniard, has made it impossible for the white man to impose his speech on the vanquished. To this day masters must address their servants in the beautiful Maya tougue if they would have their orders executed. Was it not then possible that this same language, a most perfect one in its construction, should be the one hidden in the mural inscriptions ? Time and study brought an affirmative answer to this query. But first a few words about that language, yet spoken by the people, not only of Yucatan, but as far south as Guatemala and Tabasco. It is a very old form of speech, and it affords simple and natural etymologies for names of places and tribes in Asia and Africa, as well as for those of divinities worshipped by Egyptians, Chaldees, and other civilized nations of antiquity, even for the names of the various parts of the the Indian cosmogonic diagram called Sri-Santara. The grammatical forms and syntaxis of the Maya and Egyptian tongues are almost identical, while it is well known that the Egyptian language has no cognates in Asia or Africa ; and, moreover, Dr. Le Plongeon's discoveries have proved that the hieratic alphabets of the learned men of Egypt and Mayax (as Yucatan was anciently called) are almost identical. The very word Maya must be familiar to all of you, since in India it means illusion, for which reason the Brahmins call the earth *Maya*. We find this word scattered over a great portion of the globe in India, Chaldea, Greece, Egypt, and even in modern times in Central Asia, Afghanistan, in the interior parts of Africa, and in tropic America as far back as Sonora. In one place, it is the name of god or goddess; in another, of hero or heroine ; elsewhere, of a cast or tribe ; in a fourth, that of place or country.

The Rig-veda teaches us that Maya is the goddess by whose union with

Brahma all things were created. In Greece, Maya is daughter of Atlas, mother of Hermes, the good mother Kubêli, mother of the gods, whose worship has survived to our day in Spain, France, England, Germany, in the feast of the Maya, or May Queen. Did time allow, it could be shown that the word Maya is scattered over a broad extent of the earth ; and everywhere in connection with wisdom, superior knowledge, and power. In Tahiti and other islands of the Pacific, the banana-tree is sacred, and is called Maya.

Even the Greek Alphabet, *i.e.*, the names of the letters, form a poem in Maya language, which reads as follows :—

FREE TRANSLATION.

ALPHA.	Heavily break—*the*—waters
BETA.	extending—*over the*—plains.
GAMMA.	*They*—cover—*the*—land
DELTA.	*in* low places where
EPZILON.	*there are*—obstructions, shores form, and whirlpools—
ZETA.	strike—*the*—earth
ETA.	with water.
THETA.	The water spreads
IOTA.	*on*—all that lives and moves—
KAPPA.	sediments give way.
LAMBDA.	Submerged is—*the*—land
MU.	*of*—Mu—
NI.	the peaks—*only*
XI.	appear above—*the water.*
OMIKRON.	Whirlwinds blow round
PI.	by little and little,
RHO.	until comes
ZIGMA.	cold air. Before
TAU.	where—*existed*—valleys,
UPZILON.	*now*, abysses, frozen tanks—In circular places
PHI.	clay—is—formed.
CHI.	*A* mouth
PSI.	opens ; vapours
OMEGA.	*then*—come forth—*and*—volcanic sediments.

With these few words about the Maya language we must return to the point whence we diverged—namely, the decipherment of inscriptions carved on the old walls. It began by Dr. Le Plongeon one day finding that certain signs were exactly like those of old Egypt, which led him to think that others might also be. Nor was he disappointed, and by giving them the same value, he found that they resulted in words in the Maya language. A key to those mysterious hieroglyphs was indeed found !

Beside stone inscriptions, we also have Maya MSS.—because a few of the books in use among the inhabitants of Yucatan at the time of the arrival of the Spaniards were saved from destruction; how, or by whom, is not known. The Spanish priests burnt all they could lay hands on. The volumes that were saved found their way to European libraries. The text and illustrations are in colours on parchment prepared from deerskin. The Mayas also made paper from the bark of the mulberry-tree, by a pro-cess similar to that used by the Egyptians in preparing papyrus. Strange to say, Bishop Lunda, who ordered the burning of the books, kept a copy, made by himself, of certain alphabetical and other signs, but these alone would not suffice to read the books, while on the walls only two or three of those signs can be traced, such inscriptions being graved in hieratic characters.

At the time of the Nahualt invasion, about the sixth century of the Christian era, owing to many political troubles, the use and knowledge of the hieratic or sacred characters were lost. Then only a few antiquaries knew the meaning of the mural inscriptions. In time, no one was able to read them; and they became a sealed book, which modern antiquaries have heretofore not succeeded in bursting asunder. At the Lowell Institute in Boston, last March, Dr. Le Plongeon, having on the screen pictures of sculptured façades, read the stones to his audience. Though it is a strict law of the Lowell Institute that no lecture shall exceed one hour's duration, that lecture did, and even the President failed to remind the lecturer that his time was up.

Not having it in our power this evening to show you any of the carved inscriptions, I can only say a few words about the general character of such writings. The name Can, that of a dynasty of kings, is found in many forms; and most of the inscriptions are records of certain deeds, or pane-gyrics of members of that family. We also find accounts of national catas-trophies and other events. Of these inscriptions we have made moulds, and hope to fully interpret them later on. Many of the ornaments are in themselves descriptive of cosmogonic and religious conceptions, prominent features being the serpent form, and a conventional representation of the mammoth's face, embodying certain letters, giving its name. The walls, covered with elaborate carving, and brilliantly coloured, as they originally were, must have been very grand in effect.

Passing now from stones to books we find that the historian Landa gives this description : " They wrote their books on long sheets that they folded so as to form pages (like a fan), enclosing them between two boards elaborately ornamented. They wrote in columns on both sides of the page. This paper was made from the roots of a tree, and coated with a white varnish, on which it was easy to write." Do not these books recall the papyri found in Egyptian tombs ? Many of the volumes were illustrated with designs and colours. Some pages contained text only, others were illustrated.

Cogolluds, another historian, tells us : " In those books were recorded the dates, the wars, the inundations, hurricanes, famines, and other events." Those volumes, in fact, contained not only the history of the Maya people, but of nations of a very distinct cast of features and colour with whom they entertained friendly relations, or against whom they waged war ; also a record of geological and meteorological phenomena, and the art of medicine, archæological studies. It was dreadful to burn such books, but the fanatical priests only followed the example of Paul, who, in Ephesus, instigated the Christians to burn books that were valued at fifty thousand pieces of silver.

The four Maya books which have reached our hands are written in the characters of an alphabet, which seems to have been formulated after the invasion of the Nahualts, in the early centuries of the Christian era. The volume called " Troano MS." has been closely studied Dr. Le Plongeon, who hopes to fully translate it. It contains something of geology, of mythology, and of history. We there find that the Mayas believed in *elementals* and personified the forces of Nature. One chapter is a most interesting account of the submersion of a great island called *Mu* in the Atlantic Ocean. It seems to have been the same island known to us as Atlantis. Again we must regret the want of pictures here to-night. However, though not able to show you, sentence by sentence, I can give Dr. Le Plongeon's translation of the paragraph describing the last scene of the terrible cataclysm. It is as follows: " In the year 6 Kan, on the 11th muluc, in the month Zac, there occurred terrible earthquakes, which continued without interruption until the 13th Chuen. The country of the hills of mud, the land of *Mu*, was sacrificed ; being twice upheaved, it suddenly disappeared during the night, the basin being continually shaken by volcanic forces. Being confined, these caused the land to sink and rise several times, and in various places. At last the surface gave way and ten countries were torn asunder and scattered helter skelter. Unable to withstand the force of the seismic convulsions, they sank, with their 64 millions of inhabitants, 8,060 years before the writing of this book."

This would seem to be an account of the greatest of all deluges, which, the Egyptian priests told Solon, was recorded in their temples, as in those of Chaldea and India. The author of another Maya book, now known as " Codex Cortesianus," also wrote a lengthy description of the same cataclysm, agreeing with that in the Troano, which I have just had the pleasure of reading to you.

We have reason to believe that if circumstances permitted, we could bring to light several Maya volumes which have lain concealed since the early part of the Christian era, when the wise men hid them in a certain building to save them from being destroyed by Nahualt invaders. Such books would doubtless illumine the dim past, and it is our sincere hope that if we are not able to bring them to light, some other explorer, in no distant future, may attempt the task, and have his efforts crowned with success. Setting aside literary treasures, there are many beautiful objects of art hidden among the ruins, safe for the present from mischievous hands. We ourselves have unearthed many pieces of sculpture, and have again carefully buried them because it was not in our power to convey them to a place of safe keeping. Our first excavations were made at the tomb of a certain individual, whose name—Coh, or Chaacmol, *i.e.*, Leopard—has since become famous through his statue, which we unearthed. It may interest you to hear a brief account of this, because it will make known to you how the Mayas disposed of their dead. A study of the fresco paintings which I have mentioned, and of certain carved inscriptions, led us to seek in one spot for the resting-place of the remains of an individual who, many centuries ago, played an impor- tant *role* in the history of that country. The once beautiful mausoleum had become an almost shapeless pile. Happily the corner stones were yet in place, and stairs could still be counted, leading to the summit, on the four sides of the quadrangular structure. Even the largest ornamental stones were in place, four at each corner; two having macaws sculptured on them, and two leopards. These were the totems, or figure-names of a famous warrior prince and his sister and wife, Princess Mo. There were many sculptured stones scattered over the ground, some representing skulls, others gigantic snake heads; of these, a few were still in place at the foot of the stairs. Among the *débris* we found a body, in the round, a reclining leopard, with three holes in the back as the leopard in bas- relief also had. It was headless, indicating spear wounds, the cause of death, inflicted by a jealous brother, but near by we found a human head, with the features of a dying man. With a faint hope that it might belong to the leopard we brought them in contact, and were rejoiced to find that the broken parts fitted into each other. Here, then, in Yucatan, we had a veritable sphinx! Its original place had been on the top of the monument, where we still found the oblong stone on which the sphinx had rested. After carefully measuring everything so that Dr. Le Plongeon might make, as he since has, a restoration of the once beautiful mausoleum, we proceeded to excavate. An arduous undertaking, because we were unprovided with implements of any description. A wall five feet thick of solid masonry formed the shell of the monument, and to our surprise we found the interior filled with loose stones, none weighing less than twenty pounds; liquid mortar had been poured among them, not sufficient, however, to make a solid body to hold them together. The removal of these stones was a tedious task, because after we had made a shaft down into the centre, to touch one on either side entailed the falling of a hundred. We had no planks, no ropes, no nails; the great knife, called *máchete*, had to serve all purposes. With saplings from the forest we constructed a palisade to prevent the stones from crushing us. The saplings were tied together with thick vines, called in India *jungle ropes*. With such primitive means Dr. Le Plongeon also succeeded in constructing a derrick —or at least what served as one—a lever like those used in Egypt and other parts of the Orient to draw water from deep places. We drew stones. Our Indian workmen were unwilling to have the tomb opened, believing that if they touched anything there the soul of the prince would bring upon them sickness, if not death, before a year elapsed; consequently they worked badly and slowly. Six feet below the summit we found a perfectly level floor, a few inches thick, made of concrete, the upper surface covered with fine plaster, painted bright yellow. (I need hardly tell you that among the Mayas each colour had its special meaning.) Beneath the floor there were more stones, down to the level of the ground; then a second floor. Through this we likewise broke, and again our expectations met with nothing but loose rough stones. But after a few hours' work we began to pick up from among them curious round buttons, apparently bone, with double holes bored through their backs. Soon a large round stone urn came to view. It required three men to remove the heavy lid. Notwithstanding its size, the urn contained only some dust, which we took to be the remains of a human brain, and a large round apple-green jadite bead. On a level with that urn, and quite near, a finely-sculptured white stone head was soon discovered. The workmen immediately called the figure "an enchanted King." The head was nearly double life-size, and there was much speculating as to the form and posture of the lower part of the statue, yet hidden beneath rough, heavy stones. On the following day we found a third floor, the head and shoulders of the statue rising through a hole in the middle of it. This floor being removed we discovered a second urn, larger than the first and containing partially cremated matter, the heart and viscera of the person represented by the statue. These remains have been analyzed. There was also an oblong head of jadite, of that peculiar, apple-green colour which is found only in Burmah, being the rarest of all the jadites. It would be interesting, indeed, if some person, having psychometric powers, could trace the history of this stone. In the same urn were small flat rings of mother-of-pearl, and some red cinnabar.

On the base, which was one piece with the statue, we found 64 beautiful arrow points, 32 on each side, some white, others green, said to be of jade, though we are inclined to doubt this, jade being too hard a substance to be worked, as these points are apparently, by chipping. The statue was too large and too heavy, weighing 3,000 pounds, for our men to hoist up a shaft without proper machinery, so we made an opening in the side of the monument, and an inclined plane down to the statue, which was some feet below the earth's level. Then, from the forked trunk of a tree, and a stone ring, a rough capstan was formed, with which to draw out the monolith. Ropes were indispensable. These our men manufactured from the pliant bark of a tree called *habin*. By these means, and after surmounting much obstinate disobedience on the part of our men, we at last brought the statue above ground. The posture is shown in the volume S. M. already mentioned, but it conveys a very imperfect idea of the beauty of that ancient work of art, as it was when we first looked at it. One side of the body was perfectly white, the other a light brown, the flesh-colour of the natives. The garters, bracelets, and sandal-straps were of red and yellow; a ribbon round the neck was also red. From this hung a very curious breast-plate, like some now in use among high officials in Burmah. Between the extended hands, and resting on the abdomen, was a circular plate, like a modern soup-plate, representing Honduras Bay, the posture of the figure being intended, as said, to indicate the contour of what was once the Maya Empire.

Without nails or screws, Dr. Le Plongeon managed to contrive a cart on which to remove the statue. We also had to open and level a road over which to convey it. At the end of fifteen days we had it away from the territory of the Indians, and within the military lines of the State. At that time a revolution broke out in favour of Porfirio Diaz, actual President of Mexico. Our men were no longer permitted to bear arms, and we could not ask them to work in such exposed places without means of defence. In the forest we built a house over the statue, and went to study the ruins existing on islands near the east coast of Yucatan. During our absence, and at a time when Dr. Le Plongeon was grievously wounded, the statue was seized by Mexican authority, and conveyed to the capital, where it now is in the Mexican National Museum. It was not properly taken care of, and when we visited that museum we found not only all the colour gone from it, but moss forming on it. Nevertheless, when Dr. Le Plongeon asked permission to take a mould of it, the Mexican Government sent him a written permit, *provided he would not injure the statue !*

The American Government, always apathetic in protecting its citizens, refused to take any steps toward defending us against the robbery of that statue, notwithstanding the fact that by the laws of the

State of Yucatan the finder of any art treasure, or any antiquity, has a right to one half its value.

Concerning the individual whose status we have been discussing, there is very much to be said, more, indeed, than can possibly be crowded into this discourse. Startling as it may sound, I assure you that that personage seems to have been the living origin of the myth of Osiris in Egypt. There are so many facts pointing to this conclusion that we cannot close our eyes to it, and when Dr. Le Plongeon's new work is published, many readers will probably agree with us.*

I have already mentioned some fresco paintings which we found in one room. It was in a shrine, built to the memory of that same person. The dedication on the outer entablature of the edifice reads thus: "Mó" —(this was the name of his wife, and we all know that Isis is likewise called Mo, spelt Mau)—"Mó craves to fervently invoke Coh, the warrior of warriors." A grand portico led into the shrine, and there we excavated from beneath the fallen roof a superb altar, supported on fifteen figures, after the manner of caryates. It reminded us of altars erected at the entrance of Egyptian tombs, on which fruit and flowers were presented every year, as among the Mayas, to the souls of the departed. But the altar itself is almost a *facsimile* of certain ancient structures yet existing in the old city of Angor-Thom, Cambogia. Not two of the caryates are alike. Some have a triple breast-plate, triangular apron, and curiously fastened girdle; three things exactly as we see them used by officers of high rank in Burmah. It is only one more link added to a long chain of similarities, connecting certain eastern and western lands, and showing that in remote ages intimate relations must have existed between them. Could you see the Maya and Indo-China altars side by side, you would be amazed at the astounding similarity! You will remember that Valmiki, in his beautiful poem, the "Ramayana," tells us that Maya, the terrible warrior, magician, and architect of the Davanas, took possession of, and established himself in, the southern part of India, in Dekkan particularly,† that Maya was a great navigator, whose ships sailed from the western to the eastern ocean, from the southern to the northern seas. And, strange to say, the etymology of the word " Davana " is, in Maya language, " He who has his house upon salt waters." I must ask your kind forbearance if, without bringing forward the many facts on which we base

---

* It will be interesting, indeed, to have it shown that Osiris was ever a living person, and not merely a solar myth. But the Troano MSS. show that the Mayas "personified the forces of nature," as did the Egyptians.—T.P.S.

† Maya is here spoken of under the male aspect, as the chief of Kabiri, the warrior kings. Maya is as frequently seen under its female aspect as Mai, Ma, Mo, or Mo-on, *i.e.*, the Moon, or Isis—passive nature.—T.P.S.

our opinion, I say that we have been forced to the conclusion that ancient American civilization, if not the mother of ancient historical nations, was at least a great factor in the framing of these cosmogonic notions and primitive traditions, and in teaching them many of their arts and sciences. Is it not admitted by geologists that the western continent is the oldest? Hence it is the one on which biological conditions necessary to man's existence must perforce have been first developed. Would it not seem that civilization, like the heavenly bodies, following an eastward course, after completing a cycle of 10,000 years, at the end of which, according to the Egyptians, the souls gone west must return and begin a new earthly existence—civilization, I say, after many ups and downs, is returning to its birthplace to gather in its mother's lap fresh vigour before starting anew on its peregrination around the world? Watch its course. See how western civilization is already invading Japan, China, India, and other Asiatic countries. History repeats itself. Its actual line of travel is that which it followed in bygone ages.

During a second expedition to the ruins of Chichen, we opened the tomb of the elder brother of the warrior Coh, that of a high priest named Cay, or Huancay, a word meaning in that language " the wise fish," which brings to mind Oannes, the personage, half-fish, half-man, said by Berosus to have brought civilization to Mesopotamia. The exterior of the monument was ornamented with beautifully carved stones, the greater number of which had fallen. [Some represented fish, others sacred symbols. On the largest slab was a human face within the distended jaws of a snake. Around the face we found the name Cay, written in Egyptian as well as Maya hieroglyphs. The tomb itself, like that of Coh, was square; its four sides facing the cardinal points. Thirteen steps on each side led to the top platform, which was 13ft. above the ground and 52ft. square. In its centre was a large slab, on which formerly was a statue, about double life-size, in the same posture as that of Coh. At the base of the monument we found the lower half of the statue. On the north side of the monument we opened a trench, and found it constructed similarly to the one previously opened. We had to prop back the stones as before. After ten days' work we reached the monument. There we found, on a level with the earth, a figure lying on its back, thickly coated with loose mortar. One leg was broken off below the knee, but we found it underneath the figure, and adjusted it in place to make a picture. The head rested on a stone painted bright red, representing a snake's tongue. The statue was in a squatting posture, but if standing would have been six feet high. It was of white stone, and was painted dark brown. The head was small and apparently hairless, painted blue, and over that, from the forehead down to the shoulders, were red streaks.

Doubtless everyone of these things had a significant meaning. The eyes were open, and the lids painted blue. The lips were red. The ears were pierced, and so was the back part of the top of the head. In the palm and wrist of the right hand there was a groove, as if for a rounded stick to fit in. The figure is apish-looking, and the hands quite peculiar; but fingers and toes were furnished with nails of polished shell, neatly fitted in. Nearly all had fallen. The loins were covered with a scanty garment, like that anciently worn by Egyptian labourers. The right foot is turned in, as if the person had been club-footed. The sandals were fancifully ornamented and secured with red ties. After clearing off stones and mortar, we found that the statue had rested on conoidal pillars, placed horizontally side by side. There were four, 3ft. 3in. high, one foot in their greatest diameter, and painted blue, a colour emblematical of sanctity and mourning among the Mayas, and largely used at funerals by the old Egyptians. Besides these four pillars we found 178 more. They extended over a space of twenty square feet, and were in places three or four feet deep. Two-thirds of them were blue, the others red. These conoidal pillars remind us of that which represented the Phœnician god, Baal. These found by us were probably emblems of sun-worship. The number 182 was the number of half the days of our year, and of that of Mayas, which had the same number. They also divided the year into lunar months, and like the Egyptians, had an epact of five unlucky days, and at the same time of the year as the people of the Nile. On a level with the pillars were also twelve serpent heads, with feathers and various signs exquisitely sculptured on them. These were placed so as to face the various points of the compass. From the top of each head there stood up a kind of plume or flame, and on either side of the upper nostril was a perpendicular ornament, like horns. This, we have discovered, represents the opening pod of the Ceiba-tree, which was sacred to the Mayas, a tree being one emblem of their own country. The feathers painted on the snakes' bodies were coloured green, the scales of the belly yellow, as also the edge of the jaws. The inside of the mouth and the forked projecting tongue were red, the fangs and teeth white. The whites of the eyes were beautifully polished shell, neatly fitted, with a round hole where the pupil should be. These twelve snakes, totems of twelve kings of the Can dynasty (Can being the Maya word for serpent), whose portraits are found in "alto-relievo" on a *façade* in Chichen, call to mind the twelve gods said by Herodotus to have governed the Egyptians before the reign of Menes, their first terrestrial King. On the south side of the excavation, at the statue, but lower down, was a round white urn, about two-and-a-half feet in diameter. With difficulty four men pushed off the lid, discovering within only a little red substance and a square piece of green jadite, with a human face, and letters carved on it. There was also a tube of the same precious stone, but the ends crumbled when we handled it. Besides these we found among the red matter many small pieces of turquoise and a ball of natural crystal, the special possession of the high priest and prophet. The urn and serpents being removed, we stood on a level floor. Two feet below we discovered a small pile of bones, those of a crocodile, and on each side of it was a smoke-coloured obsidian spearhead, about seven inches long; also many fragments of pottery, greatly varying in quality. Below the bones was a concrete floor, perfectly level, and painted bright red, extending throughout the mound. Two feet below again there was yet another floor, the *seventh* in the mound, and bright yellow. Believing there might still be something more concealed we continued the opening on the south side, in which direction the spearhead had pointed. We soon found a solid block of masonry, and within it, its carved surface turned eastward, stood an oblong stone covered with symbols, painted blue, yellow, and red. Later on we found two others like it, and also a sculptured fish, painted red.

We came to the conclusion that the various things found in the tomb of Cay were sacred objects from the temple in which he had officiated, even the curious statue which we have described; while that of the priest himself was on the upper platform, his ashes being preserved in the urn within. The Mayas cremated their dead, preserving the viscera in urns, as the Egyptians did. Elsewhere we found a most beautiful portrait of Cay, carved in the round in pure white marble, not polished, but made to imitate the texture of human skin. We had the joy of seeing that exquisite piece of work just as it was when the artist put his finishing touches to it; for, owing to some event which we cannot now guess at, the beautiful sculpture had been concealed within solid masonry as soon as completed. In order that such a fine object should not be injured, and remembering the fate of the Coh statue, we again thoroughly concealed the portrait of Cay.

An unillustrated lecture is perforce dull, and I sincerely hope that it may be our happiness to bring before you on some future occasion the many pictures which we have; then we can go more deeply into the subject, and speak of many interesting points which it is impossible to make clear without illustrations. To give you an idea of the vastness of the subject, I may say that when Dr. Le Plongeon, in March last, delivered seven lectures, he and his audience would have preferred fourteen. Dr. Le Plongeon's MSS., now ready for publication, have been examined by scholars, who affirm that it will create a sensation among historians and scientists, and they are kind enough to add that it is bound to be recognised as one of the great works of the age.

INDIVIDUALITY AND PERSONALITY.

In the study of Theosophy, which is the synthesis and ultimate issue of all Science, Philosophy and Religion, the range of subjects to be considered is so vast and far-reaching, that the mind of the student is liable to be at first dazzled, then confused, and finally a feeling of hopelessness sets in which causes him to withdraw altogether from the pursuit of the Higher Wisdom. In the face of this discouragement it is often well, instead of trying to deal at one and the same time with many new doctrines in seeming opposition to all one's former teachings, to examine some one point in detail, to become familiar with its various aspects, and finally to view it from a distance in order to observe its relation to the whole.

The neglect of this latter part of the proposition seems to be one cause why many abandon further study of the subject in impatience, and in their failure to see what good it can do, turn away in disgust at the monstrosity of the view presented. A fact, for instance, may be put forward for their observation, the truth of which they cannot well deny, but finding nothing in their too material consciousness to which it can be linked, the newly-discovered treasure falls from their grasp, as they find that they have been truly trying to " hitch their waggon on to some star," which had (to them) no existence. The fact fades from their mind like a dream, and they return to their old materialistic " grind," declaring that " all is vanity " which cannot be cognised by the animal senses.

A stranger at one of our meetings for discussion of Theosophical subjects lately, remarked that some of our arguments were very good, but why mix up with them sentimental ideas, *such as Karma.* Had he patiently examined this doctrine the gentleman would have found it to be nothing but an exposition of the fundamental natural law of cause and effect acting on human lives, and would have seen its reasonableness and its importance as a basis of Theosophical teaching. He would then probably have been led on to the consideration of other aspects of Theosophical truth, till one by one all were conquered.

Among these aspects there is none the right understanding of which is more important than the distinction between those two divisions of man's nature, called in Theosophy, the Individuality and the Personality. Without a right knowledge of all that is involved in these terms, no true system of ethics can be built up, for it is the constant tendency of mankind to cultivate the one at the expense of the other, and having thus destroyed the balance and harmony of Nature, he proceeds to attribute to her or to his fellow-beings, the mischievous results which he has himself brought about. The relation of the Personality to the Individuality is a little corner of the field of Theosophic study, which we may examine with profit in order to obtain a better understanding of the whole. And as analogy is useful, and since we are thinking of a field, we may without moving from the spot, lift up our eyes, and notice the tree whose leaves are beginning to fall. One by one they fade, and as the sap, the vital principle, is withdrawn from their cells, they drop off and die ; they are trodden into the soil beneath, their tissues disintegrate, their gases are dispersed in the atmosphere, they are gone into the " grave of things." Will they return again ? no, not with the same bodies, but the tree will clothe itself anew with other leaves which it will feed and inform with the sap, the vital principle that is stored up within itself, and which proceeds from the One Life which animates all Nature. Year after year this process is continued, and yet the tree remains always the same individual oak tree, or lime, or cedar, distinct not only from every other species, but even from every other tree of the same species. It is only by these continual changes and renewed lives that the tree attains its full development. The leaves are not meant for its adornment only, nor for the mere shelter of birds, nor to make glad the heart of man, but they are the means towards a fuller life in the tree itself. They are its breathing apparatus, and as they lift up their surface towards the sunlight, they draw in through a thousand pores the elements which are transmitted in their chemical laboratory into that colouring matter which gives such beauty to the forest and the garden, but which has its primary use in the economy of the tree itself. If the leaves are attacked by blight or grubs, and do not properly perform this function, the tree will remain stunted, and make no growth during that particular year ; another year, however, they may shoot forth with vigour, and the tree will increase in height and girth, and add to its permanent live stock, to its individuality as a tree. Without carrying our analogy too far, we may liken our personality to the leaves of the tree. It is the garb which our individuality, our incarnating Ego, dons for each life as the most appropriate expression of its actual state and needs. Certain physical traits will doubtless be due to heredity, but even these often become modified or disappear as the character develops, and the real self comes to the front. Now, the error of the ordinary human being, especially one under the influence of the prevalent materialism, is to mistake the personality for the real man, whereas it is but as the clothes of the actor, appropriate to the part he has to play. " Each man in his time plays many parts," is true even in our sense, whether Shakespeare intended it so or not, "each man," standing for the *real* Ego, and "many parts" for successive lives or personalities. The doctrine of Reincarnation, in itself a wide subject for study, is inseparably bound up with that of the Individuality and personality, as well as that of Karma, which determines the course of the Ego throughout its various lives. But on that we need not dwell just now. The personality being, to the uninstructed eye, more discernible than the individuality, men are apt to make it the object of their whole attention their striving and their love. They work for its welfare in life, exhausting their best energies in its behalf, and when it dies, they mourn for its outer shell with excess of grief, tending with infinite care the grave which holds it, though its component parts remain even there but a short time in cohesion. Christians say of course that the "spirit returns to God who gave it," but they do not generally behave as though this were their living belief. Even the religious man's ideas are sorely tinctured with a scepticism he dares not admit in words. It is because he does not understand the true relation of the personality to the individuality.

Let us try to define more exactly what is meant by those two words: Theosophy teaches that man's nature is sevenfold, the three higher parts constituting his spiritual and imperishable, the four lower his material and perishable nature. These two divisions are linked together during life by the fifth principle, the Manas or Ego, which on the one side is immersed in the matter in the lower quaternary, and on the other side aspires upward to the Divine. Mathematically it may be represented, the higher

triad by an equilateral triangle : △, the lower quaternary by a square :

□ . Placing one over the other the Manas or Ego may be conceived

of as a double triangle uniting and intersecting the two with one point

turned downwards, the other heavenwards, thus : ⧖. The lower quaternary furnishes to the Manas a personality which is perishable and variable, and is but the "flowing vestment of and unchanging reality." But, says the sceptic, of what use is life on earth? Is it not the materialist argument that man's life is blotted out and leaves no trace, and that even what is called his higher nature perishes with the physical brain? Just so; but then the materialist recognises only the personality, holding that for the entire man, and ignoring that which Theosophy understands by the Higher Self, the Immortal Ego, the

Individuated Spirit. And how do we think that pure spirit, which has neither form nor parts nor differentiation, can become an Individual? Theosophy answers: By its descent into matter, by its conjunction with the human consciousness, which, without its presence, would be scarcely a degree above that of the higher animals.

The question most frequently asked in these days is this: "Is life worth living?" The answers are various, but are mostly tinged with pessimism. The political economist tells us that the end of man's being is happiness, the greatest happiness of the greatest number; but in the face of the rampant misery of the many, he can scarcely believe even his own panaceas for their abatement, and his so-called science is becoming as much discredited as theology itself. Now what does Theosophy answer to this question? It tells us that life on earth is only a phase in the evolution of the individual by means of the struggle with matter, and of the specific experience gained through a material personality. It does not teach that life or happiness is an end in itself, although right living in, in each successive stage of existence does induce that harmonious condition which may be called happiness. But it is at best only a fleeting state, for as soon as the higher stages of consciousness are reached, happiness can only be attained in living for the higher by the complete conquest of the lower, a life which connotes both struggle and sadness—struggle with the lower principles which, if they get the upper hand, drag man downwards, and sadness at the sight of so many who cannot be convinced of the necessity for the upward striving. The Christ must, of necessity, be also the Man of Sorrows, he must bear the cross not only for himself but for others. Well did Jesus teach that man must lose his life for his sake (the Christos) ere he can find it; in other words, the riot of the personal must give way to the grave footsteps of the divine in man. The two cannot co-exist except in the due subordination of the one to the other, the lower must minister to the higher. And by this it is not meant that the personality is to be starved, or that ascetism, as ordinarily understood, is to be practised. The personality has a work to perform, and the body must be maintained in a state of efficiency for action. But the personality is much more than the mere physical body. It embraces the affections with all their multiform activities for good and for evil, the intellectual faculties and their potentialities, it is concerned in all the relations of social life, it is concerned with the whole sphere of human duties. Each one of us in his place has to work out his salvation by means of his personality. And in accordance with the use we make of our opportunities will be the future we prepare for ourselves, so that, though, on the one hand, our position here is the result of causes formerly set in motion by us, we are, on the other hand, creating fresh causes, the effects of which may reach us in this life, or may be postponed to some future existence. If we realized this to the utmost, there would be no room for that discontent with our surroundings which is so rife in the present day; the thought expressed by the religious poet is correct :

> Thou cam'st not to thy place by accident,
> It is the very place God meant for thee.

St. Paul says somewhere : " Art thou a slave, care not for it." It is of very little importance into what position we are born, the only important thing is that we should learn what lesson we can from it, do the duty that lies nearest to us, and try to teach others, by our sympathy, to do the same, bearing one another's burdens where we can, and thus fulfil the law of Christ. Those who hold positions of great influence in the world, can work for others on a larger scale, but their work will not be more blessed than the cup of cold water given by unselfish love. Our personal surroundings are the channels for the stream of activities which go to make up what we call our life here; the true function of the personality is to gather such materials as our experience affords for the building up of a character, an individuality which shall endure when the personality, after due service rendered, shall return to the elements, leaving behind only the impress of its unselfish deeds, its truly noble acts of love and self-denial to be incorporated with the immortal Ego by which those acts were inspired. And thus " he that loseth his life shall find it," nothing of good shall die, nothing of high and pure.

What we want is to separate in our daily life the chaff of that which pertains merely to the personal or lower self, from the true grain that is to fortify and build up the enduring fabric of the individual character. In the present state of society, artificial and unreal as much of it is, this cannot be done without making a decided stand in favour of the real and true. It is a step gained to recognise the position, a greater gain still to act upon our knowledge. It needs but that a few should be courageous and act up to their convictions, for there is a groaning and travailing under the superficiality from those who would gladly break through the crust if someone would strike the first blow. Only by the due proportions being kept between the upper and the lower parts of man's nature, by training the personality to be the handmaid of the Higher Self, can man's true emancipation be effected. It is not for another to prescribe the details; each one must work out the problem for himself by the study of the Divine Wisdom—Theosophia.

Part 1.

KEELY AND SCIENCE

(COMPILED).

"The only hope for science is more science."—DRUMMOND.

"Matter is infinitely divisible."—SCHOPENHAUER.

"We seem to be approaching a theory as to the construction of ether. Hertz has produced vibrations, vibrating more than one hundred million times per second. He made use of the principle of resonance. You all understand how, by a succession of well-timed small impulses, a large vibration may be set up."—PROF. FITZGERALD.

Dr. Schimmel, in his lecture on "The Unity of Nature's Forces," says:
—"The Greek philosophers, Leucippus, Anaxagoras, Democritus, and Aristotle, base their philosophies on the existence of an ether and atoms. According to Spiller's system, both ether and atoms are material. The atoms are indivisible. Chemistry, being based on the correctness of this statement, forces us to accept it."—We are "forced to accept it," only until it is proved by demonstration to be false. (*See note at end.*)

The discoverer of the connecting link between mind and matter, the Newton of the *mécanique céleste* of the mind, foretold both by Kepler and Macvicar, has now reached a stage in his researches at which he is able to demonstrate the truth of the hypotheses which he is formulating into a system; and consequently the stage where he can demonstrate whether theories, that have prevailed concerning the cause of physical phenomena, are sound or without basis in fact. Until this stage was reached, it would have been as useless to make Mr. Keely's theories known, as it would be to publish a treatise to prove that two and two make five. Scientific men reject all theories in physics in which there is not an equal proportion of science and mathematics, excluding all questions of pure metaphysics. They were right; for, until the world had undergone a state of preparation for another revelation of truth, the man who demonstrated all that Keely is now prepared to demonstrate would have been burned alive as a wizard. To use the words of Babcock, one of Keely's staunchest adherents, in 1880 :—"This discoverer has entered a new world, and although an unexplored wilderness of untold wealth lies beyond, he is treading firmly its border, which daily widens as with ever-increasing interest he pursues his explorations. He has passed the dreary realm where scientists are groping. His researches are made in the open field of elemental force, where gravity, inertia, cohesion, momentum are disturbed in their haunts and diverted to use; where, from unity of origin, emanates infinite energy in diversified forms," and, to this statement I would add—where he is able to look from nature up to nature's God, understanding and explaining, as no man before ever understood and explained, how simple is "the mysterious way in which God works His wonders to perform."

Mr. Babcock continues:—"Human comprehension is inadequate to grasp the possibilities of this discovery for power, for increased prosperity, and for peace. It includes all that relates mechanically to travel, manufacture, mining, engineering, and warfare." Up to within two years, Mr. Keely, the discoverer of unknown laws of nature, having their sole seat, origin, and function in the human mind, has been left partially to the mercy of men who were interested only in mechanical "possibilities." In the autumn of 1888, he was led into a line of research which made the mechanical question one of secondary interest; and yet the present results are such as to prove that on this line alone can he ever hope to attain mechanical success. The course then adopted has also been the means of placing his discoveries before the world, endorsed in such a manner as to command attention to his views and theories. It has been said that if extreme vicissitudes of belief on the part of men of science are evidences of uncertainty, it may be affirmed that of all kinds of knowledge none is more uncertain than science. The only hope for science is more science, says Drummond. Keely now bestows the only hope for science—"more science." He accounts for the non-recognition by scientists of his claims, in these words: "The system of arranging introductory etheric impulses by compound chords set by differential harmonies, is one that the world of science has never recognised, simply because the struggles of physicists, combating with the solution of the conditions governing the fourth order of matter, have been in a direction thoroughly antagonistic, and opposite to a right one. It is true that luminosity has been induced by chemical antagonism, and, in my mind, this ought to have been a stepping-stone towards a more perfect condition than was accepted by them; but independent of what might be necessary to its analysis, the bare truth remains that the conditions were isolated—robbed of their most vital essentials—by not having the medium of etheric vibration associated with them."

In order to subdivide the atoms in the atomic triplet, after release from the molecule, the molecular ether, thus liberated, is absolutely necessary in order to effect the rupture of the atoms, and so on, progressively, each order of ether, molecular, inter-molecular, atomic, inter-atomic, etheric, inter-etheric, the ether so liberated in each successive division is essential to the next sub-division.

The keynote of Mr. Keely's researches is that the movements of elastic elements are rhythmical, and before he had reached his present stage in producing vibrations, on the principle of resonance, he has had problems to solve which needed the full measure of inspiration or apperception that he has received.

Hertz has produced vibrations about one metre long, vibrating more than one hundred million times a second. Keely has produced, using an atmospheric medium alone, 519,655,633 vibrations per second; but, inter-posing pure hydrogen gas beween soap films and using it as a medium of acceleration, he asserts that on the enharmonic third a rate of vibration may be induced which could not be set down in figures, and could only be repre-sented in sound colours. He has invented instruments which demonstrate in many variations the colours of sound, registering the number of necessary vibrations to produce each variation. The transmissive sympathetic chord of B flat, third octave, when passing into inaudibility, would induce billions of billions of vibrations, represented by sound colour on a screen illuminated from a solar ray. But this experiment is one of infinite difficulty, from the almost utter impossibility of holding the hydrogen between the two films long enough to conduct the experiment. Keely made over 1,200 trials before succeeding once in inducing the intense blue field necessary, covering a space in time of six weeks, four hours at a time daily, and should he ever succeed in his present efforts to produce a film that will stand, he anticipates being able to register the range of motion in all metallic mediums. On this subject Keely writes :—" The highest range of vibration I ever induced was in the one experiment that I made in liberating ozone by molecular percussion, which induced luminosity, and registered a percussive molecular force of 110,000lbs. per square inch, as registered on a lever constructed for the purpose. The vibrations induced by this experiment reached over 700,000,000 per second, unshipping the apparatus, thus making it insecure for a repetition of the experiments. The decarbonized steel compressors of said apparatus moved as if composed of putty. Volume of sphere, 15 cubic inches; weight of surrounding metal, 316lbs."

Recently some questions, propounded to Mr. Keely by a scientist, elicited answers, which the man of science admitted were clear and definite, but no physicist could accept Keely's assertion that incalculable amounts of latent force exist in the molecular spaces, for the simple reason that science asserts that molecular aggregation is attended with dissipation of energy instead of its absorption. The questions asked were :—

" I. In disintegrating water, how many foot-pounds of energy have you to expend in order to produce or induce the vibratory energy in your acoustical apparatus?

"Answer.—No foot-pounds at all. The force necessary to excite disintegration when the instrument is sensitized (both in sensitization and developments) would not be sufficient to wind up a watch.

"II. What is the amount of energy that you get out of that initial amount of water (say 12 drops) when decomposed into ether?

"Answer.—From 12 drops of water a force can be developed that will fill a chamber of seven pint volume no less than six times with a pressure of ten tons to the square inch.

"III. In other words, if you put so many pounds of energy into vibratory motion, how many foot-pounds do you get out of this?

"Answer.—All molecular masses of metal represent in their interstitial molecular spaces incalculable amounts of latent force, which, if awakened and brought into intense vibratory action by the medium of sympathetic liberation, would result in thousands of billions more power in foot-pounds than that necessary to awaken it. The resultant development of any and all forces is only accomplished by conditions that awaken the latent energy they have carried with them during molecular aggregation. If the latent force that exists in a pound of water could be sympathetically evolved or liberated up to the seventh sub-division or compound-inter-etheric, and could be stored free of rotation, it would be in my estimation sufficient to run the power of the world for a century." . . . .

This statement gives another of Keely's discoveries to the world, viz., that molecular dissociation does not create energy, as men have asserted Keely has claimed, but supplies it in unlimited quantities, as the product of the latent energy accumulated in molecular aggregation. This is to the physicist as if Keely had asserted that two and two make a billion, but as a man of science, who is held to be "the scientific equal of any man in the world," has come forward to make known that, in his opinion, "Keely has fairly demonstrated the discovery of a force previously unknown to science," the discoverer at last feels at liberty to make public the nature of his discoveries. Until Dr. Joseph Leidy had taken this stand, Mr. Keely could not, without jeopardizing his interests, and the interests of the Keely Motor Company, make known in what particulars his system conflicts with the systems upheld by the age in which we live.

After the warning, given in the history of Huxley's "Bathybius," we may feel quite sure that if Keely had failed to demonstrate the genuineness of his claims by actual experiment, no scientist would have risked the world-wide reputation of a lifetime by endorsement of the discovery of an unknown force as Professor Leidy has done, while Keely himself was under such a cloud that, to advocate his integrity and uphold the importance of his discovery, has hitherto been enough to awaken doubts as to the sanity of his upholders. Among many others who have written of it from the standpoint of Keely's accountability for the mistakes of the managers of the Keely Motor Company—men who made no pretence of caring for anything but dividends—was one who asserted, in the *New York Tribune,* that it was a "remarkable delusion, full of tricks too numerous to mention, the exposure of which ought to be made to bring the Keely craze to an end." In the same journal an editorial states that "Mr. Keely appears to have no mechanical ingenuity, his strong point being his ability as a collector. He has one of the largest and best arranged collections of other people's money to be found in the United States. Having, a number of years ago, during a fit of temporary insanity, constructed a machine which, if any power on earth could start it, would explode and pierce the startled dome of heaven with flying fragments of cog-wheels and cranks, he now sits down calmly, and allows this same mechanical night-mare to make his living for him. This is genius; this is John W. Keely; he toils not, neither does he spin, but he has got an hysterical collection of crooked pipes and lob-sided wheels tied up in his back room that extract the reluctant dollar from the pocket of avarice without fail."

This is a specimen of the nature of the ridicule which was encountered by Keely's "upholders," as well as by himself. Until Professor Leidy and Dr. Willcox came to the front, in March, 1890, Mr. Keely had no influential supporters, and not one scientist could be found who was ready to encounter the wasps represented in Lavater's allegorical vignette; where a hand holding a lighted torch is being stung by one of a swarm.

Underneath are these lines :—

> "And although it singes the wings of the gnats,
> Destroys their heads and all their little brains,
> Light is still light ;
> And although I am stung by the angriest wasp,
> I will not yield."

Such is the position of all defenders of the truth in all ages; but the torch being held aloft, in such hands as have now seized it, the opportunity is given to see what Keely proclaims as truth.

We know that science denies the divisibility of atoms, but Keely affirms and demonstrates that all corpuscles of matter may be divided and sub-divided by a certain order of vibration. During all these years in which he has given exhibitions of the operations of his generators, liberators, and dis-integrators, in turn, each being an improvement, successively, on the preceding one, no one has attempted to give to the public any theory, or even so much as a sensible conjecture, of the origin of the force.

When Mr. Keely was asked, in 1884, if it were not possible that he had dissociated hydrogen gas, and that his unknown force came from that dissociation, he replied that he thought it might be; but he made no assertion that he had. This conjecture was repeated to an English scientist, who replied that he was willing to make a bet of £10,000 that hydrogen is a simple element. The same scientist says now that he should answer such a question with more caution, and says that he had never known hydrogen to be dissociated. Mr. Keely gives this

THEORY AND FORMULA OF AQUEOUS DISINTEGRATION.

The peculiar conditions as associated with the gaseous elements of which water is composed, as regards the differential volume and gravity of its gases, make it a ready and fit subject of vibratory research. In submitting water to the influence of vibratory transmission, even on simple thirds, the high action induced on the hydrogen as contrasted with the one on the oxygen (under the same vibratory stream), causes the antagonism between these elements that induces dissociation. The differential antagonistic range of motion, so favouring the antagonistic thirds as to become thoroughly repellant. The gaseous element thus induced and registered, shows thousands of times much greater force as regards tenuity and volume than that induced by the chemical disintegration of heat, on the same medium. In all molecular dissociation or disintegration on both simple or compound elements, whether gaseous or solid, a stream of vibratory antagonistic thirds, sixths, or ninths, on their chord mass will compel progressive subdivisions. In the disintegration of water the instrument is set on thirds, sixths, and ninths, to get the best effects. These triple conditions are focalized on the neutral centre of said instrument so as to induce perfect harmony or concordance to the chord-note of the mass-chord of the instrument's full combination; after which the diatonic and the enharmonic scale located at the top of the instrument, or ring, is thoroughly harmonized with the scale of ninths which is placed at the base of the vibratory transmittor with the telephone head. The next step is to disturb the harmony on the concentrative thirds, between the transmittor and disintegrator. This is done by rotating the syren so as to induce a sympathetic communication along the nodal transmittor, or wire, that associates the two instruments. When the note of the syren becomes concordant to the neutra centre of the disintegrator, the highest order of sympathetic communication is established. It is now necessary to operate the transferable vibratory negatizer, or negative accelerator, which is seated in the centre of the diatonic and enharmonic ring, at the top of disintegrator, and complete disintegration will follow (from the antagonisms induced on the concordants by said adjunct), in triple progression, thus:—First, thirds: Molecular dissociation resolving the water into a gaseous compound of hydrogen and oxygen. Second, sixths:

resolving the hydrogen and oxygen into a new element by second order of dissociation, producing what I call, low atomic ether. Third, ninths: The low atomic ether resolved into a new element, which I denominate high or second atomic harmonic. All these transmissions being simultaneous on the disturbance of sympathetic equilibrium by said negative accelerator.

Example:—Taking the chord mass of the disintegrator B flat, or any chord mass that may be represented by the combined association of all the mechanical parts of its structure (no two structures being alike in their chord masses), taking B flat, the resonators of said structure are set at B flat, first octave, B flat, third octave, and B flat, ninth octave, by drawing out the caps of resonators until the harmony of thirds, sixths, and ninths are reached ; which a simple movement of the fingers on the diatonic scale, at the head, will determine by the tremulous action which is highly sensible, to the touch, on said caps. The caps are then rigidly fixed in their different positions by set screws. The focalization to the neutral centre is then established by dampening the steel rods, on the scale at the back, representing the thirds, sixths, and ninths, drawing a piece of small gum tube over them, which establishes harmony to the chord mass of the instrument. Concordance is thus effected between the disintegrator and the ninths of the scale at base of transmittors with telephonic head.

This scale has a permanent sympathetic one, set on the ninth of any mass chord that may be represented, on any and all the multiple variations of mechanical combinations. In fact, permanently set for universal accom modation.

The next step is to establish pure harmony between the transmittor and the disintegrator, which is done by spinning the syren disk, then waiting until the sympathetic note is reached, as the syren chord, decreasing in velocity, descend the scale. At this juncture, the negative accelerator must be immediately and rapidly rotated, inducing high disturbance of equilibrium between the transmittor and the disintegrator by triple negative evolution, with the result that a force of from five to ten, fifteen, twenty, and thirty thousand pounds to the square inch is evolved by the focalization of this triple negative stream on the disintegrating cell, or chamber, whether there be one, two, three, five, or ten drops of water enclosed within it.

GRADUATION OF MACHINES.

Mr. Keely gives a few introductory words concerning the necessary graduating of his instruments, for effecting conditions necessary to ensure perfect sympathetic transmission, which will serve to show how great are the difficulties that have been attendant upon getting his machines into a condition to control and equate the differentiation in molecular masses, requiring greater skill than in researching the force of a sunbeam. He writes:—The differentiation in molecular metallic masses, or grouping, is brought about in their manipulations in manufacturing them for commercial uses; in the forging of a piece of metal, in the drawing of a length of wire, and in the casting of a molten mass to any requisite form.

The nearest approach to molecular uniformity in metallic masses is in the wire drawn for commercial uses, gold and platina being the nearest to freedom from differentiation. But even these wires, when tested by a certain condition of the first order of intensified molecular vibration, for a transferring medium between centres of neutrality, I find to be entirely inadequate for the transfer of concordant unition, as between one and the other, on account of nodal interferences. We can appreciate the diffiulty of converting such a medium to a uniform molecular link, by knowing that it can be accomplished only by removing all nodal interference, by inducing between the nodal waves a condition in which they become subservient to the inter-sympathetic vibratory molecular link of such structure or wire.

Therefore, it is necessary to submit the wire to a system of graduation in order to find what the combined chords of these nodal interferences represent when focalized to one general centre. Then the differentiation between these nodal waves and the inter-molecular link must be equated, by what I call a process of vibratory induction, so as to induce pure concordance between one and the other. To elaborate on this system of graduation, for effecting conditions necessary to ensure perfect and unadulterated transmission, would make up a book that would take days to read and months to study.

The graduating of a perfectly constructed instrument to a condition to transmit sympathetically, is no standard whatever for any other one that may be built, nor ever will be, because no concordant conditions of compound molecular aggregation can ever exist in visible groupings. If it were even possible to make their parts perfectly accurate one to the other, in regard to atmospheric displacement and weight, their resonating qualities would have a high rate of sympathetic variation in their molecular groupings alone. If one thousand million of coins, each one representing a certain standard value, and all struck from the same die, were sympathetically graduated under a vibratory subdivision of 150,000, the most amazing variation would present itself, as between each individual coin throughout the number, in regard to their molecular grouping and resonance. KEELY.

It will be realized in the future what immense difficulties have been encountered by Mr. Keely in perfecting his system of graduation, and in constructing devices for the guidance of artificers and mechanicians, whereby those who are not as abnormally endowed as he is for his work, can bring a proper vibratory action into play to induce positive sympathetic transmission, as well as the stupidity of the men who still seek to confine his researches to perfecting the so-called Keely motor, before his system is sufficiently developed to enable others to follow it up, should his physical strength give out. His system of graduating research, when completed, will enable men to take up the work, *not* from the standard of an already completed structure that is true in its operation, though a perfect duplicate as to size and gravity be made; for each successively constructed machine requires a knowledge of its own conditions of sensity, as regards its mass chords. Keely writes :—

That tuning forks can be so constructed as to show coincident or concordant association with each other, is but a very weak illustration of the fact which governs pure acoustic assimilation. The best only approach a condition of about a fortieth, as regards pure, attractive, and propulsive receptiveness. By differentiating them to concordant thirds, they induce a condition of molecular bombardment between themselves, by alternate changes of long and short waves of sympathy. Bells rung in vacuo liberate the same number of corpuscules, and at the same velocity as those surrounded by a normal atmosphere, and hence the same acoustic force attending them, but are inaudible from the fact that, in vacuo, the molecular volume is reduced. Every gaseous molecule is a resonator of itself, and is sensitive to any and all sounds induced, whether accordant or discordant.

ANSWERS TO QUESTIONS.

The positive vibrations are the radiating or propulsive; the negative vibrations are the ones that are attracted towards the neutral centre. The action of the magnetic flow is dual in its evolutions, both attractive and propulsive. The sound vibrations of themselves have no power whatever to induce dissociation, even in its lowest form. Certain differential, dual, triple and quadruple chords give introductory impulses which excite an action on molecular masses, liquid and gaseous, that increase their range of molecular motion and put them in that receptive state for sympathetic vibratory interchange which favours molecular disintegration; then, as I have shown, the diatonic enharmonic is brought into play, which further increases the molecular range of motion beyond fifty per cent. of their diameters, when molecular separation takes place, giving the tenuous substance that is necessary to induce progressive subdivision. This molecular gaseous substance, during its evolution, assumes a condition of high rotation in the sphere or tube in which it has been generated, and becomes itself the medium, with the proper excitors, for further progressive dissociation. The excitors include an illuminated revolving prism, condensor, and coloured lenses, with a capped glass tube strong enough to carry a pressure of at least one thousand pounds per square inch.   To one of these caps a sectional wire of platinum and silver is attached; the other cap is attached to the tube, so screwed to the chamber as to allow it to lead to the neutral centre of said chamber.   KEELY.

MINERAL DISINTEGRATION.

I have been repeatedly urged to repeat my disintegrations of quartz rock; but it has been utterly out of my power to do so. The mechanical device with which I conducted those experiments was destroyed at the time of the proceedings against me. Its graduation occupied over four years, after which it was operated successfully. It had been originally constructed as an instrument for overcoming gravity; a perfect, graduated scale of that device was accurately registered, a copy of which I kept; I have since built three successive disintegrators set up from that scale, but they did not operate. This peculiar feature remained a paradox to me until I had solved the conditions governing the chords of multiple masses; when this problem ceased to be paradoxical in its character. As I have said, there are no two compound aggregated forms of visible matter that are, or ever can be, so duplicated as to show pure sympathetic concordance one to the other. Hence the necessity of my system of graduation, and of a compound device that will enable anyone to correct the variations that exist in compound molecular structures, or, in other words, to graduate such, so as to bring them to a successful operation.
                                                             KEELY.

DISTURBANCE OF MAGNETIC NEEDLE.

If Keely's theories are correct, science will in time classify all the important modifications of the one force in nature as sympathetic streams, each stream composed of triple flows. Mr. Keely maintains that the static condition which the magnetic needle assumes, when undisturbed by any extraneous force outside of its own sympathetic one, proves conclusively that the power of the dominant third, of the triple combination of the magnetic terrestrial envelope, is the controlling one of this sympathetic triplet, and the one towards which all the others co-ordinate. All the dominant conditions of Nature represent the focal centres towards which the surrounding ones of like become sympathetically subservient. The rapid rotation of the magnetic needle of a compass which Mr. Keely shows in his experiments, rests entirely on the alternating of the dominant alone, which is effected by a triple condition of vibration that is antagonistic to its harmonious flow as associated with its other attendants. A rapid change of polarity is induced, and rapid rotation necessarily follows. Quoting from Keely's writings,—The human ear cannot detect the triple chord of any vibration, or sounding note, but every sound that is induced of any range, high or low, is governed by the same laws (as regards triple action of such) that govern every sympathetic flow in Nature. Were it not for these triple vibratory conditions, change of polarity could never be effected, and consequently there could be no rotation. Thus the compounding of the triple triple, to produce the effect, would give a vibration in multiplication reaching the ninth, in order to induce subservience, the enumeration of which it would be folly to undertake, as the result would be a string of figures nearly a mile in length to denote it.

When the proper impulse is given to induce the rotation with pure alternating corpuscular action, the conditions of action become perpetual in their character, lasting long enough from that one impulse to wear out any machine (denoting such action), and, on the sympathetic stream, eternally perpetual. The action of the neutral or focalizing centres represents molecular focalization and redistribution, not having any magnetism associated with them; but when the radiating arms of their centres are submitted to the triple compound vibratory force, representing their mass thirds, they become magnetic and consequently cease their rotation. Their rotation is induced by submitting them to three different orders of vibration, simultaneously giving the majority to the harmonic third.

Theory of the Induction of Sympathetic Chords to excite rotation by vibrophonic trajection to and from centres of neutrality as induced and shown to Professor Leidy, Dr. Wilcock, and others, on revolving globe.

All hollow spheres, of certain diameters, represent, as per diameters and their volume of molecular mass, pure, unadulterated, sympathetic resonation towards the enharmonic and diatonic thirds of any, and in fact all, concordant sounds. In tubes it is adversely different, requiring a definite number of them so graduated as to represent a confliction by thirds, sixths, and ninths, as towards the harmonic scale. When the conditions are established, the acoustic result of this combination, when focalised, represents concordant harmony, as between the chord mass of the instrument to be operated, and chord mass of the tubes of resonation. Therefore, the shortest way towards establishing pure concordance between any number of resonating mediums, is by the position that Nature herself assumes in her multitudinous arrangements of the varied forms and volumes of matter—the spherical. The great difficulty to overcome, in order to get a revolution of the said sphere, exists in equating the interior adjuncts of same. In other words the differentiation induced must be so equated as to harmonise and make their conditions purely concordant to the molecular mass of the sphere. Example: Suppose the chord of the sphere mass represents B flat, or any other chord, and the internal adjuncts by displacement of atmospheric volume differentiates the volume one-**twentieth**; this displacement in the shell's atmospheric volume would represent an antagonistic twentieth against the shell's mass concordance, to equate which it would be necessary to so graduate the shell's internal adjuncts as to get at the same chord;—an octave or any number of octaves that comes nearest to the concordance of shell's atmospheric volume. No intermediates between the octaves would ever reach sympathetic union.

We will now take up the mechanical routine as associated with adjuncts of interference, and follow the system for chording the mechanical aggregation in its different parts, in order to induce the transmittive sympathy necessary to perfect evolution, and to produce revolution of the sphere or shell.

Example.—Suppose that we had just received from the machine shop a spun shell of twelve inches internal diameter, 1-32 of an inch thick, which represents an atmospheric volume of 904·77 cubic inches. On determination by research we find the shell to be on its resonating volume B flat, and the molecular volume of the metal that the sphere is composed of B natural. This or any other antagonistic chord, as between the chord mass of the shell and its atmospheric volume, would not interfere, but would come under subservience. We now pass a steel shaft through its centre, ½ inch in diameter, which represents its axial rest. This shaft submits the atmospheric volume of the shell to a certain displacement or reduction, to correct which we first register the chord note of its mass, and find it to be antagonistic to the chord mass of the shell, a certain portion of an octave. This must be corrected. The molecular volume of the shaft must be reduced in volume, either by filing or turning, so as to represent the first B flat chord that is reached by such reduction. When this is done the first line of interference is neutralized, and the condition of sympathy is as pure between the parts as it was when the globe was minus its axis. There is now introduced on its axis a ring which has seven tubes or graduating resonators, the ring being two-thirds the diameter of the globe, the resonators three inches long and ¾ inch diameter, each one to be set on the chord of B flat, which is done by sliding the small diaphragm in the tube to a point that will indicate B flat. This setting then controls the metallic displacement of the metallic combination, as also of the arms necessary to hold the ring and resonators on shaft or axis. Thus the second equation is established, both on resonation and displacement. We are now ready to introduce the diatonic scale ring of three octaves which is set at two-thirds of the scale antagonistic to the chord mass of the globe itself, which is done by graduating every third pin of its scale to B flat thirds, which represent antagonistic thirds to the shell's molecular mass. This antagonism must be thoroughly sensitive to the chord-mass of one of the hemispheres of which the globe is composed. The axis of the scale-ring must rotate loosely on the globe's shaft without revolving with the globe itself, which it is prevented from doing so by being weighted on one side of the ring by a small hollow brass ball, holding about two ounces of lead. The remaining work on the device is finished by painting the interior of the globe, one hemisphere black and one white, and attaching a rubber bulb, such as is used to spray perfume, to the hollow end of the shaft. This bulb equates vibratory undulations, thus preventing an equation of molecular bombardment on its dark side when sympathetically influenced. It is now in condition to denote the sympathetic concordance between living physical organisms, or the receptive transmittive concordance necessary to induce rotation.

KEELY.

PHILOSOPHY OF TRANSMISSION AND ROTATION OF MUSICAL SPHERE.

The only two vibratory conditions that can be so associated as to excite high sympathetic affinity, as between two physical organisms, are :—

Etheric chord of B flat, 3rd octave, and on

Etheric sympathetic chords transmission

E*b* on the scale 3rd, 6ths and 9ths ; octaves harmonic ;

having the 3rd dominant ; the 6th enharmonic, and the 9th diatonic.

The chord mass representing the musical sphere, being the sympathetic etheric chord of B flat third octave, indicated by the focalization of its interior mechanical combination, as against the neutral sevenths of its atmospheric volume, makes the shell highly sensitive to the reception of pure sympathetic accordance, whether it be physical, mechanical, or a combination of both. Taking the chord mass of the different mechanical parts of the sphere and its adjuncts, as previously explained, when associated and focalized to represent pure concordance, as between its atmospheric volume and sphere mass, which means the pure unit of concordance, we have the highest position that can be established in relation to its sympathetic susceptiveness to negative antagonism. The beauty of the perfection of the laws that govern the action of Nature's sympathetic flows is here demonstrated in all the purity of its workings, actually requiring antagonistic chords to move and accelerate. The dark side of the shell, which represents fifty per cent. of its full area of pure concordant harmony, is the receptive area for the influence of the negative transmittive chords of the thirds, sixths and ninths to bombard upon ; which bombardment disturbs the equilibrium of said sphere, and induces rotation. The rotation can be accelerated or retarded, according as the antagonistic chords of the acoustic forces are transmitted in greater or lesser volume. The action, as induced by the mouth organ, transmitted at a distance from the sphere without any connection of wire, demonstrates the purity of the principle of sympathetic transmission, as negatized or disturbed by discordants, which, focalizing on the resonating sevenths of resonators, or tubes attached to ring, the sympathetic flow is by this means transmitted to the focalizing centre, or centre of neutrality, to be re-distributed at each revolution of sphere, keeping intact the sympathetic volume during sensitization, thus preventing the equation or stoppage of its rotation.

Again, the sphere resting on its journals in the ring, as graduated to the condition of its interior combinations, represents a pure sympathetic concordant under perfect equation, ready to receive the sympathetic, or to reject the non-sympathetic. If a pure sympathetic chord is transmitted coincident to its full combination, the sphere will remain quiescent; but if a transmission of discordance is brought to bear upon it, its sympathetic conditions become repellant to this discordance.

KEELY.

"There is no such thing as blind or dead matter, as there is no blind or unconscious law," the Buddhists have taught for centuries. Keely demonstrates the truth in this teaching; and Hertz in his conjectures that a knowledge of the structure of ether should unveil the essence of matter itself, and of its inherent properties, weight and inertia, is treading the path that leads to this knowledge. Professor Fitzgerald says :—"Ether must be the means by which electric and magnetic forces exist, it should explain chemical actions, and if possible gravity." The law of sympathetic vibration explains chemical affinities as a sympathetic attractive, but inherent, force; in short, as gravity. This opens up too wide a territory even but to peer into, by the dawning light of Keely's system of vibratory physics. The boundary line is crossed, and the crowds of researchers in electro-magnetism are full of ardour. Hertz constructed a circuit, whose period of vibration for electric currents was such that he was able to see sparks, due to the increased vibration, leaping across a small air-space in this resonant circuit; his experiments have proved and demonstrated the ethereal theory of electro-magnetism :—that electro-magnetic actions are due to a medium pervading all known space; while Keely's experiments have proved that *all things are due to conditions of ether*.

Prof. Fitzgerald closes one of his lectures on ether in these words :— There are metaphysical grounds for reducing matter to motion, and potential to kinetic energy. Let us for a moment comtemplate what is betokened by this theory that in electro-magnetic engines we are using as our mechanism the ether, the medium that fills all known space. It was a great step in human progress when man learnt to make material machines, when he used the elasticity of his bow, and the rigidity of his arrow to provide food and defeat his enemies. It was a great advance when he learnt to use the chemical action of fire; when he learnt to use water to float his boats, and air to drive them; when, by artificial selection, he provided himself with food and domestic animals. For two hundred years he has made heat his slave to drive his machinery. Fire, water, earth, and air have long been his slaves, but it is only within the last few years that man has won the battle lost by the giants of old, has snatched the thunderbolt from Jove himeslf, and enslaved the all-pervading ether. CLARA JESSUP MOORE.

Schlangenbad, August 5th, 1890.

NOTE.—In Professor Fitzgerald's lecture on " Electro-magnetic Radiation," delivered in March before the Royal Institution of Great Britain, he says of Professor Hertz's experiments in inducing vibration in ether waves :—If we consider the possible radiating power of an atom, by calculating it upon the hypothesis that the atomic charge oscillates across the diameter of the atom, we find that it may be millions of millions of times as great as Professor Wiedemann has found to be the radiating power of a sodium atom in a Bunsen burner; so that if there is reason to think that any greater oscillation might disintegrate the atom, we are still a long way from it." . . . . . .

Does not this statement border on an admission that the atom is divisible ? Keely stands alone in utilizing sound vibrations to increase the range of molecular motion ; not (as scientists have been allowed to infer) to induce dissociation of themselves alone. (*See p.* 9.) The lecture closes with "a possible theory of ether and matter " :—" This hypothesis explains the differences in nature as differences of motion. If it be true, ether, matter, gold, air, wood, brains, are but different motions. Where alone we can know what motion in itself is, that is, in our brains, we know nothing but thought. Can we resist the conclusion that all motion is thought? Not that contradiction in terms, unconscious thought, but living thought; that all Nature is the language of One in whom we live, and move, and have our being."

The truth of this theory Keely demonstrates in his experiments.

The remainder of this Number is included, at the express request of Mrs. Bloomfield-Moore, as a sequel to T.P.S, Vol. 1, No. 9. Mrs. Bloomfield-Moore is alone responsible for the contents of this paper, the T.P.S. having no connection whatever with financial articles of any kind.

Part 2.

KEELY MOTOR BUBBLE.

Causa latet, vis est notissima.—Proverb.
(The cause is hidden, the power is most apparent.)

Each day he wrought, and better than he planned,
Shape breeding shape beneath his restless hand;
The soul without still helps the soul within,
And its deft magic ends what we begin.

Legend of Jubal.—GEORGE ELIOT.

"For it is well known that bodies act upon one another by the attractions of gravity, magnetism, and electricity; and these instances show the tenour and course of Nature and make it not improbable that there may be more attractive powers than these. For Nature is very consonant and comfortable to herself."—Sir Isaac Newton.

THE Scotch author, Macvicar, from whose "Sketch of a Philosophy" has been compiled "Ether the True Protoplasm," published this year in the *New York Home Journal*, says in his "Enquiry into Human Nature" (written in 1852), "Modern science is certainly on the way to the discovery that, so far at is cognizable by us, throughout the whole universe the same laws are as work and regulate all things. The *mécanique céleste* of mind is still waiting its Newton to disclose them to us."

Knowing that "the words lie in the bosom of God, like children," and that with all a mother's watchful solicitude and attention, their Creator "supplies their wants, *as they arise*," Macvicar, with the extended vision of a seer, prophesied that, when our world is ready, a Newton would appear to reveal the connecting link between mind and matter; proving that, as Buckle said— "On the one side we have mind, on the other side we have matter, so interwoven, so acting upon and perturbing each other that we can never really know the laws of one unless we know the laws of both; that everything is essential, everything hangs together, and forms part of one single scheme, one grand and complex plan, one gorgeous drama, of which the universe is the theatre," and that "*the laws of Nature have their sole seat, origin, and function in the human mind.*" This is Keely's discovery; this is Keely's secret; which, with the highest degree of moral courage, he has, while endeavouring to solve mechanical difficulties, guarded from all who are incapable of comprehending it. He is still slowly treading, step by step, a pathless, unknown region in his efforts to formulate his system; but he has reached a stage at which he is able to demonstrate in mechanics all that he affirms.

When Buckle was asserting that "the highest of our so-called laws of Nature are as yet purely empirical," that giant in intellect, Macvicar, was contending that the fact that it is so should not discourage searchers after truth from efforts to reduce to their most general forms those laws which, reviewed as in emanation or operation at the fountain head, cannot but be dictates of mind. If not, he said, then they are not laws at all, but only manifestations of something inconceivable, which, without knowing what we mean, we call Fate. As surely, therefore, as generalisation is the grand operation of all science, and the discovery of laws, still more and more general, the grand aim in every branch of philosophy, all science, in proportion as it makes true progress in the direction it aims at, must ever tend towards the philosophy of mind, and must culminate in it. He continues: "Let us not, then, be discouraged from viewing man as a spiritual as well as a corporeal being, either from the undoubted difficulties, or the reputed hopelessness of, mental science. Let the worst that can be said of it in these respects be held as true. Let it be that, while physical science has been advancing gloriously and gaining new victory over the hostile elements of nature, and fresh laurels for those who have devoted themselves to the conflict with ignorance in this field, age after age, nay, year after year of late, little or nothing that is of interest or importance has been discovered in the science of mind, since the days of the ancient Greeks. Let it be true that men, of otherwise admirable genius, have been landed by their metaphysical speculations, and that, even in modern times, in the most ridiculous conclusions, let it be admitted that they have gone wide from the dictates of common sense; let it be that human nature, though it be so near and so familiar as to be the home of every man, is yet not so well known as the solar systems in the sky; let all these things be, still we ought not to despair, or regard the true theory of the human mind as undiscoverable. There is in wait to be discovered a *mécanique céleste* of thought and feeling as there was of the starry heavens. And if so, ought not the boasted state of astronomy, and of physical science generally, to serve rather as an encouragement to the study of mind, than as a dissuasive against it? Only since the time of Galileo, nay, only since the time of Newton, has natural science fully emerged from a state of uncertain description, and heterogeneous hypotheses, and what though it may perhaps be true, that the science of mind still remains in this state? Compared with the whole period of philosophy, the epoch of Newton is but as yesterday, nay, it is still to-day. Why, then, despair of the science of mind? The future will bring to it a

Newton too." Instead of being turned away from the pursuit of mental science by considering the more advanced state of physics, Macvicar contends that the student of mind ought rather to seek his revenge by adopting and pursuing to the utmost possible, for the advancement of mental philosophy, the methods which have proved so successful in natural philosophy. Physics may vanish into psychology, he says, and become a branch of what is now called metaphysics, but the science of mind can never cease; having the inexhaustible and ever new domain of free thought and feeling for its object, it has a root in the nature of things which must keep it alive for ever.

Looking upon the discoverer of etheric force as the Newton, whose coming was foretold by Macvicar, it is satisfactory to see that Keely, in his field of research, eventually adopted the methods which his forerunner advocated nearly forty years ago; but not until after many years of blind grappling with the mechanical difficulties which he encountered, in his efforts to control the unknown Genii, which he himself declares that he stumbled upon in quite another field of research. Keely was experimenting in 1875 on what he called a hydro-pneumatic-pulsating-vacuo engine, when, "accidentally," the first evolution of disintegration was made. The focalization of this quadruple force, acting on one general centre of concentration, produced partial molecular subdivision, resulting in a power of some three thousand pounds per square inch. Mr. Keely was himself amazed at this evidence of the energy which he had evoked, and at once turned his attention to researching its nature, with the result that he came to the conclusion that he had partially resolved the gaseous element of water by crude molecular dissociation. This was his first step, and the necessary introductory one, towards the elimination of ether; but at that time, to use his own words, he had not the remotest idea of the etheric element proper. Since then he has constructed innumerable machines to subdivide or dissociate the molecular; but it was not until he had instituted certain acoustic vibratory conditions that he began to realize the magnitude of the element that he is now controlling with his vibratory disintegrator. Yet, even this instrument was only the stepping-stone towards polar-sympathetic-negative-attraction.

In 1878, Mr. Keely conceived and constructed an instrument which he called a "vibratory lift," and, while experimenting on the improvised multiplication by this medium, he had occasion to put a piece of marble, weighing 26 pounds, on a steel bar to hold it in place, when then and there his first discovery of the disintegration of mineral substance took place. From that time progressive research of the most arduous nature has brought him to his present standard in vibratory physics. In the winter of '81-'82, when threatened with imprisonment by the managers of the Keely Motor Company for not disclosing his secret to them (which then would have been like pricking a bubble), he destroyed his vibratory lift and other instruments that he had been years in perfecting. At this time so hopeless was Keely that his plans were made to destroy himself, after destroying his devices. At this critical juncture he received unexpected aid. Again, in 1888, before he was taken to a felon's cell in Moyameusing Prison by decree of Judge Finletter for alleged contempt of court, he broke up his vibratory microscope, his sympathetic transmitter, and other instruments, which have taken much of his time since to reconstruct. It would seem to be incomprehensible that a man who believes he has been specially endowed by Providence to convey great truths to the world, should have destroyed instruments which were the result of the labour of many years of research; but Schopenhauer tells us that genius possesses an abnormally developed nervous and cerebral systemth at brings with it hyper-sensibility, which in union with intensity of will energy, that is also characteristic of genius, occasions quick changes of mood and extravagant outbursts. Schopenhauer also explains why it is that men of genius are ignored by the age in which they appear:—"The genius comes into his age like a comet into the paths of the planets, to whose well-regulated and comprehensible order its entirely eccentric course is foreign. Accordingly he cannot go hand in hand with the existing regular progress to the culture of the age, but flings his works far out on the way in front (as the dying Emperor flung his spear among the enemy), which time has first to overtake. The achievement of the man of genius transcends not only the power of achievement of others, but also their power of apprehension; therefore they do not become directly conscious of him. The man of talent is like the marksman who hits a mark the others cannot hit; the man of genius is like the marksman who hits a mark that the sight of others cannot even reach." In one sense this truth applies to all men, for, says Cicero, no man is understood excepting by his equals or his superiors.

Admitting all that has been said of the difficulties attendant upon the comprehension of a genius by the age in which he lives, it does not require genius to understand the blunders which, perpetrated by the managers of the prematurely organized Keely Motor Company, have placed Mr. Keely, as well as themselves, in false positions with the public; leaving him since the winter of '80-'81 to bear the whole burden of the infamy brought about by their having offered stock for investment which could possess no tangible existence in the shape of property until the laws governing the unknown force that he was handling, had been studied out and applied to mechanics in a patentable machine. To those informed that this company ceased to hold annual meetings as far back as '81 it will be a matter of surprise to hear that, sitting up in its coffin, seven or eight years after its burial, it called another *annual* meeting, and that now its managers are again applying the thumb-screw, as in past years; pressing their claims and threatening a suit for obtaining money under false pretences, unless Mr. Keely renounces his plan of progressive research, and gives his time to the construction of engines for the Keely Motor Company. This requirement, as was said in 1881, of a similar effort, is as sensible, under existing conditions, as it would be to require Keely to devote his time to growing figs on thorn trees. It is from the "Minority Report to the Stockholders of the Keely Motor Company from the Board of Directors" (made by a member of that board in 1881, John H. Lorimer), that the material is gleaned for disclosing facts which it is due to Mr. Keely should now, since this last attempt to intimidate him, be given to the public. The stock of that company is not lessened in value by the mismanagement of its officers and directors; for Mr. Keely's moral obligations to its stockholders are as sacred to him as if the company had not long since forfeited its charter. When Mr. Keely became financially independent of the company last March, speculation in the stock of that company received its death blow, and the "Keely Motor Bubble" burst, leaving to the stockholders all that ever had any tangible existence in the shape of property in a more valuable position than it had ever been before. Mr. Lorimer is a gentleman of Scotch birth who was elected a director of the Keely Motor Company in '81, and who resigned in '82, because he was "unable to carry the enterprise," and unwilling to fall in with the policy of the old directors. Before resigning, he set himself to studying the position of affairs with a view to forming for the Board a definite plan of action which ordinary business principles would justify.

This course resulted in a thoroughly business-like letter to Mr. Keely in which, under nine heads, Mr. Lorimer set down the conclusions he had reached as to the cause of the difficulties that had culminated in a threatened law suit, and Mr. Keely was ordered to ask that a special meeting of the Board should be called at once, to consider any proposition he should see fit to make towards settling the question whether he should proceed with the company's work or be permitted to defer it, as he so much desired, until he had fully developed all the adaptations of his power already known to him or hereafter possible of discovery by him. Mr. Lorimer added :—"And now, in conclusion, I may say to you that the above deductions from the history of your motor are the result of patient and laborious inquiry on my part, and I am truly at a loss to understand how, or in what manner, other than that herein suggested, you can honourably vindicate your position; and as no one I have met connected with the enterprise, or personally acquainted with you, hesitates for an instant in crediting you with the most unswerving integrity, I have no hesitation in offering the above suggestions for your consideration; and I trust you will so far adopt them as to enable the active portion of your friends to bring the organization rapidly into harmonious accord with you in the development of what all seem to think is the greatest wonder of our civilization, the early completion of which will lift you to the highest pinacle of fame as a scientist, and make them co-dispensers with you of the God-given wealth of which you hold the key." The date is 10th of February, 1881.

This letter was followed by another dated February 11th, in which Mr. Lorimer submitted certain conclusions, arrived at after meeting in New York with several members of the Board of Directors, one of which reads:—"It seems to be generally understood that without your hearty co-operation and good will, the company cannot realize value upon any existing contracts, or any they may hereafter make with you."

At this time Mr. Lorimer states that he had the opportunity presented of studying, semi-officially, the very peculiar man whose genius held his friends so spell-bound that they lost their power (if such they possessed) to adapt business methods to the enterprise. "To meet him socially in his shop," Mr. Lorimer writes, "after his day's work, was, I think, invariably to be impressed with his earnestness, honesty of purpose, and, above all, with confidence in his knowledge of the plane of science he was working in (acoustics), and at the same time, to be impressed with the folly of basing calculations for the government of the business details of the organization upon the statements made by him while contemplating the possible result of his researches."

With the hopeful spirit of an inventor, Mr. Keely always anticipated almost immediate mechanical success, up to the hour in which he abandoned the automatic arrangement that was necessary to make his generator patentable. From that time his line of perspective extended, and he began to realize that he had been too sanguine in the past. He had been like a man grappling in the dark with a foe, the form of which had not even presented itself to his imagination; but when, in 1884, Macvicar's work on the structure of ether came like a torch to reveal the face of his antagonist, what wonder that he, with the enthusiasm of Paracelsus, felt his

> . . . . . " fluttering pulse give evidence that God
> Means good to me, will make my cause his own,"

and, as in 1881, again rashly bound himself, anew, by fresh promises, made to those who had the power to give or to withhold the sinews needed in the warfare he was waging?

To return to the report. During the negotiations which followed, facts in the history of the company were developed which convinced Mr. Lorimer that Mr. Keely was totally unable to measure time, or define his plans, because of the ever changing results attained by him, in researching the laws governing the force he was trying to harness. At this time the treasurer of the company was proposing to bring over from New York to Philadelphia a number of capitalists to witness an exhibition of the production of the force, in order to dispose of 500 shares at 25.00 dols. a share to them. To this plan Mr. Lormer objected, writing to the treasurer, "I fear that you would be putting yourself in a false position with the friends you might induce to take stock at the figures named," and Mr. Keely himself at first refused to give the exhibition, but upon the application of the thumb-screw, kept in readiness, it took place. At this time Mr. Lorimer wrote to the president of the company, "If Keely gives us the benefit of his discoveries, it will require all our energies to guide our enterprise; and, on the other hand, if he dies or is forestalled, it will need all our care and attention to take care of our reputations. . . . . The fact that the Board has some delicate and important work to perform, brings us to the question, are we properly organized to perform our part? If we are, let us show it by our acts, and, if not, let us act like men, worthy the important trust before us. If I am over-estimating the character and importance of this work, you can show it to me, and *per contra*, if I am correct, you can and will accept the responsibilities of the position you hold, no matter how unpleasant, no matter how irksome, if understood by you and honourably supported by us."

Mr. Lorimer then prepared this summary, or analysis of the situation.

SUMMARY.

26th July, 1881.

First.—The existence of a discovery or invention which, from evidences of its adaptability (when complete) to the industrial arts and sciences, may be esteemed the most valuable discovery of civilization in modern or in ancient times, inasmuch as it revolutionizes all known methods of generating power.

Second.—The retention by the discoverer and inventor of all the secrets whereby these discoveries can be utilized by the public, thus making their future existence, so far as the Keely Motor Company is concerned, depend entirely upon his life and goodwill.

Third.—The existence of a corporated company, organized for the purpose of furnishing funds for the development and completion of the discovery, and for the final control of certain specified inventions, in certain specified localities.

Fourth.—The contracts under which the above-mentioned control of certain inventions is vested in the Keely Motor Company, being mere evidences of intention, have no real value until the inventor has received his patents and verified the contracts by transfer of the same to the company.

Fifth.—If any conflict should arise between the company and the inventor, in which the latter *felt justified* in withholding the transfer, the existing contracts might be a good foundation to build litigation upon but not good for investment in.

Sixth.—The uncertainty of the future of the enterprise, as thus indicated, must of necessity invite a speculative management; and while speculation under some circumstances is legitimate and laudable, under other conditions it may become illegitimate and reprehensible.

Seventh.—The existence of a speculative management in Keely Motor affairs has, of necessity, developed two interests—one which holds that the completion of the discovery in all its possible grandeur should ever be the sole object of its management, and the other, believing that on account of the human uncertainity of the completion of the invention, they are in duty bound to make quick recoveries on their investments, so that they may be safe financially, in the event of a failure by Keely to perfect his inventions.

––––––

It is not necessary to pursue this summary farther, as the manner in which Mr. Lorimer has set down the facts already given, makes clear the nature of the conflicting interests that brought about the antagonism which he attempted to subdue, bringing such a spirit of fairness and justice into his efforts as must have crowned them with success, supported as he was by Mr. Keely, had it not been that those who advocated following a policy which, at best, aimed no farther than at the recouping of losses to themselves were in the majority. It was at this time that Mr. Keely manifested his willingness to assume, on the one hand, all the responsibility of the proper development of his discovery; or, on the other hand, all the disgrace accompanying failure by his offer to purchase a controlling interest in the stock, fifty-one thousand shares of which, in order to prevent speculation, he agreed to lock up for five years, and to give the company a bond restraining him from negotiating or parting with a single share of it in that time, the stock to be paid for as soon as certain deferred payments had been made to him. This propositon of Mr. Keely to the Board of Directors, October 25th, 1881 (and laid upon the table by a large majority as unworthy of consideration), was made from his earnest desire to control the presentation of his life's work to the world in a just and honourable way; having recognized, with Mr. Lorimer, the utter impossibility of reconciling the numerous interests created by mistakes of himself and the mismanagement of the Board, unless he could thus obtain the power to deliver an unencumbered enterprise to the world. In the opinion of Mr. Lorimer, during the negotiations which he conducted between the management and Mr. Keely, the latter was the only one who had manifested any consistency or strength of purpose, so far as the facts gave evidence, which were brought before him, of the history of the company. When the validity of the contracts made with Mr. Keely while he was president, or director of the company, were disputed, he was called upon to resign, which he did; and yet no steps were taken to ascertain the value of the existing contracts, which had all been made with him while he was both president and director, and which were therefore, illegal. Proceedings in equity were commenced against Mr. Keely, by the Committee of the Board of Directors having the matter in charge, late in the year 1881, while Mr. Lorimer's report was still in the hands of the printer. "The spectacle of a Board of thirteen Directors, composed of business men," writes Mr. Lorimer, "claiming that they have been foiled in their business calculations by a man whose mind has been so thoroughly absorbed in researching the problems presented by his wonderful discoveries that he could not possibly compare with any of them in *business* tact, is truly a phenomenon which is not easy of explanation on any hypothesis, but the one that their visions of prospective wealth have been so overpowering as to undo their prudence; and then having in due process of time discovered their error, it certainly is an edifying spectacle to see them now trying to throw all the blame on one poor mortal wholly absorbed in his inventions, and by these efforts disturbing that mental equilibrium of both the inventor and themselves, which is absolutely necessary to ultimate success. When boys, in early summer, pick unripe fruit and eat it, because of their unwillingness to await the ripening thereof, they sometimes suffer acutely for their haste. Yet no one ever thinks of punishing the tree because of their sufferings; nor is it deemed necessary to justice to preserve the fruit of the tree, when ripe, for the sole use of the impatient ones as a recompense for their early sufferings! So it has been with the Keely Motor Company; undue haste to gather the golden fruit that was to come from it has led to a great deal of suffering financially among a few impatient believers. Still it does not seem to me to be wise to curse the inventor, or his inventions, because he has not given us the fruit when we expected it would be ripe." . . . .

The effort to force Keely to divulge his secrets failed, for at that time he had nothing of a practical nature to divulge, and though possessing no business qualifications, he was too shrewd to cut off any of his resources for supplies, necessary to enable him to persevere in his efforts to attain some practical result, as he surely would have done, had he said, "I know very little more than you know of the laws governing the force I have discovered. I can only control their operation by experimental research, and the more time that is wasted in building engines, until I have made myself acquainted with these laws, the longer will you have to wait for your golden fruit." Mr. Keely was no more able at that time to give the faintest idea of the present stage of his researches than Professor Leidy or Dr. Wilcox could now, after witnessing the experiments in sympathetic attraction, write out a clear formulation of its governing law, and an inductive substantiation of it. Even were it possible no reader could understand it, because the discovery made by Mr. Keely is not in accordance with any of the facts known to science. Mr. Keely's experiments in disintegrating water prove that incalculable amounts of latent force exist in the molecular spaces; but in the opinion of scientists, molecular aggregation is attended with dissipation of energy, not with absorption of energy. If the men of science are right, then there must be an absolute creation of energy, for only by admitting its absorption in aggregation, could molecular dissociation supply the force witnessed. Yet Keely denies any creation of energy, claiming only that he can produce an indefinite supply by the expenditure of an infinitesimally small amount of energy. Every new discovery necessitates a new nomenclature. The vocabulary coined by Mr. Keely, to meet his requirements in formulating his hypotheses into theories as he progresses, conveys as little meaning to those who read his writings, as the word electricity conveyed 200 years ago. Professor Crookes said that to him reading Mr. Keely's writings was like reading Persian without a dictionary. Another learned Professor said that they seemed to him to be composed in an unknown tongue, so profoundly unintelligible had he found the extracts sent to him. One must be familiar with Mr. Keely's instruments and their operation, in order to comprehend even the nature of his researches.

At some experiments illustrative of varying chords of mass, an author of philosophical works was present, whose theories had not been in unison with those of Mr. Keely on that subject. He sat for some time after the demonstration with his eyes fixed upon the floor, wearing as serious an expression of countenance as if he were looking on the grave of his most cherished views. The first remark that he made was, "What would Jules Verne say if he were here?" The rotation of the needle of a compass, the compass placed on a glass slab and connected with the transmitter by a wire, 120 revolutions in a second, had the same effect upon the scientists present, one of awe; so completely were they transfixed and unable to form a conjecture as to the mysterious influence from any known law of science. There was only one professor present, *a very young man*, who ventured the whispered suggestion of concealed mechanism under the pedestal; and as Mr. Keely soon after had occasion to wheel the pedestal across the room, showing that it was not stationary, and could have no concealed connection within or without, the young professor took up another line of conjecture. As Macvicar says, it has grown to be the fashion, to a marvellous extent, to give predominance in education to physical and mathematical studies over moral and mental. Hence a very general and growing prepossession in favour of material nature. Astronomy, natural philosophy, chemistry, natural history, geology, these and the like are in our day held to be everything. He continues :—

Now, all these branches of study, however various in detail, agree in this, that they exclude the conception of a true self-directive power from the field of thought. They offer for consideration nothing but figures, movements, and laws. And thus they tend to form the popular mind to the habit of looking for figures, movements, and laws everywhere, and for rejecting all other conceptions as intruders. But of all such other conceptions, there is nothing so difficult and so intractable, under physical modes of investigation, as self-directive power. It therefore runs a great risk of being rejected, and thus the mind, from its first training, having been in physics, carrying out here, as it usually does everywhere, its first love into all its after thoughts, shuts up the student surreptitiously with materialism as his philosophy. Thus it is easy to see how materialism should come to be a current opinion, when the popular education runs all in favour of physical pursuits. But if philosophy must yield to the demands of the logical faculty for an extreme simplicity, unity, identity, at the fountain head of nature, it were more logical to regard those phenomena and laws named physical, such as the laws of motion, elasticity, gravitation, etc., as manifestations, when existing under certain limiting conditions, of substances or beings which have also in them, when not so limited, and when existing under certain conditions ability to manifest self-directive power. That every body is compounded, constituted, or made up of molecules, is universally agreed. Every body is therefore a fit subject for analysis But when any body is submitted to analysis in reference to its mere corporeity or bodily nature, that is, its extension and impenetrability, what do we ultimately arrive at ? Do we not, in reference to the attribute of extension, arrive at particles, of which the physical limit is that they have at last ceased to be extended, and are but mere points in space ? And as to the attribute of impenetrability, what do we in the last analysis arrive at, but the idea of a substance that can resist the intrusion into its place of other similar substances, and, therefore, ultimately, a centre of force. And thus, under a logical analysis, which must be admitted to be legitimate, it may be maintained that a body or chemical element resolves itself into a system of centres of force balancing each other at certain distances, and thus rendering the whole molecule or mass extended, as body is known to be. The elements of body, therefore, are things of which these attributes are to be affirmed in the first instance, that they possess unextended substance and extensive power. But, if so, do they not touch upon the confines of the spiritual world to say the least ? asks Macvicar; and the Newton whom he foretold answers the question (and demonstrates the truth of his answer) in his discovery of the cerebelic stream or mind flow.

Body and spirit, one at the fountain-head, when rising into existence, form, as it were, the first breath of creation; for, as Sir Wm. Thompson says: "Life proceeds from life and from nothing else." They are the opposite poles of being, and constitute the two principles by the harmonious interweaving of which the beautiful system of creation is constituted, and its economy worked out. Such a view, far from being contrary to the canons of science, is even the necessary complement of science. That unity, which is the last word of science, must always include two objects, existing in contrast after all. The law of couples, of opposites, of reciprocal action between two contrasted yet homogeneous and harmonising elements, each of which opens a field for the other, and brings it into action, is of universal extent. In the organic world, also, no less than in the purely physical and chemical, all is framed according to the same law of couples. In the sphere of sensibility, in like manner, everything turns on the antagonism of pleasure and pain, and in the moral sphere of good and evil. Nor is the world of pure intellect exempt from this law, but on the contrary displays its influence everywhere. Hence faith and sight, identity and difference, finite and infinite, objective and subjective, space and time, cause and effect, the world of realities and the world of ideas. In a word, every system of thought and of things, when complete, present as its basis two co-ordinate elements, the reciprocals of each other; or one parted into two reciprocally, and by the harmonious antagonism of both the beautiful web of nature is woven. If we are to be consistent, mind and matter ought always to be viewed as distinct, and the opposite poles of being; *inertia*, or unvarying submissiveness to the laws of motion being the characteristic of the one; self-directive power the characteristic of the other.

The universal analogy of science sanctioned Macvicar in the characteristic he thus arrived at as that of animated nature, for if inertia, or the obedience to pressures and impulses from without, be the characteristic of matter, then that which is needed as the other term to complete the couple is just what has been insisted on, viz., self-directive power. Here is shown the symmetrical relation in which this power, when viewed as the characteristic of the whole animal kingdom (which plainly points to man, and culminates in human nature), places the animal in relation with the vegetable and the mineral kingdoms. Of minerals or crystals, the characteristic is simply self-imposing or *self-concreting* power. They are, so to speak, merely insoluble seeds without an embryo. To this, *self-developing* power is added in plants, and forms their acknowledged characteristic, while of animals the characteristic, according to the view here advanced (the same seed-producing, self-developing, powers continuing) is *self-directive* power superadded. This relationship between these three kingdoms of nature is as homogeneous and symmetrical as is necessary to appear to be legitimate, and is a true expression of the order of nature.

Granting these two principles, the inert and the self-directive, the necessary and the free, we obtain the materials for a universe, without disputing the fact of human liberty and bringing into suspicion even the possibility either of morality or immorality. If man be really free as well as under law, in this union of body and spirit, then in human nature heaven and earth truly embrace each other; and no reason appears why, as the ages roll on, our own free thought may not have the run of the universe. . . . . What study then can be more replete with interest, what researches can possess more of fascination, than those which Mr. Keely's discoveries are preparing the way for? His are no speculations, such as have been indulged in by atheistic evolutionists or hair-splitting imaginative metaphysicians, leading their students into the position of Socrates when he recounted to Cebes the result of his studies in physics:—"So far is it from me now, by Jove, to think that I know anything about the cause of these things, that I cannot settle it with myself whether, when to one one is added, it is the one to which that one is added that makes two, or whether the added one and the one to which it was added, because of the addition make two," etc., etc. But quoting Anaxagoras that "mind is the disposer and cause of everything," Socrates grows delighted, and affirms that he would "most gladly become the disciple of any one who would teach him the thing without which the cause could not be a cause, which the many appear to be seeking for, as it were in the dark, and making up to a name which is not its own, dub it a cause." How delighted would Socrates have been with the discovery of the cerebellic stream. "Metaphorically," writes Keely, "I associate the mind flow (to a certain extent) with all organisms that are sensible to negative attractive vibration that I can reach in my field of research." The immense region thus laid open has no limits. It extends as far as the universe extends, for all to explore who are willing to "chip the shell of ignorance," and allow themselves to be led by their apperception into the sanctuary of Truth, the threshold of which has been crossed in the discoveries of laws by which a *mécanique céleste* of mind will in time be revealed to the world.

The discoveries of Mr. Keely (demonstrated—as he is now prepared to demonstrate them) cannot be disputed, though his system may be called in question. With the humility of genius, he calls his theories hypotheses, and his hypotheses conjectures. The solidity of the principles, as laid down by himself, cannot be decided upon by others until he has brought to light the whole system that grows out of them. But it is time the public should know that the odium thrown upon him by the Keely Motor Company, he does not deserve. It is time that the Press should cease its sneers, its cry of "Crucify him, crucify him!" morally speaking, and extend to him that discriminating appreciation of his work and encouragement which the *New York Home Journal,** Truth, Detroit Tribune, Chicago Herald, Toledo Blade, Atlanta Constitution, The Statesman,* and *Vienna News* have been the first to do. Let the Press contrast the past history of science with the present position of Keely. "Fancy the discoverer of electricity having succeeded in inventing the modern dynamo machine! Such a fact would mean the concentration of hundreds of years of scientific discovery and invention into the single life of one man. Such a result would be simply marvellous," writes an English scientist. *Thousands* of years, he might have said, counting Thales as the discoverer; for Gilbert did but re-discover electricity. It is time that capitalists should step from their ranks to protect Keely from the selfish policy of the managers of a speculative company, which has long since forfeited all claims upon him, to continue mechanical work for it, even admitting that it ever possessed that right; and, more than all else, it is time that science should send her delegates to confer with the broad-minded men who have had the courage to give testimony, without which Keely could not have stood where, this year, he stands for the first time, fearless of threats, pursuing his researches on his own line, to acquire that knowledge of the laws governing his discoveries by which alone he can gain sufficient control of machinery to insure financial success. Meanwhile, are there no men who are able to feel an interest (without reference to commercial results) in a discovery which sweeps away the *débris* of materialism as chaff is swept before a whirlwind?—giving indisputable proof that, as St. Paul teaches, "we are the offspring of God;" or, as Aratus wrote, from whom he quoted :—

> " From God we must originate,
> Not any time we break the spell
> That binds us to the ineffable.
> Indeed, we all are evermore
> Having to do with God; for *we*
> *His very kind and offspring be :*
> And to his offspring the benign
> Fails not to give benignant sign."

CLARA JESSUP MOORE.

From *New York Truth*, 3rd July, 1890.

* I think it is safe, for even the most conservative and pig-headed of scientists, to admit that Keely, the contemned, the scoffed at, the derided, the man whom every picayune peddler called charlatan because he could not harness the hitherto undiscovered forces of ether in less time than one might hitch up a mule, is the most original and the most straightforward of inventors, and that in his own good time he will give to the world a power that will throw steam and electricity into disuse, open the realms of air as a public highway for man, and send great ships careering over ocean with a power developed by sound. His theory of etheric vibration is now conclusively established, and it is only a question of time and material that delays its use as a servant to man. The fact is patent, so that he who runs may read, but the ox must have the yoke, the horse the collar, the engine the cylinder, and the dynamo the coil, ere they can work their wonders. While Keely was hampered by mere tradesmen, who only looked to the immediate recoupment of their outlay, men more anxious for dividends than discoveries, he could do little save turn showman, and exhibit his partial control of the harmonies of nature as springs catch woodcocks, and was forced to open his crude contrivances to divert the eternal will of the cosmos to work-a-day uses, that he might coax from the greed and credulity of mere mammon worshippers the sorely grudged means to continue his exploration of the infinite. His genius was prisoned in a test tube, and only let out to play monkey tricks before muddleheaded merchants, who could see the effect, but not the means, and so the greatest discovery of the age was turned into a raree show, and the eternal music of the spheres was set, figuratively speaking, to play tunes to attract custom like a barrow organ before a dime museum.

ALLEN, SCOTT AND CO., 30, BOUVERIE STREET LONDON, E.C.

A NEW YEAR'S GREETING

THEOSOPHY AND PRACTICAL OCCULTISM.

SIMON MAGUS.

London;

THEOSOPHICAL PUBLISHING SOCIETY,

7, DUKE STREET, ADELPHI, W.C.

—

Path, P.O., Box 2,659, New York, U.S.A.

1891.

ON THE TREATMENT OF CRIMINALS
AND LUNATICS.

In considering this subject of the treatment of Criminals and Lunatics, we have thought it could best be dealt with under three heads, which naturally suggest themselves to the mind; these are (1) the object or objects in view supposed to be held in the treatment of criminals and lunatics; (2) the means adopted to secure those ends; and (3) the degree of success which has attended these methods. And first with regard to criminals.

I. Without entering into a comparison of the various offences termed "criminal", we may regard the treatment of all such cases as having respect to (a) the protection of Society, or (b) the cure of the evil. Both these objects commend themselves to the mind as being based upon a true conception of the social constitution, and the value of human life. While the condition of the human race is such that no system of Ethics can be uniformly conceived of and applied, it is clear that, in order to preserve the civic and social interests of any community, there is a necessity for an external law, applicable to the treatment of individuals in whom the sense of probity and justice is not sufficiently strong to prevent them from committing acts which endanger the common weal.

It is difficult to decide, at once, as to the respective merit of the two objects which the treatment of criminals is supposed to aim at. Looking at the question from the standpoint of Economics, one would suppose that the protection of Society (in the broadest sense of the word, of course) was the first and essential object; and it might be argued that the cure of the evil implied by the term "criminal offence", would be but the means to that end; yet in no case would the true Economist allow us to disregard the criminal unit. But then we are forced to admit that it is from the internal state of Society the offence proceeds in the first place, and that if such evil did not exist, there would be no need for protection, so that we are led to consider the cure of the evil as of primary importance; and the cause of it must be sought in the life of Society, as a disease having its root therein, and not as an evil of a foreign nature happening to it from without. Leaving this point, however, to individual decision, let us pass on to the consideration of the ways and means adopted to these ends. As we are dealing with the modern methods of criminal treatment, we may say they are of two kinds, viz. :—corrective and punitive ; and of these the reformatories represent the one, while the prisons, treadmills, stone quarries and gallows of our country represent the other method.

Now the fitness of any treatment cannot be properly apprehended apart from a consideration of the case in hand ; for on the " corrective " principle, the treatment would naturally depend on the diagnosis ; while the punitive method would have regard to the measure of the offence, and thus entail a consideration of the causes which induced it, and the responsibility of the criminal in the act. Here we at once see how really different are the two objects proposed to be attained in the treatment of criminals, or rather, how differently they are regarded by those who administer, or are supposed to administer, justice to the criminal, and to Society against which he offends. Is it possible to regard the two objects as distinct from one another, and at the same time to ensure the attainment of either ? We think not ; for clearly, unless the evil *is* cured, and the cause of the offence removed, the community is in no way secured against a repetition of its effects. Yet Society has all along held the criminal act, as an offence against its rights, to be of greater importance than the cause of crime, which exists as an evil within itself. It is the old tale of " the beam and the mote ", beginning in the ignorance and ending in the selfishness and cruelty of the world. And yet, until the factors which operate in the production of crime are properly perceived and understood, we cannot hope that any means whatever will avail for either the cure of crime or the protection of Society. The constitutional defects observable in the confirmed criminal are to be traced very frequently to the social conditions bearing upon his heredity, such as unhealthy modes of living ; lack of proper education, mental, moral and physical training, &c. ; and these adverse conditions are frequently aggravated by direct injustice and dire necessity.

That such conditions should exist at all is a manifest injustice, and only serves to show how blind, even to self-advantage, a selfish world can be ; but when absolutely no allowance is made, in the punitive method of criminal treatment, for such unequal conditions, the injustice of a severe punishment only tends to exasperate the convicted person, and destroys the very object which the punishment is supposed to subserve. In *Remedies for Perils of the Nation* it is said, " It is just because the reigning philosophy of the day has taught us that it was better worth our while to improve our steam engines than to nurture our population ; it is because honours and rewards have been showered on those who taught how to cultivate capital for the few, while contempt was poured on those who contended for the greater necessity of cultivating the people's happiness. . . . From these fancies and fictions it has come to pass, at last, that the bloated wealth on the one hand, and the squalid poverty on the other, have gone on increasing, till all calm and considerate observers begin to ask themselves whether it is possible for a framework, the parts of which are so grievously disproportioned to each other, to hang together much longer ".

With regard to the *corrective* method of treating criminals, it is wholly just and beneficent if properly conducted, and the only method which should find a place in the government of a civilised country. It should, however, apply uniformly, and as much to the adult as to the juvenile criminal; and in every case the *cause* of offence should concern us more immediately than the offence itself. On this point the *Irish Quarterly Review* has said :—" The time has arrived when the Government of this country must adopt those admirable rules of other nations, by which the health, the morality, and the education of the people can be secured. The preacher has implored, the economist has complained, the patriot has urged, the physician has warned. We punish those who are criminal, but we never try to shield them from the blasting contamination of vice. The Churchman thunders forth God's curse on sin, and we suffer the grasping house-owner to cram his wretched rooms with human beings—age and sex unnoticed. Our manufactories are the seminaries of sin; the cottages of our labourers are the schools of vice; our coal mines are only the working-places of biped brutes. Drunkenness is the common luxury of our poor; murder, incest and infanticide are common entries in our assize calendars ". These and such as these are the crimes which stand to our charge—I say " our charge " with intention, for it is that " mote " in our poor brother's eye which warns us of the " beam " within our own. The welfare of the community is, after all, made up of the individual welfare of its members, not forgetting the least of them; for the head cannot say to the foot " I have no need of thee ". Yes, these are the evils which lie at our doors,—and in our very houses. What is the remedy we have applied, and are still applying ? A system of punitive revenge, as disastrous to ourselves as it is ineffectual to erase the red stain of crime which mars our records year by year. A system which neither repairs the evil effects of crime, nor seeks to correct the incentive cause; and which considers corporeal punishment, hard labour, solitary confinement, and the forfeiture of money, to be sufficient compensation to Society for the evil done by any of its members. Of course in many cases it is impossible for anyone to repair the evil effects of crime, as, for instance, in the case of murder. And this brings us to the question of Capital punishment, " the extreme measure of the law ".

The old laws of absolute barbarism, when men were hanged for such offences as sheep-stealing, &c., have given place to milder forms of punishment, and a modification of most of the laws bearing upon the treatment of crime. A far higher and more rational conception of freedom, than entered into the minds of people in those days, is gradually spreading itself, and is changing the whole attitude of society with regard to this and other questions of equity.

Equality, before the law, is becoming more and more a fact. The real worth of a human being is better understood; *i.e.*, his worth as an individual, on his own account, and not merely as a useful tool for others. In these days, there is not a single case of the sentence of capital punishment being passed, but efforts are made in all directions for a commutation of the penalty to some milder form. This is not from any condonation of the sin, on the part of Society, but partly from condolence with the wretched being whose crime is most frequently the result of an extremity of suffering, and partly from a sense of the inefficacy of any further blood-shedding. Let us for a moment consider our position in this matter. Why does Society continue to recognize this form of punishment? Why do we who have the making and repealing of the laws in our hands, permit this worse than useless and inhuman law to continue? What is the end in view? Is it to revenge our dead, to protect our own lives, or to cure crime by intimidation? If any of these be our object, the method adopted is *an unqualified failure.* Surely, if the taking of human life be a crime, it is as criminal in us to kill the murderer, as it is criminal in him to have killed another. The balance of justice is not restored by a *repetition* of the crime! Nor do we *protect* ourselves by such an act. We may learn a great truth concerning this matter from the teaching of Lord Buddha, as set forth in the 8th Book of the "Light of Asia", where, speaking of the law of Karma, it says: "Fresh issues on the universe that sum which is the lattermost of lives"—and, "also it issues forth to help or hurt. When death the *bitter murderer* doth smite, red roams the *unpurged* fragment of him, driven on winds of plague and blight". You would cure crime by intimidation? The occult *law* is against you; you cannot do it. You cannot prevent this "*red and unpurged fragment*" of the murdered murderer, from fastening on the mind of man wherever it finds congenial soil, as "the feathered reed-seed flies, o'er rock and loam and sand, until it finds its marsh and multiplies"! You cannot cure by intimidation, as each new case will prove. Does the criminal stay in his deadly work to count the cost of his crime? Facts seem to say otherwise. What then shall we do to compass the double evil? Something of an answer is contained in the words of Lord Palmerston:—"There is *one* power which knowledge gives us, which is more important than all others; it is the power of man over himself. It is by knowledge that men are enabled to control their passions, regulate their conduct, and devote their energies and exertions to the welfare of their country." While men are in ignorance of the inviolable laws which hedge them in as offenders on every side like walls, and which become to the truth-seeking lover of justice, wings of beauty and of strength; what can we hope for but a continuance of those evils for which we have no better remedy than evil itself! Knowledge of the laws which govern our existence as responsible agents, and education of the right sort, applied physically, mentally and morally, after the best methods, can alone solve the problem of our great social evils, and comprehend at once their cause and cure. "When," asks Dr. Channing, "will statesmen learn that there are higher powers than political motives, interest, and intrigue? When will they learn *the might which dwells in truth?* When will they learn that the past and present are not the future; but that the changes already wrought in Society are only forerunners, signs, and springs of mighty revolutions? Absorbed in near objects, they are prophets only on a small scale. They may foretell the issues of our next election, but the breaking out of *a deep moral conviction* in the mass of men, is a mystery which they have little skill to interpret. In all the grandest epochs of history, what was it won the victory? What were the mighty all-prevailing powers? Not political management, not self-interest, not the lower principles of human nature, but the principles of freedom, of justice, of moral power, moral enthusiasm, and the divine aspiration of the human soul." But whatever may be the objects, and whatever the means which control this matter of the treatment of Criminals, let us glance at the *results* before leaving the subject. The statistics for London alone, of crime and dissipation, are as follows :—

16,000 children trained to crime.

5,000 receivers of stolen goods.

15,000 gamblers by profession.

25,000 beggars.

183,000 habitual drunkards.

150,000 persons subsisting on profligacy.

50,000 thieves.

These figures are made up from cases under notice. Those that escape notice may be as many more; but these alone give a total of 784,000 *souls!* And this is what the nation suffers for neglecting to make efficient provision for the education and physical welfare of the masses; and all through *selfishness!* It costs us over two million pounds sterling, per year. How long we shall suffer the double stress of this moral and physical burden, we alone can decide. The cause and cure is within and from *ourselves!*

II.—It may not be immediately apparent why we have elected to deal with the subject of lunacy and its treatment, in connection with that relating to criminals. Before tracing the connection which we find to exist between the two subjects, it may be best to consider the nature of lunacy, and the provision that is made for its treatment. Of course the only complete method of dealing with the diseases of the brain and their effects upon individuals, would be to gain a proper knowledge and understanding of the normal conditions and proper functions of the various parts of the brain. This of course we cannot attempt. We must therefore content ourselves with a summary view of its functions in their normal and abnormal conditions. The normal brain has three chief and distinct functions, viz.—

1. To be affected by impressions.
2. To express consciousness.
3. To affect other bodies within its sphere of action.

The complete interaction of these three functions is held to constitute *sanity*. Any departure from the perfect manifestation of these qualities is attended with more or less danger of an eventual loss of certain healthy conditions of thought and action. This deterioration of the physical condition of the brain is not always to be discerned during life time, nor is there always an indication of cerebral disorganization to be found in the post mortem examination of certified maniacs. This is an *important fact* and one which should concern the occultist very greatly in his consideration of the treatment of lunatics.

Dr. Winchcomb, of the Warwickshire County Lunatic Asylum, testifies to this fact in the following words:—" I have long come to the conclusion that, the outward appearance of the brain being normal, is no proof that the mind is sound." From this, and other evidence to the same effect, we may conclude that the border line between sanity and insanity, from the purely physical standpoint, is not as yet determined. Professor Windle, of the Queen's College, says:—" It is only with the greatest possible care that even the most experienced are able to detect between a common illness and the most advanced conditions of insanity; between nervous affections and brain disorganization."

However, not to lengthen this subject indefinitely, we may state that there are three primary affections arising out of the disorders of the brain. They are :—

1. Illusions.
2. Delusions.
3. Hallucinations.

The first of these disorders is said to lie in a defective condition of the sensorium whereby wrong impressions are received, and thus the individual becomes the dupe of his senses.

The second of these unhealthy conditions of brain function, delusion, consists in a mis-shapen impression being conveyed to the mind and received by it as real and consistent, being uncorrected by the application of logical thought. In the first case the false impression begins and ends in the sensorium—but here it extends to the mind; and just at that point where sensation is translated into consciousness, illusion becomes delusion. *Hallucination* is unlike either of these; for whereas they are objective, and proceed from without, hallucination, on the other hand, has its origin in the mind itself. In its expression lie almost all the symptoms and conditions of morbid insanity. In this state, the mind receives not only imperfect impressions as in cases of illusion, but *absolutely false* and unreal ones; and not only believes them to be true, as in the cases of *delusion*, but cannot be reasoned out of them. Perception, memory, and imagination, each runs its own *mad race*. Neither faculty corroborates the others. Impressions are false, memory imperfect, imagination contorted, reason nil.

These are the three chief disorders of brain functions, and those in whom these conditions *persist* are held to be insane.

The statistics show that out of every 100 cases of insanity 20 are due to hereditary disease, 14 to bad marriages, 10 to intemperance, and 6 to epilepsy, the remaining 50 being from distinct causes of a diversified nature.

So far we have considered the nature and cause of insanity; we must now determine how far its treatment is provided for, and how far the cure of this evil is effected. Until a very recent date the number of *private asylums*, for the treatment and safe keeping of lunatics, in this country, was comparatively very large, and the system adopted in most cases was of the nature which characterizes the average " baby-farming " establishment.

We believe it is a well-known fact that many a well-conditioned and perfectly sane child, whose prospects from all points were bright and hopeful, but whose presence in the world was particularly unfortunate for certain "interested" relatives, has been secretly incarcerated in one of these private asylums, and left there to be treated indefinitely for " aggravated symptoms of insanity ". All that was required was the doctor's certificate. This could be obtained for a consideration; and forthwith the victim of this diabolical scheme was committed to the hands of the " keeper ", under whose treatment he rapidly developed symptoms which rendered the position of the conspirators a comparatively secure one. However, since the Government of this country has undertaken the supervision of asylums, and in the case of lunatic asylums is responsible for the appointment of duly qualified resident physicians, the case is very different. Those who, under medical certificates, are received into these places, are cared for and attended in a manner in no way inconsistent with our ideas of true philanthropy. The greatest possible freedom, consistent with the circumstances of each case, is allowed to them. They are provided with various means of amusement, and are encouraged to take part in physical exercises of different kinds conducted by one or more of the overseers. In some places they have a theatre attached to the institution, where plays and spectacles of an amusing and instructive nature are presented. Their food is ample and wholesome; and only in the most rabid cases of mania or frenzy is there the least evidence of any restraint or harshness; but even this is mostly assumed by the overseers for the safer keeping of the maniac, and for self-protection. The tax upon the energies and watchfulness of these overseers is enormous; almost every case requires separate and special attention, but as often as possible the inmates of the asylums are grouped together according to the nature of their affections.

Such is the plan usually carried out in our lunatic asylums to-day. The method of treatment is generally that of *counter irritation* in the case of monomaniacs, of *stimulation* in that of hypochondriacs, and of *palliation* in that of demoniacs; applied on the physical or mental principle as the diagnosis of the case suggests. We have not been able to get at the figures which represent the cures effected under this method, but there can be little doubt that, wherever the disease is not deep-rooted and chronic, it would readily yield to such a course of treatment; and in mere functional disorder of the brain I know that several cures are effected every week, within the walls of one asylum in this country alone.

Now, regarding this subject in connection with that already treated, the point of connection lies in the fact that thousands of persons, including our highest medical authorities, are convinced that the cause of crime is *insanity, i.e.,* not only an imperfection existing in certain undeveloped faculties of the *mind;* but actual physical disorganisation of part or parts of the brain; and thus of consequent functional disability. Take only one case, that of drunkenness, responsible for the production of half the crime in our land. It is held that the *immediate* cause of this failing is in a diseased condition of certain physical functions; the *secondary* cause being the insufficiency of moral strength to resist the gratification of the abnormal appetite caused thereby. Now drunkenness is not held to be a crime, but a disease; and yet, if, in a state of intoxication, a man were to do harm to another, the effects of this disease would be held as *criminal,* and the culprit subject to punishment which may affect his pocket or his physical comfort, quite as much as does his particular failing, but which does not in any way aim at a redress of the injury inflicted by him, or the cure of the disease, of which his culpable action is only one symptom.

In the case of the suicide also, we see the same inconsistency of judgment maintained by the law. If, from one cause or another, one puts an end to his life, the invariable verdict returned by the coroner is:— "Suicide while in an unsound state of mind." But if, on the other hand, the attempt at suicide were unsuccessful, or partially so, the law ¡would regard the act as criminal, and deal with the unfortunate being accordingly.

In a satirical novel entitled *Erehwon*, a play upon the word "nowhere", the fallacy of our methods of criminal treatment is thus portrayed :—In a remote and hypothetical part of this world, there is said to exist a nation, whose laws with regard to disease and crime are as follows : If a man be found guilty of stealing, lying, defrauding, or other action which indicates a lack of moral rectitude, he is taken to a hospital, where his friends go to visit him and offer their sympathy and condolences. But if one falls sick, is stricken with the fever, or becomes insane, he is taken to a public prison, and severely punished by flogging and other harsh treatment, &c.; and to carry out the satire, it is said that the cures effected by these means are enormous, and, in most cases, immediate. Nothing could be more pointed and justly critical than this parody on our modern methods.

In conclusion, we venture to say that the application of Theosophic teachings to this subject of the treatment of criminals and lunatics, would result in the conclusion that impartial justice,—which is no respecter of persons, and values life, as such, in one man as much as in another,— demands that similar measures of humane treatment should extend to the criminal as to the lunatic. Theosophy would teach us that action begun on the physical plane, ends there ; and that no reform which is to be permanently good can begin with the world of effects, to which the transitory veil of the flesh belongs. Therefore, it is the *cause* of crime, rather than crime itself, which concerns us as immortal Egos, bound to be born and reborn, never except as parts of that One Humanity, whose degradation is our suffering, and whose freedom is our Rest !

SEPHARIAL.

FROM FLESH-EATING TO FRUIT-EATING.

VEGETARIANISM has been much discussed on its scientific interest, and also on its advantages in health and economy. Comparative analyses of food abound, so do persuasive lists of comparative prices, as well as marvellous histories of longevity; what is not so abundant is simple and practical instruction for those who wish to adopt the diet.

This can scarcely be because the course is plain and easy, for it is, on the contrary, beset with difficulties on every side. Yet this question of diet is not without its importance at the present time. Vegetarianism claims to be the basis of long life and economy, of contentment and temperance, and of the cure of disease; such a claim, if made good, should solve most of the bewildering problems of social life. The motives on which a trial would be made of any such panacea would certainly be of various kinds, and methods of making the experiment would be as various as motives, for both would be the outcome of individual idiosyncrasies. But before considering the success or failure of any particular method in any individual case it will be well to go over common ground, considering how far rules can be found to fit all alike, and how far exceptions will have to be made.

There is no doubt that numbers of people attempting a change of diet from the best possible motives, ignominiously fail. It may be that some natures lack endurance for the battle against prejudice and ridicule that the vegetarian has to face in the beginning. This sort of persecution shows itself in so many different forms and in such insidious ways that the mere nervous strain of the strife is enough to dishearten a timid nature. Or it may be that the change is made very suddenly, health is upset by its suddenness, and this is taken for proof that vegetarian diet is unfitting or unwholesome. Again, it may be that the novice does not study the science of the question and so never discovers the nourishing food lying close at hand.

In so momentous a change as that from flesh-eating to fruit-eating the first secret of success is to go slowly, as Nature does. Nature never developes anything hastily—except perhaps ill-weeds—she is joyous, but never eager; active, but never hurried; determined, but never rash. There is about her processes something of the peaceful calm of the higher consciousness, as well as the weight of the enduring will; and so it should be with those who are avowedly forsaking the lower for the higher—the cruel for the kind—the civilised for the natural.

Next in importance comes diligence, especially in learning the science of the question, and for this an impartial and unprejudiced mind is needed; a mind that will consider all things with equal favour—as the sun shines alike on all, whether good or bad—knowing that civilisation is not infallible in its labelling even in the rough distinctions of good and bad.

In the controversy between flesh-eaters and vegetarians there are certain points on which the two sides agree. They agree that animal differs from vegetable food not so much in its chemical constituents as in being altogether of a different class. All animal food is second-hand; it has already been eaten and digested—this is so even with eggs and milk, but actual flesh is a stage further on towards decomposition. They agree also that in both can be found the same chemical constituents, though the large proportion of what figures in tables of chemical analysis as "Ash" in foods from the vegetable kingdom would seem to point to valuable additions. There are plenty of chemical analyses in print to prove these points.

There remain two points on which the two sides of the controversy do not agree. The first is that of stimulant. It is proved by practical experiment that a concentrated essence of beef, that is to say the concentrated extractives or stimulating element of beef is a more rapid restorative than wine or even spirits. There are drugs still more powerful even than beef, and probably less harmful, so that beef, need not be produced on purpose for those suffering from fainting or weakness; but investigation would certainly be needed on this point if animal food were altogether abolished.

The second point of disagreement concerns the assimilation of food, one side contending that animal food is more easily assimilated than vegetable food, and drawing arguments in support of this view from the fact that those who have been meat-eaters all their lives become sooner or later unable to digest anything else; the other side showing that those who become vegetarians continue even to old age able to digest such things as nuts and cucumber, which to the meat-eater are almost poisonous; and arguing from this that the digestive organs being freed from the enormous labour of digesting meat are able to digest the most indigestible of fruits. The argument against the vegetarian would probably break down however if any line of distinction could be drawn between the two causes—the merely stimulating and the easily assimilated. Preparations from meat are found to produce an immediate effect in restoring strength, and from this fact the conclusion is hastily drawn that they are easily assimilated; whereas the result would be precisely the same if they were (as contended by the other side) merely a very strong stimulant.

In the mixed diet of a flesh-eater there is a rough classification of food into solids with the accompanying vegetables and sauces; fruits and sweets regarded as unwholesome; bread and butter considered as of little value; and drink. It is important that the vegetarian novice also should classify his food. To do this he must begin at the beginning and learn his dietary tables all over again, like an Englishman does about money and weights when he goes into a country where the decimal system prevails. He must banish from his mind all that he has learnt from his childhood upwards about meat being so strengthening, and making his mind a blank imprint upon it either in figures or proportionate spaces what he learns from chemistry about foods of different kinds compared with meat. He will principally need to study two points; first, the chemical constituents required to support life in man; and secondly, how to supply them from the vegetable kingdom, as if meat did not exist. When this is well fixed in his mind let him try to supply them from the animal kingdom, and he will be astonished to find how difficult and complicated a process right feeding is when flesh is admitted as food. Beyond this he will discover, sooner or later, that change of diet once begun will not end in a mere transition from the animal to the vegetable kingdom, but will go on to a more radical change in the chemical constituents required. First of all, however, there must be merely the transition from one kingdom to another, and even this slowly and carefully.

The first practical question then is to examine the diet of a meat-eater, to discover its chemical constituents, and to supply these from the vegetable world. This is step the first.

Shall we roughly classify the flesh-eaters solids, or meat and flesh of all kinds, as nitrogenous or flesh-forming food? Meat as usually eaten without fat contains little else than nitrogenous elements in addition to its enormous proportion of water. Then the meat-eater's carbonaceous or heat-forming food would be such things as sweets, cakes, and puddings, and there would then remain only that mysterious element called stimulant or extractives about which so little seems to be known, and which is supposed to reside chiefly in meat, wine, and spirits. This last element is a necessity to most meat-eaters, but its necessity disappears with the disappearance of meat. This is proved by universal experience—a vegetarian drunkard is unknown. It is curious to observe how even in the case of meat-eaters nature will assert herself and insist upon due proportions. How few of those who eat eagerly of meat ever like milk or brown bread. Fewer still can digest nuts or beans. The reason of this will be seen from what follows.

The evidence of analysis goes to prove that a human being requires about 15 oz. to 20 oz. of food daily (reckoned as dry food, not counting water) and that of this about $\frac{1}{6}$ should be of a nitrogenous or flesh-forming character, the rest being carbonaceous or heat-forming chiefly. Dr. Allinson confirms this by some very interesting personal experience of living on $1\frac{1}{2}$ lbs. of wheat-meal a day, this containing about 3 oz. of nitrogen (or flesh-forming food) and about 17 oz. of carbon (or heat-forming food). There are, however, well authenticated cases where even so little as 12 oz. was the entire weight of food consumed including water. A meat-eater in order to get 3 oz. of nitrogen would have to consume nearly $1\frac{1}{2}$ lbs. of meat daily, and he would then lack nearly 14 ozs. of his 17 ozs. of carbon. This he would probably supply by means of potatoes (each pound of which contains about 3 ozs. of carbon) or pastry made of fine flour and fat. But in doing this he would consume a volume of water three times the weight of the nourishing elements, and quite as much as the $1\frac{1}{2}$ lbs. of wheat-meal would require (in addition to the water naturally contained in it) to make it into bread or porridge.

The vegetarian on the other hand not only finds his food arranged ready for him in right proportions in grains, and therefore in whole-meal bread and porridge, so that he could live and grow on these alone, requiring nothing else, in a most admirable simplicity; but he can also take a mixture of beans and roots, or of nuts and fruit, with the same result, and with the addition of valuable salts and acids not found in flesh.

A little reflection will show how great a change this would be, and how very well calculated it would be to upset the digestive organs were it carried out too suddenly. Let the novice begin then by changing his diet at one meal in the day only. Which this should be depends very largely on circumstances too varied for general discussion, but in the large majority of cases it would be breakfast, if only because in the case of breakfast there would not be any question of drink—the vegetarian can choose amongst tea, coffee, and cocoa just like a meat-eater. He would, however, do well to choose coffee, if it is served without any admixture of chicory. We are thus only concerned with actual eatables.

The novice should not begin with a breakfast of bread and butter merely, if he is used to more variety. But he must emphatically replace ordinary baker's bread with good brown bread, and he should also take his drink, whether tea, coffee, or cocoa, half milk if possible. To this foundation he should add some little dainty dish, as mushrooms on toast, rissoles made of beans and potatoes, porridge, or muffins or cakes; otherwise his stomach being unaccustomed to monotony will refuse to take a sufficient quantity, and there must be no diminishing of quantity at first. To this there should be added fruit; cooked fruit in preference to raw as a beginning. More than this vegetarian breakfast should not be attempted for some time, nor should the next step be taken until all craving for meat at breakfast has disappeared and the vegetarian breakfast become a standing habit. This will generally take about three or four months.

Most people who are not huge feeders—and Lancelot Gobbo does not often turn vegetarian—most people take one large meal a day and two smaller ones, without counting afternoon tea: breakfast, dinner, afternoon tea, and supper; or breakfast, lunch, afternoon tea, and dinner. Breakfast has been suggested as the first meal for experiment; the next meal for experiment should be the other smaller meal, lunch or supper. The best way to deal with it is to make it another meal very much like the breakfast just described, a meal in which brown bread and butter and milk are the solids, and fruits, pudding, porridge, salad, or other vegetables the accessories, maigre soup being a useful addition. Supposing this to be impossible, as in cases where there would be a very substantial lunch and a slighter meal for late dinner, it is not difficult to keep lunch as the heavy meal still devoted to flesh food, and at late dinner to make a selection that leaves out meat. Maigre soup, vegetables, and such sweets as are not made with dripping or suet. If this is not sufficient, the cheese course can be made to fill a large gap, and the dessert that follows is the vegetarian's paradise. Let the novice devour as fast as he can the fruit that is forbidden to the degraded stomachs of flesh-eaters.

Then whatever may be the time of the year at which the first start is made, nothing more must be attempted until green peas are in season. The novice must continue his one meal a day of meat until June, and he may then safely leave off meat altogether and supply its place with green peas and new potatoes, taking plenty of butter with both. Duly he should eat four times the quantity he would have eaten with his meat, that is about half a vegetable dish full of peas and about six good sized potatoes, and a piece of butter about the size of an egg. Even so the novice will probably be obliged to return to meat once a day when winter sets in, but with the following summer he will find himself a full blown vegetarian ready to take his vows after a novitiate of about two years altogether.

The vegetarian at this point will have discovered that as no one can live on flesh alone, so there are vegetable foods which alone would not support life. But he will also have proved what has been asserted above, that there are other vegetable foods which not only support life alone, but which also contain all that man needs for nourishment in proportion proper for his needs; some for health and some for sickness.

First and foremost amongst those proportioned for health is bread— to the Englishman at least the staff of life, and the fundamental food of adult man. The vegetarian in every stage of his career, whether as a novice or as a practised hand, should never forget that in England at least bread is the one thing needful. He should agitate perpetually for pure bread; bread made from whole-meal, but without husk of any kind; bread made without yeast or salt or alum or potatoes or any other adulteration; bread that is neither sour nor white; but sweet and brown, and soft and fresh, and fit for the food of the lords of creation.

Another food of the same kind is milk—not a vegetable food, but one that can be used without taking life, often very usefully during the transition stage. Eggs are of the same kind, but are for many reasons les admissible in vegetarian diet.

The largest class of all is food in which one element is found predominating over others. These should be roughly divided into two heads; the nitrogenous or flesh-forming class, consisting of peas, beans, and nuts of all kinds; and the carbonaceous or heat-forming class, consisting of the lighter grains, such as rice, sago, and the like, as also the interior portions of heavier grains, such as white flour and oswega.

Besides these there is the watery class such as turnips and potatoes, which contain little else than water; and the fruit class, about which less is known.

Vegetarianism would regard these classes as follows :—

The nitrogenous is strong meat.

The carbonaceous is vegetable and pudding.

The watery is for purposes of flavouring.

The fruit is wine and beef-tea.

It is perhaps unnecessary to act cookery book further than to say that all peas, beans, and lentils, most heavy grains, and nearly all nuts, should be thought of as meat, cooked as meat, and eaten as meat; as should also milk and cheese; that the lighter grains are best as soup or jelly; fruit at the end of a meal as wine; and roots only for flavouring or thickening.

There is, however, another aspect of food—its magnetism. Very little is really known about magnetism of any kind, and that of food has perhaps been less studied than any other, yet most people are well able to perceive not only the imparted, but also the inherent magnetism of food. Is there anyone who cannot tell whether their food has been prepared with kindness and care or the reverse? And who would ever mistake an earth-fed from a sun-fed food? About imparted magnetism it is useless to say much, for few persons can choose the hands through which their food should pass, but it is the more desirable that food should come as directly as possible from the place where it grows to the mouth it is to fill. Every hand it passes through has power to poison it: every process it undergoes deprives it more and more, not only of its genuineness, but also of that intangible something which is the more likely to be its essential goodness, because it eludes our perceptions.

But even this subtle essence can be of different sorts; it can be the rough and homely—of the earth, earthy; or it can be the ethereal, produced not by mere growth, but by the unfolding of leaves, the budding of flowers, and the ripening of fruit—processes not of the damp, dark soil but of the warm bright sun.

Thus the novice, finding himself at the end of about two years to have surmounted the difficulties of a change of diet, will see above him still further heights to scale. It is true that he no longer destroys life to find food like a savage tiger, nor does he bolt flesh like a dog, nor purr over it like a cat; but he still perhaps drinks milk like a calf, eats cheese as greedily as a mouse, and drowns himself in cream like a fly.

Soon however a change comes, and all animal food becomes distasteful; eggs first, then cheese, butter, milk, and even cream, disappear from his dietary, and along with this a more sparing use of nitrogenous foods begins, while an inexplicable craving for fruit, hitherto unknown or unrecognised, begins to assert itself irresistibly. The whole quantity too, of food required diminishes, appetite is satisfied and strength maintained, and even increased, on much smaller rations; stimulants and condiments are no longer needed; and thirst is unknown.

In this more advanced stage the vegetarian is fast becoming a fruit-eater, and besides bread, eats little else than fruit. But as he is no longer a beginner it is no longer useful to follow him into the chronic stage of the old hand who lives joyfully on bread and fruit, never wishes for alcohol, only bargains that he may not be obliged to feed in the same room with meat-eaters, and that he may be spared the disgusting odour of burning flesh. Here then are the watch-words: endure, go slowly, learn, and aspire. The rocks on which success may be wrecked are: persecution, hurry, ignorance, and heedlessness. But in the end the vegetarian will find that he has not only accomplished a most important change in his diet, but that he has also added independence and discretion to his stock of virtues.

The question of mere diet is in this way disposed of; not so the whole difficulty of the change from flesh-eating to fruit-eating. There still remains for discussion one of the greatest trials of the whole course, that of persecution. There are those whose endeavours are stunted, if not eventually destroyed, by the solicitude of friends and the opinions of doctors. It needs no little courage to face the jeers of brothers, but much more to resist maternal entreaties. The novice who is really in earnest will be ready to turn over in his mind the question of leaving home altogether, but so serious a complication as this does not arise until meat is entirely abandoned. So long as the novice can manage to swallow a square inch of flesh, the attention of friends is not drawn to his plate, but even the square inch at last becomes impossible, and the novice must then make plans to secure freedom. Nevertheless, the exercise of patient diplomacy and quiet but persistent will is in itself a step on the upward path—a path so thorny that we can scarcely begin too early to accustom our feet to the pricks, with the deliberate intention of developing the higher nature at the cost of the lower.

Amongst the many who change carnivorous for vegetarian diet, these aspirants to the path above all others claim the sympathy of Theosophists ; yet these are the very people who so often go astray in changing their food. It may be that they are too eager in asceticism ; too inattentive to their own wants ; too keenly bent on higher things ; but in one way or another if they do not suffer in health, it is a sort of miracle, due, probably, to an unusually healthy mental or spiritual condition. It is for vegetarians of this class that this paper is more especially written.

These are not, however, the only persons who change their diet. There are those who do it from motives of economy or as an interesting experiment. Such seldom encounter persecution. A gentle shower of pity is usually their reward. But there are others who have as great a claim to sympathy as the aspirants : those who well-nigh despairing in search of health grasp eagerly at any system carrying the banner of hope. And these are of all others the most difficult to guide. In some cases a vegetarian doctor is a great help ; in others a sudden change of diet will produce so marvellous a change for the better in health, that all but a prejudiced minority will be won over and the sufferer will have a party of support ; in others again, a simple and truthful following of nature's cravings for fruit and brown bread for instance, even at the risk of being accused of invalid caprices, will disarm persecution. But the invalid too must aspire to the higher life, or effort will be defeated by indiscretion. If the mind be fixed rather upon the right than upon the desired, the fixed mind will in the end shape the surroundings. It is, however, well that vegetarians should know something about sick diet, otherwise they may easily be impeded in their progress by such unworthy opponents as headache, sore-throat, or biliousness. It is good in the first place to know a few grandmother's remedies, such as a juice of an onion to squeeze into a wasp sting ; a raw potatoe to scrape over a scald, or to rub on an aching head ; coffee for sickness ; hot water to drink for indigestion ; and lemon juice in boiling water for a shivering cold. It will be found, too, that carbonaceous foods—or rather drinks—are most useful with a raised temperature ; and fruits and nitrogenous food for a low state of the system. Again, in all cases of inherited or organic disease large quantities of fruit should be taken habitually, and in some cases there are spices which will prove beneficial, the need for them being generally indicated by a natural craving for them. Whether in health or in sickness, nature itself is the only safe guide, but by far the larger proportion of mankind is unable to understand her. For these let the rule be to go slowly step by step; to learn carefully with a free and open mind; to bear patiently with a peaceful soul; and to cure likes by likes.

For these—the favoured few—who have the light to perceive natural instincts truly, and the courage to follow them honestly, no rule is needed; and with such even important changes may take place in a short time without danger. Still it is a rare gift either to see what is true, or to act without fear, and therefore rules for following nature are not altogether out of place for those who are striving to give up flesh-eating for fruit-eating.

E. FRANCES WILLIAMS, F.T.S.

The nutriment of the rational soul is that which preserves it in a rational state. But this is intellect; so that it is to be nourished by intellect; and we should earnestly endeavour that it may be fattened through this, rather than the flesh may become pinguid through esculent substances. For intellect preserves for us eternal life, but the body when fattened causes the soul to be famished, through its hunger after a blessed life not being satisfied, increases our mortal part, since it is of itself insane, and impedes our attainment of an immortal condition of being. It likewise defiles by corporifying the soul, and drawing her down to that which is foreign to her nature. And the magnet, indeed, imparts, as it were, a soul to the iron which is placed near it; and the iron, though most heavy, is elevated, and runs to the spirit of the stone. Should he, therefore, who is suspended from incorporeal and intellectual deity, be anxiously busied in procuring food, which fattens the body, that is an impediment to intellectual perception? Ought he not rather, by contracting what is necessary to the flesh into that which is little and easily procured, be *himself* nourished, by adhering to God more closely than the iron to the magnet? * * * * O that, as Homer says, we were not in want either of meat or drink, that we might be truly immortal!—the poet in thus speaking beautifully signifying, that food is the auxiliary not only of life, but also of death. * * * * Democrates says, that to live badly, and not prudently, temperately and piously, is not to live in reality, but to die for a long time.

PORPHYRY; On abstinence from animal food; trans. by THOMAS TAYLOR.

Women's Printing Society, Ltd., Great College St., Westminster S.W.

CPSIA information can be obtained at www.ICGtesting.com
Printed in the USA
BVOW07s1144090314

347022BV00009B/456/P